praise for
Goodbye 20th Century

"As much a chronicle of the combustion of music and popular culture Sonic Youth helped ignite as it is an earnest portrait of the band and examination of their work. . . . Browne's book will suck you in. . . . He fleshes out the personalities and occasional tensions behind the band's deadpan image."
—*Los Angeles Times*

"The most comprehensive book yet on slackerdom's greatest musical legacy."
—*New York* magazine

"The whole scene in you-are-there detail."
—*New York Post*

"A rollicking, epic biography . . . Browne cannily opts to tell, in a crisp, novelistic style, the compelling story of the cultural tornado of galleries, rock clubs and unique personalities (Lydia Lunch, Kurt Cobain and Chloë Sevigny, to name a few) Sonic Youth swirled around in, the band's ongoing fight to maintain the purity of their vision, and above all, their shared passion for new ideas and sounds."
—*Salon*

"A much-deserved biography."
—*Rolling Stone*

"A purposeful, detailed pleasure, describing the day jobs and the tensions, and animating the real story: how a group of smart twentysomethings repurposed half-broken instruments and thrived by feeding back—just like their amps—into the world around them."
—*Times of London*

"Browne's game for the task of finding fresh ways to describe Really Noisy Guitars. . . . He goads the band (everyone's on board here, even Jim O'Rourke) into uncharacteristic chattiness, and he milks intrigue from the mysterious cultural and sexual magnetism of the Kim Gordon/Thurston Moore union that drives the band."
—*Village Voice*

"Deeply reported . . . entertaining and insightful . . . Browne smartly humanizes the most aloof of rock's great bands."
—*The Stranger*

"This copious amount of research . . . renders Browne an expert not only about the band but also about the scene. *Goodbye 20th Century* delivers the

only thing you really want from a rock & roll biography: it enhances your
listening experience." —*Pop Matters*

"Comprehensively captures Sonic Youth's unorthodox legend in full . . .
Browne's willingness to probe every facet of every member's activities and
proclivities adds an extra dimension." —*Detroit Metro Times*

"Thoroughly researched and passionately written . . . Browne had full,
unfettered access and tells a complete version of the band's story.
Recommended." —*Library Journal*

"Compulsively readable . . . Browne traces each phase of the band's career
with the easy, anecdotal grace of an accomplished journalist. . . . he succeeds
at capturing the personalities and debates that shape the band's character."
—*Publishers Weekly*

"A wonderful evocation of the '80s no wave, downtown standard-bearers
and their uneasy alliance with the major label system. . . . An effective
remembrance of times past." —*Hits*

"Whether you've heard of the band or not, whether you're a fan or only
dimly aware of their 25-year existence, you've probably felt the effects of
Sonic Youth. Like Gertrude Stein to the lost generation, Sonic Youth
either directly paved the way or actively encouraged the young careers of
the grunge generation. . . . Browne warns in his introduction that 'you
also won't find the usual litany of rock-star foibles here.' Sound boring? It
would be if it weren't for Browne's ability to portray the band's very lack
of cliché as such an exceptional feat." —*Men's Vogue*

"Browne chronicles the band's quarter-century career from avant-garde
noisemakers to indie-rock pioneers. Members weigh in on the culture that
influenced them, but it's the culture that they influenced—ranging from
Nirvana to *Guitar Hero*—that stands as their real legacy."
—*Cleveland Free Times*

"[Browne] found a neat narrative to work with, charting the group's determinedly paced journey from under-populated gigs in the arty early-'80s
downtown scene to its brush with alt-rock fame in the mid '90s to its
current status as an inspiration to a nation of young experimentalists."
—*Time Out New York*

"Browne does a fabulous job of detailing the setting, technical details and artistic temperament in the group's creative process without hyperbole. The book can't help but feel nostalgic for a cozy time before punk broke."

—*Time Out Chicago*

"Browne acknowledges the band's impact on popular and underground culture without descending into the obnoxious sentimentality that characterizes so much of rock journalism."

—*VenusZine*

"Sonic Youth's journey, meticulously documented in *Goodbye 20th Century*, unfolds much like a Sonic Youth song, slowly and deliberately . . . Browne digs deeply into the band's democratic decision-making process, which gives each distinct personality ample voice."

—*The Huffington Post*

"A vivid and fascinating picture of the rise of the independent music scene in '80s America."

—*RTE Guide*

"Through amazingly thorough recollections, Browne takes the reader through nearly thirty years of recording and touring with Sonic Youth. . . . Browne doesn't just go through the motions, but analyzes the connections between albums and songs, showcasing the band's taste for irony and innovation . . . Sonic Youth's music is both art and poetry and, similar to those vehicles, takes on new meaning when its inspirations are revealed throughout the book."

—*Feminist Review*

"Compelling and thoroughly researched . . . A refreshing look at a hard-working band that stands out in the culture of unrealistic industry hype."

—*Charleston Post and Courier*

"An essential history of an essential band."

—*Record Collector*

"Terrific . . . Virtually no important detail is spared . . . You'll get a sense of Sonic Youth's roots, what was going on around them at the time, the inspirations behind much of their best-known (and least-known) work and personal insights into the marriage of Thurston Moore and Kim Gordon. Highly recommended."

—*The Big Takeover*

"An extraordinary job capturing the whole history of a band . . . *Goodbye 20th Century* is truly like one of those great freeform jams they would later release, ebbing and flowing as it weaves a tale."

—*Bookgasm*

Also by David Browne

Dream Brother: The Lives & Music
of Jeff & Tim Buckley

Amped: How Big Air, Big Dollars, and
a New Generation Took Sports to the Extreme

Goodbye 20th Century

A Biography of
Sonic Youth

David Browne

DA CAPO PRESS
A Member of the Perseus Books Group

Library of Congress Cataloging-in-Publication Data
Browne, David, 1960-
   Goodbye 20th century : a biography of Sonic Youth / David Browne. —
1st Da Capo Press ed.
       p. cm.
     ISBN-13: 978-0-306-81515-7 (alk. paper) 1. Sonic Youth (Musical group)
2. Rock musicians—United States—Biography. I. Title. II. Title: Goodbye
twentieth century.
   ML421.S615B76 2008
   782.42166092'2—dc22
   [B]
                                                                 2008004228

First Da Capo Press edition 2008
ISBN-13: 978-0-306-81603-1
First paperback edition 2009
Published by Da Capo Press
A Member of the Perseus Books Group
www.dacapopress.com

Da Capo Press books are available at special discounts for bulk purchases in the U.S. by corporations, institutions, and other organizations. For more information, please contact the Special Markets Department at the Perseus Books Group, 2300 Chestnut Street, Suite 200, Philadelphia, PA 19103, or call (800) 810-4145, extension 5000, or e-mail special.markets@perseusbooks.com.

1 2 3 4 5 6 7 8 9 10

For Maggie, who will always be a kool thing

CONTENTS

INTRODUCTION

GROWN-UP RIOT

OR, SEVEN WAYS TO START
AN INTRODUCTION TO A BOOK
ABOUT SONIC YOUTH

1.

ALTHOUGH I HESITATE to say this after several iPods have ignominiously flamed out on me, every so often a certain computer company may know best. In the early stages of researching this book, I crammed a batch of Sonic Youth albums onto my iTunes. With each disc, the description that popped up under "genre" changed. Certain albums were designated "rock"; a few others were "alternative." One particularly grimy-sounding bootleg was "noise." (I didn't even know that *was* an iTunes category.) My favorite moment, though, came when I downloaded a copy of their first album. As if iTunes' operating system had been utterly mystified by what it heard, the music was given another designation I'd never seen before: "Unclassifiable."

As random and silly as those tags sound, they also make a certain amount of sense. Over the course of almost three decades, Sonic Youth have been all of those things at one point or another. They've been called rock or alternative or indie or noise, yet in the end, they've never sounded like anyone but themselves. And they've operated in their own universe for so long that it was easy to take them, and their achievements, for granted.

2.

IN THE BEGINNING, Sonic Youth scared me. Only a few years out of college, I was immersed in what everyone at the time quaintly called "college rock." R.E.M.'s *Murmur* and *Reckoning*, the Replacements' *Hootenanny* and *Let It Be*, and Hüsker Dü's "Diane" and *Zen Arcade*, among others, spoke to me. In their respective, ramshackle ways, they (and so many other bands that I'd need an entire page of this book to list them all) seemed to be fighting for a way to make rock & roll fresh, wonderful, and *real* again after years of the likes of Styx, Journey, and REO Speedwagon turning it into an oxymoron—innocuous bombast. But more importantly, these new bands, recording on small labels I'd never heard of, were my age and seemed to be grappling with something larger: life in the '80s and in one's twenties. They didn't seem to know what lay ahead and what was and wasn't meaningful, and neither did I.

Even given my awareness of their world, I didn't know what to make of this *other* indie band, the one from New York. I was familiar with their milieu: I'd graduated from college the same year Sonic Youth released their first EP, and my school, New York University, was in the same part of town where they played many of their earliest shows. The first album of theirs I ever owned was *Bad Moon Rising*, which confused me even further. I recognized the title from an old Creedence Clearwater Revival song I'd grown up hearing, but I didn't understand the way it was being used: Was the appropriation ironic? Or, given that Ronald Reagan had just been reelected, was it frighteningly serious? They certainly *looked* normal enough, especially the tall guitarist who resembled a good Catholic boy who'd strayed but was, deep down, still a good Catholic boy. But the cover, a scarecrow with a flaming pumpkin head, was spooky even to someone who'd grown up on a regimen of horror and sci-fi films.

The music inside was foreboding and inexplicable even by indie rock standards. Intentionally or not, the guitars sounded out of tune; the singing wasn't straightforward, either. Every once in a while, a melody would lurch out, as if seeking to reassure me that everything would be okay. But then the rattling, suffocating intensity of it all would reassert itself. I listened to the album several times but never managed to get a handle on it or the band.

Yet something about it pulled me in; sometimes it's the music you can't figure out, on first or subsequent listens, that makes you keep listening. Two years later, an advance cassette of another Sonic Youth album, *Sister*, arrived. I popped it into the boom box of the office where I was toiling and got to work copyediting stereo-equipment reviews. I was concentrating so hard on the computer screen that I wasn't always able to completely focus on the music in the background, but at one point, I stopped: Something astonishing was emanating from the coffee-can-size speakers. The music was a slow, tough-gnarl crawl, but the melody was beautiful, and it sounded as if the married couple in the band, whom I'd come to identify as Kim Gordon and Thurston Moore, were singing together in something approaching harmony. It might have been even a love song. I stopped what I should have been doing (that is, working) and listened to the song until it was over, then let the rest of the tape play out. When the album finished (warning: extremely old-school audio reference approaching), I madly rewound the tape to find that exact song, which turned out to be "Kotton Krown." With that, my full-on fascination with Sonic Youth truly began.

3.

LET'S PRETEND you're not overly familiar with the name Sonic Youth. There's a good chance you aren't. They've never had a hit single or Top

10 album, never been on *Saturday Night Live*, never had any of their songs over-emoted on *American Idol*. Yes, "Kool Thing" was included on *Guitar Hero III*, leading to video game–playing teenagers across the country semi-learning to play that song, and the indie film sensation *Juno* included the band in both its dialogue and soundtrack. (In some ways, to paraphrase one of their vintage projects, 2008 was the year Sonic Youth broke.) But if Sonic Youth still doesn't register, then some or all of these names should: Nirvana. Beck. Sofia Coppola. Courtney Love. Spike Jonze. Todd Haynes. Chloë Sevigny. Jason Lee. Raymond Pettibon. These are just a few of the people the Group You've Never Heard Of befriended early in their career and helped shuttle into the mainstream, and that tells as much of the Sonic Youth story as their music itself.

Even if the general populace has never heard "Kool Thing" or "The Diamond Sea" or any of the few other Sonic Youth songs that briefly snuck onto radio, Sonic Youth has shaped the pop culture zeitgeist of the last two decades. Theirs is not just the tale of a band but of an era, community, and sensibility that has infiltrated and altered the culture. Over nearly three decades, they've tapped into a separate and parallel arts universe of illustrators, graphic designers, directors, painters, poets, actors and actresses, zines, and underground comic artists—even extreme sport video makers. And that world all flows through the saga of Sonic Youth. As with the Beatles, Bob Dylan, and only a few others, Sonic Youth's is the place—but for a different generation—where music, art, and culture intersect; nothing afterward was quite the same.

4.

AS I WAS CONTINUALLY REMINDED while researching this book, everyone has his or her take on Sonic Youth. Leaving their World Trade Center–area studio one day in the months after September 11, I found myself talking with a New York City cop patrolling the neighborhood. When he saw I was carrying a vinyl LP, he asked what it was; as it turned out, he'd heard of Sonic Youth and had seen them perform in the '80s in nearby Hoboken. "My buddy took me to see them—they had a girl in the band, right?" he said, as the memories came back. "Right. I remember them. But they were *nev-uh* mainstream."

Later, when I mentioned this project to my chiropractor, he smiled and said, "Lollapalooza!" To him, Sonic Youth embodied something else entirely: the crazy, carefree, "alternative" '90s.

5.

I CAN STILL RECALL the first time I interviewed the members of Sonic Youth. In the fall of 1988, I ventured out to the office of their record company in New York's Little Italy. They'd just returned from a European tour, and with their careworn guitars and equipment cases piled up behind them, the four of them sat down in front of me. I was aware of their cooler-than-thou reputation, and they didn't disappoint. Kim Gordon mostly stared at me as if this were the last place on the planet she wanted to be. Lee Ranaldo and Steve Shelley were more affable, but Thurston Moore spent most of the time trying to figure out how to break a Crime and the City Solution LP in half; from time to time, he'd interject wry or acerbic comments. Although I'd interviewed dozens of musicians by then, I was even more intimidated than the time I faced a clearly hung-over John Cale.

Sonic Youth's vibe was, of course, part of their appeal; although I'd never interviewed Bob Dylan in his prime, I now knew how that must have felt. Although I'd never felt "cool" in my life, I'd never felt so unhip. Somehow an article emerged from it all, but I'll never know how.

That conversation was the first of several I had with the band (or individual members of it) over the next fifteen or so years, for publications that included *Entertainment Weekly*, the *New York Times*, and the now defunct *Musician* magazine. When their twenty-fifth anniversary was suddenly in sight, it seemed like the time had come to tell their story and get them to finally answer a few basic questions that lingered from that first chat: How had they changed, or not, over the years? Exactly what impact did they have? How had they managed to stay together for so long? Why did their guitars *sound* like that? Thus began this book.

6.

"YOU'RE GOING TO GO THROUGH all those records?" one of Sonic Youth's past colleagues asked me after we'd finished an interview for this book. When I told him yes, he added, "Wow—that's quite a job."

He was right, of course. A collection of Sonic Youth group recordings, side projects, solo albums, and compilations featuring one or more of their songs came to take up almost two long rows of shelves in my home. Yet in this vast, sometimes overwhelming pile of records lies the saga of one of rock's most unique and influential units.

7.

A WORD OF WARNING for every reader of this book: Do not expect any sex, drugs, and rock & roll.

Well, let's rephrase that. Two of the band members are married to each other, and one of the others has a wife, too; between them they have four children. So, yes, there has been sex. There have been a few drugs, but a laughably small amount relative to most rock & roll sagas. And yes, there is rock & roll, but not of the traditional sort: The voices, guitar sounds, and song structures have rarely been standard. You also won't find the usual litany of rock-star foibles here: no car crashes, drug overdoses, hotel room trashings, or other tales of excess that sustained *Behind the Music* for years. When one of their former associates checked with the band to see if it was okay to speak with me, Kim Gordon told him it was fine; maybe, she said, he could add some spice to what she considered an uneventful story.

It's true that a Sonic Youth episode of *Behind the Music*, in the unlikely chance it ever came to pass, would be one of the least sensationalistic installments in the history of that show. Yet the ordinariness of their story, its *lack* of cliché, is what drew me to it. The Sonic Youth saga is the tale of a young couple who meet, start a band, find equally driven and compatible musicians to further their vision, and then proceed on a winding creative journey now entering its third decade. Along the way they attempt to push rock forward, meet plenty of like-minded creative types in various media, and receive any number of promotions (that is, bigger record deals and such) for their work. It's a story of stability and relative well-adjustedness, of creating chaos onstage but not off it. In its contrariness, it's almost, well, punk.

Sonic Youth have had their share of ups and downs, their tiffs and turmoil. During the research for this book, they were fairly candid with me about it all. But ultimately, theirs is a story that has less to do with rock overindulgence and more to do with the reality of life. It's about the ways in which life generally isn't filled with big *Behind the Music* blowouts but is instead a steady stream of ups and downs, highs and lows. It's about balancing work, career, and family, about doing what you love in spite of what everyone tells you, about trying to find that balance between integrity and the demands of living and growing older. Much in the way iTunes called their first album "Unclassifiable" when I downloaded it, Sonic Youth's story is pretty unique, too.

PART 1

RISE

Chapter 1

ON THE NIGHT THEY MET, the summer evening when it all began, the first thing he noticed about her was her height. Since she was a good foot shorter than he was, he had to bend down to say hello. Even when he did, it was hard to see her petite, lean face. She was wearing a cap and sunglasses, the latter with the shades flipped up, and only her long, slender nose poked through. A friend would later describe the look as "this sort of blocking," as if she were hiding from or behind something. Many years later, he would still remember the striped shirt and pants she wore that night; they reminded him of prison garb and seemed as exotic as shades worn long after the sun had descended.

The evening itself, in 1980, felt like the end of something, not the beginning of anything. It was simply another gig, taking place at one of those Manhattan clubs that would welcome you when no one else would. Most of the venues everyone desperately wanted to play could be found further south; this one, called Plugg, was tucked away in a two-story, redbrick brownstone squashed between two larger buildings on West 24th Street. It was a particularly desolate stretch of Chelsea with nothing approaching any other form of nightlife on the block. Even in a city that often felt ravaged and forlorn, the locale was remote and isolated—the last stand for anyone who wanted to make a stand.

When he walked in, he took note of the club's trademark decor— its lengthy, bowling-alley configuration and array of couches and chairs. Plugg felt like someone's living room; if thirty or forty people showed up, it felt like an especially crowded living area. In fact, someone did live there. The space belonged to Giorgio Gomelsky, a music business mover and shaker who'd made a name for himself nearly two decades before when he was involved as either a promoter, producer, or manager for the Rolling Stones, the Yardbirds, and other new, mangy rock bands who emerged from London in the middle of the '60s. After relocating to Manhattan, Gomelsky decided that one way to keep his hand in the business would be to offer up his loft for another generation of musicians looking to make their mark—and perhaps a few dollars—in rock & roll.

That evening, the featured band, the tall kid's band, was called the Coachmen. They'd been knocking around the fringes of downtown Manhattan for several years—four kids from neighboring states who'd arrived in the city two or three years before, shared a loft space in the bowels of Wall Street, and joined together to see if they could become a New York punk-style band. They had all the right influences—one could hear punk-rock antecedents like the Modern Lovers and the Velvet Underground in their songs, as well as current local luminaries like Television—and they had the appropriately unpretentious street-clothes look. Yet all their effort was getting them nowhere; no one seemed to be championing them beyond family, friends, and girlfriends, and the pay, if one wanted to call it that, was laughable. On a good night, they might score twenty dollars, but when it came time to clear out, John King, the band's leader, singer, and guitarist, would usually have to pay someone at whatever dive they'd played about twenty-*five* dollars to help them pack up their gear. And the cycle never seemed to end.

Since the scene appeared to be passing them by, they decided to play whatever shows they'd already committed to, and then it would be over. The Coachmen would be history, at least for anyone who cared to remember them. The refrain to one of their original songs— "I could be a household word/Can I call you on the phone?"—rang sourly in their ears.

King wasn't the only guitarist in the band; the other was a towering, gangly twenty-two-year-old from Connecticut. In many ways, he didn't fit the image of a New York punk of the period; his sandy brown hair was cut in an updated Beatle mop and combed neatly to the side, and his attempt at a nasty snarl always seemed more comical than vituperative. He had an easy, dry laugh, and each of his features—his ears, hands, even lips—seemed a bit over-sized. His name—Thurston Moore—was more appropriate for a Baptist minister or a passenger on the *Mayflower* than it was for a disaffected rock star; his mother would later say that his wholesome looks accounted for the nickname "Opie" when he was younger. Because of his height, the sleeves on the button-down shirts he favored were always too short, and his elbows often poked through the sleeves of the used clothes he'd pull out of cardboard bins at downtown's no-budget emporium, Canal Jeans. He, King, and the bass player, Bob Pullin, were each over six feet, which led to plenty of jokes about how they should've been named the Basketball Players instead of the Coachmen. Few understood the ironic use of a generic '60s band name like the Coachmen anyway, especially in a landscape dotted with bands dubbed Teenage Jesus and the Jerks, Suicide, and the Dead Boys.

She was already there when he arrived at the club, shortly before the band was scheduled to start playing. He'd heard something about her from Stanton Miranda, who was also at Plugg that night. Moore had met Miranda through a coworker at one of his day jobs. With her short dark hair, South American background, and olive-toned skin, Miranda—who preferred to be known as "Miranda Stanton" in the States since it sounded more normal—was an international woman of mystery even to those who knew her. With her rudimentary keyboard skills, she would invite friends and acquaintances over to her loft to play music and see what new sounds they could devise; the only requirement, of Miranda and the times, was that they not sound like anyone else. During one of those get-togethers, Miranda had told him that her best friend was a girl named Kim, Kim Gordon in full, and that she could play a bit of guitar and perhaps they should get together at Miranda's loft and try to make some type of music together.

He hadn't thought much of it at the time. It struck him that Miranda may have been playing matchmaker, which interested him even less. He'd had a high school girlfriend back home in Connecticut, but since moving to New York City, he hadn't had much success in the romance department. He'd obsessed fairly heavily over one girl he'd met, but when it turned out she was actually dating one of his neighbors in his apartment building—one of his *friends* in the building at that—he was devastated. Then there was the time he actually had been set up and wound up at a woman's apartment, eating cheese, sipping wine, and talking about everything except what he wanted to discuss: punk rock.

At Plugg, the two newly introduced acquaintances started talking casually about rhythm and when it should and shouldn't be used. She had a subdued, scrutinizing way about her that could give way to a wide, welcoming smile, and it intrigued him that she worked in an art gallery; his late father had always been interested in that area. But again, his personal life was not his focus right then, especially since the Coachmen were about to collapse. He liked John King just fine; after all, King had invited Moore to New York in the first place and had been supportive of his very rough-hewn guitar skills and even tried, with no success, to force the kid to sing once in a while. Moore already had something else in mind—although, in his reserved, slightly jokey way, it was nothing he could articulate to anyone at the time.

Once the set ended, Miranda invited him to grab a bite with her and her friend Kim. After helping to pack up the Coachmen's gear, he took them up on the offer and jumped on a subway to a bar downtown. Again, he didn't think much of it. If anything, he was thinking more about his next band, his next sound, and some way to make a name for himself in a town that was forcing him to pay his dues for what felt like an eternity.

THURSTON. *Thurston.* For a time, especially when he was young, he had regrets about the name. There were, of course, the *Gilligan's Island* jokes; the sitcom about the stranded sightseeing boaters had premiered just as he'd entered first grade, and he had to endure references to one of its characters, Thurston Howell III, throughout his adolescence. "You don't want to have something that stands out," he says, "that calls attention to any weirdness about you. And the name certainly was weird." It was bad enough that he was tall—so much so that, in the house where he spent his teen years, he would frequently bump his head on the frames of the doors. When he was little, he would ask his mother if he was going to be a giant; she reassured him no, of course not.

He knew the somewhat roundabout history of the name and who it was meant to honor. His grandfather, Harold Moore, was the family's black sheep, an alcoholic who vanished early on, leaving behind a wife, Dorothy, and a son, George. After the family relocated from New Jersey to the Coral Gables area of Florida, Dorothy would eventually get remarried, and to quite a character: Thurston Adams, known around the household as Doc. A crew-cutted, gregarious social dandy, Doc hailed from Pine Apple, Alabama, which would eventually name a pond and dam after him for his school football success; later, he would move to Florida to be a basketball coach at a small college. Dorothy, called Dotty by the family, was a concert pianist who gave recitals at the Coral Gables Music Club, where she was president. They met after Doc had taken a job as director of student activities at the University of Miami campus in Coral Gables; the kids on campus called him Doc, too.

Dorothy's love of music was passed on to her son George Edward, who, in 1950, could be found in the practice rooms at the University of Miami, where he majored in music. In one of those rooms, he encountered a nineteen-year-old fellow student with long, brown hair and an ample smile. The vivacious Eleanor Nann always dreamt of meeting a man who was big and blond—the opposite of her—and George fit that bill; he also had a high forehead and a relaxed, easygoing manner. He stood her up on their first date, her first indication that he could be what she called an "absentminded professor type—always up in the clouds." Eleanor, by comparison, was the grounded one. But he made up for the screwup by taking her, on early dates, to the record stores in Miami Beach. There, he would select classical records—his real passion, since he played flute, piano, and piccolo— and escort her into listening rooms in the back, introducing her to music she'd never heard before. These were far from typical dates, but with his love of Matisse and Picasso, George Moore didn't seem like a typical student, either.

Little would be predictable, not for a while anyway. After graduation, George briefly left Eleanor behind and moved to New York City to work toward a master's degree at Columbia; in due time, Eleanor would follow him, landing a job as a secretary. Soon they were engaged and, his degree in hand, they returned to Florida, where he began teaching. They married shortly thereafter, but with the start of the Korean War, their honeymoon didn't last long; George was drafted, and the young couple moved to Fort Jackson in South Carolina, where George played in the Navy band. Then it was back to Florida again, where George worked as a band director at a local Catholic high school. That job, like others that followed, lasted only a short time. "If my husband didn't like anything," Eleanor would say, "off he went." He didn't like confrontation and avoided it as much as possible.

Starting in 1953, they had three children: Frederick Eugene (whom everyone called Gene), Susan, and finally, on July 25, 1958, Thurston Joseph. The youngest was named in honor of the charismatic family patriarch, who'd never had children of his own. A large baby, more than ten pounds at birth, Thurston was soon caught up in the family's ongoing uprooting. He was only two when they relocated to Tennessee, where George took his first position as a professor; after that, they were back in Florida, where George taught in a community college for a lengthy—for him—four years. Through it all, George was composing instrumental classical music of his own; an article in a local newspaper described his style as in "the modern idiom." He began sending his sheet music to song publishers in New York, eager to have someone publish his work, but there were no takers; the music may have been too modern for most.

By 1967, George was restless yet again, and for reasons even his wife never fully understood, he announced he wanted to move to

New England, especially when a position—associate professor in the Humanistic Studies and Philosophy department—opened up at Western Connecticut State College in Danbury. The family piled into a station wagon and drove north, arriving in the town of Bethel that summer.

Bethel was the home of Duracell batteries and the birthplace of P. T. Barnum; it was also a sprawling, woodsy town in the southwestern part of the state with a population that hadn't yet reached ten thousand. At first, the family rented homes, but eventually they bought a charming, and very old and drafty, two-floor house on Cod Fish Hill Road for $40,000. The curvy street was easy to miss; so were some of the statelier homes hidden behind stone walls.

Much like his father, the Moores' youngest son could drift off with the best of them. During first grade, at a Catholic school in Florida, one of the nuns told his mother that Thurston was staring out the schoolroom windows and daydreaming too much. He sensed he was different from an early age; few of his friends' homes had collections of books and records like those in his, and he would sometimes venture out to the family garage in Bethel and see his father laying out newspapers on the floor and fashioning them into collage art. When he wasn't working on those projects, George could be found in the den on the first floor, writing philosophy papers by hand that Eleanor would type out. Soon Thurston too began to write: stories, poems ("There's nothing as beautiful as a flower/Its beauty grows while under a rain shower"), then bemused letters to his parents when he would visit his grandfather in Alabama, where he would refer to his new home as "Ice Land CT" and ride horses. At home he would hang out at the local Friendly's ice cream parlor. "I wouldn't say nerdy, but he came from a conventional family," says Eleanor. "What was that show back in the fifties? *Father Knows Best?*"

Music was everywhere; little else, including sports, made much of an impression. George would play piano and his classical LPs, and Gene, the oldest son, brought rock & roll into the Moore household. Gene was the one who came home with the Beatles and Jefferson Airplane records, the one who played "Louie, Louie" for his kid brother and convinced him (for a short while, at least) that that was *him* singing and playing, and Gene was the one who first began strumming a guitar upstairs, where the kids' rooms were found. Everyone thought it would be Gene who would form a band and become a professional musician. Eventually, he taught his younger brother a few basic chords. Wary of Thurston messing up his instrument, Gene would lock his electric guitar in its case, yet Thurston would still somehow snap the lock, fool around with the guitar, and break a string, after which he would replace the instrument in its case and tell his brother "some weird temperature thing" must have caused the string to snap. Thurston signed up for group guitar instruction in his teens but found it intimidating and bailed out after one lesson. He would eventually learn to a play a riff from a Deep Purple record, but he didn't seem particularly interested in learning to play actual songs.

Soon the kid brother began buying his own records, starting with the Youngbloods' peace-and-love anthem "Get Together," his first 45 rpm single, and his first album, Iron Butterfly's *In-a-Gadda-da-Vida;* he was fascinated by the way the title song of the latter stretched out across the entire side of an LP. Yet something about the established rock of the era didn't appeal to him, perhaps because it belonged to his brother and his friends; he wanted music and records—and an identity—all his own.

He found them in the cutout bins of the local department stores, which were filled with the detritus of the music business—LPs with vivid artwork, and even more colorful band names, that had been marked down to a dollar. Sometimes he'd buy them merely for the covers and be disappointed; other times, he'd stumble upon a band and a sound he'd never heard, like the grinding punky garage snarls of the Stooges or the Transylvanian prog rock of Amon Düül, and be instantly attracted to its strangeness. "Nobody had those records, since they weren't considered cool records to have," he says. "But they were certainly affordable, and they were *your* records." He played them even when his older brother and his friends gave him strange looks for showing up with those LPs or better-known ones by shock-rock ringmaster Alice Cooper.

Gene and his friends weren't the only ones puzzled by the kid's tastes. Although Thurston's emerging class-clown image made it easy for him to make friends, few understood what he saw in music so freakish—not even the music nerds at school who approached him one day at the cafeteria, having heard he was a rock fan. Sitting down next to him, they asked him to run through his favorite bands. "Theater rock," he replied, meaning the glam and glitter of the time, from Cooper to David Bowie. He was greeted with dead silence: "I knew I was going down the hole on this, really fast. They looked at me, like, 'This dude is a total loser.'" Almost instantly, the kids got up and walked away.

Finally, during his senior year, he found his first musical soul mate. After school one day in March 1976, a kid approached him and asked if he wanted to accompany some friends to nearby Westport; Patti Smith was playing a club that night. Moore had seen Harold Paris around school; Paris was the flamboyant kid a year younger who always seemed to be wearing scarves. Immersed in gonzo rock magazines like *Creem* and albums like Smith's *Horses*, which he'd bought the previous fall, Moore eagerly took Paris up on the offer. So began a mad, after-school driving dash to the club, where the high schoolers saw Smith in all her leather-jacketed, androgynous-priestess glory.

Visiting the Moore home later, Paris found himself flipping through his new friend's LP collection; to his pleasant surprise, here finally was someone else in Bethel who owned records by Smith, John Cale, and other underground pop subversives ignored by radio and the mainstream press. Living in the Connecticut woods, surrounded by fellow teenagers who gravitated toward the mainstream rock of the time—bands like Kansas and Styx—Paris and Moore bonded immediately. They began making regular trips to any local record store they could find before ending up at one of their respective homes to play their new purchases. "How boring is that?" Paris says. "But it was good enough for us."

The emerging duality in Moore was seen in his high-school prom photo, taken that June: The white tuxedo contrasted with his newly long, brown shag and the hint of disaffection on his face. He applied to the same college where his father taught, telling everyone he would be a journalism major. More important, though, it seemed far more legitimate than what he wanted to say: guitar player in rock band in New York City, a goal that seemed both within geographic reach yet insanely unattainable, even for a dreamer.

THE FIRST SIGN that something was seriously wrong came when Susan, the Moores' daughter, heard from her fellow students at WestConn that her father was going blank during his lectures. George was always a little preoccupied to some degree; three months could go by before he'd remember to pick up his paycheck from the college office. Then he began complaining about pain in his eyes—which his wife had long noticed were bloodshot—and then, even more distressingly, he began stumbling during walks. Eleanor described the enigmatic symptoms to her sister-in-law; her husband, a doctor, said the family should immediately take George to a hospital in New Haven. There, doctors confirmed the relative's suspicions: George had a brain tumor.

At first, everyone, including George, was almost relieved; finally, here was an answer to his sudden mood swings and argumentativeness. Up to that point, Thurston had never seen his father and mother argue. The operation seemed to go well, and Eleanor and her children returned home to Bethel, only to be awakened early the next morning by a call informing them that George's brain had hemorrhaged overnight. The tumor was malignant, not benign. At the Moore home, relatives began arriving, huddling worriedly in the living room.

During one of the family's trips to the hospital, Thurston found a local record store, Cutler's, where his mother bought him a copy of the first album by the overlords of the downtown New York punk scene, the Ramones, released that spring. Putting it on the family stereo in the living room, the youngest son watched, amazed, as his mother, aunts, and uncles danced around the room to the rivetgun pop of "Blitzkrieg Bop" and "Beat on the Brat." It wasn't the reaction he expected at all: Didn't they know they were listening to radical punk rock from the city? Maybe they did, but maybe, he realized, they simply wanted to shed their troubles for a night and laugh and dance.

The sons visited the father in the hospital soon thereafter. "It was kind of heavy," Thurston says. "He looked like he'd been run over by a car." He talked a bit to his father, told him about college and his interest in being a journalism major; George seemed happy to hear it, even if his son wasn't sure that was the route for him. George too was thinking of moving on; before his illness, he told his wife that office politics at WestConn were wearing him down, and he was thinking of relocating the family back to Florida. But a few days later, on the morning of October 1, 1976, a far more devastating call came into the Moore home: George had died overnight, of cardiac arrest as a result of the tumor. He was fifty years old.

Even though the family had been warned that his chances of survival after the initial surgery were slim at best, everyone was stunned. "His father was charming and wonderful," says Paris. "It shouldn't have been happening." Eleanor went into shock, but it was Thurston who seemed to take it hardest; when the unthinkable news arrived, Eleanor saw her youngest son rip apart a wool sweater with his hands. To her distress, his acting out didn't end with that gesture. He dropped out of college after only a quarter semester and took a night-shift job at a local doughnut shop; his new best friend was a local hood named Mark, who would pick up Thurston after work to get stoned. "I was at kind of loose ends," Moore says. "It was a fucked-up time." One snowy afternoon, he found himself standing outside his next-door neighbor's house; Mark, who claimed to have burglary experience, proved it by smashing a pane on the back door and entering the unoccupied home. The two snuck in and stole some electronics gear; Moore also swiped a copy of Joni Mitchell's *Court and Spark*, an album he'd always been curious to hear.

The next morning, Susan told her mother that a couple of policemen were sniffing around in the family's backyard. The cops informed Eleanor of the break-in and that footprints in the snow led from the scene of the crime right to the Moore house. At first, Eleanor couldn't believe her son would do any such thing, but the truth was confirmed when Thurston and his friend picked up and left town—just jumped into the Moores' white Volkswagen and headed for Mark's family's home in Michigan. The trip was a debacle; they had no food or money, Mark's parents weren't happy to see their son, and the car broke down, after which Thurston hitchhiked back to Bethel (following a brief layover in New Jersey with someone who picked him up and turned out to be gay, much to Moore's confusion). A policeman spotted him sitting in a park in Bethel and drove him back to Cod Fish Hill Road. "He's home!" Eleanor exclaimed to Harold Paris over the phone.

Arriving at the Moore house, Paris saw his friend acting as if nothing had happened; he seemed happy to be back on familiar ground. Eventually, he was put on probation and made to pay a fine. The matter would be put behind him, rarely discussed in the family, although the repercussions of his father's swift passing would be felt in many ways, and for years to come.

He already had one escape valve in place. In November 1976, a month after his father's death, Moore and Paris finally took the plunge into the world of live music in New York City. They'd been reading about it for so long—all the clubs hosting all the new music they were hearing on record—and the time came to finally experience it firsthand. Borrowing the Moore family car, they headed for Max's Kansas City, then the city's leading entry point into fringe rock & roll.

Located on Park Avenue between 17th and 18th Streets, Max's was in a tonier, slightly more upscale area than where most of the city's other punk clubs could be found. Yet the cruddiness of the city—the trash-strewn streets and overall feel of urban depression that engulfed it after a paralyzing recession the previous year—was hard to avoid. They could taste it as soon as they parked the car and headed toward the large, black, and slightly cheeky "steak, lobster, chick peas" sign that hung over Max's entrance. The drive had taken an hour and a half, and they were so naïve they arrived two hours early and had to wait in the bar downstairs until the doors opened. They had no idea who was performing—some new band called the Cramps, another one called

Suicide. The latter, the headliners, were particularly eye-opening. The two Connecticut teenagers sat, jaws scraping the floor, as the band's singer, Alan Vega, emitted whoops, pushed over customers' tables, and jabbed a lit cigarette into his arm. Behind him, Martin Rev coaxed grim electronic bleats out of his keyboards. The performance—a demented urban yawp—was like nothing they'd seen or heard. Stunned and disoriented by the performance, they fled halfway through it, barely talking during the drive back home.

As jarring as the evening was, it nevertheless pushed them to return for more. In what became a routine, they would find the latest issue of the *Village Voice* in Bethel, jump in the VW, zip down Interstate 84 to the curvy Saw Mill River Parkway, park wherever they could, and try to get into whatever club seemed to have a punk band they'd heard of. Their timing couldn't have been better. Punk had made itself known in the city a few years before, at clubs like CBGB, a former country and bluegrass bar on the Bowery where a new group of scruffy anti-stars were offering an alternative to the sort of arena concerts—Rick Wakeman, Kiss, Blue Öyster Cult—that Moore had grown up seeing.

For anyone living outside New York City, the scene, like the city itself, was scary, magical, dangerous, and alluring all at once. Only a few years old, it already seemed mythical, dominated by larger-than-life characters like Smith, the Ramones, and Tom Verlaine and Richard Lloyd of Television. Moore owned an album called *Live at CBGB's*, and the first time he and Paris wandered into the club, entering its narrow, darkened tunnel of an entrance, he says, "it felt like we were walking through the front cover, like we were entering the Alice in the Looking Glass thing and actually walking into the cover of the record and into another dimension." The reverie ended when a bottle smashed over his and Paris's heads soon after they wandered in.

The ritual of driving and concertgoing would continue for months. Moore always insisted they arrive early so that they could be at the front of the stage; sometimes they would be so jammed in that they would have to forget about peeing until late in the evening. They would see Blondie or John Cale, Philip Glass performing a new composition,

North Star, at a loft in SoHo, Patti Smith reading poetry. Record shopping at the iconic Bleecker Bob's one night, Paris poked Moore in the side; looking up, Moore saw Smith wander in, eating a piece of pizza. "We looked at all these people as stars," Paris said. "It was a dream come true to see them."

It wasn't merely celebrity that attracted them. Given George Moore's interest in art, foreign films, and literature, the avant garde was no stranger in the Moore home. Whether it was George's influence or simply another consequence of the anger that still hovered in light of his sudden death, the words of punk songs appealed to Thurston as much as the music. The Beat-generation connection was clear enough; he would read interviews in which Smith would gush over the work of William S. Burroughs and Allen Ginsberg, and then track down those writers' books. Yet punk songs were also bursting with visceral, primal rage, the sort that didn't come naturally to him in conversation. "I thought Led Zeppelin were great, but all their lyrics were either veiled references to groupies and sex or this mystical podunk stuff," he says. "But the Stooges' lyrics, like 'Search and Destroy,' were amazing to me. 'Your Pretty Face Is Going to Hell' struck a chord with me, lyrically." The demented humor of the Dictators' *Go Girl Crazy* spoke to a kid who'd played the part of a serial killer in one of his school plays.

Another record store, this one closer to home, proved to be equally pivotal. One day in December 1976, Moore returned to Cutler's, the New Haven shop where he'd purchased the Ramones album two months earlier. There, flipping through the Velvet Underground bin, was another towering record buyer, seven years his senior, named John King. At the time, King worked at a local art supply store but fantasized about a life as either a musician (he'd been playing guitar for a decade and had a band in Providence) or an underground cartoonist. They began talking about how sparse the Velvets bin was; on the way out, Moore recommended King buy the Ramones album. King thought his new acquaintance was curious: a punk rock kid who loved the Dead Boys but had a haircut straight out of *A Hard Day's Night*. "He was calling David Byrne and Tom Verlaine the great poets of their generation," King recalls, "but he was also into stuff like Al Stewart." They exchanged addresses and phone numbers.

Months after the traumatic incident he would later refer to as his "crime spree," Moore received a letter from King, informing him that King had just moved to New York—in September 1977—and was thinking of putting together a band. They needed a bass player—was the punk rock kid interested? Although he'd never played in a band before, much less performed on any sort of stage, Moore had few other alternatives. He and Paris drove into the city one day, meeting King at a midtown welfare hotel where he was staying while his downtown digs passed a fire-inspection code. Moore brought one of his brother's guitars, and he and King sat down and strummed out a few ideas. Upfront, King said he didn't know if he could play that fast. But to Paris, the matchup seemed to instill in his friend an urgency he hadn't seen before. "It just seemed that after his father's death, he got serious about what he wanted his future to be," Paris says. "It was a catalyst for him saying, 'I know what I want to do with my life. I want to play music. I want to have a band.'"

FROM HIS LOFT at 85 South Street, King could smell the fish; their odor wafted through the windows of the space he and his musician (and art-school) friends John Miller, Randy Ludacer, and Danny Walworth had rented for $500 a month. The Fulton Fish Market, with its docks, ships, and freshly shipped-in seafood, was down the block. So was Wall Street, but when the workdays ended, the area became instantly deserted.

Yet it seemed like the only place to go. SoHo, the artists' colony below Houston Street in the Village, had not only been revived but was already seeing signs of gentrification. As a result, finding living space soon became difficult, especially for broke musicians barely making ends meet with day jobs. Heading south, King and his friends moved into the loft in the fall of 1977, building little bedroom areas for themselves in the space. The roommates had to walk what seemed like a mile to find a supermarket; the only nearby bar catered mostly to the grimy fish market workers. But the space allowed the fledgling band, with Ludacer and King on guitars, Walworth on drums, and Miller on bass, to set up their equipment and practice in a windowless room with exposed brick. Friends and fellow musicians could easily crash if there was nowhere else for them to go.

The kid from Connecticut took King up on his offer not only to play with the band but to sleep on their floors; with little happening in Bethel, he was happy to take the long drives (or train rides) into the city to bang out chords with them. Stationed at an army base in New Jersey after he'd enlisted in the air force, Gene Moore began hearing from friends back in Bethel who'd see his younger brother Thurston on the train with his guitar, either heading into or returning from the city. "What the hell is your brother doing?" they'd ask him, as if the kid was engaging in something utterly incomprehensible and dangerous; Gene didn't know how to answer.

From the start, the band wasn't quite fully formed. King had ambitions to play what he calls "progressive garage rock," borrowing freely from sources like the Modern Lovers to more recent bands like Talking Heads. With his horn-rim glasses and AV-club haircut, King even looked the nerd-rocker part. As far as the newest addition to the band, King immediately noticed Moore didn't always show up for practice on time, never seemed to have a spare set of strings, and never seemed to have any money (yet somehow always came with the latest punk singles). But King was thrilled to have what he called a genuine teenager in the band and noticed how natural a guitar player he was; the kid's wrist seemed so loose.

The group was originally called Room Tone, a transparent attempt to make themselves sound appropriately arty; one night, the roommates and bandmates took one of many alcohol-fueled strolls around deserted downtown, spray-painting the band name on random walls. After Ludacer decided to form his own group, a lineup eventually coalesced with King and Moore on guitars, Walworth still on drums, and John Miller on bass, although Miller soon left, replaced by Bob Pullin. In the kitchen of the loft one day, King joked they should change their name to the Coachmen as a tongue-in-cheek homage to all the garage bands around the country who once used that name, and the idea stuck. At their first gig, at a loft co-owned by an emerging conceptual artist named Jenny Holzer, they played the Modern Lovers' "She Cracked" and a few originals, the new kid cutting his finger during some frenetic double-strumming with King.

"We've got a radical lifestyle," King intoned in one of the band's originals. Like most of their repertoire, "Radical Lifestyle" (and another song, "Girls Are Short") felt like one long nervous tic; the buzzy guitar drone, spare drum rhythms, and deadpan singing were so taut they sounded neurotic. King sang all the songs, with Moore strumming along or coming up with guitar ideas, like what King calls a Beatles-influenced part for "Girls Are Short." On "Household Word," King and Moore dual-picked so fast they approached a New York version of bluegrass. It wasn't the new kid's preferred style of music—it barely approached the wild giddiness of punk—but it was a band and an opportunity.

Thanks to King's determination, the Coachmen managed to score one show at Max's and another couple at CBGB. The gigs weren't particularly well attended and usually took place on off nights with bands with whom the Coachmen had little in common. But to Moore's high-school friend Paris, who attended them, the impact on his friend was evident: "He walked offstage at CB's," Paris says, "and he didn't want to look back."

With the help of a real-estate broker, Moore soon found his own place, a one-bedroom hellhole on East 13th Street near Avenue B, a part of the East Village overrun with drugs and squatter buildings. The bathtub was in the kitchen, the old toilet had a pull chain, and he couldn't afford a telephone; the pay phone down the block would have to suffice. He painted the walls strange colors to make it look, he says, "like an insane asylum." The Puerto Rican family downstairs had a large Jesus statue in their living room that was visible from the street; on certain nights, they would get drunk and start fighting. One night he returned home to find the front door ajar, his cassette deck and guitar—the Stratocaster given to him by his brother Gene—gone. To make enough money to pay the rent, he began working a series of day jobs, including ones at a recording studio and a furniture store called Design Research. For twisted kicks, he would watch the TV sitcom *Three's Company*, about two women and a man who live together by pretending the man is gay. His mother, still coping with the death of her husband, never saw the apartment; reports from her daughter of its decrepitude made her glad she never did.

By late 1979, the Coachmen had a new, more commanding drummer, a recently relocated Pittsburgh kid named Dave Keay who replaced the barely proficient Walworth. But the scene, and any opportunities therein, was still far from welcoming. In the little over two years since King and his friends had first arrived in the city and set up shop, the community had changed. The bands King worshipped had either scored hit records and moved on to larger venues (Blondie and Talking Heads) or had disbanded (Television). What arose from the ashes of the original punk was no wave, a rattling, amelodic clatter that prided itself on the absence of traditional melody or instrumental chops. A short-lived movement led by bands like Teenage Jesus and the Jerks, DNA, and Mars, no wave was centered in the squalid, drug-heavy streets of the East Village. Its rival scene, the punk jazz bands, was based several blocks south, in SoHo. The no-wavers saw the SoHo crowd, epitomized by the nattily dressed Lounge Lizards, as soft and wimpy; the SoHo crowd saw the no-wavers as antimusical.

In that context, the Coachmen were an almost overnight anomaly: too melodic for the punk and no-wave crowd, too quirky for anyone else. Their button-down shirts didn't project any particular image. They experimented with a funk beat on "Stay in My Room" and tried to sound grimmer and grimier like DNA and Mars, but neither move felt quite right.

"We were naïve," says Keay. "We just figured, 'We'll play the gigs and sooner or later someone will respond to it.'" But hardly anyone seemed to. "We'd go to the *SoHo Weekly News* with our flier and ask them to announce a show," says Moore, "but nobody would." King began growing tired of calling CBGB every week and hoping the line wasn't busy, and, if it wasn't, that the gruff guy on the other end of the line wouldn't give them another bad day or time slot. They began rehearsing less and thinking about other options, and eventually King decided enough was enough. They would play a few more gigs, then pack it in. Their show at the Plugg Club would most likely be their swan song; it wasn't meant to be.

IN A SCENE FILLED with people who were anything but inconspicuous, she still managed to stand out. It wasn't merely those flip-up sunglasses, which were both impossibly bookish and practical (she wasn't yet able to afford contact lenses). Her hair fell in a straight, brown shag, and instead of the black jeans and tights preferred by her friends, she tended to wear layers of clothes or men's shirts. She also had an Australian sheepdog that made her seem outdoorsy and athletic in a way no one had quite seen before, at least not anywhere south of 14th Street in Manhattan in the early months of 1980.

In fact, she wasn't from there, nowhere close. Her father, Calvin Wayne Gordon—everyone called him Wayne—was born in Kansas, where he taught elementary and high school. A tall, gangly farm boy, he met Althea Coplen, a blond, blue-eyed girl with a knack for sewing her own clothes, at Emporia College in Kansas; each was studying for a degree in library sciences. Wayne eventually wound up teaching and working as a guidance counselor at a high school in Ferguson, Missouri, and he and Althea married in 1942. A son, Keller, came first, followed by a daughter, Kim Althea, on April 28, 1953.

Wayne was no typical farmhand; his training in education and his masters and PhD in sociology paved the way for a book, *The Social System of High School: A Study in the Sociology of Adolescence*, which the Free Press of Glencoe, Illinois, published in 1957. With its charts and graphs, its dissection of social groups like "clydes" and "big wheels," the book constituted the first major study of adolescent school cliques and factions; it was also plainly the work of an analytical, curious mind.

A year after the publication of his book, the family relocated to Rochester, New York, where Wayne began teaching in the sociology department of Rochester University. In later years, the daughter would have no memories of that town; when she was barely kindergarten age, they picked up and left for California, where Wayne took a job in the sociology department of UCLA. As a result of sabbaticals related to Wayne's job, the family spent one year in Hawaii, during their daughter's sixth grade, and another in Hong Kong. In Hong Kong, she found her first boyfriend, who drummed in a local band; in Hawaii, as a blond white girl, she learned how it felt to be a minority.

But most of their time was spent in West Los Angeles, in a small house on Prosser Avenue with a compact front yard and a vegetable garden in the back. For Althea—who was born in Los Angeles, after which her family relocated to Wichita, Kansas—it was a homecoming of sorts. Decades before, her grandfather had sold his farmland in Beverly Hills to developers. One of its streets, Swall Drive, was named in his family's honor. While Wayne taught, Althea made clothes at home for the family, sometimes selling them for extra cash. She'd learned the trade as a teenager; during the Depression, her family had been so poor they had no choice but to create their own apparel. One of her earliest creations—an orange-and-brown polka-dot dress with an orange cape—made people in Wichita sit up and notice. As her younger sister Marian would say, "She was determined to be somebody."

Both parents were modest and quiet. "Wayne wasn't the joking type," Marian recalls. "But then again, Althea wasn't either." One of Wayne's UCLA colleagues would later describe him as "courteous but aloof . . . always calm, under control." Many described Althea the same way, and they would also say the same of their daughter, who was blond and comely in a surfer-girl way and was, by her own admission, rebellious and angst-ridden during high school. "My mom didn't say much and was very quiet," Gordon says. "And at one point, I decided to take after her." A self-described tomboy, she took dance lessons (her mother enrolled her, but then warned her that a dancer's life was a bad one and that she shouldn't pursue it as a profession) and made clay sculptures in school, some of which would share space in the house with her father's extensive collection of jazz records. Sometimes she would arrange her father's album covers in a particular order, make up a story to accompany them, and then act out the story as a dance.

As in the similarly academic- and art-minded Moore household, jazz (courtesy of her father) and the classic rock of the '60s (by way of her older brother Keller) were in the air. One of her closest friends, William Winant, discovered that for himself when, during their sophomore year at University High School in West Los Angeles, she introduced him to the music of Pharoah Sanders and painted the speakers in his garage stereo to resemble the cover of Miles Davis' *Miles in the Sky;* another day, she brought over a copy of Joni Mitchell's new album, *Blue*. She and Winant wound up in the same dance class; together, they performed a modern-dance routine to Crosby, Stills & Nash's "Wooden Ships," a song of her choosing and one very much of the Southern Californian culture of the time.

She and Winant, who had a crush on her, were part of the school's creative crowd, the teenagers interested in music, film, dance, and art. The crowd soon came to include Danny Elfman, a newly arrived transfer student from nearby Baldwin Hills. Elfman met Gordon in dance class—his way of avoiding being in gym, which he loathed—and before long, they began dating. Visiting Gordon in her family home, Elfman loved nothing better than to hang out in her room, take in her Billie Holiday records, and listen to his girlfriend's voice, which always felt soothing and comforting. For a teenager, Gordon struck Elfman as centered and calm, almost adult—"a grown-up bohemian," he recalls. Like many kids in school, he'd also been impressed when he heard she'd been busted, so to speak, at Disneyland while smoking on one of the attractions.

Far from strict disciplinarians, Wayne and Althea sent both children to progressive schools early on and rarely badgered them to get straight As and do their homework. Between her parents' less restrictive tendencies and her brother Keller's increasing rambunctiousness, she was often left to her devices, some wilder than others—hitchhiking to Malibu or sometimes up to San Francisco to see bands like Jefferson Airplane and Cream at the Fillmore.

During the times he was invited over for Thanksgiving dinner, Winant was always struck by the normalcy of the Gordon home, especially compared to his own family's hectic life; his father's career as an actor led to many absences. But something was a little off, too. Keller had always been a handful, always getting into trouble. He was taking a lot of acid at the time, and in his twenties, when his sister was in her teens, he was diagnosed with schizophrenia. For Wayne and Althea, the situation was devastating; Althea especially had looked to Keller to be the star of the family, the one who wouldn't have to work so hard to prove himself as she and her husband had. When Keller's diagnosis came through, "it broke her heart," says her sister Marian. The Gordons didn't believe in therapy; they felt families should deal with problems on their own. For a while Keller lived a reclusive life in Malibu; when his sister next saw him, he was wearing a robe and quoting the Bible. But he was also verbal and an intellectual, adept at spouting Shakespeare. When he finally returned to the Gordon home, he parked his mobile home in the driveway and lived there by himself; his sister would pop in and smoke hash with him.

After graduating from University High in 1971, she'd hoped to attend the California Institute of the Arts, highly regarded for its art and creative programs. But the family couldn't afford the tuition, so instead she enrolled at Santa Monica College. During her brief time there, she reunited with Elfman. They'd broken up during their senior year in high school, but now the two began sharing a home in Venice, where Elfman bought her a gray sheepdog they named Egan (inspired by a joke related to a sci-fi movie they'd once watched). Then, with her other high-school friend Winant, she transferred to York University in Toronto in 1975, where she immersed herself deeper in dance and the arts, directing (but not starring in) a student film about '70s rich-girl-hostage-turned-renegade Patty Hearst. She also had her first taste of onstage performance when, for a class project, she, Winant, and two other fellow students formed an ad-hoc band. Their debut, at the Ann Arbor Film Festival, was auspicious, Gordon dancing and screaming along to what Winant calls "noisy no-wave songs. But that's where she got the bug to perform."

York didn't prove to be satisfying, either, so soon she returned to Los Angeles to enroll in the Otis Art Institute of Los Angeles County, which would prove to be the most important stint in her nomadic post-high-school life. It was there she attended a lecture by Dan Graham, a cantankerous New Yorker (although born in Illinois and raised in New Jersey) who was busting open the world of conceptual art in any way he could by way of photography, video installations, and writing. At Otis she met Michael Gira, a "vituperative, raging, and deluded young male," in his words, also interested in art and music. Gira remembers Gordon as "a mousy post-hippie girl" and "sort of opaque" yet one who was intelligent and "a real challenge intellectually." Gira's class work was dark and fueled by anger; with their emphasis on nudity, body piercing, and S&M imagery, his projects were intended to make everyone squirm. Gordon's, by comparison, were more whimsical in their humor and sensibility; they seemed to be straight out of the postmodern art world of the Fluxus movement. To Gira, one of Gordon's most memorable projects was a blank postcard that read, "This Is Space."

At Otis, appropriation began playing a larger role in her creations. She began using advertisements cut out of magazines as the basis for class assignments, although not always to the amusement of her teachers: One failed her for a project in which she painted in the windows of cars in automobile advertisements. "Proposal for a Story," written in 1977, took its cue from the movie rating system, but with a twist: "Stylized Italian animation/Some strong language," it began, before devolving, with subtle dry wit, into parodies of the same language: "Subtitled romantic tragedy . . . Some bathroom humor . . . Amoral, crude disrespect for law, some sex . . . Considerable bloodshed." It was both a playful poke at Hollywood and a jab at the increasing nihilism of its products.

"West Coast pop art was very different from British or East Coast," recalls John Knight, an artist and Otis teacher who was one of Gordon's instructors. "It was about montage, text, suburban America and, of course, film and pop culture. Kim was interested in all of that." In January, 1977, she was handed her diploma. Yet she still had no particular direction, especially when it came to a life or a career in Los Angeles.

SHE'D VISITED NEW YORK CITY once before, in early 1979, around the time Sid Vicious was stabbing his girlfriend Nancy Spungen to death. A bad relationship had sent her out of Los Angeles, and she was instantly attracted to the city's art scene and its music, particularly the no-wave bands she saw during her initial stay. She stayed in a place on Fulton Street, mere blocks from where John King and some of the Coachmen had a loft. Returning to Los Angeles, she decided New York would be her next home, but first she had to save up some money by waitressing at an Indian restaurant. Later in the year, she drove across the country with her friend Mike Kelley, a fellow art student; by the oddest of coincidences, Kelley had seen Gordon, Winant, and their class rock project at the Ann Arbor Film Festival, where Kelley was a student. Kelley later transferred to the California Institute of the Arts.

Upon arriving in the city, Gordon immediately called Dan Graham, who, as it turned out, was friends with Knight—not just Gordon's teacher at Otis but a later boyfriend as well. Gregarious, flirtatious, and intellectually rigorous, Graham had become the city's conceptual-art godfather, and his fascination with rock & roll—he had had a side career as a music critic—led him to discover not only punk and no wave but the connections between music and art. "The art world was going toward more business in the late sixties," he says, "so we had a kind of communalism that took place in rock clubs." Gordon needed a place to crash, and Graham directed her to a large loft owned (and rented out) by a boyfriend of artist Jenny Holzer. A recent arrival herself, from Ohio, Holzer was just beginning a career as a conceptual artist, creating pieces in which words and phrases would be transposed onto billboards, walls, and other public spaces; the effects were both playful and monolithic.

The intermingling of artists and musicians wasn't brand new: In Michigan, Kelley had been in a band called Destroy All Monsters and later formed another crude, punk-rooted band, Poetics, in Los Angeles with another rising artist, Tony Oursler. In downtown New York in 1980, the intersection of art and music felt even more natural. Up-and-coming artists like Robert Longo and Richard Prince could be found playing guitar in noisy no-wave bands. "At that time, being in a band was the hot thing to do," recalls Christine Hahn, a visual artist who'd moved to the city from Cincinnati several years before. "The artists weren't getting enough feedback from being artists, so they did music too, which is where they got the most feedback." Hahn, who was painting and designing album covers, experienced the thrill first-hand: During the city's 1977 blackout, she sat down at an empty drum kit—no electricity required—and began playing the instrument for the first time in her life. Taking to it immediately, she decided she was a drummer despite having nothing close to training. So it would be in the new scene, where one could be whatever one wanted to be; ideas and raw drive were as important as raw talent.

Hahn's transformation was standard for the time. Artists and musicians alike flocked to the empty warehouses below Houston Street for cheap, ideal, and sometimes illegal work spaces and homes. They also shared a postmodern sensibility, a deconstruction of everything that had come before. Art, music, illustration—all were in the process of being torn down, reassembled, and combined with other media. Conceptual art not only toyed with the notions of what art should be but how audiences should respond to it. Rap, emerging from the streets, party rooms, and gutted buildings of the Bronx, placed its emphasis on sampling and recycled beats. The music was finding a home downtown as well, personified by the way Blondie integrated rapping and graffiti art in the single and video of their hit "Rapture." Graffiti art had become the scourge of the city, thanks to renegade spray-painters who'd splatter subways; it was still illegal, but galleries began showing the graffiti taggers' work, further throwing the idea of what constituted art on its head.

"There was nothing sacred, and anything that was perceived as sacred had to be reduced," recalls Richard Edson, a musician who arrived in the city during this time. "It was the beginning of a whole new age, in which the whole modern era, the modernist era, came to an end. What took its place was irony: *Nothing* is serious now. It was a really exciting time, like when Communism fell."

With her interest in appropriation, art, music, pop culture, and painting—as well as her growing distaste for the traditional, moneyed art world—Gordon fell into a scene seemingly conceived to accommodate her interests. Graham was more than happy to help guide her. To him, Gordon was "totally lost. She had no real direction. Maybe she was shy because she was out of her element." He took her to clubs and gallery openings, introducing her to his network of artists and musicians. Graham felt she could be a writer ("that's the way you learn about things—to write about other artists"), and with his help and connections, she published some of her first work. "Trash Drugs and Male Bonding," printed in the underground *Real Life* magazine in March 1980, was a nearly beat-by-beat description of a performance by avant-guitarist and composer Rhys Chatham and his band; the article's title referred to the discussion of the way (in Gordon's words) "drugs are for the musicians so they can indulge in their playing"—a philosophy a child of the California '60s lifestyle most likely identified with. When an apartment became available in Graham's building on Eldridge Street, in an old Jewish neighborhood on the Lower East Side, Graham even found her a home, right below his.

Each day or week seemed to bring a new connection. She took a secretarial job at the Annina Nosei Gallery, and, at Graham's suggestion, started a semi-serious company, Design Office—"furniture arranged for the home or office," read one of their fliers—with a friend, Vikky Alexander. One of she and Alexander's first projects, very much in keeping with Gordon's interest in conceptual art, involved repainting and rearranging Graham's kitchen as an art space; the centerpiece was an 8-x-11 piece of white paper containing a Gordon sketch of Blondie's Debbie Harry.

Soon enough, Graham also introduced her to an intense, cockily confident guitarist and composer named Glenn Branca. An expatriate from Boston, Branca had grown up a rock fan—he loved the early Aerosmith albums—but gravitated toward a career in the theater instead. With a friend, he formed a company called the Bastard Theater, writing his own admittedly vicious and violent songs to accompany the productions. But New York beckoned. In 1976, with only $900 in his pocket, he moved to the city with the idea of furthering his theatrical interests. "People were so afraid of New York," he says. "When I told people I was moving, they said, 'Are you out of your fucking mind?' But we *needed* to be here. It was the last place left. For punk rock and new music and experimental performance art, it was the only place to come. There was *nowhere else.*" Branca, who had the hardened mug of a city detective, soon found himself surrounded by kindred spirits in all art forms, and theater began taking a back seat to rock. With a keyboardist and songwriter named Jeffrey Lohn, Branca formed Theoretical Girls, who made tense, nervy rock before breaking up after a year. Afterward, with his girlfriend Barbara Ess and drummer Christine Hahn, he put together another band, the Static.

Gordon soon became friendly with Branca and Ess, even giving them an art gift—what Branca recalls as "a photograph she had cut out of some *Architectural Digest*, crumpled up and put inside of a sandwich bag and ziplocked it. It was fucking brilliant." In California, Gordon had already begun wearing flip-up sunglass shades, but it was Branca who suggested she wear them indoors as a fashion statement. Branca also left his musical mark on her: Gordon saw the Static perform and found it inspiring. She'd never been especially fond of the moshing gyrations of Los Angeles hardcore, yet the way the new downtown music required its bands to have no musical requirements intrigued her: "I never thought I was a good singer. I was a *terrible* singer. But in punk rock that didn't matter."

Before long, Hahn began noticing the new girl in town at Static shows, where Gordon would ask Hahn questions about what it was like to be in a band. Gordon asked so many questions that at first Hahn thought she was being interviewed. To Hahn, Gordon seemed "intense and laid-back at the same time. If she wanted something, she was going to get it. It wasn't obnoxious; it was just very tenacious."

The Static disbanded soon thereafter, but Hahn and Gordon, who'd become friendly by then, were soon drafted into a band—or, more to the point, an art project. Playing off his article "New Wave Feminism"—about, in his words, "how exciting female bonding is to men in the audience"—Graham had arranged for a performance piece at the Massachusetts College of Art in early 1980: an intentionally crude all-woman band. All he needed were participants, and as a way to encourage Gordon to dabble in music, he asked her, Hahn, and Stanton Miranda to become that group.

Miranda became especially supportive and encouraging of the shy, somewhat aloof girl from California, telling her to pretty herself up by wearing makeup and encouraging her to take off her glasses. ("Kim wore the worst, ugliest dresses," Graham says. "But all the women back then were afraid of rape. These were sexually oriented women trying to look unsexual.") Congregating at Miranda's loft with a guitar, bass, and drum kit, the three began figuring out who would play which instrument and writing primitive songs. In an early indication of the way she would take her interest in collage and extrapolation and adapt it to a musical setting, Gordon brought along an advertisement from *Cosmopolitan* magazine and turned its ad copy into lyrics. During another song, Gordon began singing. Her voice was soft and hesitant, yet Hahn was struck by its surprisingly smoky quality. "It was very pure sounding," she recalls. "She couldn't sing on key very well, but she had a very nice vocal quality."

The band was dubbed CKM, after their first names, and its one and only performance, at the festival, was something of a debacle. Hahn recalls Miranda freezing up onstage, unable to sing a word, followed by a dispirited train ride back to New York. Gordon felt it went better: "I remember the next day feeling, 'That was rock and roll. That was so exciting. I want to do that again.' Music had this emotive, visceral quality I felt I couldn't find in my art. I enjoyed art but intellectually I wasn't sure where it fit in—how it hit me, what it meant to me. But I liked the physicality of music."

By that time, Miranda had had another visitor to her loft, the kid from Connecticut named Thurston. He and Miranda's boyfriend, Michael Shamberg, worked together at one of Moore's many day jobs of the time, Design Research. Shamberg suggested Moore and Miranda meet: "We lived in a place where they could make a lot of noise, and they made a lot of noise." One day, the sandy-haired kid showed up with a guitar and an interest in playing something other than the recycled chords of the Coachmen or punk rock, which, to his mind, was more steeped in Chuck Berry and therefore conventional. Miranda began playing electro pulses and patterns on a keyboard; in turn, the kid started thrashing about wildly on the guitar.

"Do you always play like that?" she asked when he finished.

"*Now* I do," he replied, in a deep, deadpan tone that would become his manner.

"It was about being challenged," he would say later. "'What if we really just played *anything* on the guitar?' It totally destroyed any pre-conceived idea of rock and roll as a rhythm-and-blues-based music. It was totally liberating."

Not long after, Miranda told her friend Kim about Thurston, calling him "sweet and a special guitar player." Gordon had also heard he had a number of female friends, which intrigued her further; it made her think he was, in one way or another, a good person. They finally met that night at Plugg, and when the band began its show, Gordon immediately noted how collectively tall the Coachmen were—everybody did, the first time they saw the band—and admired the herky-jerky, Talking Heads influences in their songs. She'd always dated men either her age or older, never younger, but there was something about him: the harmonics he was playing on guitar or what she would later call the "little glow" around him.

It wasn't long before they encountered each other again. One night he went to the Ear Inn, a watering hole with the Hudson River in sight, and as he was leaving, he saw her walking Egan. He remembered her immediately, and she said, "I knew you'd be here." No one had ever said that to him before. They walked around the block, talking music and upcoming club shows that sounded worth catching. At one of them—8 Eyed Spy at Tier 3 on August 1—there she was, once more. Other casual meetings at clubs ensued, and one day he received a postcard from her when she was in California vacationing with her parents at their favorite fishing camp. He was struck by the unexpected gesture.

Finally, one night, they found themselves near his apartment. He had a feeling that if he were to ask her up, she would take him up on his offer. But he was too much of a coward to ask, and he wasn't sure he knew how to handle the situation anyway. Instead, he offered up a meek "See you later," and she headed back home. Later, he wondered if he'd blown it for good and if something else within his grasp had slipped away.

Chapter 2

As IT TURNED OUT, the courtship period was brief, as short as one of the wham-bang punk songs he couldn't get enough of. A few days after the night at Plugg, Christine Hahn ran into Gordon at an audition for a performance piece, where Gordon, Egan straining at his leash, began talking excitedly about the cute punk rock boy she'd just met. "I knew that was the guy for her," Hahn recalls. "That was who she wanted to be with, and she knew it the first time she met him. It was love at first sight, and she was going to get him and that was that. She was very determined."

After the first aborted night out, she eventually invited him back to her place at 84 Eldridge Street. The first time he visited, he saw a strangely familiar sight—a black guitar that had been floating around the scene, from guitarist to guitarist. A friend of the Coachmen's had once owned it, and as it turned out, Gordon knew the girlfriend of the previous owner. In what amounted to either a sign or the strangest of coincidences, the guitar was now in her home. He was a little surprised to see it there, but it also relieved any possible tension. Taking it in his large hands, he sat down and started playing it as they began to talk.

From the start, they were different in ways other than physical stature. She was college educated; he wasn't. ("He had a way of pretending he knew about things," she says. "He was confident.") He had a prankish side that people would sometimes find jarring, like the way he would suddenly burst into a scream just to throw someone off.

Even when he would make a serious point, he'd almost always end the remark with an offhand joke and a quick chuckle. As her art projects revealed, her humor was drier and terser. And yet the matchup somehow felt right. They shared a disdain for the big-dollar art world springing up around them, one she'd been witnessing firsthand by working at galleries and seeing the way the owners would fight over artists. He was her entry into the rock world; she was his into the art scene. They made each other feel legitimate—cool—in their respective worlds.

Her strongest memory of his apartment on East 13th Street was the mountain of dirty clothes rising up in the middle of it. Within a few months, he'd moved into her place at 84 Eldridge; he'd begun staying over anyway, so it made sense. Her home, a standard tenement railroad apartment, was bigger than his, although not by much. The kitchen in the front housed a grimy, crackled tub that doubled as a serving table when a metal plate was laid over it. The sink was mounted in an odd, sideways manner. Since the stairways were in the middle of the building, the apartment's second room was slanted and sagging; years later, their friend Mike Watt would visit and feel he had to get his sea legs as soon as he walked in. The small space in the back was generally given over to the bedroom, which amounted to a mattress on the floor. Often they would hear their upstairs neighbor, Dan Graham, running around or dropping pieces of art onto the floor with a huge *thud*. The building had no intercom, so visitors would have to call from a pay phone down the block and wait for the third-floor window to crack open and a sock with keys to fall onto the street.

Graham was quickly struck by one trait of his protégée's new boyfriend: the way the kid would get headaches and worry it was a sign he had a brain tumor, like the one that had afflicted his father. To Graham, Moore seemed unduly frightened about that. Although Graham was fascinated with Gordon—some, Moore included, sensed he was unusually smitten with her—the older artist also sensed Moore was the right person at the right time for her. "That was a time when people's relationships were very fast," says Graham. "There was no stability. Kim thought Thurston could be a stabilizing force for her. He was someone she could trust, and he projected a certain stability."

Moore's move also made sense in terms of personal safety. Gordon found his block too scary for her taste, not that hers was any less dodgy. Ira Gershwin had been born down the street, at 60 Eldridge, one of many traces of the neighborhood's Jewish roots. But the drug trade sweeping through the East Village—one so seemingly out of control that dealers would take over abandoned buildings and build underground tunnels to facilitate swift escapes from police raids—was within sight. Up the street, on Eldridge between Stanton and Rivington, junkies scavenged for used needles in lots. One block west lay Roosevelt Park, a slice of land carved out in the middle of the block; hookers gathered there nightly, slipping on leg warmers and lighting up garbage cans when the temperatures plunged in winter.

But the apartment was rent-controlled, a mere $125 a month. Their Belgian landlord was convinced he and his building were the last holdouts against the rising numbers of Chinese immigrants moving into the neighborhood, so he was determined to hold onto the property as long as he could. For Moore and Gordon, it was not just a home but a place to escape from messy, troubled recent pasts and family sorrows and reinvent themselves. Many others, an army of musicians and artists dating back decades, had fled to the city for the same reasons; now it was their turn, or so they hoped.

ON THE EVENING OF December 17, 1980, they left their apartment with their guitars, walked up Eldridge, took a left at Grand Street, and, on the other side of Roosevelt Park, arrived at a brown brick building wedged in the middle of Broome Street. They pulled open a metal door, trudged up the gray stairs to the third floor, and set up their instruments for their first live performance together.

It was inevitable they would make music together. "It was all Thurston's doing," says Graham. "He saw her as a Patti Smith and wanted to teach her how to play music. It was his project." Yet what sort of music or racket it would be wasn't immediately clear. Moore's guitar thrashings-about with Stanton Miranda had opened a few new doorways for him, but the specific direction remained unformed: Songs or no songs, rhythm or no rhythm?

Miranda herself was now out of the picture; she'd formed her own band, the Same, and was off on her own escapades. But another, equally provocative woman soon arrived. Always in need of money to help pay the rent and food bills, Moore had taken a one-off job at the recommendation of Miranda and Shamberg: moving pieces of art for Vito Acconci, an iconoclastic artist whose many creative hats—poet, writer, deliberately provocative performance artist who once mastur-bated during an installation—embodied the boundary-crossing arts scene of the moment. As soon as he entered Acconci's Brooklyn loft, Moore noticed a striking blond: Anne DeMarinis, a St. Louis native who was Acconci's younger girlfriend (and former art student). Visu-ally, DeMarinis reminded everyone of glamorous Hollywood actresses of the past—"a female James Dean," says one. She was both feminist and feminine, and half the downtown music community seemed to have a crush on her.

At Acconci's loft, Moore and DeMarinis bonded over their love of cigarettes and Acconci's punk records. DeMarinis, it turned out, was a skilled pianist, and before long, as Acconci watched, they were trading musical ideas and riffs. Soon after, Dave Keay, the Coachmen's last drummer, was invited along, and the seeds of a group were planted. The music was largely unformed, just random chords and ideas, electro keyboards bumping up against Moore's irregular guitar strums and Keay's brawny drumming. One day, Moore casually mentioned that Gordon would be playing too. From the notes she began plucking out on a bass guitar—"completely primitive, one-finger stuff," Moore re-calls—it was clear Gordon was still finding her way with the instru-ment. But at the time, not knowing how to play was as important as playing, so no one seemed to mind or notice. "Kim was learning," says Keay. "But right from the beginning she had the right attitude. When you're playing experimental music, that's the most important thing."

Well-read, intellectually curious, and aggressive, DeMarinis was a good match for Moore and Gordon, and she was willing to play with anyone just to see what came of it. They somehow cobbled together something close to a set and began rehearsing at Acconci's loft. One night, as they were trying to fashion a new style of music out of the old, John Lennon was shot and killed in front of his uptown Manhattan apartment, and the four gathered around a television to watch the news reports.

Quickly, the formative band—Moore, Gordon, Keay, and DeMarinis—picked the first of several names, Male Bonding, a Moore brainstorm. By the time they assembled at the space on Broome Street in December, though, they already had another, odder moniker, Red Milk. The building's third floor was owned by Arleen Schloss, a lovably loopy teacher and performance artist who, with a few artist friends, had bought the building years before for a mere $58,000. It quickly became apparent why no one else wanted to live there or on the block. Drug deals and paraphernalia littered Broome; hookers cruised the block so regularly that one night, Schloss grabbed her Super 8 camera and filmed a blow job for posterity.

With her boyfriend and partner Todd Jorgensen, Schloss decided to turn the loft space, with its sixteen-foot ceilings and wood floors, into a place to present musicians, poets, artists, and whoever was around and couldn't land a gig anywhere else. It was also for friends who couldn't afford the trendier Mudd Club and were more likely to have the three dollars Schloss charged for admission. Since she herself had little extra cash for ads in the *Village Voice*, Schloss and Jorgensen settled for fliers slapped onto buildings up and down the Bowery, right up the block. People either knew about the space or didn't.

They called it A's—mostly to stand for "anarchy," but also reflecting Schloss' love of the alphabet, which she used as a basis for art projects and teaching. Starting October 27, 1979, A's opened as a Wednesday night performance space; two weeks later, the Coachmen gave the first of several shows there. (Another show, on New Year's Eve 1979, paired them with another band, Harry Toledo, that included Keay on drums.) Like most, Schloss recalled the Coachmen as very tall and very loud, although noise wasn't a problem, since the block was so deserted at night that no one was around to complain anyway. Anyone who wasn't fond of whoever was performing on a given night could hang out on a back deck and smoke. A's was the kind of place where, says Keay, "you could play one chord for an hour, and if you did it with conviction, people would respond to it."

In such an atmosphere, Red Milk should have fit right in, but Moore's plan to break from traditional guitar and song patterns remained unfocused. As soon as the four began playing, it was clear something was off. The songs, such as they were, sounded like randomly strung-together parts and chords. DeMarinis' and Gordon's voices circled around each other uncertainly, and Moore interjected, now and then, a gulpy yelp. Keay's drums were so loud Moore could barely hear anything. The music was a muddle, and after fifteen minutes, it all came crashing to a depressing halt. Afterward, they and Acconci went out to grab a bite, and Acconci bluntly told them he thought it was a disaster.

Yet they were determined. By the following month, the quartet had taken yet another new name, the Arcadians, almost as if to make everyone forget about Red Milk. The change came about when Moore read about the ancient Greeks who communicated by way of music and song, and it seemed as good (and new wave) a name as they could find at the time. The Arcadians secured slightly tonier gigs, landing slots at CBGB on January 20 and March 11. But as winter turned to spring, it was apparent DeMarinis wouldn't be long for the band. "I want to be in a band that's *great*," she told Moore one day. The two had been speaking about Public Image Ltd., the mold-breaking band John Lydon had put together after the Sex Pistols had imploded, but Moore felt she was also referring, in some way, to the Arcadians. "I don't think she thought we were going to go that route," Moore says. "Which at the time was very possible."

Walking along Eldridge Street one spring day, Moore told Keay he'd decided to call the nascent band something else. It was, he said, a name he'd had in mind for some time but had never brought up before. It was inspired in part by Fred "Sonic" Smith, the guitarist in the MC5, whose anarchic '60s hard rock paved the way for punk, and in part by revered Jamaican toaster and DJ Big Youth. The deep, undulating rhythms of reggae and dub had infiltrated the downtown music scene. Moore was so invested in the genre he'd begun taking subway trips to a warehouse in Queens that specialized in reggae LPs, and he told Gordon to practice at home by playing along with the bass lines on a Black Uhuru album. With DeMarinis' future with the band in question, Moore felt the new name—Sonic Youth—better reflected his vision of a harsher, more violent band without any electronic keyboards.

"I always thought it looked real good on paper," he recalls. "With Anne, it was always democratic. But I said, 'I'm going to do a show with Kim and a drummer. And if you want to play, it'd be great. But I'm gonna call it Sonic Youth.' It was the first time I ever really enforced something. It was one of my few dictatorial decisions." The band remained wildly in flux in every regard, but the name Sonic Youth implied more of a sound and direction than any of the earlier monikers; Gordon liked it from the start. That problem solved, she and Moore assumed everything else would follow in good time.

IN THE SPRING, they and their music plunged underground. One afternoon, Moore, Gordon, and DeMarinis found themselves in front of a bodega on Second Avenue, not far from Eldridge Street. They pulled open a steel grate on the sidewalk and walked down the metal stairs into a dark, murky hallway that, in turn, lead to a door. Inside a small room were a steam pipe, a couple of amplifiers, and a window so dirt-encrusted it was impossible to see out of it. And waiting for them there was their potential new drummer.

Sonic Youth, this new entity that seemed to exist more as a concept than a reality, would have to exist without Dave Keay. Keay had been offered a job with former Television guitarist Richard Lloyd, who had a major-label record contract and a string of concerts set up to promote his album. Moore seemed surprised Keay wouldn't be playing with *both* bands, telling Keay he was making a mistake to choose Lloyd: "You're going to miss out. I'd think about this." But like others, Keay wasn't sure where Sonic Youth were headed; the sound was foggy, the gigs poorly attended and few and far between, and De-Marinis' role increasingly shaky. For Keay, the Lloyd job seemed like the more promising of the two opportunities.

Musicians, especially drummers, appeared to be everywhere, but Moore and Gordon didn't actually know that many—except for one they'd seen playing around and hanging about A's. Like Gordon and Moore, Richard Edson had arrived in the city fairly recently—in his case, from San Francisco, where he'd done time in funk-oriented bands. Funny, brash, jive-talking, and sporting a nose that looked like it had been broken in a boxing match (but hadn't), he'd grown up in the nearby suburb of New Rochelle but moved to the Bay Area to attend the Berklee School of Music. Realizing the San Francisco punk scene was too limited for his eclectic tastes, he left for Manhattan when he began hearing about a new breed of punk-jazz bands in New York. The idea of combining the energy of punk with elements of jazz and funk so excited him he even left his old drum kit behind in San Francisco.

Edson saw himself as not just a musician—he was adept at not only drums but trumpet, which he'd begun playing in high school—but as a painter and writer. The arts community he discovered in Manhattan couldn't have been more like-minded. He was soon hitting the clubs to meet people and search out work opportunities. To support himself, he took a job in the photo lab at the *SoHo Weekly News*, getting by on working only twenty hours a week. Edson had seen the Coachmen perform at A's; in fact, he lived above the space for three months, subletting from Schloss during the summer of 1980. As he wasn't much of a guitar-rock aficionado, the band hadn't struck him in any particular way except to remind him of New Rochelle's high-school basketball team. But when Moore approached him, saying his new band could use a drummer, Edson, twenty-five at the time, was intrigued and invited them over to a space where he'd been practicing.

The basement room actually belonged to Konk, the heavily percussive avant-funk band in which Edson played trumpet. (He also played in yet another band, Body, at the time.) Gordon, Moore, and DeMarinis plugged in their guitars and keyboard, and almost immediately, Moore began playing his instrument at top volume. "I was like, 'Well, *that's* interesting,'" Edson recalls. "No warming up here." DeMarinis and Gordon joined in, at a similar volume, for what ended up extending to forty-five minutes—no songs, no real jams, just flailing. The tempos, Edson says, were "medium fast, fast, and fast fast."

At one point, Edson noticed small red drops on his drum kit. At first he thought something was dripping from the ceiling—maybe out of the pipes?—before he looked around and noticed blood on Moore's right hand. One of the tone knobs on his guitar had fallen off, leaving only a thin piece of metal sticking out, and Moore, standing several feet away, was playing so frenetically he hadn't realized he was cutting up his hand in the process. Edson immediately stopped; the drum kit was his only possession of any value, and he didn't want it stained, especially with human blood.

Confused, Moore asked Edson why he wasn't playing. When Edson pointed out the problem, Moore looked at his hand and casually acknowledged the dripping cut with an "oh yeah" and a shrug. "Thurston probably thought it was punk rock," says Gordon, "but Richard was totally grossed out." At Edson's request, Moore moved a little further away, and the jamming continued.

Edson couldn't tell if this tall kid was amazing or pretentious, and he didn't know what to make of the rest of this so-called band either. DeMarinis struck him as a bit uptight, and Gordon barely said anything. Gordon's lack of expertise on bass was apparent, but Edson liked the way she stayed on the downbeats and plunked a root note of whatever chord they were playing. For their part, the three of them were puzzled by this new-wave beatnik behind the drum kit. To Moore, Edson, whose style was polyrhythmic in its complexity, "was good, and he had an interesting vibe about him. And we certainly didn't know anyone else." At the end, they asked Edson if he wanted to be in the band, and Edson agreed. "I would just say yes to everything," he says, "because I needed more situations, more practice. I felt that exposing myself to as many different people as possible would be helpful to my playing."

With Edson behind the drums, the new band played its first two shows as Sonic Youth, one on May 8 at Club 57 on St. Mark's Place and another a month later, on June 3, at Great Gildersleeves, a club on the Bowery mostly known for less fashionable hard rock and metal bands from the nearby boroughs. At Gildersleeves, Sonic Youth opened for Glenn Branca, Gordon's acquaintance from her connections with Dan Graham. Edson had a penchant for wearing baseball caps—"an ironic statement on Americanism"—and Gordon asked him to wear one during their shows as an homage of sorts to heavy-metal drummers who did the same. "It was a reference I didn't really care about," says Edson, "but Kim was always making references to pop culture, and because she was so sweet, I did it."

A downtown drummer with a sports hat was not the only unusual thing about them. Seeing some of their early performances, Dan Graham told Gordon that her boyfriend was certainly an unusual frontman. Most would fall down onstage *after* they started playing; this kid always seemed to do it before.

THERE STILL WASN'T A NAME for what they, and anyone else in their circle, was doing. It was neither punk nor no wave, at least not in the traditional senses, and it certainly wasn't what most people in the rest of the country would call rock. In much the same way, there weren't always venues for them and their friends to perform at. They took what they could get, and for one week in June 1981, what they got was fifteen hundred square feet of scuffed wooden floors and white walls, with floor-to-ceiling pillars that gave the space its name, White Columns.

Even in a part of town permeated with performance spaces—lofts, basements, tiny clubs—few felt as fringy as White Columns. It was actually a gallery, one of dozens that had sprung up in area just south of Greenwich Village. Getting there, even from Eldridge Street or points east, was a hike, since White Columns was located at the furthest point west, on the edge of the Hudson River; the bustling West Side Highway (and, on the other side of the river, waterfront New Jersey) was in plain sight. Because of the locale, the area was especially frigid and windy during the winter; during the summer, the fact that White Columns was down the block from a garbage dump was abundantly clear. With its primitive PA and wood floors, the space was not conducive to perfect sound, either. To Branca, who occasionally performed there and had an office on the third floor of the building, it was "the worst possible piece-of-shit place you could do a show. But those were the days when you had to play where you could."

First known as the 112 Workshop, after its previous address on Greene Street, the gallery, which included Philip Glass on its board of directors, later moved to Spring. The new owners were the Port Authority, which also oversaw the city's bridges and tunnels. Josh Baer, the son of minimalist artist Jo Baer, had been hired to run the space, and starting with a show by a fast-talking, caustic spoken-word auteur named Eric Bogosian, Baer began booking performance-art shows into White Columns. (The name was not simply a reference to the space's interior architecture but a sly swipe at the Caucasian hierarchy of the art world.)

Yet from its relatively low monthly rent ($400) to its booking policies, White Columns was far from a traditional gallery. In one of the earliest installations, Baer covered the floor with sand and hired homeless men from the nearby Bowery to sit in the space; emerging graffiti artist Fab Five Freddy was part of another early installation, as was Kim Gordon, who made a project out of chairs belonging to her artist friends. Through their mutual friend Graham, Baer had met Gordon, whom he considered a "punk intellectual concept artist." To help her and Moore pay the bills, Baer gave Moore $50 to put up fliers around town—dangerous work, since the fliers were legally dubbed litter and pasting them around town was illegal.

No one remembers whose idea it was to put together a few nights of music at the space; Baer may have mentioned it to Gordon. But as a way to showcase all the new outsider music cropping up downtown, little of which seemed to have a home, a festival was conceived, and Moore and DeMarinis were put in charge of organizing it and selecting the bands. So many musicians telephoned Moore or dropped by the gallery with tapes in hand that the newly christened Noise Festival (so named by Moore after the owner of Hurrah, an Upper West Side club, declared that all these new musicians were merely making noise) was soon expanded to nine nights. One afternoon, as a few of the musicians were setting up the sound system, John Belushi walked by, poked his head in, raised an eyebrow, and moved on. He lived nearby and indicated he might stop by, but never did.

Starting with its first evening, the Noise Festival was one long, casual party. The crowd, usually a little more than one hundred people a night, consisted mostly of the bands and their friends, who sat on the gallery floor to listen; if the music grew too deafening and abrasive, they wandered outside and spilled onto Spring Street, adding to the block-party atmosphere. As with A's, the absence of neighbors played to the space's advantage; there were no noise complaints, although Baer had to stop selling alcohol after the first night when Port Authority police saw the "beer for sale" sign and asked if he had a liquor license. (Baer didn't, so anyone who wanted refreshments had to go across the street to the Ear Inn.) The result, says David Linton, who performed as part of a duo called Avoidance Behavior, was "a defining moment for our generation. The Noise Fest was really our gang, so to speak." It also defined the connection between art and music scenes; as the musicians played, the gallery walls were filled with artwork by, among others, Robert Longo.

The music itself, performed on a wooden plank stage only a foot above the floor, was as unconventional as the setting. Mofungo and the Avant Squares made bumpy, scraggly guitar rock that went out of its way to zigzag around melodies; Branca's ensemble and another, the Blue Humans, featuring guitarist Rudolph Grey, created instrumental screeches; Borbetomagus assaulted the audience with skronking free jazz. Every so often, as with Longo's band Built on Guilt, more traditional (and cohesive) rock made a cameo. But those moments were rare. During their roughly twenty-five minutes onstage, the still nascent Sonic Youth sounded as if they were searching for their identity as people listened. One number, which primarily featured Moore clomping hard on his guitar, sounded like an extended intro for a song that never actually began; others, with DeMarinis' piano weaving in and out, balanced melody with clatter. Another began percussively, with bangy, clanky noises; DeMarinis' celestial keyboards soon drifted in. A wordless chant by Gordon then entered, followed by one from DeMarinis; the two voices intertwined in counterpointal harmony.

The uneasy tension in the music was mirrored offstage as well. Gordon felt DeMarinis brought a melodic sense to the band but also felt the situation was "mutually frustrating—it was always a battle with the keyboards, which tended to take over. It was kind of a struggle. Everything would end up sounding kind of pretentious." As Acconci recalls, "Anne wanted to do something more modulated and structured. She wanted a semblance of melody; she didn't want it to dissipate into noise."

Before the show, DeMarinis had made it known she would be leaving the band, but Moore, who noticed her spending more time with musicians who seemed to be belittling Sonic Youth, asked her to stay on for at least a few more gigs. The Noise Festival would be the last of those, and Edson himself was on the way out. "The scene was just too straight and too white and too middle class, so I didn't take it that seriously," he says of the Noise Festival crowd (and the SoHo arts community he also viewed warily). For him, shows like the festival were just a job; he was drawn more to his other band, Konk, who seemed to be on a faster track to success than this little four-piece avant-no-wave band.

Six months had passed since their disastrous A's debut, and Moore and Gordon were once again at a loss; their band was collapsing. But on the sidewalk outside White Columns, Gordon noticed another local guitar player, a guy with short dark hair, eager, alert eyes, and a vaguely swarthy Mediterranean complexion. She'd seen him play with Branca; a few months before, he'd sat in with the Arcadians at a show at Inroads, a boxy performance space where the Coachmen had once gigged. In her timid but determined manner, Gordon suggested the guitar player could perhaps hook up with her boyfriend; the two men seemed to have a similar aesthetic and be excited by similar things.

Sonic Youth had imploded only hours before, but there was no time to waste and everything to accomplish.

HIS FIRST NIGHT in the city had been auspicious, to say the least. Two summers before, in 1979, Lee Ranaldo and two college friends, David Linton and Stuart Somer, decided the time had come to move to the East Village. Their van pulled up to a tenement building on East 11th Street, near Avenue B, on an afternoon that was at first sunny and inviting; in daylight, everything looked fine. But the skies quickly turned dark and soggy. A pregnant junkie slumped on the stoop; fire trucks whizzed by, seeming to set off alarms everywhere. They began hauling their belongings upstairs to the apartment they planned to rent, but when they walked in, they discovered one of the window gates was rather ominously broken. On their way back down for more boxes, an old man with a frazzled tornado of hair stuck his head out a window and yelled they'd be sorry if they moved in. The lightning began, adding to the modern-hell experience of it all. Taking a quick vote, they all agreed they weren't *that* no wave and gathered up their belongings and fled. It would be months before they returned to take another stab at living in the city.

Manhattan freaked Ranaldo out for good reason; he'd grown up on Long Island, about an hour away from the city's border. He was the first child of Nicholas Ranaldo, a quiet, hardworking hardware store manager (and later high-school custodian), and Josephine Claro, a seamstress and amateur piano player. Nicholas' parents had hailed from Italy, as had Josephine's father, whose arrival in New York had truly reflected the immigrant experience: Upon arriving at Ellis Island, his last name, Quagliariello, was changed by a clerk to Claro in honor of a nearby cigar box.

During World War II, Nicholas had been stationed in Guam and Iwo Jima, and brought home a Bronze Star. He met Josephine in 1945, after the war ended, and they married two years later and moved to Long Island—first Oyster Bay, then Glen Cove, and finally to a new suburban development in East Norwich, a hamlet within

Oyster Bay. They would be close enough to all their Italian relatives nearby and in Brooklyn, where Josephine was born and raised (and where she briefly worked as a piano player at a dance school). It was in nearby Glen Cove that their son Lee was born on February 3, 1956, followed three years later by a daughter, Donna.

Situated on the water, unhampered by much of a crime rate, Oyster Bay and East Norwich brought to Lee's mind the fictional Mayberry he grew up watching on television. Some of his friends would spend weekends on sailboats and motorboats; he would wander over to his father's Italian-American club and watch the old men play bocce. He was on the track team in high school and was a decent pitcher and hitter when playing baseball with the neighborhood kids. From his mother he had inherited an outgoing personality (Jeff Cantor, an early friend, immediately noticed the way his pal could fit in with either the Italian or Jewish kids in town); from his father, whom he rarely saw given his father's long hours at the hardware store, he adopted a can-do work ethic.

His father also helped instill a love of music in him: The store where he worked sold LPs, and after his seven-year-old son was mesmerized by the Beatles' appearance on *The Ed Sullivan Show*, along with everyone else in the country under the age of twenty, Nicholas began bringing home the group's LPs from the store. During lunchtime at school, the young Lee and his friends would run around and pretend they were Beatles, recreating scenes from *A Hard Day's Night*. "Half the kids in the school would think we were daft," he says. His favorite television show was *The Monkees*, itself an obvious knockoff of the Beatles' film.

He grew into a fairly typical teenager of the late '60s and early '70s. After seeing the Monkees wear bell bottoms, he asked his mother to make him a pair. When his friends first saw the pants on him, they mocked him so much he didn't wear them again for weeks. Later, during high school, he let his hair grow long, down to his shoulders. He favored ripped jeans that upset his mother; to her, bad clothing was a sign parents weren't looking after their children. He eventually had a van with a shag carpet, paneled walls, and speakers, and he'd retreat to the newly finished family basement, where he hung posters for *Butch Cassidy and the Sundance Kid* and the iconic Milton Glaser drawing of

Bob Dylan. New York City was an enigmatic, faraway place he would only occasionally venture into with his parents.

As an eighth-grader, he went to local anti-Vietnam protest rallies and, thanks to the older sister of one of his friends, was introduced to pot. A high-school buddy presented him with the music that needed to be played while stoned—the Grateful Dead's *Workingman's Dead* and *American Beauty*, along with LPs by Jethro Tull and Jefferson Airplane. The pot eventually lead to dabblings in opium, LSD, and the requisite stoner-life literary accompaniment of the time—books by Timothy Leary and Carlos Castaneda and *The Tibetan Book of the Dead*. "Lee was into all that hippie-dippy, lovey-dovey shit," says one of his childhood friends, Thom DeJesu. By his senior year of high school, he'd grown a beard and would sometimes arrive home from school a little wasted, but his grades were good enough that his parents didn't seem concerned—although his father, like many at the time, frowned on his music, lifestyle, and hair. Josephine Ranaldo wasn't thrilled to see her son's hair drop to his shoulders, either, but she knew there wasn't much to be done about it.

The concept of playing music entered his life around the same time the drugs did. In early high school, he took guitar lessons and persuaded his parents to buy him an instrument from a mall in Brooklyn. A girlfriend taught him a few chords, and an older cousin showed him how to tune to an open chord, which meant he suddenly could master songs like Crosby, Stills & Nash's "Suite: Judy Blue Eyes" fairly easily. He was soon playing with two bands in high school—one that specialized in Steppenwolf and Cream covers, where he was primarily just the singer, and a flannel-shirted folk group, Tumbleweed, with whom he played his first song in public, Stephen Stills' "4 + 20," during a high-school talent show. ("That was my *a-ha!* moment," recalls Cantor. "I thought, 'His singing is unbelievable.'") Later, he wound up with his first electric guitar, a beaten-up model that, thanks to what he'd learned from his father, he stripped down to bare wood and painted glossy black. Alone in his bedroom, he tried to imitate the feedback he heard on Jimi Hendrix records.

Despite his proclivities, his grades were good, and after graduating Oyster Bay High School in 1974, he enrolled in Harpur College, the liberal arts division of the State University of New York at Binghamton, just northwest of the Catskill Mountains. His plan was to major in math, science, or something equally disciplined; he had a good head for numbers. He'd done a fair amount of painting during high school, but the idea of attending school for music or art didn't occur to him, just as it hadn't to Thurston Moore in Connecticut during the same time. On his first day of class, in an English course called "The Quest for Enlightenment" that focused on the work of Herman Hesse and Jack Kerouac, he met Linton, who was a year younger and from Newburgh in upstate New York. After class, a bunch of the students, including Linton and Ranaldo, would retreat to the dorms and toke up; the rooms, Linton recalls, were like "clouds of smoke."

With his flannel shirts, wire-rimmed glasses, and long dark hair and beard, Ranaldo struck Linton as "a cross between a Deadhead and John Lennon. He was a total Long Island hippie," albeit one with a sense of humor Linton considered charmingly whimsical. To Linton, Ranaldo always seemed to be giggling, which may or may not have had something to do with all the pot floating around.

Linton and Ranaldo didn't see each other much after that first semester. By the time they met up again, nearly two years on, everything had changed for Ranaldo. Finding himself in crowded, impersonal classes he found boring or difficult, he soon grew disillusioned with math and science, and his grades fell off. Sensing his art-major friends were having a better time, he changed academic course and began studying film and attending drawing classes, the latter featuring actual nude models. He fell in love with a girl from Brooklyn, a fellow art major, and moved into a communal house on campus where tofu dominated the menu. The Grateful Dead and the other music of his youth fell by the wayside; although he would still practice his fingerpicking guitar chops on campus, learning the songs of Jorma Kaukonen, his new plan called for a career in art.

Whether or not he initially meant to, Linton helped change all that, and fast. Linton had gone through his own transformation, shedding his long red shag and Fry boots—the requisite look for the counterculture-minded '70s teenager—in favor of a buzzy punk haircut. By way of a nearby record store that sold import 45s, Linton discovered punk, and even though the music professors at his school looked down on it, Linton's life was changed with one listen to Patti Smith's *Horses*, released midway through his sophomore year. Before long, Linton, who'd learned how to play drums as a child but abandoned the instrument by the time college arrived, had returned to drumming and hooked up with a bass player, Richard Brewster, and two guitarists. He called the band the Fluks, inspired by the Fluxus art movement of the previous decade but also a nod, he says, to "the idea that culture was immediate and unfolding in the moment and disposable in that sense—in flux."

When a singer was needed, Linton tacked up a flier answered by none other than his former literary-class friend. To Linton's surprise, Ranaldo's voice reminded him of the Long Island blue-eyed soul of Felix Cavaliere of the Rascals, and he also realized Ranaldo was willing to tackle just about anything and had an equally strong sense of song structure and live performance. "In the back of your mind," Ranaldo says, "you always wanted to be in a band. It was this huge rush." In an empty college classroom one day, Linton introduced Ranaldo to Television's *Marquee Moon* and other music Ranaldo had barely heard as an East Norwich kid. The revamped Fluks, with Ranaldo joining in, landed gigs at a few quasi-redneck roadhouses. They were, Linton says, "a nerdy new-wave band" doing covers of "Venus" and "Don't Let Me Be Misunderstood," but not everyone appreciated them; after one show, they found the tires on their car slashed.

Unhappy with their two ostentatious guitar players, Linton and Ranaldo broke up the band but reformed it a few months later as a four-piece: Linton, Ranaldo, Brewster, and, this time, an organ player, another student named Stuart Somer. The turning point for them all came when the classmates went to a local club, the Other Place, to see

Talking Heads, three preppy-looking types who'd attended art school in Rhode Island. With their twitchy sound and bass lines, the Heads weren't anyone's idea of a punk band, and the prim preppiness of singer and guitarist David Byrne didn't look ravaged either; Ranaldo in particular was struck by the fact Byrne wore a wristwatch. "Rock and rollers didn't wear watches," he recalls. "You were there to play all night. You didn't *want* to know what time it was." But maybe the normal rules no longer applied.

"Lee absorbed a lot of things in those days," Linton says. "He absorbed this wiry guy [Byrne] with a short haircut holding everyone's rapt attention putting those songs over." The day after the show, the four friends went to a local barber, who gave them all military-short haircuts; immediately after, they found a photo booth and had group pictures taken. Taking his cues from Byrne, Ranaldo began sporting black sneakers, black pants, and gray short-sleeve shirts. The reconfigured Fluks began writing original songs about—what else—nerdy guys, with Somer's organ lending their sound a hint of the calliope rock of the Doors' Ray Manzarek. Based on tapes the band recorded in Binghamton, the Talking Heads influence was also apparent in Ranaldo's gulpy, tightly wound singing and song titles—"Creep," "Repressed Boys," "Mighty Stiff Guy," "Nervous Jerks"—that conjured Byrne's uptight-preppie character.

Their college careers ended in 1978, after which the friends all hung around Binghamton, Ranaldo working at an art studio. But if they were to be serious about becoming a successful new wave band, they had no choice but to head for New York City. It finally happened in May 1979, when they found a cheap, huge space far uptown on Riverside Drive. The setup turned out to be too good to be true. The neighborhood was too far from downtown, where everything seemed to be happening, and after realizing the building's management was less than trustworthy, they packed up their van one night; darkness would make it harder for anyone to see them escape. The next day, they headed for what they'd been told was the East Village apartment of their dreams but wasn't. Ranaldo, twenty-three and with no employment options on the table, had little choice but to return to his parents' home in East Norwich.

Eventually he and Linton returned, but to Brooklyn. Downtown, and the music and art communities that swirled around it, had too great of a pull to resist; they had to try one more time.

Shortly before their journey to the Lower East Side, Linton and Ranaldo had made the pilgrimage to Max's Kansas City, the same club a young Thurston Moore and his friend Harold Paris had first attended nearly three years before. This time, on a late Tuesday night in July 1979, the performer was a twenty-six-year-old guitar player and student of modern avant-garde music named Rhys Chatham (the same musician whom Kim Gordon would write about the following year in an early article). Surrounded by a dozen other curious paying customers, Linton and Ranaldo, who went thinking the evening's name, "Melt Down," was funny, watched as Chatham—along with two other guitarists, Branca and David Rosenbloom, and a drummer, Wharton Tiers—played one extremely loud note for half an hour.

The effect was hypnotic, especially when hints of raga came out in the guitars' overtones. Chatham, who later told Tiers he'd just come from the dentist and was still on medication, was equally riveting: lurching around the stage, he swatted customers with his guitar, stood on tables, and knocked over drinks. When the piece ended, he and his band did the unthinkable: They played it *again*, driving away half the audience in so doing. Where some were appalled, though, Ranaldo was captivated: "I felt like it was something I'd heard in my head for my entire life and I was only then hearing it aloud for the first time. It was amazing."

Linton was less enthralled, but the show left an impression on them both; seeing it made them realize they still wanted in. All around were college-educated types steeped in art, theory, and cinema studies, as well as musicians applying theories they'd glommed from the art world or university classes—like minimalism—to music. In the remaining months of 1979, they returned, this time securing a loft in

Brooklyn near Flatbush Avenue to which they'd been tipped by Michael Gross, a fellow Binghamton student and guitar player. The space was raw, the area not particularly inviting, but it was affordable and became their home for nine months, Ranaldo paying the bills working as a waiter and cook.

During their first drive into Manhattan the previous summer, Fluks bass player Richard Brewster had been so adversely affected by the mere sight of the city that he asked to be dropped off at the Port Authority terminal, where he immediately caught a bus back to his native Pennsylvania. By the time they relocated to Brooklyn, they'd found a replacement, and the Fluks carried on, sending their crudely recorded Binghamton demo tape to clubs. By then, their sound was already changing, leaning toward dronier sounds driven by Somer's keyboards. Throughout the winter of 1979 and into 1980, they landed a few gigs; one night, they found themselves on a triple bill at CBGB with an equally upright new-wave band called the Coachmen. Ranaldo had seen the Coachmen before when, in search of bars with cheap covers, he ventured into a Chelsea club called the Botany Talkhouse and saw the band for the first time.

Ranaldo and Linton considered changing the name of the band to the more exotic-sounding Flucts, inspired by the name of a memoir by dada founder Hugo Ball. But before they'd had a chance, the Fluks suffered a similar fate as the Coachmen: They were not, as Linton says, "cool enough," and the scene was giving them a collective cold shoulder. By the spring of 1980, the band had essentially petered out. Through mutual friends, Linton met Chatham and soon became a drummer in one of his bands.

By that point, Chatham's chief rival on the scene was Branca. Branca's band, the Static—the one that had so impressed Gordon— had crumbled, stung by an especially bad review in the *SoHo Weekly News*. Yet the Static, and Branca's previous band, Theoretical Girls, proved to be an extended prologue to far more audacious music. In 1979, Branca began writing instrumental pieces intended for multiple electric guitars—a sort of bludgeoning, charged, contemporary classical music. He had no idea what six guitars, each tuned only slightly differently from regular tuning, would sound like, but the effect—an overpowering assault layered with overtones and surprising nuance—was, he recalls, "unbelievable. It was, 'Okay, fuck these rock bands.'"

Branca's first work in this vein, an instrumental piece for six guitars, debuted in 1979, was followed in quick succession by two even more ambitious works. The small battalion of scraping guitars on *Lesson No. 1* built to a quiet, drum-driven fury. *Dissonance* added subtle, almost noticeable, sections, as if he truly were composing a symphony. The approach was as remarkable as Branca's look: ragged clothes, a shock of seemingly uncombed hair, and a perpetual dissatisfied scowl that owed a huge debt to the punk scene around him. In both look and sound, he came across like a descendent of Beethoven, but for the nuclear age.

Branca always needed guitar players, partly due to his interest in having as big a guitar orchestra as possible and partly because he didn't pay much, sometimes only a handful of dollars a show. "It wasn't hard to get a job in Glenn Branca's band," recalls Ned Sublette, a New Mexico–born, new-music-trained guitarist and urban cowboy who'd moved to the city in 1976 and joined Branca's ensemble several years later. Word would filter out, sometimes by way of fliers Branca would post at downtown record stores like Rocks in Your Head. Young guitar players with dreams of playing deafening, assaultive music—metal for intellectuals—would stream toward Branca's apartment on Spring Street for auditions that consisted of Branca telling them how to strum while waving his arms like a conductor. One of them was Moore, recommended by his girlfriend Kim Gordon. To Moore, Branca was "changing the name of the game." Although he doubled-strummed up a storm as Branca watched, Moore didn't get the job; Gordon later told him Branca thought he was too unbridled a player, even for Branca.

In December 1980, Branca was preparing to leave for his first tour of America. Several days before the scheduled departure, three of his musicians dropped out—he felt some of them didn't actually believe he *had* a tour lined up—and into Branca's apartment walked Ranaldo. Ranaldo had given Branca a call after seeing one of his ads; they also had several mutual friends, including pianist Anthony Coleman, who lived in Ranaldo's building in Brooklyn, and Michael Gross, who had joined Branca's group but was already on the way out. Having seen Branca and his ensemble perform at the Kitchen—one of downtown's most important performance spaces, curated by Chatham—Ranaldo was eager to join up. The thought of traveling, playing in a band—*that* band particularly—and meeting other musicians was one he couldn't resist. Branca didn't know anything about Ranaldo (he wouldn't learn for decades that he was from Long Island), but he was desperate, so he told the kid to plug in and play. Sensing he had talent and was readily available, he told Ranaldo they were leaving in a week and to learn ninety minutes of music by departure time.

The band—Branca, Ranaldo, Sublette, and David Rosenbloom on guitars, Jeffrey Glenn on bass, and Stephan Wischerth on drums—left New York in December 1980, winging around the country by way of Eastern Airlines' fly-around passes; the musicians were paid $175 each a week. Playing *Lesson No. 1*, *Dissonance*, and another early Branca piece, *Commodities*, they touched down in Minneapolis, San Francisco, Buffalo, and Toronto. As Sublette soon discovered, Branca was "absolutely the opposite of everything I had subscribed to before or since about how you should treat musicians. 'That was good' was not in his vocabulary. If it was good, he would stop complaining." Yet Sublette was struck by the tremendous clarity of the music, the way all the musicians would be hammering away on an E chord, get the nod from Branca, and then shift to an F, with Wischerth bashing along in a futile attempt to be heard over the aural tidal wave. Since there were no singers, nothing was held back; holding back was far from the point.

From the start, Branca intimidated Ranaldo as few others would. "He was like the megalomaniacal composer, like Toscanini," he says. "He was really authoritarian, and he was so overbearing and so determined about what he was doing that there was something frightening about him." But like many, Ranaldo sensed the rewards of tolerating Branca's personality would be plentiful. Branca himself realized that the latest, last-minute addition to his band wasn't as musically sophisticated or well trained as some of his bandmates, but that he liked to play louder than everybody; on stage, Branca could always hear Ranaldo above anyone else.

During the tour, Ranaldo, playing a soprano guitar strung with six high-E strings, became Branca's onstage foil, engaging in playful but aggressive head- and guitar-butting as Branca pushed the music and the physicality of his performances to extremes. "Being onstage with Glenn was like having rough sex with six men," says Sublette, who noticed that his fellow guitarist Ranaldo was "the most into making the rock moves on stage. He was a rock kid from Long Island. But *not*." Sublette was not the only one who felt assaulted: At some shows on the tour, some in the audience would come up to the musicians screaming about how damn loud it was or how it was the devil's music. At one performance, a woman tried to stop the show halfway through on the grounds that she found it offensive.

"Coming from New York, you had a slight superiority because it was obvious New York was miles ahead of everywhere else in terms of sophisticated and intellectual goings-on," says Ranaldo. "But you also just felt like an alien everywhere you went. People didn't relate to you. Nobody had any frame of reference for the music Glenn was making. Nobody knew what art music *was*." Several years later, Ranaldo realized this lack of connection even extended to his family, when his parents, sister, and relatives came to see him perform with Branca at the St. Marks Church in the East Village. After about fifteen minutes, everyone in his clan was either outside or cowering in the back of the church—except for Nicholas Ranaldo, who stayed put in the first row. Either he was proud or merely accustomed to the sound of clattering machinery after years working in a hardware store.

For Ranaldo, the days of singing Crosby, Stills & Nash songs and learning Jerry Garcia solos were gone, possibly for good. Thanks to Branca, he grew even more fascinated by sound and less by singing and songwriting. From Branca, he says, "We all learned what that meant to completely forget everything, even who the hell you are, and then walk on stage and do things you never imagined doing before in your life."

Waiting for a BART train to arrive on the way to their show in San Francisco, the musicians heard John Lennon had been shot and killed three thousand miles away. Given how life-changing the Beatles had been to him from early childhood, Ranaldo couldn't begin to process the news; Lennon had been one of the people who'd inspired him to want to become a rock star, and now he was being told Lennon was dead while embarking on his own first tour as a mini-rock star of sorts. It felt like the end of something, although, at the same time, the beginning of something else.

IN THE MONTHS THAT FOLLOWED the end of the Branca tour, he rummaged around for the next step. There was another Branca tour, this time of Europe, in the spring of 1981. The audiences were more receptive than they were in America, although Branca could still be antagonistic toward promoters and audiences alike. During a show in Munich, he was so upset that he had all the amplifiers set up in a wall in the center of the stage and ordered the musicians to play behind the amps. Yet when it worked onstage, as it often did, the thrilling violence of the music compensated for all of the aggravations. Sublette noticed Ranaldo's interest in art—Ranaldo always seemed to wander out to a museum during his time off—and his ability to network by making notes of the venues they played for future reference.

By that point, Ranaldo had a new home—a huge, cheap loft on Duane Street, downtown near City Hall, that fell into his lap. He and David Linton had secured the place during the waning days of the Fluks. Through Linton, Ranaldo soon met Truus de Groot, a singer, songwriter, and keyboard player from Holland who led a loose-knit band, Plus Instruments, in her home country. Moving to New York and in search of musicians to accompany her, de Groot asked Linton—whom she had met in Holland, when he was on tour with Rhys Chatham—to join up; Linton, in turn, recruited Ranaldo. Together, they recorded an album, *Februari–April '81*, based around de Groot's droogy synthpop songs and electronic keyboards. Ranaldo's guitar and occasional voice jutted in, but the band was clearly a showcase for de Groot. Taped in the early months of 1981 (hence the title) at a studio in Chelsea, it marked Ranaldo's first—but not most representative—appearance on record.

That particular edition of Plus Instruments barely lasted as long as the Fluks. There were arguments over money, particularly payments for the album, and Linton and de Groot had unresolved romantic issues. "We were all getting tired of each other anyway," says de Groot. Linton and Ranaldo were about to leave for Europe for another Plus Instruments tour when they heard about the Noise Festival. Sensing it would be a gathering and networking place for other searching downtown souls—in ways both musical and social—they signed up, leaving a startled de Groot to find last-minute replacements.

Billing themselves as Avoidance Behavior, Ranaldo and Linton played into tape loops separately—Linton banging his arm on the metal sculptures hanging on the wall behind him—then combined the loops to create a big, wall-of-noise sound collage. The noise was so eardrum-bursting that some fled the volume and stood outside on Spring Street. It was there, at another point during the festival, that Ranaldo also found himself, and where he heard Kim Gordon's interesting musical proposition.

THE AMPLIFIERS WERE STILL SET UP at White Columns, so it made sense for the new trio to meet there and see if the combination made any sense. Sitting around on the floors of the gallery right after the final Noise Festival evening, the artwork from the event still on the walls, Moore, Ranaldo, and Gordon looked at each other and decided to simply start playing. No one had any real songs, so they began strumming the simplest and crudest of riffs to find a common ground. Tentatively, they started working on what were essentially instrumental pieces—riffs and chord changes that would be played, repeatedly, until something resembling a shape emerged from them.

In some ways, the union was surprising. Although he once joined the Arcadians onstage, Ranaldo hadn't been overwhelmed by the version of Sonic Youth he'd seen at Gildersleeves and at the Noise Festival. He was intrigued by the call-and-response voices of Gordon and DeMarinis and sensed potential in the band as a whole, but it was still, in his words, "an arty, shambling thing. It wasn't a very together band." Ranaldo and Gordon shared backgrounds in art school and each had strong ties to '60s rock, yet most of the hippie rock Ranaldo had grown up on was music Moore considered anathema. They were each at different levels of competence—Ranaldo the most experienced, Gordon the least, Moore somewhere in between.

By that point, though, they each needed help moving to the next level, and in each other saw possibilities and connections. "Lee was very positive," says Moore. "He had ideas for gigs. He was ready to go. He was ready for anything. He seemed to have the *fire*, as opposed to the rest of the nerds." Despite the differences in the music of their teen years, Ranaldo sensed his and Moore's parallels: Both were about the same age (only two years apart), both were refugees from the nearby suburbs who'd moved to New York City to make it. In the process, both had confronted a hostile environment and an even more hostile—and indifferent—music business, which still didn't know what to make of the post-punk discord emanating from the clubs and galleries south of 14th Street.

The new band would retain the name Sonic Youth; Ranaldo seemed fine with it, and the use of the word "sonic" appealed to his post-Branca interest in the possibilities of sound. They had few if any finished songs and no drummer, but in a move that revealed their drive and churning ambitions, they decided it was time to work regardless. Based on a few connections they had and their associations to various degrees with the revered Branca, the trio lined up a few early shows. During the sweltering summer of 1981, they began performing, starting at Just Above Midtown, then over to Stillwende, the new name for what had once been known as Tier 3. "Thurston was a go-getter," says his sister Susan. "He had a lot of confidence in himself. Some people, they're just driven to be successful."

Onstage, they were still finding themselves, both as individuals and a performing unit. With his short, newspaper-delivery-boy haircut and suburban-wholesome look, Moore seemed normal, but his spastic, live-wire moves were anything but. With his rugged look and equally neat, short hair, Ranaldo had the dramatic flamboyance of a guitar hero. Wearing her sunglasses and playing with grim-faced intensity, Gordon barely moved, as if she was spending all her time focusing on which bass notes to play. They were far from a cohesive unit, and neither were their early performances. The show at Stillwende was particularly chaotic and brief. At one point, Moore put aside his battered guitar and bashed away on a snare drum, while Ranaldo took the assault a step further by hammering on a metal pipe. Using a suction cup and gaffer's tape, Ranaldo then attached a microphone to the side of a power drill; the cable from the drill was plugged into an amplifier or a wah-wah pedal, resulting in a stereophonic dental-patient nightmare. Of all the tools at his disposal, Ranaldo thought the drill worked best; it gave off the most musical sound. As the performance wound down, Moore fell into the audience and ran out. "That for me," he says, "established what we were going to be doing." Outside, Ranaldo and Moore whooped and hollered on the street in what Ranaldo's friend Jeff Cantor, watching from the sidelines, remembers as an exhibition of "spontaneous exuberance."

Whether anyone else would be interested in such an approach to music remained to be seen. Few if any independent labels existed in New York, and the one everyone admired, 99 Records, didn't seem interested in signing the band. Based out of the record store of the same name on MacDougal Street, a place where collectors and music fanatics would regularly visit to flip through bins and find the latest talked-about singles, 99 was run by a local luminary named Ed Bahlman. Bahlman released Branca's first two records on 99; Branca, in turn, recommended Bahlman sign Liquid Idiot, a dance band renamed Liquid Liquid, whose first record had small but respectable sales. But when Branca pushed for Bahlman to record and release an album by Sonic Youth, he was rebuffed; Bahlman, he felt, was probably jealous of fellow record buff Moore, who frequented 99.

Branca longed to start his own label, but cash was always the obstacle. In 1981, though, Branca told Sonic Youth he'd found an "angel investor" who had given him $5,000—a fortune at the time—to get a label off the ground. The backer was none other than White Columns' Josh Baer, who happened to have $30,000 in the bank. (In a scene full of broke musicians—Sublette would loan $20 to Chatham, who would then loan it to another friend, who would in turn loan it back to Sublette—the sum qualified Baer as a millionaire.) When Branca told Baer he'd make his money back in a month, Baer, who'd never worked in any aspect of the music business, agreed to fund the label.

"It was really about getting out records by bands we loved," Branca says. "Great fucking bands that *no one* was going to release." The new company was to be called Systems Neutralizers until both men realized that one-name record labels, like Stiff, were all the rage; the name was then shortened to Neutral. Branca would decide which bands to sign, and Baer would do the rest—getting the records pressed and distributed, sending copies to the press and radio, even hauling the actual records to the post office from his Lafayette Street apartment. The business arrangement called for the bands and the owners to split the profits equally after expenses were paid off.

Branca and Baer were both dismayed when, soon after starting the label, DeMarinis left Sonic Youth; both Baer and Branca had crushes on her and loved what she brought to the lineup. "We had no idea what Sonic Youth was going to sound like with Lee," says Branca. But his concerns were alleviated once he began seeing the second version of the band perform during the summer of 1981. "Anyone who was my fan automatically became a Sonic Youth fan, and I knew *why*," says Branca. "Sonic Youth gave them what I had, but sugarcoated it. There's *no one* who was around in the early '80s who doesn't know that. They knew I'd come up with all these incredibly cool sounds that could be used in the context of a rock song. At the time I wasn't going to do that. It helped to be on the inside where you knew what the tunings and fingerings were and how the scores were structured. So I liked their candy-coated version of my music. I *loved* it. I came in my fucking *pants*." Branca wasn't the only one who heard a bit of himself in their music: "When Lee joined," says Sublette, "I started to recognize a lot of the sounds and the approach."

The fall of 1981 blew in with much promise. First came their most prominent and distinguished job to date, a slot in the ironically named Music for Millions festival at the New Pilgrim Theater, a venue deep in the East Village, on Avenue D and East 3rd Street. The show was an important one—they would be playing an actual theater, complete with plush seats—and for it, they would need a drummer to firm up their sound. Without many options, they reached out to Richard Edson, who decided to return to the fold: "I remembered it fondly enough," he says. When the new quartet began rehearsing, Edson noticed an immediate change in Sonic Youth. Physically and musically, Ranaldo made for a stronger presence than DeMarinis, and he and Moore had clearly different, but complimentary, styles of playing: Moore's more rhythmic, Ranaldo's more fluid. It was if the group was suddenly freed up. "You can use the metaphor for a tree," Edson says, "It's rooted but it also expands."

Edson's feelings were borne out when the band began its performance on the night of Friday, September 18. While still fragmentary, the songs also felt more structured than they'd been a few months before. The music was anchored by Edson's casually sophisticated rhythmic patterns—he played as if his sticks were bouncing off plastic tubs—and Gordon's swooping bass notes; Moore's and Ranaldo's guitars buzzed and hummed around the rhythm section. ("Kim didn't play the logical bass part, because she didn't know what it *was*," Ranaldo says.) Revealing the evident influence of Branca's work, the two guitarists double-strummed from one harmonic to another during "Hard Work" and "Loud and Soft." They attempted a fleshed-out version of "Cosmopolitan Girl," the song Gordon had first written during her brief CKM experience the previous year, and which she now sang in a combination of bark and scream.

With the exception of "Cosmopolitan Girl," fully formed lyrics were not necessarily the point: "Hard Work" mostly seemed to consist of Moore chanting "I don't want to push it" over and over, and "Loud and Soft" featured Ranaldo reciting random lyrics culled from one of his journals. Yet sometimes they didn't need words: The music conveyed as much of a mood as anything that came out of their mouths. During "Destroyer," an instrumental, they wove their instruments in and around each other as if they were still learning how they could complement each other; the effect was captivating. The guitars sounded slightly out of tune, and more dreamlike and expansive, on another wordless performance, "Where the Red Fern Grows."

During rehearsals, Edson had ridden the band particularly hard on another partly developed song, "The Burning Spear." Named after the reggae icon, it had started to gestate before Ranaldo had joined, inspired by Moore's fascination with what he calls "the really spooked-out bass on dub records." Thinking it had the most potential of their songs, Edson thought it needed to be more firmly arranged: "He kept saying, 'Is that a hook?'" Gordon recalls.

Onstage at Music for Millions, the work clearly paid off. A sole, ominous thump of Edson's bass drum started it, followed by a simple, four-note bass line from Gordon that didn't actually hint at reggae but instead some kind of unseen dread. Ranaldo's drill pushed in soon after, grinding along in tandem with Moore's equally harsh voice: "I'm not afraid to say I'm *scared*!" he howled. Even though it was possible to pick apart each song and trace its direct influence, what emerged was nonetheless a distinctively pungent musical stew.

After the performance, Ranaldo remembers Branca approaching the band and, in that very Branca-like way, ordering them to make a record for his new label. It may have been the first the band had heard of his interest, but in Branca's mind, the decision had been made months before. Although this particular edition of the band had only been together a few months, the time had come to unleash them on the world above and beyond downtown Manhattan.

Chapter 3

THE RECORDING STUDIO was unlike anything they'd seen, in a part of town where they rarely ventured. With its gauntlet of decaying department stores encircling the battered Union Square Park, 14th Street was, as Richard Edson puts it, "the northern demarcation. It was a wasteland above that." And yet, here they were on a chilly December morning in 1981, at the corner of Sixth Avenue and 50th Street. The air reeked of day jobs, lunch hours, paperwork, and everything else they were hoping to avoid for the rest of their lives.

Radio City Music Hall, known for the dancing Rockettes and annual Easter and Christmas family-fun extravaganzas, was not their kind of place, either; the last time any of them could remember being there was when Ranaldo's parents took him, as an eight-year-old, to see *Mary Poppins* on the hall's massive movie screen. But Branca had proposed they use it as a place to put their songs on tape, so they took the elevator to the ninth floor of the Radio City building, walked up one flight of stairs, and entered a gymnasium-sized room in order to put their barely six-month-old vision onto a record.

Two months earlier, at a studio in Chelsea, they'd taken an initial stab at recording their material. Although Branca had set it up with the goal of using the tapes for the band's Neutral Records debut, the sessions proved desultory. They found themselves facing an engineer who didn't seem to understand anything about them and made condescending, dismissive comments—"kind of a bozo," Moore says. They were able to lay down rough takes of some of the songs they'd worked up with Edson, but the experience was so unsatisfactory that, except for a recording of "Where the Red Fern Grows" that would be unearthed many years later, the tapes were never released.

As soon as they stepped into Radio City Music Hall Studio, they had a feeling this time would be different. Originally designed as a broadcast studio for NBC, the large, rectangular room had high ceilings, an imposing recording console, and corrugated walls six feet thick. Conductor Arturo Toscanini had rehearsed the NBC Symphony Orchestra in that room; taped versions of Little Golden Books, the best-selling children's book series, were recorded there as well. Designers had worked hard to isolate the space from the rest of the building and had largely succeeded, although the studio's employees would sometimes feel the floor shake when the Rockettes practiced their precision steps in the next room. Although Ranaldo marveled at the space—"it felt like what you read about, a real studio like Abbey Road"—it seemed almost perverse that they were there. "The buildings themselves represented some kind of enemy," says Edson. "I couldn't help but feel two things—being in awe of it and feeling like we were in the belly of the beast."

At the same time, though, the studio's history wasn't alien to them. When it was called Plaza Sound Studios in the mid '70s, the Ramones, Richard Hell, and Blondie had recorded there. In 1978, a young, easygoing recording engineer (and experimental-music aficionado) named Don Hunerberg had started managing the studio, after which the name was changed to Radio City Music Hall Studio and punk was banished: Radio City executives weren't happy about the noise emanating from the studio (nor the pot smoke that seeped over to the nearby offices). The space was on the verge of closing when Hunerberg made the owners an offer: He would pay *them* to run the studio as long as he could bring in whatever clients he chose. After they agreed, Hunerberg received a call from Glenn Branca, who heard about the studio from a friend and was looking to record.

Ultimately, that session went so well ("I want to hear the angels sing!" Branca shouted to Hunerberg over a mass of guitars) that

Branca asked about booking time for one of his label's new signings, a band called Sonic Youth. Like the engineer who'd been hired for their first, aborted sessions, Hunerberg knew little about them, yet he was intimately acquainted with their community. Under the name IMA (Intense Molecular Activity) and using a batch of synthesizers and prerecorded tapes, Hunerberg and partner Andy Blinx, a percussionist, had performed a static-driven tape collage piece on the Noise Festival stage six months before. Hunerberg wasn't offended by eccentric sounds; he welcomed them.

As Hunerberg sensed from the start, the four musicians who stepped into Radio City that December day were prepared, if only because they had to be. The rate, $300 for ten hours, may have been relatively affordable compared to other midtown studios, but Baer and Branca's limited funds meant they could only pay for two days' worth of sessions. "The schedule," Gordon says, "made us pull the songs into a structure before we recorded them." With little time to waste, they laid down a few takes of each number before committing a final version to tape.

By the end of the first day, they had the basics for five songs. "Loud and Soft," which had featured a Ranaldo recitation when it had been included in their set at Music for Millions, became an instrumental called "The Good and the Bad"; in the way Ranaldo and Moore would pick a fret, hit the fretboard, and then move up another fret, it became a type of tribute to the repetitive drones of Branca and Rhys Chatham. "Hard Work" had morphed into "I Don't Want to Push It," named after its refrain. Inspired by the way the B-52's and Laurie Anderson were using overlapping male and female voices, the band had begun toying with a similar approach for "Where the Red Fern Grows." At Radio City, the song transformed into "I Dreamed I Dream." Ranaldo sang his part, the words taken from his ongoing journals, but Gordon's spoken portion hadn't yet been finished. Utilizing an approach that harked back to Gordon's roots in appropriation and collage, everyone in the band contributed lyrics, after which Gordon picked and sang random lines as the song was being recorded. "They were working hard, and they had *songs*," Hunerberg says. "They had a direction. I thought, 'This is a group that's going to have legs.'"

As Hunerberg saw, it was also a group unafraid to mess with those songs and that sound. During the taping of "She Is Not Alone," Ranaldo threw metal pipes around on the floor for additional clank; the resulting clatter could be heard in the final mix, in the moments just before Moore began to sing. Hunerberg was initially worried when Ranaldo pulled out a drill for "The Burning Spear," because the din of the tool was throwing off the amplifiers and console. "But they said they *liked* it," Hunerberg says, "and if anyone says they like it, that's fine and okay with me." Due to either time constraints or lack of interest, a few of the older compositions, like "Cosmopolitan Girl," were left behind, unfinished relics from another era.

When they returned the next day to begin the mixing process, they and Hunerberg had only five hours to wrap it up. In the final hour, they begged Hunerberg to rerecord Moore's vocal on "I Don't Want to Push It." They were pushing it, all right: At that late stage in the process, Moore would have to sing it directly onto the tape, no mistakes. But even with a cold, he somehow pulled it off. A few hours later, their time was up and, with a light snowfall blanketing the city, they headed back downtown. Almost a year to the day after the disastrous debut of Red Milk, they seemed to have been reborn, although where it would take them was anyone's guess.

On foot in SoHo in early 1982, John King instantly recognized his former Coachmen cohort Moore—with that height, it was hard to miss him. It had been almost two years since their band had petered out, and King had stopped making music altogether and had begun pursuing a career as an underground comic artist. During their catch-up chat, Moore, who was strolling with his mother Eleanor, told King that his new band, Sonic Youth, was about to release a record and that a few thousand copies had been pressed up. King couldn't believe it—not just that there was a record, but that there were so many copies being distributed. A few *thousand*, for a band from *that* scene? It seemed unfathomable, as if Sonic Youth already were rock stars.

When it arrived in April, in whatever stores Baer could get it into, the record, simply called *Sonic Youth*, was nothing if not an homage to their musical and creative influences, even if some of those inspirations escaped the few people who saw the EP. In the black-and-white photos on the cover, taken by Ranaldo, they greeted the world with expressionless or skeptical faces. The way the two portrait shots were laid out side by side was a nod to Dan Graham's penchant for using mirrors during performance pieces. For the band's name on the cover, Gordon chose a typeface that reminded her of fonts used by art galleries. An even more obscure East Village reference point was embedded on the cover: Edson folded his hands on the cover in imitation of a Jesus statue he'd walked by on the way to the photo session.

The EP began the way they, Moore in particular, wanted it: with the simple bash of a drum that would, in his words, be a "primitivist announcement to the world" that the band had arrived. The rest of that track, "The Burning Spear," blared the announcement in capital letters. If the throb of Gordon's hollow-body bass and the way the rain-on-tin buzz of Moore's and Ranaldo's guitars slowly escalated weren't enough to announce this wasn't normal rock, the entrance of Ranaldo's power drill about ninety seconds in—a hailstorm of sound that overwhelmed everything else—rammed the point home. When Moore opened his mouth, he sounded as if he were hollering to someone down the street—even when singing a line like, "In my bed, I'm deep in prayer," the first (but perhaps most straight-faced) of his lyrical references to his Catholic upbringing.

"We didn't have an established Sonic Youth identity at that point in terms of songwriting," concedes Moore, which accounted for the way in which none of the four songs that followed "The Burning Spear" sounded much like it. Coming after the jangled-nerve drive of "The Burning Spear," the final incarnation of "I Dreamed I Dream," with its metronomic pulse and its contrast between Ranaldo's lazy-afternoon croon and Gordon's chilly recitation, was a mesmerizing mantra that toyed with beauty; it had the discomforting stillness of a late-night walk on a deserted East Village street. Edson's polyrhythmic approach rose up in "She Is Not Alone"; even as Ranaldo's and Moore's guitars ping-ponged off each other in scrappy, skeletal discord, the rhythm held the track together like a teacher scolding wayward students. ("I was trying to play like James Brown drummers, soft and so deep into a groove and hoping everyone else would approach it that way," Edson recalls.) Both the rhythms and the guitars intensified on the next track, "I Don't Want to Push It," but minimalism returned in the closer, "The Good and the Bad." As if coming full circle from the opening of "The Burning Spear," Edson was again the star: He crashed about his kit while the other three (Moore taking over the bass while Gordon switched temporarily to guitar) clicked into a steady drone, as if playing while standing stock still.

Since there wasn't time to "gum it up in any way," as Ranaldo says, the guitars sounded cleaner than they would've preferred, and the lyric writing was far from developed. The record's influences—Branca, Public Image Ltd., even the German art-rock band Can—were more apparent than on any other record that would follow. "We were lucky how well it came out, considering we had so little time," Gordon says. "But it wasn't a representation of what the music was like live." Yet *Sonic Youth* was its own enigmatic creature: Neither punk nor no wave, clubby dance rock nor pure noise.

Neutral Records did indeed press up about three thousand vinyl copies of the record, and Baer began calling distributors to see who wanted to buy it. Some did, although in some cases only a few copies at a time. Baer even hired Moore for a brief period to make some of those calls. But thanks largely to the Branca connection—he was already a brand-name figure in the city's new-music community—the record received more notice than anyone expected. In the *New York Times*, Robert Palmer wrote that the album "sometimes recalls Mr. Branca's carefully formal, numbingly loud overplays of massed electric guitars" while adding that the "concern with order and clarity is still evident." (Given the way in which their lyrics would only be written once the music had been finalized, Palmer was also prescient in noting that the vocals, "when there are any, sound like afterthoughts.") Across the country, the *Los Angeles Times* opined that "The Burning

Spear" could be "a dance club smash given a promotional push." Even the far-off *Milwaukee Express* weighed in, comparing them to the Cure ("in mood and music"). *Billboard* made an analogy to Public Image's "angry sound experiments" while, not surprisingly for an industry publication, admiring the way "this band settles down into what could be developed into pop ballads." To Moore, the most meaningful review came from the Michigan fanzine *Touch & Go*: "Interesting as shit and from NYC no less."

In what was most likely their first proper interview to promote the record, for the city's leading underground rock magazine, *New York Rocker*, the band convened at the Eldridge Street apartment. There, writer Mark Coleman, one of the first music critics to track them, found a band that wanted to take chances without falling into what Ranaldo called "New York art wave." Ranaldo and Moore told him that neither of them could play standard guitar chords. Yet, as Moore told Coleman, "We don't want to be an experimental jerk-off band, either. That can be fun, but there's really no use for it. We like the idea of songs."

As Coleman also learned, Edson was no longer a member of Sonic Youth. Edson's commitment to the band had been shaky from the start; he'd already left once before, after the Noise Festival performance. Although he liked the people in it, Edson had complicated feelings about Sonic Youth music and the scene from which they sprang; he felt many of the SoHo artists were phony. He'd been excited by the rhythmic direction of songs like "I Don't Want to Push It" but wasn't sure if Moore, Ranaldo, and Gordon had a feel for dance rhythms or were even interested in them. "Sonic Youth needed something different, much more traditional rock playing," he says. With its manic Afro-Cuban party mood, his other band, Konk, was more to his liking and sensibility. He rarely socialized with Moore, Gordon, and Ranaldo outside of shows or rehearsals: "I kinda felt like it was me, and then the three of them." During his last shows with them—a two-night stand at the Mudd Club in the middle of February—Edson threw his jazz and funk leanings out the door and let loose, but was taken aback when, backstage, one of his Konk bandmates cracked that Sonic Youth were "squares."

To the three of them, Edson's announcement came as a jolt and an inevitability. During rehearsals, Ranaldo would often see Edson with his fingers in his ears, cringing behind the drum kit at the volume. "We had a record deal, so Richard wasn't about to turn that opportunity down," says Ranaldo. "But what we were doing was a little *too* out there for him. We were just a bunch of downtown ruffians creating this crazy noise music, and I don't know if he saw much future in it, really." The band had equally mixed emotions about Edson. "He was kind of flaky and hard to pin down," Gordon says. Moore was somewhat jealous that Edson was in Konk, which had much headier local buzz, and Ranaldo also feels Edson made it clear that Konk was his priority. "I think he thought what we were doing was interesting but was too art school for him," says Moore. "Which is what I really *liked* about it."

When the Mudd Club shows were over, they began a process that would repeat itself several times over the following months: Finding a new percussionist, teaching him the material, playing a show or two, deciding that drummer wasn't right in one way or another, and then moving on to someone new—at which point, thanks to their particular demands, requirements, and lack of a very specific musical direction, the routine would begin anew. David Linton, Ranaldo's former Fluks bandmate, was one of these people. Dave Keay, the former Coachmen drummer, was another. Keay got as far as traveling to Washington, D.C., with the band for a show, but the three had reservations about his playing and whether or not he shared the same art-world background. When Keay called Eldridge Street one day to ask about future rehearsals, Gordon informed him bluntly that they already had someone else in mind. When Keay dropped by the Moore-Gordon apartment to pick up some of his gear, Moore followed him outside, telling him it was one of the others who wasn't sure about Keay. It would be neither the first nor last time such a nonconfrontational, good-cop-bad-cop approach would be used in dealing with business or personnel matters.

As so many bands had done before and so many would after, they resorted to fliers: "Sonic Youth Needs a Drummer" read the scrawl, with the numbers for both Ranaldo's and Moore and Gordon's apartments penciled in underneath. Passing one on the street, Moore noticed that someone had scratched out "a Drummer" and written "Ideas" over it. ("I thought, '*That* was kind of snarky,'" he recalls.) One day, the phone in Ranaldo's loft rang. The caller said he'd seen the band perform a few times and had heard their EP, and he wanted the chance to audition.

Those who'd grown up in nearby Clifton, New Jersey, would have known him as Bob Bertelli, the son of Angelo Bertelli, a Notre Dame quarterback and Heisman Trophy winner; in his later years, Bertelli ran and owned liquor stores in northern Jersey. His son was another child of the '60s and its attendant rock culture: J. Geils Band and Humble Pie concerts, LSD, and Jefferson Airplane albums were all part of his backstory. He took art classes in high school and worshipped Andy Warhol, especially after a class trip into New York City for a Warhol exhibition. Another city trip, to see the New York Dolls at Max's Kansas City in 1972, turned him into a fan of the new punky glam rock emanating from the city; afterward, he discarded all his Grateful Dead records. Following his high school graduation in 1973, he stopped playing drums, an instrument he'd taken up at age twelve, and decided to become an artist and learn to print using silk screens. Like the members of Sonic Youth, he too eventually moved to New York City and became immersed in the CBGB world, albeit sooner than any of them; he'd witnessed early performances by Patti Smith and Talking Heads, developed a crush on Heads bassist Tina Weymouth, and then discovered the no-wave scene, which made him realize "talent is one thing and concept is another."

Anyone who saw a no-wave band was not only brutalized but oddly inspired: If these people with barely any discernible training could be onstage, they could too. Bertelli—or now Bob Bert, as he was calling himself—was one of them. With his soon-to-be-wife Linda Wolfe, Bert—an agreeable and all-around congenial sort with a hearty guffaw of a laugh—moved to Hoboken, New Jersey, in 1980 and returned to drumming with Drunk Driving, a loose, chaotic band that mixed punk thrash and poetry. The group didn't last long—he'd had enough of the lead singer's borderline-psychotic onstage behavior—but Bert was back to playing the drums. The training came in handy when he noticed the Sonic Youth flier at 99 Records on MacDougal Street, one of the stores he, like Moore, most frequented in search of new releases, imports, and the best new records to own.

Bert, then twenty-six, knew of Sonic Youth: He owned a copy of Branca's *Lesson No. 1*, and word of a new band inspired by Branca intrigued him, so he bought *Sonic Youth* when it was released, shortly before he spotted their flier. He'd already seen several of their shows, including one with Edson, and was astounded by how long they took between songs—hours, it seemed—to retune their shabby guitars. He thought they were "downtown arty-looking people, maybe a little pretentious. But they seemed to be the next step." They didn't seem as intent on destroying rock as no-wavers like Mars and Teenage Jesus and the Jerks had been, but rather in taking what the fleeting no-wave scene had started and fusing it with some of the conventions of mainstream rock. Bert pulled the flier right off the wall—he didn't want anyone else to get the gig—and dialed the number. When they suggested a meeting, he wrapped rubber bands around his drumsticks, took the train into the East Village, and met them at a Polish restaurant. They bonded over seeing punk bands at CBGB, and Moore said he recognized Bert from the band's shows—not a terribly hard thing to do, given that some of their early gigs drew only a dozen or so paying customers.

After food and more talk, they all walked a few short streets to a rehearsal space on nearby East 6th Street, where Bert played along with the three of them. His style was crude and pounding, and since he hadn't played much in the few years before, he was, he admits, terrible. He had no idea whether or not he passed the audition, if that's even what it was, since no one had used the word. But soon enough, they called back, and Sonic Youth had a new drummer. "He wasn't tight, but he seemed to be proficient," Ranaldo says. Another crucial factor played a role in the decision: No one could recall anyone else responding to any of those fliers.

ONLY OUTSIDERS WOULD CALL IT a rehearsal space; to everyone else, it was simply "the bunker." In truth, it had been a Pentecostal church long before, but the windowless, two-room space on the northeast corner of 6th Street and Avenue B was far from sacred ground. It was home base for Swans, a newly formed band led by Michael Gira, Gordon's former classmate at the Otis art school in Los Angeles. Like Gordon, Gira had made the trek to New York, traveling across the country with his girlfriend (and eventual Swans manager), Susan Martin. He'd formed one early group, Circus Mort, which quickly lead to Swans, a band intent on making the most bludgeoning, claustrophobic music in the city, if not the planet.

All urban-pitbull intensity himself—he always looked angry, even when he wasn't, and he would sometimes perform shirtless—Gira had come to New York with lofty expectations but found the experience distinctly unwelcoming. "I quickly realized the New York City art and music scenes were infested with careerist, climbing, self-important and scheming, duplicitous snobs," he says. "And I reacted probably in the worst way—by insulting and attacking anyone that came in my path, guilty or not, at random and without any good judgment at all on my part. I didn't feel a connection with any 'scene.'" The dark, aggressive force of Gira's personality manifested itself in the way he furbished the space he'd found and rented for his new band: The walls were decorated with drawings of black snakes and a painting of a man hanging aloft by meat hooks.

Drug deals regularly went down right outside the bunker, and the battering-ram music emanating from it, by Gira and drummer and cofounding band member Jonathan Kane, matched the surroundings in ugliness. "I just basically at first stuck to the idea of rhythm and sound, without much if any concern for melody or anything else except *rage*, and any *power* I could generate from volume and sound and words," Gira says. As Kane recalls, finding other members for the band was hardly easy: "People either wouldn't have the necessary intensity, or they would walk in and listen and say, 'This is horrible.'" Arriving at the studio one day, they found a beheaded chicken in a bag, left by an angry former parishioner who resented the horrible noise coming from the space.

"We liked the idea of having fun with music," recalls Moore, "and Mike once said to me, 'This is *not* fun.'" Gordon and Gira's shared art-school background in Los Angeles was an obvious point of connection between Swans and Sonic Youth, though, and the two bands found other common ground. Neither attracted a large crowd, and both felt like outsiders even in an outsiders' community. "Nobody liked either of our bands that we knew of," says Moore, "so we bonded." They were comrades in sonic assault and in isolation.

Starting in the spring of 1982, Sonic Youth and Swans began doubling up for bills at whatever clubs would have them; one combined show at the Mudd Club was free of admission, perhaps as a way to persuade anyone to be subjected to not one but two deafeningly thunderous bands. "Typically, Swans would drive people out of the room with volume and the violence of the sound," says Gira, "so Sonic Youth was happy to play first, so they'd at least have whatever paltry audience we both drew before Swans scared them away." To Gira, who joined Sonic Youth onstage at least once during one of their dual shows (Moore returned the favor with Swans), "Sonic Youth were very awkward, almost comical in the early days. Very under-rehearsed, almost like a haphazard gesture, like swatting publicly at the hovering gnat of an idea. But there was something about Thurston's willingness to make an idiot out of himself onstage that I admired. I don't mean this disparagingly. He wanted to push the performance and make it actually 'happen' in a real, uncomfortable way, at the risk of being seen as a fool."

Coincidentally, the sound of Sonic Youth began to grow harder—rougher, more distorted, more abrasive—during the spring and summer of 1982. Their association with Swans was one factor, and another was Moore's growing fascination with the emerging hardcore movement. The uncompromising power of screaming skinheads spoke to him; with the original punk and no-wave scenes having expired, hardcore was perhaps a replacement for their energy and primitiveness. He also idolized the self-contained, self-sustaining community that had built up around hardcore, a network of bands, fans, fanzines, indie labels, and clubs that existed outside the traditional music industry. "I was really enamored of it," he says, adding, perhaps only half-jokingly, "I still had this desire to give it all up and be in a hardcore band." Neither Ranaldo nor Gordon shared his obsession with dropping into the "hardcore matinee" shows at CBGB; Moore recalls Ranaldo once telling him he was "bummed out" that Moore wanted the band to play faster and cruder like a hardcore band. But to Lyle Hysen, a Long Island kid who drummed in the hardcore band the Misguided and soon became a close friend of Moore and Gordon's, the connection was obvious. "Just the way hardcore bands really couldn't play and didn't give a shit is what appealed to Thurston," Hysen says. "Here were these kids putting out records themselves, and Sonic Youth were excited by that."

Other aspects of hardcore—or the sound emanating from it—crept into their sound as well. One night, Ranaldo and Moore went to see Black Flag, the all-powerful, all-overwhelming hardcore band from California. During a break in their set, guitarist Greg Ginn and bassist Chuck Dukowski turned around, faced the speakers, and proceeded to create a wave of feedback that enveloped the club. Ranaldo and Moore were immediately inspired and began thinking of ways to incorporate that approach into their sound. "We all had this similar idea at the time of ways to mine these ideas that were floating around from post–no wave," says Ranaldo. "We all thought we could see ways to take what was happening at the time on the scene and graft them to create something we could do together."

Of course, the escalating harshness of the band's sound was also rooted in their continually unpleasant surroundings, the increasing grimness of living in the city during the early '80s, especially the Eldridge Street area. "I believe they *had* to live in that environment to get that sound," says Hysen, who visited the apartment many times during that period. "It was crazy down there, super-hardcore Chinatown. It was *nuts* walking around there."

All of it—the music and the physical environment—swirled around them as they began working up new songs at the bunker with a drummer who was an ideal fit for their evolving approach. "Bob was the perfect person for us at that moment in time," Ranaldo says. "It was a little more bludgeoning." Visiting the bunker one day, Swans' Jonathan Kane heard Sonic Youth rehearsing and opened the door to the room. Out ran a cat, hair standing on end in horror from the racket. It was, Kane thought, like something out of an R. Crumb cartoon.

RELATIVELY QUICKLY, their roles in the band began to be carved out. As the artwork for the EP demonstrated, Gordon brought her art aesthetic and a broader sense of what worked—and didn't—for the band, visually, conceptually, and often musically. Moore, far less concerned with day-to-day business, brought the overarching vision, the guitar chords or ideas that would be the basis for band-written songs, and the beat-on-the-brat humor. "Thurston was always pretty much the instigator, maybe because he's a Leo," Gordon says. "He would always figure out what our next move should be." Ranaldo would be the technician, the one ever more obsessed with tinkering and refining an arrangement in a way Moore, who prided himself on spontaneity, rarely would; Ranaldo would also book many of the shows and collect whatever money they made at the end of each show. Gordon sensed another emerging role as well: "I would help mediate communication and get people to talk. Guys don't always communicate with each other."

Their determination manifested itself in the fall. Although they were barely known beyond the parameters of lower Manhattan—the EP was far from a best-seller, and they were still playing to tiny crowds in small quarters—they decided to undertake a tour. Unlike many of their peers (not that they had many beyond Swans), they had a basic press kit, which consisted of a copy of the EP and a few clippings, such as Coleman's *New York Rocker* article. Ranaldo began making calls to clubs where he'd played during the 1980 Branca tour as well as those with good word of mouth. They mailed their media package to the clubs, and soon enough, they and touring mates Swans had lined up gigs in the Southeast and Midwest. They rented a van and a truck, hired a driver (a local musician and poet, Joe Chassler, member of another band, the Avant Squares), and, in the second week of November, met up at the bunker. After stopping off for beer and cigarettes, they drove off to see how this new music would play in America, or at least one small part of it.

Nothing about the first leg of the road show, which Gira dubbed the Savage Blunder tour, was traditional; it wasn't even much of a tour, since it encompassed six clubs in six shows, from Chapel Hill, North Carolina, to Baltimore. Not surprising for bands who were both extreme and virtually unknown, attendance was sparse. The first night, at the Cat's Cradle in Chapel Hill, North Carolina, ten people showed up. On a tour where both bands sometimes found themselves playing to only a bartender and one other customer, that would be considered a good night. If a club was lucky enough to even have a sound man, he would often tell the two bands they were too loud or set up the microphones and flee in disgust; as a result, both Swans and Sonic Youth suffered from poorly set up sound systems. They drew a respectable crowd at the 40 Watt Club in Athens, Georgia— home to a burgeoning indie rock scene that included R.E.M.—but in the main, says Moore, "We were just playing for ourselves at that point."

Of the two bands, Swans were the most intimidating onstage. With their two bass players and banging metal plates, as well as Gira stalking the stage and glaring at the crowd while singing about rape, they must have seemed like aliens, and particularly hostile ones at that. "Swans sound was so extreme and nihilistic," says Gordon, "so compared to that, we were kind of uplifting." During their own time onstage, Sonic Youth introduced some of the new songs they'd written: the hardcore-influenced "Confusion Is Next" and "Making the Nature Scene," set to a Gordon lyric about the prostitutes who congregated near their apartment. Even if Sonic Youth were comparatively easier on the ears than Swans, catcalls and screams of "you suck!" peppered many of the shows. As Ranaldo recalls, "Half the patrons thought we were just a bunch of jive art nerds from New York."

The situation inside the van could be equally taxing. In the back, ten musicians found themselves sitting together on a bare metal floor with no seats and a few pillows; the only windows were next to the front seats. Given the amount of cigarettes and pot everyone was inhaling, the van would quickly fill up with smoke, a situation that Bert, the only one who didn't smoke regular cigarettes, soon found intolerable. Swans always seemed to be arguing amongst themselves, with Gira being particularly testy, accusing others of taking the last smokes. No one had any money, especially from the shows themselves, which could pay them all of twenty dollars, so they would sleep on the floors of whatever friends or acquaintances they had in those cities. After working their way back to New York, they headed out again a few weeks later when they were offered a chance to play the Walker Arts Center in Minneapolis. As a warm-up before both bands drove to the Midwest, they did a set at Maxwell's in Hoboken, where only three people, one of them Bert's girlfriend Linda, showed up. Gira demonstrated the hard-hitting sound he wanted the sound man to attain by slapping him hard on the chest.

As Bert and others noticed, traveling with a couple proved less problematic than anyone would have thought. On the road for the first time, Moore and Gordon made a point of avoiding obvious intimate gestures. "You wouldn't have even known they were a couple," says Bert. "They never were extremely affectionate in public or anything. If she rested her head on his shoulder in the van, that would be *it*." Kane sensed the two were in love, but that they "didn't want to annoy people with mushy romantic moments." The decision was a conscious one, akin to a couple toiling in the same workplace who didn't want to make their romance overly apparent. "We decided we weren't a lovey-dovey couple," Moore says. "That was fairly conscious. We tried to separate ourselves from each other."

To Gira, the Savage Blunder shows amounted to "a discouraging nightmare, and the responses for Swans were complete and absolute rejection." Sonic Youth, though, took what they could from the experience. After each show, they would assemble in the van and pass around a Walkman, listening back to a tape of a show from the previous night to analyze the set and the music. Gira saw for himself how Sonic Youth made the most of it: "They seemed to garner some fans. They were very good at networking, too. They were very likable people. They made friends and gathered addresses along the way." Kane, who left Swans not long after the tour wrapped up over disagreements with Gira, noticed the fierce determination of his tour mates. "Sonic Youth had attitude," he says. "They were convinced that what they were doing was right. They were like the Three Musketeers."

When they finally arrived back home in late December, the relief was palpable; as Gordon says, the overall experience "wasn't all that much fun." One consequence was a developing chill between Sonic Youth and Swans. "Any vague friendship any of us had for each other was probably erased after that tour," Gira admits. "*Everyone*, individually, in both bands, hated every other person on the tour by the end of that debacle, I'm sure." Yet Sonic Youth had made a number of important contacts and were able to work out their new material onstage. As Ranaldo says, "We came back from that tour a much more ferocious band than we were."

They also returned with an unexpected problem. At rest stops, Moore would often spot Bert standing off by himself, not looking especially happy. (Given the circumstances within the van, it was hard to blame him.) Onstage, during the Midwest shows, Moore and Ranaldo began growing dissatisfied with their new drummer. "We felt he wasn't cutting it," Ranaldo says. "There'd be lots of times when you'd be onstage and you'd glance back like, 'Come *on*, dude!' He was having trouble keeping the beat steady." Part of the problem was beyond Bert's reach. The onstage volume meant he had to bash even more frenetically (and off base) in order to hear his own playing, and his style—heavy on the tom-toms—wasn't right for the driving, hardcore-influenced rhythms Moore craved. They liked and respected Bert—he'd seen most of the classic New York punk bands before any of them had—but to Moore, Bert was less ambitious than the rest, and Bert noticed Moore growing testier with him onstage. "I was not satisfied with where we were at," Moore says. "I was really focusing on Bob in a way. I thought, 'We really need a drummer who can kick ass.'"

Not long after their return to the city, Moore made the decision to fire Bert, but the task was easier thought than done. Bert first began thinking something was wrong when the calls for practice stopped coming, but the reality only hit him when he received a call from Gordon telling him in no uncertain terms he was no longer a member of Sonic Youth. Although he was aware of his limitations, Bert was nevertheless upset and confused: He thought they were all getting along well.

As with the way Dave Keay had been dropped as a possible drummer a year earlier, the course of action revealed another facet of the band's growing internal dynamic and which roles everyone would take. Moore was, by his own admission, "too much of a wuss" to make the call to Bert; by nature, he was nonconfrontational. Ranaldo was reluctant to have the business of the band hamper friendships and connections. That left Gordon—"the most adult, the one most capable of doing it," Ranaldo says. "She had more of that attitude; she was able to just go, 'Okay, you're out.' Cut and dry—that's the end of it. Thurston and I were more concerned with how *Bob* would take it."

With little choice, Gordon took on a chore neither Ranaldo nor Moore had much stomach for. "Lee and Thurston were cowards," Gordon says. "They wouldn't tell him. And as all girls feel, if some guy doesn't want to see you again, the worst thing is *not* to be called. So even though I didn't *want* to do it, it was like a Band-Aid you pull off quickly. I wasn't happy to do it, but I felt it needed to be done. I felt awful." It wouldn't be the first time she would be called upon, almost by default, to pull the trigger on some of the more difficult decisions in their career.

THEY FIRST SPIED EACH OTHER on a subway platform, back when he was living on East 13th Street, before the move to Eldridge. He knew who *she* was, certainly, but not that she lived a mere block away. To her, he was "the cutest thing ever," but then, she had a thing for tall, young blondish guys, the anti-bad boys. "He was," she says, "like an innocent angel. How sexy! And opposites attract."

Lydia Lunch had arrived in New York in 1976, several years before Moore, with a background that made those of her peers seem pedestrian. She'd been born Lydia Koch in 1959 in Rochester (where, coincidentally, Gordon had briefly lived as a child) but was far from an ordinary upstate girl. Alone in the blacked-out basement of her parents' home, listening to Lou Reed's *Berlin* album, she was, in her words, "hateful and depressed" and ran away to the city when she was fourteen. She loved it there—everyone downtown seemed to be like her—but soon returned home. A few years later, she left again, this time for good, earning spare change by pretending to collect money for cancer research on the streets of the Village. A ravaged kewpie doll with a dark mop and a lasciviously smoky voice, she had no problem confronting local icons like David Byrne and Patti Smith guitarist Lenny Kaye on the street, where she would scream her nihilistic poems in their faces.

Admittedly anti-everything, she saw Smith as musically conventional and gravitated instead toward no-wavers like Suicide. Her nickname arrived when, while working in a cafeteria downtown, she began sneaking food out to her musician friends, and one of them—she thinks it was Willy Deville of the CBGB band Mink Deville—called out to his friends, "Here comes Lydia Lunch!" Adopting hard-boiled urban identities was not unusual on the scene: For a while, Richard Edson referred to himself as "R. Smith" during Sonic Youth shows and put up a sign on his apartment door that read "R. Smith Detective Agency."

She soon hooked up with another downtown misanthrope, James Chance, and together they formed the provocatively named Teenage Jesus and the Jerks. Fueled by Lunch's poking-you-in-the chest voice and the band's caveman riffing, Teenage Jesus didn't sound completely like their no-wave contemporaries: DNA, with their flagellating tempos and Arto Lindsay's strangulated singing, and Mars, who made what sounded like an electrified shovel-scrape, were more adroit. But as Lunch says of the genre, "The point was the primal," and all the bands lived up to that billing. Claustrophobic and clenched, sounding as forbidding as the East Village looked, no wave was the sound of a city dying—and angry at having to fight for its survival. It made the Ramones or Blondie truly sound like the modern-day pop classicists they were. Walking home from a CBGB show to the squalid apartment she and her lover Chance were sharing on East 2nd Street, Lunch was approached by a man who screamed at her, "Do you want to fuck my dog?" She didn't think twice about it: Of *course* someone would say that, in that city at that time.

Moore had idolized her from afar; it was at a show by 8 Eyed Spy, the band she formed after Teenage Jesus had collapsed in 1979, that he'd run into Gordon before their first date. Finally, Moore and Lunch met by way of their mutual friend Edson, who lived across the street from Lunch. By then, Sonic Youth had formed, and Lunch approached Moore with the idea of accompanying one of her spoken-word shows. She met him in a small park on the Lower East Side and told him about the time she'd been raped. "Uhhh . . . yeah, wow," is all she remembers him saying, as he listened intently. "He was kind of shocked but enthralled," she says. "He didn't run away." It was exactly the kind of response she was hoping for. For her show, Lunch recreated the experience onstage: her telling the story, Moore listening. During the fall of 1982, she asked him to play bass on *In Limbo*, a solo album she was recording, and their sonic alliance began.

To Jim Sclavunos, who was also backing Lunch at those sessions, "Thurston embodied a breath of fresh air for Lydia compared to a lot of musicians she'd worked with. He was younger and more unabashed about it and very enthusiastic and positive, whereas a lot of the people from the no-wave scene were misanthropic grumps. Also, he was really cute, and she always liked the idea of corrupted innocence." Tall and thin, a wave of blond hair falling to the side of his face that made him look almost like a New York version of a Beach Boy, Sclavunos well knew Lunch's appetite. He'd met her while interviewing her for his Brooklyn punk fanzine, and later she asked him to join her band to play bass even though he'd never picked up that instrument and had only taken a few lessons on drums and saxophone during his teen years. Lunch didn't care: "She likened the idea of a rhythm section to a good hate-fuck," he says. "Just sort of relentless pelvic pounding. And I wholeheartedly endorsed that approach." The other part of his audition involved losing his virginity to Lunch—"quite willingly, mind you"—even though she scared him more than the menacing junkies who approached him on the street (so often, in fact, that he took to carrying a knife and brass knuckles).

By early 1983, Lunch was a looming presence around Sonic Youth, both as an inspiration (especially to Moore) and a friend. To their surprise, given her status on the scene, she would often hang out with *them*, and despite her sexual reputation, she and Gordon clicked better than expected. "She was very flirtatious," Moore admits. "She was kind of a man-killer." Seeing some of their early shows, Lunch swooned over the moments when the melodies stopped and the feedback squalor began. She was no fan of the guitar—"one of the most repugnant instruments ever invented," she says—but they were an exception. "When Sonic Youth were awful, they were pretty fucking awful," she says. "But at that point, almost all their shows were amazing. It was about letting your soul leak out of your fingers. Something was leaking out of them, and that's what was most moving to me. They were doing something that went beyond words, trying to get beyond something, even beyond themselves."

The Lunch connection became particularly valuable when, in light of Bert's dismissal, the band needed yet another percussionist. Shortly before the second, Midwestern leg of Savage Blunder, the band had begun rehearsing with a new drummer, a transplanted California art school student and experimental musician named Tom Recchion who'd met Gira at the Otis school. During rehearsals at Gira's bunker, the matchup seemed to click; Recchion felt at home bashing away on songs that were equal parts punk and improvisation, music with what he calls "lots of freedom to move." After playing a solid show with them at the Mudd Club in early December 1982, Recchion wanted to continue on in the band. But when he heard about plans to drive out to the Midwest with Swans—in a van and without any clear idea where they were going to sleep—Recchion abruptly quit; he knew he didn't travel well, and he also knew how difficult Gira could be. (When someone in the Mudd Club crowd yelled out, "Who's the new drummer?" Recchion thought it was an in-joke but didn't realize until later that the wisecrack had some basis in reality.)

Given Sclavunos' no-wave roots, talent as a drummer, and friend-ship with Moore (the two of them had roomed together on a brief Lunch tour to promote *In Limbo*), it was inevitable that Lunch would recommend him for the slot. Although he wasn't a thrash drummer, he was more sophisticated—"a little more cymbal washy than Bob," as Moore puts it. (During a visit to Eldridge Street, Moore played Sclavunos some of his hardcore 45s; the drummer rolled his eyes the whole time, thinking the music silly.) Rehearsing with the band for the first time, Sclavunos noticed Gordon's quietness and Moore's bois-terousness but also their democratic approach. While it was more than clear that Gordon had less instrumental experience than Ranaldo and Moore, Sclavunos was struck by how often they ran ideas by her and deferred to her. It was a noticeable change from working with Lunch, which he recalls as "a dictatorship. She would take most of the money and the credit and you were pretty much expendable." Sclavunos was impressed that Sonic Youth "didn't have to apologize for being arty and didn't have to wear their art on their sleeve, either. They could function as a rock band, but they also had more highfa-lutin ideas than your average rock band."

They were more than eager to present some of these new ideas to the world, but frustrations with their label were already beginning to mount. Only two years into its existence, Neutral Records was run-ning into financial problems. Contrary to his partner Branca's initial promise, co-owner Josh Baer had begun to realize he wasn't going to make his money back quickly and that indie distributors took much longer to pay labels than he'd hoped. No funding for a second Sonic Youth record would be immediately forthcoming, not even for a bargain-rate session at Radio City.

Looking to put some of their new songs on tape, Ranaldo rang up Wharton Tiers. By coincidence, Tiers—a wry, dark-haired twenty-nine-year-old originally from Philadelphia—had been Rhys Chatham's drummer in the cataclysmic show Ranaldo had witnessed at Max's Kansas City nearly four years prior; Tiers had also drummed in Theo-retical Girls as well as A Band, who once shared a bill with the Coach-men and the Fluks at CBGB. By day, Tiers was the superintendent of a building on 22nd Street between 1st and 2nd Avenues, and as part of an arrangement with the landlord, he was able to convert the basement into a small recording studio. On the phone, Ranaldo told Tiers the band was "sort of biding our time" while they waited for Neutral to get enough money to finance an album, but that the group had decided instead to "release a quickie single, like as quick as possible" and wanted to do it "as inexpensively as possible. . . . If the whole thing goes well, we could probably give you some cash." Tiers won them over when he told Ranaldo he'd recently recorded a single and pressed a thousand singles for a mere $400, a fact that made Ranaldo respond, with awe, *"Incredible."*

The original idea was to record a seven-inch single of one of their new songs, "Confusion Is Next," which reflected Moore's dual influences at the moment: The intentionally slothful first part had the sludgy drag of Lunch's post–Teenage Jesus work, while the second half aimed for the propulsive drive of hardcore. (The references to chaos and confusion were a nod to the work of Henry Miller; at the time, Moore was immersed in *Tropic of Capricorn*.) In the early months of 1983, the group, including Sclavunos, began filing into Tiers' studio, Fun City.

As they soon learned, the space was a long way from Radio City, both geographically and technologically. The recording room was a narrow sliver of space with an oil slick across the cement floor; it was separated from the console room by a white cinderblock wall. The setup, with its basic eight-track recording machine, was particularly jarring to the latest member of the band's loose entourage, an Ohio-born, Michigan-schooled recording engineer named John Erskine. At thirty, Erskine was the oldest of the bunch. He'd played in a punk band of his own in Michigan and had moved to Manhattan a few months before to inch his way into the city's music scene. He'd seen one of Sonic Youth's early club shows, after which he went up and introduced himself to the band (which impressed Moore, who hadn't remembered anyone else ever doing that before). Erskine volunteered his services to make them sound better onstage. Soon enough, he was honing his own craft as a sound man, attempting to make their deafening assault as sharp as possible in the tiny spaces they would play.

When the Fun City session came up, Erskine tagged along. At first, he was put off by Tiers' setup: To isolate the individual instrument sounds, Erskine had to toss blankets over the guitar amplifiers, since everything tended to bleed into everything else. But Erskine was impressed with how good the final results sounded, and Moore in particular was thrilled at the idea of having more control over the band's sound than at the more formidable Radio City.

Although Bert had always had trouble nailing the rhythm for "Confusion Is Next," particularly the hardcore-rooted portion, they managed to record it quickly with Sclavunos. Upon hearing the track, Branca was pleased enough with the results that he told them to keep recording and make a full album. All they needed was money, and soon it came from a particularly unlikely source. One evening at CBGB, the band was approached by Nicolas Ceresole and his girlfriend, Catherine Bachmann. He was Swiss, she was half Swiss and half Danish, and he had money in his family: His father was a doctor, and his grandfather had owned a newspaper and a beer company in Denmark. While living on an estate on Lake Geneva, with a sculptured garden in the back and boats on the lake, Ceresole and Bachmann began visiting New York in 1978; avid music fans—Nicolas was a collector of rare records himself—they became regular club-hoppers.

A year later, they actually moved to the city, settling into an apartment on the Upper West Side, just off Central Park at West 86th Street. At the suggestion of 99 Records owner Ed Bahlman, they went to see Sonic Youth in October 1981 and introduced themselves afterward. The band didn't quite know what to make of them: "They were taken with New York rock and we were one of the bands they liked," Moore says. A friendship began, and at least once a week, the band would take the subway up to the couple's apartment for brunch or dinner, usually pasta cooked by Bachmann on a hot plate, followed by generous amounts of pot. The Ceresole-Bachmann apartment became a sort of indie-world salon; on various days, they would invite over Lydia Lunch and her posse, Sonic Youth or Australian post-punk singer-songwriter Nick Cave. When the couple heard the band needed funds for a recording session, they borrowed $500 from Nicolas' father, telling him the money was for dental work. (According to Moore and Ranaldo, the final loan came to much more, nearly $3,000.)

With Ceresole, Bachmann, and Neutral kicking in funds, the band was able to return to Fun City and begin making a complete album. Working with no time constraints, as they had at Radio City, they, along with Tiers and Erskine, were able to indulge their creative whims in ways they'd only begun to on the first EP. For "The World Looks Red"—lyrics courtesy of Gira, who hoped to convey "just a general sense of paranoia"—Moore stuck a broken drumstick through the strings for the first time in a studio. To give the song an even rawer sound, Erskine suggested using Moore's rougher first-take vocal. Ranaldo had been working on a series of tape-loop instrumentals; Gordon called one of them "Lee Is Free" and they put it on the record. Grabbing beverages at a nearby deli one evening, Erskine and Ranaldo became so entranced by the sound emanating from inside one of the refrigerators that they returned with a Walkman to record it. As the deli worker yelled at them to keep the door shut, they stuck the machine inside and pressed record, resulting in "Freezer Burn." (The sound of the door closing could be heard on the original vinyl release.)

There were, Sclavunos recalls, "no limitations in terms of the creative imagination or how to play the songs." Sclavunos himself did a snare drum overdub for "Inhuman" in the bathroom; for the same song, Moore plugged his microphone into a broken amp to make his voice sound even more distorted. Tiers too was more than game: "Wharton was like a big brother to the band," Erskine recalls. "They had nothing but laughs."

Yet it was the most introverted member of the band who began to come into her own. Gordon's mentor Dan Graham was in the midst of making a film, *Rock My Religion*, about the connections between religious services and rock shows; when Graham first saw hardcore pogoing, it reminded him of the similar way Shakers would dance themselves into an ecstatic frenzy in a circle. In search of music for his film, he assigned Gordon the task of writing a song; out came "Shaking Hell," inspired by both Graham's vision and Gordon's feelings on advertising and male fashion designers: "The way advertising men are in control of the way women look. 'Take off your dress and shake off your flesh' was about male corporate control." Lydia Lunch was partly the inspiration for Gordon's lyric for "Protect Me You," a song about, she says, "being innocent and being ravaged." Initially reserved about singing the song—"She was very shy and not very confident in her voice," recalls Erskine—Gordon hunkered down and nailed it in two takes; to help out, Ranaldo stepped in and played her bass part.

Given that both the band and the studio were in gestation stages, mishaps plagued the project: Tape was unintentionally stretched, soda accidentally spilled on Tiers' console. ("We cleaned it up as much as we could, I guess," Moore says.) Hands cupped over his headphones, Erskine would nervously watch the needle on the console to make sure that, with the increased volume, it didn't leap too far to the right and burn out the system. Since neither he nor Tiers could physically see the band, they would have to shout out "Tape rolling!" to let the musicians know when to start. (Attentive listeners would hear one of Erskine's shouts at the beginning of "[She's in a] Bad Mood.") Gordon rerecorded her vocal for "Shaking Hell," but, after deciding she liked the first take better, everyone discovered the original had been erased; in its place, a version from a club performance was stripped in. "That record was a real struggle," Gordon says. "We didn't know what we were doing. It was a real patchwork, a labor of love."

To Sclavunos, the experience was particularly rattling. He found Fun City "fraught with peril," especially the monitoring system that let the musicians hear themselves play. "I was disappointed with the circumstances they'd decided to record under," he says. "I didn't feel they were adequate for the task at hand. If that makes me unreasonable or deluded, it's probably true. But that's what I was seeing." After he'd started asserting his opinions, Sclavunos began to feel like the odd man out and that his input wasn't being taken seriously. Another unusual factor was at work: By unlikely coincidence, Sclavunos had recently married Truus de Groot, Ranaldo's former bandmate in Plus Instruments, and the breakup of that band had resulted in lingering strain between Ranaldo and de Groot. "I was married to a woman who didn't want me to hang around with Lee Ranaldo," Sclavunos says. Nor did it help that Sclavunos was consuming a fair share of acid and speed at the time, which, he admits, probably made him edgier than normal.

The tension came to a head during the recording of "Making the Nature Scene." The song had been written and rehearsed in Gira's bunker with Bert, whose blunt style ideally suited its tribal-beat pulse. With his lighter touch, Sclavunos couldn't find his way into the song—at least not in the way the band wanted to hear it—and someone, possibly Ranaldo, remarked that since Bert had played it better, maybe they should ask him back, if only temporarily, to record the track. Although Ranaldo and Tiers have no memory of the moment, Sclavunos remembers being so offended that he stormed out of the studio. ("I was like, 'Oh, shit, what's going on?'" Erskine says.) Moore has no recall of the incident, either: "I might have been oblivious to it. I didn't have the emotional skills to deal with it. I was immature."

Whatever happened that day—in a press release issued years later, the band wrote that "Sclavunos left the band to persue [sic] foreign women and other personal hells"—Moore was soon on the phone to Bert, then working in his father's liquor store in Clifton. Bert was happy to hear from Moore but also puzzled: Moore told him the band was simply trying Sclavunos out and asked if Bert could come into the city to help them put "Making the Nature Scene" on tape.

The comments seemed to contradict what Gordon had told Bert a few months before, yet Bert didn't argue. In the interim he'd been brushing up on his drumming, hard, and felt newly confident. He took the bus in and quickly recorded the song with them, pounding so hard that Tiers had to replace the heads of the drums when they were finished. "Jim was a real clean, technical player," Ranaldo says. "He could certainly keep the beat and drive the songs. But he didn't have this wildness quality we were ultimately looking for. 'Nature Scene' was all about that—that crude, bludgeoning *Flintstones* beat—and Bob had it."

Bert also had the forgive-and-forget attitude that allowed him to return. "Considering they kicked me out of the band, everything was still friendly," he recalls. Shortly after, he received another call from the band, this time inviting him to play with them at Speed Trials, a multi-night show at White Columns. To Moore, Bert was "fabulous—he was on fire that night." Elsewhere on the bill were three snide teenage hardcore kids who complained about playing in an art gallery (not their usual style of venue) and didn't understand why they were playing to such *old* people. They called themselves the Beastie Boys, and, like Sonic Youth, their performance announced that something fresh and enthralling was happening in New York City, and beyond, if anyone would ever be able to hear it.

In the Eldridge Street home one day a few years earlier, Moore was idly flipping through a magazine, his head cocked to the left. As he read, Gordon began sketching his profile. Afterward, she showed it to him—a simple line drawing of a downturned face, with other lines cutting in and out of it. They'd used it for the flier to advertise their first show as Sonic Youth, in May 1981, but the drawing would now serve a different purpose. Moore had always felt the cover of *Sonic Youth* was too clean-looking, and he knew the new, harsher music they'd recorded needed a different presentation. In Gordon's raw doodle—one of the first pieces of art he'd seen her create since they'd met—he found the solution. He scrawled the words "confusion is sex" across the top, and before long, Sonic Youth had a cover for their second record.

Thanks in part to the circumstances under which it was made, *Confusion Is Sex*, which Neutral released in April 1983, was cruder-sounding than the debut. Its takes on everything—music, the city, sex, identity—were shot through with dread and anxiety, and the tracks sounded as if a thin layer of soot had settled atop them. This time, the album opened with guitar, not drum, but the harsh, metallic strumming that launched "(She's in a) Bad Mood" was no less disquieting. The song itself—prompted by Moore's dealings with the volatile Lunch, who, he says, "made bad mood an art form"—was a showcase for their progress. To a degree, it was a simple song, consisting of only two identical verses—one of which Moore sang carefully, as if trying to sound conventional, and the other of which he sang in his more familiar tight-throated yawp. Around those two verses, though, the band built a bloodcurdling wall of sound, building up to a section where Moore's and Ranaldo's guitars played in unison, the primitive rhythm section behind them adding a grim wallop. Then they almost casually tore down that very wall; by the end of the song, the track had purposefully crumbled.

The rest of the album was similarly electric, brittle, and unnerving. Like few other records of the time, it captured the spooky, menacing feel of downtown Manhattan in the early '80s: a world where, as Moore sang in "Confusion Is Next," "chaos is the future." That track alone, with its shift from death crawl to hardcore-inspired pummel, captured the uncertainty and trepidation that came with living in their part of the city at that time: a neighborhood where a week didn't seem to go by without news that a friend or acquaintance was stabbed or mugged. The rattled guitars and numbed-out lyrics of "Inhuman," in tandem with Moore's psycho-killer delivery, spoke to that atmosphere as well. "It totally captures where we were at," Moore says. "For my money, that was our purest record, in a way. We did it cheap and fast, and it captured the sound we had and where we were emotionally."

Emotions good and bad raced through *Confusion Is Sex*. From Gordon's elliptical words, it was hard to piece together exactly what was happening to the teenage girl in "Protect Me You," yet the chillingly calm way in which she sang, the frenzied strumming of the melody line, and Ranaldo's simple, ominous bass line amounted to an urban horror film set to music. "Shaking Hell" may have been inspired by Dan Graham and the fashion industry, in different ways, but it too could have accompanied a movie about a slasher; the slow, creepy rhythm and textures were matched only by Gordon's repeated, increasingly desperate cries of "I'll shake off your flesh." Ranaldo proudly termed the album more multifaceted than *Sonic Youth*, and it was, especially in the sounds of the guitars. He and Moore made them sound like nail-gun blasts in "Shaking Hell," shimmery keyboards in "The World Looks Red," and chiming clocks in "Protect Me You."

The album also revealed the group's expanding palette. Its fascination with pure sound was heard in the humming buzz of "Freezer Burn," which was paired with a live recording (with Bert on drums) of the Stooges' primal, carnal anthem "I Wanna Be Your Dog" taped during the Savage Blunder tour. (The crumpled-up inside photo of the band was also taken during those shows.) For all the group's dissonance, one of the record's most striking songs was its simplest: "Making the Nature Scene," Gordon's meditation on the "order of decay" in the city, was driven mostly by Bert's heavy thump, a rubbery bass line played by Moore, and intermittent injections of guitar tempest by Ranaldo.

The underground rock press of the time was accustomed to dissonance. But even those publications were taken aback by the record, which appeared at almost the same time as *Murmur*, the far more lush and beautiful (if equally cryptic) debut by R.E.M. To the influential *Trouser Press*, *Confusion Is Sex* was an "aural root canal"; the zine *Flesh & Bones* referred to it as "piles of raw hamburger meat bleeding on the turntable . . . [it's] what you'll hear when you take the final elevator ride to Hell." Those were compliments, of course, as was a review in *The Offense:* "The album is really over the top, and of course, they've probably gone too far, but who else has?" At that point, it was hard to argue.

Chapter 4

MOORE AND GORDON hadn't been apart for a single day of the previous three years, but that would now end. In the early spring of 1983, just as *Confusion Is Sex* was sent out into the world, word went out that Glenn Branca needed musicians. Branca always needed musicians, of course; every piece he wrote seemed more complex than the one that preceded it and required more players as a result. But now he really could use a horde: He'd received offers to perform his latest and grandest piece, the sprawling *Symphony No. 4*, in Europe.

Once again, he hired Ranaldo, who'd become a trusted and respected employee. But since the piece required a more expansive ensemble—people to play not only guitars but harpsichords, percussive instruments, and any variety of peculiar, often homemade stringed instruments—Branca had to cast about. Despite his initial concerns about Moore, Branca had used him for several earlier pieces, including a 1982 recording of "Bad Smells," a rhythmic piece commissioned for a Twyla Tharp dance performance, and now Branca hired him for the tour. "I was skeptical about Thurston," Branca says, "but he was a good boy, and so clearly serious and dedicated about playing music." When Gordon asked if she too could enlist in the upcoming tour, Branca demurred, saying he had enough players by that point. Visiting Branca in his apartment, Ranaldo and Moore tried to convince Branca otherwise, but, not surprisingly, Branca was intractable. ("They were young," Branca says. "Everything had to happen *immediately*. They had no patience.") To Moore's disappointment, Gordon stayed behind while he and the rest of Branca's ensemble flew to Europe.

In ways they predicted and didn't, the Branca tour became a pivotal event for Sonic Youth. Some of the instruments used for the shows were truly vexing, like the harmonics guitars that had pickups on each end, wire for strings, and a movable bridge; players pulled sounds out of them by slamming them with chopsticks. Someone had to tune each one of the dozens and dozens of guitars, and Ranaldo and Moore volunteered for the impossibly arduous task. For a few hours before each performance, the two methodically tweaked and tuned every fretted instrument. "It was either like Chinese water torture or this incredibly interesting study of sound," Branca says, "and they clearly treated it like a study in sound." During the performances, Branca saw that the towering, fresh-faced kid was inordinately attentive; whenever Branca looked over, the kid would be staring directly at him, waiting for the next cue.

The experience endeared them to Branca—never an easy thing to do—yet had a more profound impact. The guitars on their first EP, *Sonic Youth*, were tuned in the traditional E-A-D-G-B-E configuration. No longer; Ranaldo and Moore had each had a taste of alternate tunings. Ranaldo had been introduced to open tunings a decade earlier, and Moore had his own particular entry point: the day a bunch of Branca's guitars were dropped off at his home on Eldridge Street. The moment occurred shortly before Ranaldo joined the band, when Moore needed guitars for one of the early shows with Anne DeMarinis and Branca loaned the nascent version of Sonic Youth a few instruments. Kneeling in front of a slew of worn-down guitars with strings tuned in every which way, Moore picked up one instrument after another, strumming each and sensing the possibilities in guitars not limited to standard tunings. "I felt like I could write songs all day," Moore says. "It was a signature day."

For John Erskine, who worked the sound system on the Branca tour, the impact on his friends in Sonic Youth was more than apparent. "It really solidified their feeling at that time," he says, "that if you wanted a guitar to sound like something in particular, you had to design the instrument to *make* that sound."

The idea of having their guitars be not quite out of tune—but not exactly *in* tune either—appealed to them on several levels. The approach could be heard in recordings not only by Branca but by the Velvet Underground and La Monte Young, meaning Sonic Youth could tap into an historical lineage they'd long admired. "It was almost second nature to do it," says Ranaldo. "It was in the air." But it also emerged from necessity. During the early days of the band, their guitar arsenal was tiny: Ranaldo had a Fender Telecaster that dated back to his Fluks days, and Moore had a beat-up Harmony. A few cheap Japanese hand-me-down models—including the guitar Moore had found in Gordon's apartment, now dubbed the Drifter—were also floating around. Since the guitars were so patchwork and shabby, some held together with tape, they couldn't hold standard tunings anyway; they'd fall out of tune within a few minutes. With no supply of new guitars on the way, Ranaldo and Moore figured they might as well employ sounds that didn't sound normal, and they might as well try to elicit other sonics out of them by jamming screwdrivers beneath the strings or rubbing a drumstick up and down the fretboard to bring out different overtones. Both men were still working with the structures of the twelve-tone Western music scale, but it all sounded different. "It gave us an advantage that we didn't have to play by the rules of the game," says Ranaldo, "which was the main thing we were looking for."

Much more so than in his own country, Branca was embraced by European audiences, a fact that didn't escape Ranaldo and Moore. Here were venues and crowds that actively seemed to welcome and embrace especially harsh sounds. When both Branca and Sonic Youth were invited to play at a festival in Vienna, Ranaldo and Moore quickly did the math: They could use the money they made from that performance to fly Bert and Gordon to Europe and then set up a small, frugal tour of their own after Branca's had ended. Approaching the promoters or club owners at Branca gigs, they talked up their own band and asked if

Sonic Youth could be booked into the same venue; Ranaldo made sure to jot all the names and contacts down in a notebook. "Glenn's shows were really impressive," Ranaldo says, "so people were inclined to think we were part of something and willing to book us." Much like the Savage Blunder shows with Swans, the tour would be another example of seemingly contradictory impulses: a desire to make the most grating music they could possibly make and yet an equal craving to reach as many people as possible while doing so.

With a few shows lined up, they cobbled together enough cash to buy Gordon a plane ticket; she, and Erskine's wife Sherry, met up with Ranaldo and Moore in Poitiers, France, during the last show of the Branca tour. With the tour not scheduled to start for another month, they retreated to the home of Nicolas Ceresole and Catherine Bachmann in Rolle, Switzerland. There, they drank wine, sailed, ate fish (asking for ketchup while doing so, much to the amusement of their hosts), and imbibed copious amounts of pot; one afternoon, everyone picnicked near an abandoned house in the middle of a vineyard.

But the bucolic vacation ended on June 11, when they congregated at a club called La Dolce Vita in Lausanne, Switzerland, to commence the first Sonic Youth tour of Europe. It began with a manic frenzy of activity and anxiety. After making the band promise they wouldn't fire him again—to which they agreed, although Moore, for one, doesn't recall the revised arrangement—Bert packed his snare drum and cymbals and boarded a flight to Paris, at which point he asked for directions to a train (in a language he didn't speak) and then took a nine-hour train ride to Lausanne. Although Bert arrived in a jet-lagged haze, there was no time to do anything but stop off at a fast-food restaurant and stuff him with hamburgers. Afterward, he was taken directly to the club and plopped behind a drum kit at the gym-size venue just as their set was scheduled to start.

The audience was well-lit before the show began; by the end, after "I Wanna Be Your Dog" and a long noise jam, they were smashing beer bottles against the stage to the rhythm and refusing to let the band leave. Bert couldn't believe what he was seeing—his first-ever European performance, and it was insanity. The rest of the five-show tour was equally chaotic. Using Eurail passes left over from the Branca tour, they traveled by train—pushing their guitars through train windows in order to disembark as quickly as possible, scrambling from one platform to the next as tourists and locals alike stared at them as if they were crazy people. During his brief tenure in Plus Instruments, Ranaldo had met Carlos van Hijfte, a Dutch booking agent; after Ranaldo got back in touch with him, van Hijfte set up a Sonic Youth Netherlands show in Eindhoven, during which the band's amplifiers blew up and they left with no money in their pockets. "It was loud, and some things fell apart," van Hijfte recalls, "but then it would come together again and be really beautiful."

After a summer in New York dotted with shows at CBGB, the Sin Club, and even Plugg, where Gordon and Moore had met three years earlier, they returned to Europe for an even longer series of shows starting in late October. On the fliers, the words "From New York" were often printed in larger font than "Sonic Youth." But they didn't seem to care; what mattered was spreading the word in any way possible. This time they ventured deeper into the continent, and the experiences—and the venues—grew more surreal. Glue-sniffing skinheads greeted them when they arrived at a club in Switzerland, and a Milan venue turned out to be a decaying, cheesy disco. One German booking took place at a former gasoline storage tank, another at a bar in the middle of a cow pasture, the female owner feeding them shots to force them to play more. At a place in the mountains of Germany, an irritating audience member who'd been lurking by the side of the stage made his way onto the stage itself, where he was promptly wrapped in tape by the band. ("We had all this duct tape we used, so what the hell?" Erskine recalls.) They only stopped once they realized he was having something close to an epileptic fit.

They slept on whatever floor they could find, drove in their rented car to the next show, and played to curious and sometimes unruly but captivated crowds of fifty to one hundred people. Many of those people barely spoke English, yet aggression was universal: They wanted something, anything, that was high intensity. "In New York, we typically played a lot shorter, maybe twenty minutes, forty-five minutes max," Gordon says. "In Europe, people were throwing bottles at us because we wouldn't play more, so we started stretching things out because of that."

The performances lived up to—even extended—the grim ambience of *Confusion Is Sex*. Bert's style of drumming was one factor: His tom-tom throb lent a heavier, denser undercurrent to "(She's in a) Bad Mood" and "The Burning Spear," both originally recorded without him. But as their show in Triers, Germany, on November 20 demonstrated, the band as a whole was capable of pushing itself to more forbidding heights. Hardly speaking to the crowd, they turned "The Burning Spear" into even more of a deranged howl, Moore hammering on the fretboard with drumsticks and pushing his voice to the point of an out-of-tune yowl. They dragged out "The Good and the Bad" to the point where it seemed to completely fall apart but never quite did. The set, like many on that tour, was the calm before the storm, the storm itself, and then an eerie calm again, with the promise of yet another storm. "There were so many chaotic gigs back then," says Ranaldo, "but chaos was part of what we were doing in a way."

Like the venues themselves, the audience response was never predictable. The fifty people who showed up for their Eindhoven show either loved it or, as van Hijfte says, "were turned away by it." But their excitable reactions were a genuinely pleasant change from the near-empty clubs that faced them back home. Even those taken aback by their sound and volume left with an indelible image: Moore, in his untucked long-sleeve white-collar shirts, hurling his guitar behind his back or dropping to his knees and screaming into the microphone; Gordon, playing stolidly in her flip-up shades and print skirts; Ranaldo, his legs spread out as if he were jackhammering or jabbing the air, sword-like, with his guitar. The volume was such that Erskine began to stick cigarette butts into his ears; later, he found plugs made specially for army personnel who fired off cannons.

While in Berlin, they met up with the owners of Zensor, a German label that, at Branca's forceful suggestion, had released *Sonic Youth* and *Confusion Is Sex* in Europe. They also brought with them a tape they'd dashed off at Tiers' studio shortly before they left town, paid for with money they'd made when a drunken club owner in New York accidentally paid them twice for the same performance. The tape had recordings of their three latest songs, each pointing in different directions. "Kill Yr Idols" was a grizzled, grimy scream-out to *Village Voice* music editor Robert Christgau, who'd been initially chilly toward the band's music. It felt like a silly, faux-hardcore in-joke, which couldn't be said of the two other new recordings. "Brother James" was inspired by *Mystery Train*, rock critic Greil Marcus' version of D. H. Lawrence's *Studies in Classic American Literature;* it was also featured in Dan Graham's film *Rock My Religion* (Graham used it in the background during footage of a religious rattlesnake cult). The music felt completely theirs—the way it began as a threatening murmur, whipped itself up into a frenzy, then locked into a visceral hammering when Gordon began singing. Although Gordon's one-paragraph lyric was elliptical, "Early American" took its cue from bad boy literary critic Leslie Fielder's writings on the supposed homoerotic relationship between Native Americans and the original settlers. With Gordon intoning the lyric over a heartbeat-murmur drum part and buzzy guitar drone, the song was more scarily motionless than anything they'd done. ("I have a pretty limited range," Gordon admits, "so I use space and phrasing and rhythm as my guide.") Combining the songs with "Protect Me You" and "Shaking Hell" from *Confusion Is Sex*, Zensor had a new Sonic Youth record all its own—called *Kill Yr Idols* and released, for the time being, only in Germany.

In best and worst ways, the tour climaxed with a performance at the Venue in London on December 1. From the start, everything seemed to go wrong. They'd hoped to play second on the bill, but were instead forced to open the three-band show; hardly anyone was in the hall by the time they took the stage. Once they began playing, Moore's guitar broke during the first song; Bert's borrowed drum kit began to fall apart. At one point, Ranaldo turned to see the coil in his amp glowing red-hot orange, smoke rising from within it. Outraged, Moore began pushing monitors around the stage. ("Thurston had a temper back then," Gordon says.) Before they knew it, the curtain had come down, and it was over. They left London dejected. "They must have thought it was just noisy bullshit," says Ranaldo. "We left thinking, 'What a bust.' We'd waited so long to play London, and it was nowheresville."

And then the strangest thing happened: When the reviews in the British music press began appearing, everyone seemed to *like* it. A writer for *Sounds* dubbed them "demonically funny," *New Musical Express'* Gay Abandon thought they looked like "four cretinously 'normal' mop-topped Americans"—even likening Moore to Ron Howard in *Happy Days*, much like his teenage friends in Bethel once had—but found the actual performance "mindblowing, psychedelic without the amoeba slideshow" and "a fortuitous blend of the painstakingly serious and the unwittingly comic." It didn't make any sense, not even to people who knew where they were headed even if no one else understood them.

THEY SHOULD HAVE BEEN HAPPY, should have felt they'd scaled a few major mountains. Unlike the few Manhattan bands they considered part of their community, they'd put out records both in the States and in Europe, had established a network of contacts in several countries, and had exposed their music to audiences not only in the Midwest but the middle of Europe. "A lot of bands from that scene made the same mistake—they didn't tour," says Tom Surgal, a New York–born experimental music percussionist who met the band through their mutual friend Lydia Lunch. (Surgal, also a set designer, had worked with Lunch on a film.) "But Sonic Youth had vision. They had a sense of scope. They knew they had to get out there."

Yet by early 1984, they were feeling stymied again, and their relationship with Branca was growing more complicated by the month. During their European shows, the composer grew irritated when Ranaldo and Moore spray-painted "Sonic Youth" on the stage and in dressing rooms. ("They were being real pricks," he says, "and they *know* it.") Yet perhaps because they paid such homage to him in their music (as well as guitar techniques and tunings), Branca was also enamored of them. When Moore and Ranaldo informed him they wouldn't be playing with his ensemble anymore, Branca was disappointed. "They left," he recalls. "'We're doing Sonic Youth.' It was as a simple as that. I said, 'Okay, I understand. You have the greatest band in the world—go do it.'"

Business matters made the situation between the two camps more precarious. As everyone soon became aware, neither Branca nor his Neutral partner, Josh Baer, were experienced when it came to the record business. "We made it clear to the bands: 'We don't have money for PR,'" says Branca. "We said, 'We have money to put out the records, to get them to the press and to radio. But beyond that, we can't do anything.' And all of a sudden, we became the major label who's fucking them." Frustrated with the lack of distribution and funds at Neutral, Moore drew up a flier castigating the label for, in his words, ripping them off; the leaflet somehow found its way to Branca, only adding to the tension between the two parties. In the end, the band told Neutral they were leaving. Baer in particular wasn't happy, since he felt he'd helped jump-start their career, but there was little either he or Branca could do.

As the band soon discovered, though, other takers didn't exist. With each passing year, the American independent label community was expanding; every city, major or not, seemed to have its own scene and endemic label to support it. Yet encouragement for Sonic Youth outside Manhattan appeared nonexistent. Moore's fascination with hardcore had led him to idolize SST, the California-based label that had begun, in 1978, as the home of Black Flag; guitarist Greg Ginn was also SST's founder. (The name came from Solid State Tuners, the mail-order electronics business Ginn had started when he was a teenager.) But when Moore sent a cassette of Sonic Youth music to SST's Joe Carducci, along with copies of a homemade, crudely Xeroxed and stapled fanzine Moore had started called *Killer*, Carducci threw the tape in the trash; the label didn't entertain unsolicited demos from bands they didn't know. However, Carducci did keep the issues of *Killer*, since their perverse humor, fan-boy enthusiasm for underground bands, and lists of fanzines around the country (complete with addresses) intrigued him.

Compared with the activity of the two previous years, the first half of 1984 was strangely quiet. Bookings were scarce—they would only perform a handful of times during the entire year—and day jobs again beckoned as their principal means of paying their rent and eating. Gordon worked as a waitress and painted apartments, including one on Central Park West occupied by the strutting cock-rocker Billy Squier. She and Moore both took jobs at Todd's Copy Shop, the Mott Street business owned by Todd Jorgensen, also the cofounder of A's. (Anyone with even the slightest interest in art—and making reproductions—seemed to stop by; Gordon would regularly see graffiti artist Jean-Michel Basquiat and fledgling director Jim Jarmusch.) One day Ceresole and Bachmann met up with Moore in midtown, where he was selling Chipwich ice-cream sandwiches at a cart. Abruptly, Moore told them he needed to find a bathroom, leaving Ceresole, whose command of English was limited, to man the cart himself. Working for David Klass, a fine-arts and metal sculptor in Chelsea, Ranaldo learned the art of welding, making metal wind chimes in the process. The chimes became part of the band's onstage metal-shop arsenal until they were stolen right off the stage of one of their regular haunts, the Pyramid Club. Of them all, Bert had the steadiest and most time-consuming job, a forty-hour-a-week gig at a silk screen printer whose clients included, among others, Andy Warhol.

By the spring, they were beginning to work on new material, some of it in Gira's bunker space. No matter the locale—Gira's or any one of a number of subterranean rehearsal rooms downtown—the band's creative ritual was taking shape. In a pattern that would be used for years to come, someone—usually Moore—would arrive at rehearsal with a riff, a few chords, or the most basic idea for a song, but rarely a finished song itself. The band would begin playing it: knocking it around, toying with it, coming up with ideas for sections and individual parts. Once a basic structure was devised, they would then play and refine it for weeks verging on months, the song expanding in length and density. Since the songs were always instrumentals at first, the band would never bother setting up microphones. In another lesson they gleaned from Branca, sound came first.

The process was long, intensive, and laborious—the antithesis of how punk songs were written and recorded—but it spoke to their ongoing need for group democracy. Eventually, finished songs would emerge; so, too, would eviction notices from all the noise they were making (or, in a telling sign of things to come, a notice that whatever building they were in would be converting to co-ops or condos). Only after they completed a track would they divvy up the songs and figure out who would sing which, at which point either Moore, Gordon, or Ranaldo would hastily come up with lyrics.

So it would be with the latest batch of songs, although they were shaping up differently than the ones before. At Gira's bunker, Moore began playing the two low strings on his guitar in F sharp. The simple pattern appealed to him, reminding him of the rock LPs he'd heard in his youth. "It was more rocked out than anything we'd done before," he says. "It was like, 'Wow, even with these different kinds of tunings, we can get some kind of neo-Foghat vibe here.'" He worried it was too goofy but then added another section: part of a motif he'd learned in an instruction book while taking piano lessons during his youth. He transformed it into a sinuous guitar lead part and then merged the two sections together; with it, a new and very different Sonic Youth song was born. It was, Bert recalls, "really unusual, almost like a regular rock and roll riff to a certain extent."

Sitting next to Lydia Lunch on a bus heading uptown to her apartment in Spanish Harlem, Moore began telling her about the song, even singing some of the lyrics he'd already written. The whole band had grown fairly obsessed with Charles Manson and his cult, reading Ed Sanders' book *The Family* (which mentioned a girl Gordon's brother Keller had once dated and who had mysteriously disappeared, possibly at the hands of one of the Manson clan) and attorney Vincent Bugliosi's retelling of the incident, *Helter Skelter*. For children of the '60s, the Manson murders, coming as they did at the end of that decade, held a lurid fascination; it was, Gordon says, "another American utopian situation that was cracking. America is a country built on people seeking utopias, and being from California, that was all very interesting to me. The whole Charlie Manson thing was the most obvious symbol of what was wrong." On a metal oil drum they began using onstage, they scribbled the word "rise," one of Manson's favorite words and one his followers scrawled on the walls of their victims' homes.

As it turned out, Lunch had lived briefly in California with a Mansonite and was herself both fascinated and repelled by the saga. "You could not *not* love Charlie, on some fronts," she says. "You could not *not* love what he stood for. Yes, it's got to come down. Yes, this *was* injustice. The guy's a brilliant spoken-word artist. But at the same time you're embracing a mind-controlling, drug-addled ex-con killer. You've got to reconcile that." As the bus wound its way from Grand Street to Lunch's neighborhood, Moore sang the parts he'd written— words that took their cue from the Manson-directed murders of Sharon Tate and her friends in Los Angeles in 1969—and Lunch added her own lyrics. By the end of the trip, they had a nearly finished song (and, most likely, a bus full of weirded-out passengers).

But it all seemed possibly for naught. They had no record company, no manager, and few club bookings. Ranaldo was beginning to wonder if the band had peaked. "It was a bit of a limbo period," he says. "There was almost a time when it would have been possible to imagine us breaking up right then, because we wanted to make another record and nobody was interested in doing it with us." He confided to a friend that he was considering a full-time art career, since music seemed to be hitting a dead end. The friend told him to stick with it and that, in the end, musicians generally made out better than artists anyway.

ELEANOR MOORE WAS STILL IN BED the morning of April 22, 1984, Easter Sunday, when her son popped into her room. It had taken years, but she'd finally begun to emerge from the shock of her husband's death, even taking a job at his old workplace, Western Connecticut State College. Her three children were now grown and long out of the house in Bethel, but this particular weekend, her youngest son and his girlfriend were visiting for the holiday weekend. In those early days, they often made the trip up, invariably stocking up on food (including stews made by his mother) for the ride back to the city. As Eleanor noticed, they never seemed to have even the slightest bit of money.

On this particular morning, the sight of her son was not as surprising as what he held in his hand: a note that read, "We're getting married." Eleanor soon learned, when she rushed into his old room to find out more, the idea had been Gordon's. The couple had been in his small childhood bedroom, the converted closet that still had the album cover of the Rolling Stones' *Goats Head Soup* taped up on the wall; his old comic books were still stacked high on his manual typewriter. "I felt everything was so *drifty* in our lives," Gordon, who was thirty-one at the time, says. "I spent so much of my life not wanting to commit to things or analyzing things. I felt like I wanted to make a firm commitment." Since they'd been a couple for nearly four years, she suggested they close the deal. Although he'd thought the issue might be raised at some point, the question was still, he recalls, "shocking, but I was into it. I had no doubt about it."

When Gordon and Moore's friend Lyle Hysen first heard the couple were getting married, he was startled: "I remember thinking, 'You *are*? Why?'" Yet as the ceremony demonstrated, they were all fairly traditional when it came to most everything outside their music. Eleanor Moore took her future daughter-in-law to a bridal shop in Bethel and helped her select a white dress; a crown of flowers was chosen to rest on Gordon's head. During pre-ceremony meetings at Saint Mary's Church in Bethel, the Roman Catholic priest, Reverend Peter DeMarco, told Gordon she had to promise to raise her children Catholic; she said yes, but crossed her fingers behind her back.

On the actual wedding day, the brutally humid afternoon of June 9, the bride walked down the aisle with her father. Harold Paris, Moore's high-school friend and their best man, couldn't stand ties, so he wore a tuxedo without one. As the ceremony was about to commence, Bert showed up, dragging along Lunch, in full East Village goth-queen garb, and her boyfriend, Australian noisemaker Jim (J. G.) Thirlwell, who was wearing a sleeveless white T-shirt and looking similarly smudged. As the service began, Reverend DeMarco glanced around the room and remarked, with some amusement, "interesting crowd."

After the brief ceremony ("I'm surprised I didn't raise my hand to contest it," Lunch says, half-jokingly), everyone retreated to the Moore family home, at which point the groom relieved himself of his black suit and returned with a T-shirt sporting the logo of Void, a D.C. hardcore band. As the guests (who also included Ranaldo and Hysen) watched, the couple playfully sliced into a cake. For all his health problems, Keller, Gordon's older brother, struck Eleanor Moore as sweet and friendly, and she was amazed by the number of Shakespeare quotations he reeled off throughout the day. Everything was fairly standard, although, at one point, Bert looked over at Lunch, who was propped up on a bench, and realized she wasn't wearing any underwear. Since the newlyweds couldn't afford a honeymoon, they headed back to Eldridge Street with one of their most substantial gifts, a television.

As with many other newly married couples, quarrels were unavoidable. Seemingly oblivious to finances, much like his father, Moore would think nothing of wandering over to one of the many record stores in their neighborhood to buy the latest must-hear import single or album. Yet the purchases were, he admits, "a source of conflict"; Gordon even complained about it to Branca. ("She said, 'We can't *eat* those,'" Moore recalls.) In their so-called workplace— band rehearsals—Moore would sometimes grow frustrated when he felt Gordon's bass parts weren't living up to what he was hearing in his head. "I felt my job was *not* to become a good bass player," Gordon says. "My bass playing worked well because it was minimal. And it would be frustrating when there'd be a song where he'd want me to play a specific note. To *some* extent I'm a creative person, and that's not very creative." The situation would invariably work itself out, although her new husband realized he could be demeaning in his demands.

Visiting them on Eldridge Street, Paris would see Moore engage in his class-clown ways as Gordon rolled her eyes, but Paris, like many, saw the way they continued to complement each other, how her grounded qualities were a suitable match for his free-floating mind. "They completed each other," says Catherine Ceresole. "Thurston was young and crazy, and Kim had her feet on the earth. Kim had a lot in the brain, and Thurston was more like a child. We used to call him T-Moon because he seemed like he was on the moon; he dreamed like young people do." Indeed, he was still young, only twenty-five, when Gordon slipped a wedding ring on his finger.

THEIR CIRCLE OF ARTISTIC FRIENDS continued to expand; it now included not just fellow sonic assailants but photographers, underground filmmakers, and actors pushing the limits in their own ways. By way of Lunch, they met Richard Kern, who'd moved from his native North Carolina to Manhattan in 1980 with a studio-art degree in hand. Gaunt and proudly perverse, Kern was drawn to what he calls "mindless aggression"—punk, hardcore, and the exploitation films playing in the decaying Times Square.

Watching movies in those theaters, Kern, who dreamed of becoming a filmmaker, was inspired. The trailers for slasher films were so potent, why not make sexual, graphic, and disturbing films that were only ten minutes, like long trailers? "The less subtle you are, the easier it is to get noticed," he says. "It was basically this tactical plan. I wanted to make movies that said, 'Look at me—I'm the toughest guy around,' even though I wasn't. If you want anyone to know who you are, you have to find a niche that's different." Kern called his company Death Trip Films, and the movies, which he financed by selling pot out of his apartment, more than lived up to that name. Starting with 1984's *Right Side of My Brain*, which had Lunch being subjected to groping and forced to give a blow job, the Super 8 shorts reveled in bondage, S&M, and squirm-inducing violence.

Kern's associates, like Lunch, tended to be similarly twisted, and whenever Kern told someone he was friends with Sonic Youth—Moore soon began supplying instrumental guitar music to Kern's soundtracks—Kern always heard the same response. "They'd say, 'Kim Gordon's a junkie, isn't she?'" he recalls. "And I'd go, 'Are you kidding? She's the straightest person you ever met.'" As Kern and others realized, Sonic Youth were more observers than participants: "Warhol hung out with all those people from the Factory. But he was like a person above it, and they were like that. They were very levelheaded, almost business-minded in their approach." At the time, that approach seemed very straight to Kern, but then, he was in the midst of heroin addiction.

They dabbled in drugs but rarely; Dan Graham sensed that Gordon's disdainful attitude toward them had something to do with her brother's ghastly experiences with LSD. (Kern only once saw her take a drag on a joint and was shocked.) Ranaldo was surprised by how traditional his bandmates' wedding was, but by then, he and his girlfriend and new wife, Amanda Linn—a dancer who also helped the band keep track of its accounting—had taken up residence at the massive $500-a-month loft on Duane Street that Ranaldo and David Linton had found several years before. Everyone in the band (even Bert, who married his girlfriend Linda in a more low-key serv-ice soon after the Moore-Gordon ceremony) was inclined toward domesticity and a certain middle-class stability. "When Lydia and Kern came in, and no-wave artists who had weird sex and violence motifs in their work, we had no interest in being that freakish," Moore says. "We kept a bit of an arm's length from it. Those themes weren't us. We didn't feel like we needed to do that to prove any-thing. We were set apart by our conservative lifestyles. Our music was extreme and wild, and we met those people on *that* level."

The craziness would indeed continue to be relegated to the stage, as it was that spring and summer of 1984. The songs that had begun to emerge early in the year were moving toward completion. The band began working them out onstage at clubs like Maxwell's in nearby Hoboken, New Jersey, the songs taking on the feel of an impressionis-tic suite—"sort of a concept album," as Moore recalls. To ensure that the audience wouldn't be bored senseless while Moore and Ranaldo switched guitars and slowly, carefully, tuned up, they began using prerecorded tapes (of songs like the Stooges' "Not Right") between songs. Bert, for one, began to feel the shows were becoming more co-hesive, less scattered.

With their relationship with Neutral all but over and no other in-dependent label interested in them, they had no choice but to record the new songs themselves and then shop around the finished tape. Once again, Bachmann and Ceresole rode in like the European cavalry, lending the band several thousand dollars; some estimates are as high as nearly $10,000, although the couple doesn't recall. With a fresh infusion of cash at its disposal, the band decided they wanted to work someplace more professional than Tiers' basement compound, and Erskine told them about an out-of-the-way space in Brooklyn run by someone named Martin Bisi.

With his shoulder-length locks, penchant for black headbands and wristbands, and Argentine gaucho belt, Bisi was another of those only-in-New-York characters with whom the band crossed paths. Merely twenty-three, Bisi, born of Argentinean parents and raised in upper Manhattan, had learned his craft as a recording engineer working with bass player and multi-genre experimentalist Bill Laswell, who was largely responsible for Herbie Hancock's hip-hop-propelled hit single, "Rockit." With money from Laswell, Bisi had opened a studio rechristened B.C., an in-joke on the pronunciation of his name. (Moore jokingly renamed it "Before Christ," which, to Bisi's annoyance, stuck.) Having worked primarily with hip-hop and experimental music, Bisi had little experience with a rock band; to him, Sonic Youth felt almost normal, like a rootsy country-rock group. Young and eager to work, though, Bisi agreed to help on their record and sensed that his work on rap records—the most truly underground and edgiest of pop music at that moment—was a motivating factor for a band eager to be associated with the edge. "Everybody wanted in on the hip-hop connection," he says. "The hip-hop people had more credibility than *anyone*. They did their own thing and didn't give a shit about the world around them."

Starting in September 1984, they began their daily trips into the heart of south Brooklyn. The area was a desolate stretch of empty lots and dilapidated warehouses, the stench of the Gowanus Canal in the air; it looked like Sonic Youth's music sometimes sounded. Amidst those surroundings, the castle-like building that housed Bisi's studio was a fortress in more ways than one. Its previous incarnation, an armament factory during the Civil War, was evidenced by the way the band had to walk through a courtyard before they arrived at the tucked-away studio. Bisi, who lived and worked at the space, didn't have much of a street view from inside, but he'd seen enough: the packs of dogs roaming the streets late at night, the young black kids who beat up a cop one evening, the squatters in the building, the arson fires, what he called *"Clockwork Orange* stuff." Even to Erskine, who'd spent time in Detroit, the neighborhood was "frickin' scary." But Bisi's rate, $500 a day, was affordable and the space funky but usable. The band set up on a small area of parquet floor facing Bisi and his vintage recording console; with no baffles or separations between band and technicians, Bisi and John Erskine would essentially be their audience.

Most of the material had been practiced and rehearsed; the song's chord changes were set, but not the breaks where they would let their guitars run wild. At B.C., they began using a studio as a compositional tool for the first time, splicing tapes and overdubbing cymbals and layers of guitar parts. "Ghost Bitch," another Gordon meditation on the twisted underbelly of American history, had begun as a piano instrumental Moore recorded at his Bethel home; in the studio, it was combined with what sounded like a lone, lonely foghorn but was in fact Ranaldo's acoustic guitar feeding back into his amplifier. For additional effect, Bert pounded on his tom-tom with a wooden-headed mallet. To attain the proper chain-gang rhythm and clang, "I'm Insane" was peppered with church bells Ranaldo and Erskine had recorded while on tour in Europe. A backward-recorded tape threaded its way through "Brave Men Run (In My Family)," its lyrics inspired by an Edward Ruscha painting hanging in the Eldridge Street apartment: a colonial sailboat, bright blue sky behind it, the words "Brave Men Run in My Family" superimposed over it. To add to the feel that the songs were a loose suite, feedback passages connected them. (A portion of the Stooges' "Not Right" even showed up, although the band never bothered to obtain legal clearance for its use: "We thought we were so subterranean anyway," shrugs Moore.) Bisi recalls Ranaldo doing Pete Townshend guitar moves while overdubbing multiple guitar parts—as Ranaldo was increasingly wont to do, usually long after everyone else had gone home.

The Moore family, Miami, 1965: mother Eleanor, Susan, Thurston, Gene, and father George. *(Photo courtesy Eleanor Moore)*

Free suburban rhymes: Thurston Moore at 13, in his bedroom in Bethel, Connecticut, 1971. *(Photo courtesy Thurston Moore)*

Hair club for young Long Island men: Lee Ranaldo and Jeff Fleischer, aka Tumbleweed, 1974. *(Photo courtesy Lee Ranaldo)*

Young man on the verge of punk rock: Thurston Moore equipped for his senior prom, June 1976. *(Photo courtesy Eleanor Moore)*

Moore's first band, the Coachmen, New York City, ca. 1979: left to right, Dave Keay, Thurston Moore, John King, Bob Pullin. *(Photo courtesy Dave Keay)*

(Below) "Repressed boys": The Fluks, pride of the Binghamton, New York, new-wave scene, 1979— left to right, Stuart Somer, David Linton, Richard Brewster, Lee Ranaldo. *(Photo courtesy Lee Ranaldo)*

Glenn Branca, the mad symphonic-guitars prince of downtown New York, 1980.
(Photo by Stephanie Chernikowski)

(Below) Kim Gordon and Thurston Moore (center) visiting the Moore home in Connecticut, December 1980, a few months after the couple met. Thurston's older brother Gene on far left.
(Photo courtesy Eleanor Moore)

Gordon, Moore, and
Gordon's flip-up shades
onstage at CBGB,
New York, early '80s.
*(Photo by Stephanie
Chernikowski)*

Richard Edson during
his second tenure in
Sonic Youth, Danceteria,
New York, 1982.
(Photo by Catherine Ceresole)

Not quite dentist's office music:
Ranaldo and amplified drill, CBGB,
December 1981.
(Photo by Catherine Ceresole)

Pushing it: Moore onstage
at CBGB, early '80s.
(Photo by Stephanie Chernikowski)

The sound and the fury: Ranaldo and Moore, CBGB, November 1982.
(Photo by Catherine Ceresole)

Student-teacher conference: Moore onstage with Lydia Lunch, Peppermint Lounge, New York, October 1982.
(Photo by Catherine Ceresole)

Sonic Youth and Swans mutually stare down the camera, 1982. (Top row: Pascal, Ranaldo, Gordon; bottom row: Michael Gira, Sue Hanel, Jonathan Kane, Moore.) *(Photo courtesy Lee Ranaldo)*

Confusion is next: Jim Sclavunos (left) during his brief, tumultuous membership in the band, February 1983. *(Photo by Catherine Ceresole)*

Branca rides shotgun over Ranaldo and Moore (far left), live on the Lower East Side, 1983. *(Photo by Stephanie Chernikowski)*

Exploring the early limits of feedback onstage in New York, March 1983. *(Photo by Catherine Ceresole)*

Making the intercontinental scene: playing for Swiss radio, with drummer Bob Bert during the first European tour, June 1983. *(Photo by Catherine Ceresole)*

Shaking hell: live at the Sin Club, New York, September 1983.
(Photo by Catherine Ceresole)

Working for a living: Moore and his Chipwich stand, midtown Manhattan, June 1984. *(Photo by Catherine Ceresole)*

The newly wed Moore and Gordon outside St. Mary's Church, Bethel, Connecticut, June 1984.
(Photo by Catherine Ceresole)

Adhering, for once, to tradition: Moore and Gordon cut the cake in the backyard of the Moore family home after the ceremony.
(Photo by Catherine Ceresole)

Preparing for the *Bad Moon Rising* cover shot, with Bob Bert (right), Queens, New York, November 1984. *(Photo by Jim Welling)*

Moore, Bert, Ranaldo, and Gordon mug (or not) for the camera at Nicolas and Catherine Ceresole's New York apartment, March 1985. *(Photo by Catherine Ceresole)*

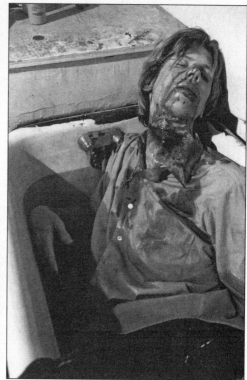

(*Above left*) Gun crazy: Gordon during the filming of the "Death Valley '69" video, Long Island, June 1985.

Gore boys: Moore (above) and Bert (below) immersing themselves in the "Death Valley '69" video, June 1985. *(Photos by Richard Kern)*

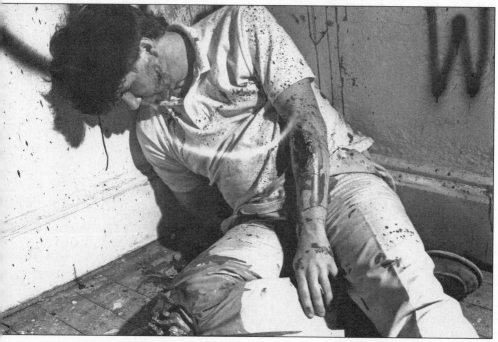

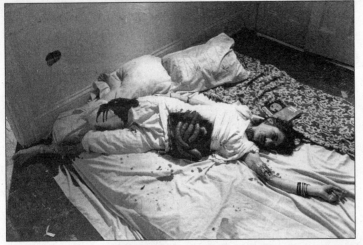

Gordon, Ranaldo, and Shelley relishing their roles as faux-Manson victims in Richard Kern's apartment for the "Death Valley '69" video. *(Photos by Richard Kern)*

New kid in town (and band):
outtake from the back cover
of *EVOL*, with new drummer
Steve Shelley, 1985.
(Photo by Lee Ranaldo)

Emerging star power:
Gordon onstage at CBGB, 1986.
(Photo by Ebet Roberts)

Expressway to many skulls: onstage at CBGB, July 1986. *(Photo by Monica Dee/Retna)*

The burning stick:
Moore drums up a new guitar
sound, live in New York, 1986.
(Photo by Monica Dee/Retna)

Minor epiphanies abounded. During the recording of "Brave Men Run (In My Family)," Gordon was unhappy with a bass part Moore had suggested and devised her own on the spot; it was the first time Erskine, who helped out on the sessions, had seen Gordon express herself so forcefully. Moore himself sensed a breakthrough when he and Ranaldo recorded an uncharacteristically delicate, multilayered guitar instrumental to precede that song. "We realized we could actually play songs that involved picking," Moore says. "We were getting into more intricate ideas on the guitar and stepping away from the chaos, and those possibilities became very exciting."

To Bisi, the personalities within the band couldn't have been more different. He found Moore goofy, Ranaldo self-assured, "very alpha," and Bert "very positive, his eyes wide open." With her sunglasses and inaudible delivery, Gordon was "in a shell beyond belief. She didn't *speak*." Bisi strained to hear the few words that came out of her mouth; during one band conversation, Bisi had to shush Ranaldo and Moore when Gordon started to talk. Later that day, as Bisi was packing up after a day's work, Gordon approached him, offered a deliberate smile, then walked away without a word; he interpreted it as her muted way of thanking him for the support.

The record was finished by the time the autumn leaves began to turn in the Northeast. From the unexpectedly lulling layers of guitars on "Intro," which opened the album, through the more purposeful rhythm section (Gordon's stronger bass lines, Bert's more intricate drum parts), the album was the work of an increasingly confident band. The music didn't ape punk or hardcore or no wave; instead, it took its own cues. "Intro" gave way to the urban rumble of "Brave Men Run (In My Family)," Gordon's voice building in intensity with each line. The song was one of the most strapping bits of rock & roll the band had put on tape, but what followed was more complex and unpredictable. "Society Is a Hole," which began as Moore's mishearing of a line from a Black Flag song, suddenly plunged the record into a dirgelike pit of darkness from which it only occasionally escaped.

Yet that was the point: The music wasn't afraid to drop down and crawl, as if searching for beauty in ugliness. Moore's ode to Gordon and the city, "I Love Her All the Time," had a slothlike raptness, heightened by the hint of raga guitars in the background. The song threatened to explode at any moment, but the band sounded as if they were doing their best to rein in the chaos, at least for the duration of the track. There were not one but three spoken-word pieces: Gordon's "Ghost Bitch" and Moore's "I'm Insane" and "Justice Is Might" (which admonishes "a genius and a sex maniac" who are "taking lots of drugs" at home and in doing so "risking [their] life"), each set to what amounted to dank sound collages. The increased number of music-poetry pieces had an unfortunate consequence of making for a bumpy ride; three mood pieces felt like at least one too many. But thanks to segues that ran between the tracks, the record felt like one very long composition—a song that stopped after "Justice Is Might" and momentarily paused before launching into "Death Valley '69," the band's crowning achievement to that moment.

They'd first recorded the song in July at Tiers' studio. In need of new product to help secure club dates in California, they'd licensed the single to Iridescence, an indie label in Los Angeles. But they thought they could improve upon that version, and at Bisi's studio, they did. The inspiration behind it wasn't hard to miss: Moore's frightening screams, which opened the song, could have been recorded in Tate's Hollywood home on that gruesome night, and "Sadie" and "the canyon" were obvious Manson references. The rock riff Moore and Bert had initially responded to was clear, too: The song began with the guitars, bass, and drums imitating the sound of a fist repeatedly hitting a punching bag, then wended its way through a slithery midsection with Moore and Lunch (who recorded her part later, when they had finished) singing in unison or apart, like two Mansonites engaged in an orgasm of sex and death. Just when it couldn't get any creepier—"She started to holler! . . . I didn't wanna . . . Hit it!"—the song returned to the pummeling intro. And with that, the album came to a nerve-shattering close.

They called it *Bad Moon Rising* as a way of "referencing the music we'd grown up on, like Creedence," says Ranaldo. "It was ingrained in us in one way or another." To Moore, the title also took its cue from the way the Replacements, impudent Minneapolis tongues firmly in cheek, had called their latest album *Let It Be*. The gestures implied that the rock they'd all grown up with needed to be taken down a notch and demythologized, especially if there was any hope for the music to renew itself. There was one difference, though: *Let It Be* had been released by the Minneapolis-based indie Twin/Tone, and *Bad Moon Rising* was a record without a home. Whether anyone would get to hear the sound of rock dismantled and rebuilt was unclear in the weeks after the Bisi sessions wrapped up.

IT WAS JUST ANOTHER HOMEMADE CASSETTE by just another band, but the man at the British pub was intrigued. Paul Smith went there regularly, especially during breaks from his job drawing buses for transportation route maps for the city council of Nottingham. At his home in that town, he held down another job, compiling and selling long-form music videos by the dark electronic dance band Cabaret Voltaire. On Thursdays, his day off from his bus-drawing job, Smith would grab a copy of the new issue of *New Musical Express*, one of England's three weekly music papers, and head down to the local pub for breakfast. But on this particular day in the late fall of 1984, he couldn't wait to get back home, where he planned to listen to a tape that had shown up in the mail two days earlier.

Thanks to Lydia Lunch, he knew it was coming. Smith had already met and been introduced to the warped world of Lunch when she was living in London earlier that year. Smith had heard she and her then lover, Nick Cave, were going to make an album together. Smith was eager to release the record, but by the time Smith reached Lunch, she and Cave were no more, both as a couple and collaborators. However, Lunch told him about another record she'd begun but hadn't finished, *In Limbo*, the one that featured Moore as one of her backup musicians, and Smith eventually released it on Cabaret Voltaire's label, Doublevision.

Far from a novice, Smith had already accumulated a good deal of music business experience in his thirty years. Raised in Nottingham, he'd worked at record stores, tried his hand at managing local bands, and worked as a promotion go-fer for EMI. Bearded, gregarious, and possessing an especially dry British sense of humor, Smith knew how to hustle and make people listen, whether they wanted to hear what he was selling or not.

Lunch tipped Smith to a band in New York, Sonic Youth; although Smith had never heard of them, he trusted Lunch's instincts, and she put stock in those of a man who referred to music as modern art. Soon enough, the cassette arrived at Smith's home. The handwritten lettering on the cover read "Sonic Youth—Bad Moon Rising" and listed five songs per side; on the spine were the addresses and home phone numbers of Gordon, Moore, and Ranaldo. Sitting in his living room, the light streaming in through the window, Smith put on the *Bad Moon Rising* tape and was flabbergasted. "It rang all the bells of quality that I associated with music I loved," he recalls. "I'm happy to use the word 'epiphany.' It was life changing."

Smith yearned for Doublevision to release the album in the U.K., but to his disappointment, the other members of the company didn't agree. Without the approval of all involved, the label would not release any album. Making dubs of the original cassette and using his contacts, Smith began making the rounds of record companies and was roundly turned down. "Nobody got it," he says. "Nobody *wanted* to get it." When Smith expressed his exasperation to his friend Pete Warmsley of Rough Trade, the eminent indie label as well as distributor, Warmsley suggested that if Smith believed in the record so strongly, perhaps he should put it out himself.

The thought hadn't occurred to Smith, but he had no choice, and before long he was making an expensive long-distance call to Ranaldo. Not surprisingly, the band was interested in a label—any label—that wanted to release its record. Skipping two mortgage payments on his house, Smith sent the band a bit of cash, and Smith's new label was effectively launched, with *Bad Moon Rising* its first release. Smith dubbed the new enterprise Blast First from the opening line—"blast first (from politeness)"—from the first issue of *Blast*, the journal of the short-lived Vorticism art movement in the early twentieth-century U.K. (Even abroad, the band couldn't escape art-scene connections.)

For Smith, the "blast first" line also connected to what he calls Sonic Youth's "whirlwind of sound." In the U.K., Smith paid for an initial pressing of one thousand copies, but with the help of Rough Trade, he was also able to license it in other countries almost immediately: five hundred in Germany, several hundred in France, a small amount for Japan. All told, Smith was able to ship five thousand copies of *Bad Moon Rising* worldwide right from the start.

The band's connection with Smith—what he calls an "accidental collision"—was the first of several breaks the band stumbled into just when matters seemed most dire. Two years before, at 99 Records, Moore had met a fellow racks comber named Gerard Cosloy. A high-school dropout from Boston, Cosloy sought salvation in indie rock: working at a college radio station, starting a fanzine, and holding down the obligatory record store job. He also booked occasional shows in the area, including an August 1982 gig at the Storyville club that marked Sonic Youth's Boston debut. Cosloy had been impressed by the *Sonic Youth* EP, which, given Cosloy's strong, take-no-prisoners opinions on all things music, was an accomplishment. Writing up *Confusion Is Sex* in his zine *Conflict* (and urging readers to attend the show, which he himself booked), Cosloy wrote that the record was "perfect for throwing in the face of anyone stupid enough to have ignored their brilliant EP" and called it "one of the great guitar records of our time." The show itself was, as Cosloy recalls, "kind of an abortion. Let's say it was sparsely attended." Despite the turnout, though, Cosloy had been overwhelmed by how violent and charged the music was. "The actual physical nature of what they were doing was pretty imposing," he recalls. "Whatever idea you may have had about loud rock and roll was kind of torn apart."

Thanks to a compilation he'd released on his own, Cosloy landed a job at Homestead, an indie label that was part of a larger record distribution company, Dutch East India, on Long Island. When he heard Sonic Youth was in search of a home for their finished tape, Cosloy jumped at the chance, especially since he adored the record. The band was suspicious of Dutch East India head Barry Tenenbaum; the label offered no money upfront, Tenenbaum loved classic rock, and Bert even tape-recorded a band meeting in Tenenbaum's office to make sure he lived up to his word. But since no other American options remained, they decided to roll the dice. By the time the band received a copy of Smith's contract, in late December, Homestead was already on board.

During Christmas, Moore and Gordon made one of their frequent trips back to the Gordon home, and in January 1985, the four of them made their first West Coast appearance. "Thurston never thinks about the future," Gordon says. "He doesn't have that sort of head. But he somehow thought it was important we establish ourselves on the West Coast." Indeed, the band broadened their network considerably in just about two weeks' time. At the Gila Monster Jamboree, a mini-festival in the Mojave Desert, they shared the stage with the Meat Puppets, the Arizona trio who'd begun integrating country and guitar solos into their hardcore songs. Making the most of their time, they played at clubs in San Francisco, Los Angeles, Santa Cruz, and Seattle. Attendance was sporadic at best. In Santa Cruz, they played a brief set to skinheads and reggae fans who thought any band with "youth" in its name played either hardcore or dub. They drew a better, more enthusiastic crowd at Seattle's Gorilla Garden's Omni Room; also on the bill was a local band called Green River, whose lead singer, Mark Arm, glanced around and saw the crowd with "jaws open, watching and listening."

David Markey, drummer in the SST band Painted Willie as well as a fledgling filmmaker, popped into their show at the Anti-Club in Los Angeles on January 17. All he'd heard about this New York band was that they played guitars with drumsticks; otherwise, they were an utter mystery. The crowd that night also included two members of one of California's most important indie bands, the Minutemen. Both D. Boon and Mike Watt thought they were doing a good job of overhauling rock & roll with their blend of hardcore, classic rock, and punk-funk bass. That evening, their confidence dipped a bit as they watched Sonic Youth attack the songs from *Bad Moon Rising* and *Confusion Is Sex,* complete with guitars that each seemed to be in very distinct tunings. "The Minutemen were trying to be very adventurous and find our own sound," Watt says. "And when I heard Sonic Youth, I felt very old-fashioned and not very new at all. I came from arena rock and then the Hollywood punk scene and stuff. It all seemed way more regular when I experienced the Sonic folks."

When Watt approached the band after the show, Moore was instantly chatty, revealing an in-depth knowledge of Watt's career. When Watt, a bass player himself, tried to compliment Gordon on her musicianship, she demurred; she didn't want to talk about it. They were perplexing and friendly, often at the same time.

ON A LATE-FALL EVENING, they assembled at a field in Queens, a patch of land near the water they'd heard about from a friend. They brought along a pumpkin, a flannel shirt, and straw they'd gathered from a police-horse stable downtown. With the help of Ranaldo's old friend Thom DeJesu, who'd launched a career designing film sets, they erected a scarecrow, propped it up, carved a demonic smile on its face, filled the pumpkin head with lighter fluid, and set it aflame. Photographer James Welling, who'd met Gordon on the art-gallery circuit, got off a few shots before the makeshift scarecrow quickly burned up. "It was beautiful," Moore recalls. "Dusk was coming and you could see the city behind it." The idea, according to Moore, was inspired by album covers by the Misfits, but the final image was uniquely their own: menacing, ominous, a hint of the gnarled, disturbed music that anyone putting on the record would hear.

The downplaying of the band's image on a second consecutive cover was intentional. "We didn't think about putting ourselves on the cover," says Gordon. "It's not like we were the best-*looking* band. Warhol talked about his artwork being ready-made, the idea of mass-producing work, and we wanted the album covers to be a space to promote art."

When he received the artwork in the mail, Smith thought it was arresting too. When he flipped the cover over, though, a red flag went up. As a way to tie in the artwork with the year 1969, the band designed a collage around photographs of themselves in their youth: a bearded, hippie-era Ranaldo emerging, seemingly stoned, from a van; Bert partying after his high-school graduation in 1973; a longhaired, teenaged Moore in the woods of Connecticut, looking very much like a rock star of the era. Smith immediately called to say the photos would send the wrong signal about who they were and how their music sounded, especially in the U.K. "The band was of the moment, but this was not the thing to sell it," Smith says. "It was this stupid thing with people getting out of vans." Bert wasn't particularly taken with the collage either, since no one knew what Sonic Youth looked like, and vintage photos of each member wouldn't help. The band didn't fight Smith ("We weren't married to the back cover, so we complied and compromised," says Moore), and the photo was replaced by a comparatively standard band portrait. Without too much trepidation, they'd given in to a record company to have their music distributed, although part of them wondered if they should ever do it again.

In the middle of March, with the album approaching release in both the States and Europe, they flew to England to meet their new label head and perform a series of concerts Smith arranged for them. Picking them up at Heathrow Airport, Smith had no idea what the band looked like, but with a photograph in hand, he scoured the crowd and quickly picked out Moore by his height. To his astonishment, Smith was told the four of them had only about twenty dollars in cash between them, which struck him as either overly confident or brave, since it meant they had enough money to cross the ocean but none to get back. For the next five weeks, they played a series of shows in the U.K. before once again traveling to mainland Europe, but this time to slightly larger clubs in Berlin and Zurich, among other cities. Staying at Smith's house in Nottingham for part of the trip, they gladly drank his tea and crashed on his floor—and, more importantly, completely eradicated any bad memories of their first, disastrous London performance nearly a year and a half earlier.

At the first British gig, at the Institute of Contemporary Arts in London, Smith, always game for a good stunt, gave a few of his staffers money to round up pumpkins for stage decor. The idea, clearly, was to play off the *Bad Moon Rising* cover, even though the small, yellow pumpkins the employees scrounged up weren't quite as fierce looking as the one on the album cover. Would the performance itself be as ferocious as that album cover? Smith himself didn't know; he'd never seen the band onstage and was worried the shows would amount to lots of banging noises. Adding to his concerns was Moore's state: Shortly before showtime, the guitarist, due to a combination of pressure and exhaustion, seemed to come down with what felt like the flu. When R.E.M.'s Michael Stipe wandered backstage to say hello, Moore could barely make out who he was.

Standing in the balcony, though, Smith watched as Blast First's initial signing put on a show of uncommon cohesion and intensity. The *Bad Moon Rising* material had grown stronger and more forceful onstage; "Ghost Bitch" transcended its mood-piece recording to become a moment of genuine terror. With each song, Moore dramatically peeled off a shirt, revealing another beneath it, and then another. The performance was so intimidating and loud that, by the end, two-thirds of the 150 people had fled. "But the fifty who stayed," Smith says, "were the right fifty people. All the journalists—or most of them, anyway." Ever irreverent, Moore asked Smith afterward if he wanted his money back; Smith said no.

Driving the band to each of the subsequent shows on the British leg of the tour, Smith took stock of Sonic Youth. Moore constantly cracked jokes or made music-geek references to rock bands, many of which Smith didn't get. To Smith, Gordon was "quiet, mysterious, beautiful," Ranaldo "a manic force" always spewing new plans and ideas. Smith would be amused by what he calls their New York rules in restaurants, as when they tried to explain to a pub owner in Sheffield exactly how dark they wanted their toast. For all their "New York po-faced image," Smith also found them "fantastic fun," albeit straight; they seemed to get sleepy after half a pint of beer in the pub.

Thanks to the network of international labels connected with Rough Trade, *Bad Moon Rising* sold all its five thousand European copies within six months, which meant Rough Trade was quickly paid back and Smith recouped most of his initial investment: "It was, 'Bang—we're in business.'" The business also included meetings with

Smith, who was not only their British label head but slowly becoming a career advisor for a band that still had no manager or lawyer. As Smith made clear, Sonic Youth needed to begin planning ahead: Where did they want to be in six months or a year? When would they start recording another record? What were their *goals?* "He wanted us to rise to the challenge," Ranaldo says, and the band slowly did; they too wanted to keep moving and making progress, albeit on their own terms and with their own steering-the-ship involvement.

However, at least one band member was not so thrilled by the discussions. Bert had had enough of the touring, the almost nonexistent pay, and the time away from his wife; sharing a room on the road with Ranaldo, who tended toward the hyperactive, was occasionally taxing as well. When talk of further tours came up, Bert realized it was time to go. "Paul was mapping out the next three years of our lives, and it petrified me," Bert says. "I was like, 'Wait a minute—I'm not even going to be out of debt from *this* tour.' I gave it a lot of thought, and then I thought, maybe this is a good time."

The night before a final band meeting with Smith, after which they would fly back home, Bert told Smith he was leaving Sonic Youth. Smith was stunned: "But Bob, this is the best band in the world," he told him. "Why would you leave?" The band was equally taken aback when talk at the meeting turned to future campaigns and Bert announced his intentions. "Bob just said, 'I won't be doing that—I'm quitting the band,'" Moore recalls. "He just said it. And we were like, Wow." Part of them could understand his reasoning: The other three were hardly enamored of sleeping on people's cat-piss-stained couches or returning home from a road trip with only a few hundred dollars to show for it.

Beyond the grueling day-to-day realities of life as an independent band in the '80s, a larger, more complex issue reared its head. Bert had stayed with the band far longer than his predecessors Richard Edson and Jim Sclavunos, but like them, he found that penetrating the tightly knit world of Ranaldo, Moore, and Gordon—a world of intertwined musical tastes, ambitions, and even downtown neighborhoods—was no easy task. "There's always been a small degree of that in the band—the three of us in the front line and then the drummer," admits Ranaldo. As a married couple able to go on tour and still be together, Gordon and Moore perhaps didn't fully grasp Bert's conflicted feelings about being away from his wife for so long. "Bob had difficulty coming to grips with what his role in the group was," says Cosloy, "rather than being an accessory to someone else's thing."

Smith was instantly concerned about the impact of Bert's departure on the band, especially now that they were beginning to make major strides. The rest of the band, however, wasn't as worried. On the plane ride back to the States, they talked about a possible and very obvious replacement for Bert (who flew back with them, no hard feelings evident). By chance, Moore and Gordon had sublet their apartment to a kid from Michigan who'd once drummed with the Crucifucks, a Michigan hardcore band. Gordon had never seen him play, but Ranaldo and Moore had, when the band had come through town for a show at CBGB. The lead singer was a small, seemingly loony guy who berated Ronald Reagan, the police, and the crowd itself in his stage patter. At one point, the show completely broke down, but the drummer—a kid with short brown hair and big round glasses who had the wide-eyed look of a suburban junior high student—kept the beat going. Both Ranaldo and Moore flashed back to that moment, and the decision was made. "We were like, 'This guy's living in your apartment—let's have *him* be our drummer,'" says Ranaldo. "'If it doesn't work out, so be it. But here he is.'"

When Gordon and Moore unlocked their front door and walked in, there the kid was, twenty-three years old but looking so much younger. His bags and drums were packed and sitting by the door, and after some quick hellos (and introducing the kid to Gordon), Moore told him Sonic Youth needed a new drummer. Stunned, the kid responded with an immediate yes—or almost immediate, since even at his age, he was savvy enough to ask if they wanted him to be an auxiliary player or a full-on member. Moore said it would be the latter, and in another of their fortuitous breaks, Sonic Youth found itself with an immediate replacement for Bob Bert.

HIS BLUE-AND-WHITE CHEVY VAN had rumbled into the city only a few months before. Since Moore and Gordon were already in Europe, Lyle Hysen—by then drumming in a new band, Das Damen—met the kid outside 84 Eldridge, handed him the keys, showed him around the place, and introduced him to Egan, the dog he'd have to watch over. The kid had been to New York once before, when his previous band had played that show at CBGB, but the city, and especially that neighborhood, was a new sensation. "If you can make it here, you can make it anywhere," Hysen cracked, although he wasn't sure the kid knew he was joking.

Yet it wasn't terribly surprising he was there, at that moment; he always seemed to know where he was heading and what he wanted to do. His father, Ivan Shelley, and his mother, Julia, had met in the farm country of Michigan right after Ivan's return from the Korean War; a mere eight months later, they married. Shortly after their third child, Steven Jay, was born—on June 23, 1962—the family, including his two older sisters, moved to Midland, a largely white town in the middle of the state with a population of just over twenty-seven thousand. There, Ivan began working for the city, organizing snow plows for the inevitable blizzards, repairing flat tires. Whether at that post or in the infantry during the Korean War, he knew he had a job to do and he did it, dutifully, and he expected everyone around him to live up to the same code of conduct and work ethic.

From the start, the son felt like an outsider. He was small and skinny, and from an early age, he realized that everyone else's family seemed to work for Dow Chemical, the vast chemical and plastics company that had opened shop in Midland at the close of the nineteenth century. It was impossible to live in Midland and not feel the company's presence. Banks, gardens, a library, and a high school were named after it; in some literature, Midland was even referred to as "Dow Town." When the Shelleys would roll down their car windows, they would inevitably smell something odd in the air. Dow and its sibling company, Dow Corning, manufactured not only plastic, chemical, paint, rubber, and cleaning products but napalm, Agent Orange,

and materials for silicone breast implants. The company would sometimes ask employees to take home samples of soap or shampoo and try
them out.

The first music the son heard was his mother's; her love for country
meant that albums by Johnny Cash and Marty Robbins were regularly
heard around the house. Her son's own tendency toward brooding,
rugged, and self-destructive singer-songwriters would begin there.
Rock culture was still a mysterious, mystical force; like his friends, he
only heard about it by word of mouth or via a rare copy of *Rolling Stone*
that would find its way to Midland. His older sisters helped introduce
him to the Beatles, who, along with Elton John during his *Honky
Château* era, became his favorites; he took to the quality of the songwriting and the band interplay.

He was wholesome enough to be an Eagle Scout, and in fifth grade,
the same year he was diagnosed with nearsightedness and had to start
wearing glasses, he took up drums in the school band. He was still so
meek and tiny—the kind of kid who would be stuffed into lockers
and regularly bullied, the kind who was hard to see behind a drum—
that even his junior-high band teacher made him the target of jokes.
(Eventually, friends taped a photograph of the teacher's face onto his
bass drum to make the kid pound harder.) He eventually bought his
own kit, and every night after dinner he'd retreat to the basement and
play along with his Beatles albums, bashing so hard he would drown
out the music. "He could be heard, that's for sure," says his mother.

In marching band, playing period pop hits like Chicago's "Colour
My World," Shelley first met kindred souls—the band nerds and
weirdos, as opposed to the kids who listened to Charlie Daniels and
Lynyrd Skynyrd and owned Confederate flags even though Midland
was closer to the Canadian border than the Mason-Dixon line. Seeing
Talking Heads perform Al Green's "Take Me to the River" on *Saturday
Night Live* tipped him to the new music coming out of the East Coast,
but he felt even more an outcast when, at school two days later, he discovered that most of his classmates had seen—and hated—the same
performance.

Their lack of understanding didn't stop him from dreaming of a different life. Lugging his drum kit to a neighbor's house in the woods, he jammed along with a friend's older brother, bashing out "Proud Mary" and his first dose of Neil Young songs, and before long he was playing with local cover bands, at lawn parties and school talent shows. No Zone, with its classic-rock repertoire, transformed into the No Zones, who specialized in Police and Jam remakes. In his senior year at Midland High, he joined a local (and very adult) polka band, who played country and rock covers at weddings. It was his first paying job as a musician (and his first upfront look at drunkards), and he would take home up to $200 a night, a fortune for a teenager. Around that time, he met a classmate a year older, Tim Foljahn, whose long, curly hair reminded Shelley of Robert Plant. Foljahn, who was learning to play guitar, was struck by how responsible the kid was; he always seemed to have jobs and even a car.

Although Shelley had little interest in attending college, his parents wanted that type of education for their son; neither of them had gone to a university. They compromised with Delta College, a local school not far from Midland. On weekends, though, he found himself visiting other local college towns, like East Lansing, and in his first act of family rebellion (he never smoked, drank, or took drugs), he dropped out of college during his sophomore year and moved to Kalamazoo, where Foljahn had relocated to play in a band dubbed the Spastic Rhythm Tarts. Their music was taut and gothy, reflecting new wave and the postpunk coming out of England. In time, Shelley also joined Strange Fruit, a new-wave band that spun out of the Spastic Rhythm Tarts; later came a slot in Faith and Morals, also based in East Lansing and featuring a lead singer with an Ian Curtis obsession (reflected in the band's ersatz Joy Division drones). "Steve was always very clear about what he wanted to do," Foljahn recalls. "He wanted to be a drummer. There weren't any other options."

By 1982, the hardcore scene that had been festering around the state began calling. During one of his trips to East Lansing, while he was still in and out of the Spastic Rhythm Tarts, Shelley met Doc

Corbin Dart, a local troublemaker and fledging hardcore singer and songwriter whose family had been involved in the invention of Styrofoam cups. Although Shelley was the last thing from a skinhead, he and another bandmate and friend, Scott Fagerston, soon found themselves playing to crowds of them as members of the Crucifucks, the band that came together around Dart's snotty-kid voice (he was like a Midwestern Johnny Rotten) and pointedly antiauthority lyrics: "Cops for Fertilizer" was a typical song title.

For several years, the Crucifucks made as much of a name for themselves as anyone could on the Midwestern hardcore circuit. The name, of course, enraged so many locals that club owners would often intentionally change it on fliers and posters to "Cruise Effects" or something similar. ("You'd almost cry after a while," says Dart. "Your band name *means* something.") Shelley was so embarrassed by the name "Crucifucks" that he never told his parents he was in the band. Just as controversial was Dart. In and out of therapy, given to drinking before he'd get onstage, Dart was an especially high-maintenance frontman. During shows, he would cut himself or mock the very hardcore kids who went to their shows; offstage, he would make prank phone calls to the police or local frats. "I was just going for shock effect," he says. "Back then you were still able to shock people. I was pushing the boundaries, and I wanted to find out what the boundaries actually were."

A few of Dart's phone pranks were included on a homemade band cassette, a copy of which ended up impressing Jello Biafra, the revered leader of San Francisco's Dead Kennedys. (Another copy, ordered through the mail, arrived in the Eldridge Street mailbox of hardcore obsessive Thurston Moore, who would play it repeatedly on Sonic Youth's European shows of 1983.) Biafra's interest led to the Crucifucks' invitation to play its first series of shows outside the Midwest, as part of the national Rock Against Reagan tour in the summer of 1983. In need of transportation, the Crucifucks ended up on a bus full of the yippies who'd been involved in organizing the tour. The experience was far from pleasant in every regard—the granola-culture food the yippies ate was utterly foreign to Michigan kids—although Shelley met other local indie bands from as far away as Austin and, with the band, played at the Mall in Washington, D.C. With Biafra's connections, the Crucifucks flew to California to open a few shows for the Dead Kennedys and record an album, *The Crucifucks*, for Biafra's Alternative Tentacles label. While they were there, they drove around Los Angeles, but it was so sprawling—and their music still so underground—that any dreams of rock stardom seemed ludicrous.

Even with an album in the can, the Crucifucks were doomed. By his own admission, Dart was mentally ill; for a time, he was convinced Ronald Reagan and his vice president, George H. W. Bush, had hired Mark David Chapman to assassinate John Lennon. The band was fairly unstable as well; guitar and bass players came and went. "Doc was known as a strange and erratic and confrontational performer," Shelley says. "And that was part of being in the band. He was confrontational when he *wasn't* onstage." Dart felt that Shelley was full of enthusiasm as well as ambition: "I just figured he would end up in U2 or Billy Joel's band, that he would just climb as high as he could." Shelley's organizational skills and dedication impressed Dart; even Dart had to concede that the band wouldn't have survived as long as it did without Shelley's devotion to it.

Just as the Crucifucks would inevitably start to fall apart, another opportunity would arise and pull them back together. When the band first rolled into New York to play CBGB, Shelley had met Moore and Ranaldo, who'd dropped by the club to see what all the Midwestern fuss was about. In a later conversation, Ranaldo suggested to Shelley that the Crucifucks make a record at Wharton Tiers' studio. Yet before the plans were set in motion, the band imploded once and for all; after a show in Ohio, Dart, chafing at Shelley's officious ways, unleashed a tirade at the drummer, who decided he'd had enough. With Marc Hauser, then the band's bass player, Shelley abruptly quit the band and decided to move to either New York or San Francisco. At Ranaldo's suggestion, they opted for Manhattan—especially when Shelley heard from Ranaldo that Sonic Youth would be out of town on tour for a while and Gordon and Moore needed someone to apartment-sit.

Shelley and Hauser drove into the city in the late spring of 1985. Prowling around, they took in New York: the steam coming from the street vents, the Tribeca neighborhood they'd long read about. At a club one night, Shelley met the lead singer of Rat at Rat R, one of Sonic Youth's peer bands at the time, who told Shelley that if he was hooked up with Moore and Gordon, he would do just fine. At the time, Shelley didn't quite know what that meant.

Soon after, Shelley wrote to Foljahn, filling him in on Gordon and Moore's offer to drum in their band. Foljahn flashed back to the day the two of them had been driving around Midland; Shelley mentioned he'd just read about Sonic Youth in the *NME* and that they sounded like the kind of band he wanted to join. It seemed like the ultimate pipedream, but to Foljahn's astonishment, it was actually happening. At least one person in Michigan was not surprised, though. Ivan Shelley knew well his son's determination: "If he wants to do something, he *does* it," he says. When Ivan heard the news, he figured his son, always so prepared and single-minded, wouldn't just be the drummer, but most likely the leader as well.

Chapter 5

THE KID HAD BARELY BEEN in the band a month when he had to pretend to be dead. On a steamy late June afternoon in 1985, he found himself sitting at a desk in an apartment in one of the most drug-ravaged blocks in the East Village. His head was down, touching the desk, a small puddle of congealed blood—fake, he hoped—clinging to his hair. When he glanced around the rest of the place, he could just about see a blood-splattered Bob Bert crumbled in a corner and Ranaldo, sprawled on the floor, intestines protruding from his chest. What the kid couldn't see from his vantage point was Moore lying in a bathtub, one of his large feet dangling over the rim, and Gordon stretched across a bed with a gaping wound in her stomach. Most of all, Shelley caught sight of Richard Kern, darting around his apartment with his camera and preparing the simulated gore—actual animal intestines bought from a nearby meat market and filled with shaving cream. The kid couldn't believe how *happy* Kern looked.

Never one to refrain from voicing her opinion, Lydia Lunch had argued against the band making a music video: "Where's it going to get played? Why waste the money?" she would bark. But more so than college radio or certainly the mass media, videos dangled the possibility of exposure in front of the new indie bands. Earlier that year, the Minutemen's "This Ain't No Picnic," from their 1984 SST album *Double Nickels on the Dime*, had actually snuck onto MTV, and a slew of local cable shows programmed by punk-rock enthusiasts were popping up around the country. Other avenues for exposure and advancement were emerging; the idea that a kid in a suburban mall might possibly become aware of a band thanks to a video was a tantalizing possibility. And with that, the time came to make the first Sonic Youth video, for "Death Valley '69," which Homestead released as a single the same month the clip was filmed.

Given the inspiration behind the song, a storyline tied in with Manson was only natural. Borrowing a truck from one of Ranaldo's cousins, they (and codirector Judith Barry, a video artist) filmed part of the video at a Long Island nature preserve where the teenaged Ranaldo and friends used to sneak off and get high. Dancing in a circle, Gordon brandishing a shotgun and smiling maniacally as she aimed it at the camera, they gleefully acted out the roles of Charlie's children. Retreating to Kern's apartment for additional filming with him, they threw themselves, pretend wounds and all, into their roles as cult-murder victims. Later, Kern interspersed the footage with a jumble of contemporary and period references: a clip from the obscure hippie movie *The Strawberry Statement* and footage of a scruffy, hardened-looking actress named Elizabeth Karr. (Under the name Lung Leg, Karr was one of the coterie of aspirant actors and actresses happy to drop by Kern's home, undress, and star in one of his films.) The video was unquestionably of a piece with Kern's films but also made obvious connections between California in the late '60s and New York City nearly two decades later. "It was a very paranoid time in New York, violent and dirty," recalls Jim Sclavunos. "There was a lot of post-Mansonite fantasizing going on."

Between the music, the mass-murder scene, and shots of Leg jabbing at the camera with a knife, "Death Valley '69" stood little chance of cracking MTV, and Kern didn't care: "I don't think I had anything in mind except to use this for myself and put it on one of my own tapes," he says. (Neither did the band: "We never expected it to get on MTV," says Shelley. "That was for the Duran Durans.") Like Kern, the band seemed more interested in pushing the gruesome envelope. When Homestead released the single as a 12-inch that included tracks from each of their first three records, the band also tacked on a largely improvised *Bad Moon Rising* leftover called "Satan Is Boring." One of the band's most unsettling pieces, the track was a sinister dirge, all glass-shard guitars, purposefully erratic rat-a-tat rhythms from Bert, and a glazed-over delivery from Moore, who intoned lines like "your flesh has a limit of too many years." Although it wasn't explicit, the song had been inspired by a horrific crime the year before: Thinking a friend had stolen his drugs, a clearly disturbed Long Island kid named Ricky Kasso lured the boy into the woods, stabbing him multiple times and gouging out his eyes.

For Shelley, the whole experience—the filming of the video, the air of East Village depravity, even the use of Bert, the drummer he was replacing, in the video—was unlike anything he'd encountered. Dissoluteness, even by association, didn't appeal to him in the way it fascinated the others. Yet he was so eager to be part of the band that little of it unnerved him. To make the point that Sonic Youth was transitioning smoothly between two new members, the "Death Valley '69" video opened with performance footage with Bert; by the end of the clip, Shelley was the one pounding away (or, rather, drum-synching).

His integration into the band was equally seamless. When they played their last show with Bert, at the Pyramid Club on May 3, Shelley was in the audience, taking note. A few weeks later, Shelley was himself behind the kit, and soon after he was joining Moore and Gordon at a rehearsal space on Houston Street, learning to play formative new songs like "Green Light." To Moore, it was instantly apparent Shelley knew how to play well. "He had a certain physicality about him," he says, "and he wasn't a too-cool-for-school no-waver." Gordon excitedly told Bisi she was thrilled to have a hard-core drummer in the band; Shelley's style was indeed tighter and more disciplined—more indebted to new wave and hardcore beats—than that of his predecessors.

Soon after, the time came to discover what awaited them outside of the city, how the rest of the country looked and felt and how amenable it would be to the kind of music they were making. Three years had passed since they'd first ventured outside Manhattan into the American South for the Savage Blunder tour, but the climate had changed; a phone- and fax-connected network of independent labels, clubs, and promoters was growing more expansive (and professional) all the time. Using his list of contacts, Homestead's Cosloy set up what amounted to the band's first cross-country expedition, a month of shows to promote *Bad Moon Rising* that would start in Ohio, work its way to Los Angeles, and wind up back in New York.

The fact that Shelley owned an automotive vehicle didn't escape the other three when it came to inviting him to join the band. ("He had a more fluid style to the music," says Ranaldo. "And he had a *van*. Case closed, basically.") But the van needed some modifications, so Shelley drove it down to a loading dock near Ranaldo and Amanda Linn's loft. Having learned the basics of carpentry from his father, Ranaldo bought a batch of cheap plywood, pulled the bench seat out of the back, and constructed a shelf that could hold a mattress for anyone in need of a nap. Beneath the shelf would be storage space for drums, amplifiers, and as many guitars—up to a dozen—as would fit. With the first show of the tour—in Columbus, Ohio, on August 1—in sight, they crammed themselves, their gear, and some clothing into the Chevy. To help with lighting in the clubs and provide Gordon with a female buddy in an otherwise all-male setting, they dragged along a new friend, Susanne Sasic, a red-haired New York hardcore kid and close friend of Lyle Hysen. Since the idea of a road crew was unimaginable, Sasic would also help the band unload their gear at each venue.

Taking to the highways, Moore and Ranaldo immediately noticed their new percussionist was far more straitlaced and regimented than they were. Relaxing and smoking in the back of the van while playing one of their many mix tapes—or Ranaldo's copy of John Cougar Mellencamp's *Scarecrow*, his favorite mainstream rock album of the moment—they noticed how the speedometer needle never moved past 55 miles per hour. They'd ask Shelley to step on the gas, but not wanting to break the law, he continually refused. "We were all grownups in a way," Moore says. "He was slow to break into adulthood. He didn't like drinking coffee and alcohol and cigarettes. He was polite and sweet and innocent. He had a strong sense of responsibility." As they also gleaned, he had an impressive list of contacts from his travels with the Crucifucks; he was friendly with bands like the Butthole Surfers and the Dicks, both from Texas, that Sonic Youth had heard of but didn't know, and connections were everything for bands who didn't stand a chance of making a fortune from their records. "Steve had covered ground we had yet to cover," Moore says. "He had connections we hadn't yet established, so we were able to integrate both of our connections."

Thrown almost overnight into the land of Sonic Youth—the group even helped him secure his first city apartment, a basement place near Ranaldo's—Shelley had to adjust to three very different people, each with a distinctive personality and quirks. Taking his job seriously, he'd quickly learned the *Bad Moon Rising* numbers and earlier songs like "Brother James," "Kill Yr Idols," and "Making the Nature Scene." At his kit behind them, Shelley could see how their onstage roles were sharpening and developing. On stage right, Ranaldo, building on the guitar-hero moves he'd initiated in Branca's band, would often end a solo or a flourish with a gesture as if was pulling a cord to start up a lawnmower. Gordon was beginning to loosen up, and not merely in the way she'd grown her hair longer and ditched the glasses; still shy yet far more animated onstage than she once was, she would either bounce up and down to the rhythm or lurch forward with her bass as if taking a step (and then lurch back). Moore was his own unpredictable beast—bumping into the others onstage, dropping to his knees, using his long arms to extend his guitar neck out as far as possible from his body.

At some point, one or another of them would turn around and begin waving his guitar in front of an amp—twisting and turning the instrument, sacrificing it to the amplifier, until an ungodly din would overtake whatever song they were playing. Eventually, Moore, Ranaldo, and Gordon would all be doing the same, transporting the crowds to some dingy gallery in the East Village where music, performance art, and noise all merged into one overpowering beast. The presentation was both anarchic and well planned, which Shelley learned on the road as well. "It wasn't like we got onstage and went crazy," he says. "It *seemed* crazy to people watching, but there was a method to the madness."

As gratifying as the road work was, especially compared with the Savage Blunder undertaking, they were still a long way from where they wanted to be. Their sound man, John Erskine, bailed out before the tour began; since he and his wife couldn't afford to live on the meager wages he earned from Sonic Youth, Erskine decided it was time, after two years, to move on. Given the tour's timing, late summer, the college towns Cosloy focused on didn't have many actual college students in them, making for a number of sparsely attended shows. None of the clubs had air conditioning, which led Gordon to refer to it as "the spa tour." With his mathematics background, Ranaldo would diligently collect the money (whatever there was of it) after the shows; then they'd find someplace to crash, usually on the floors of the homes of whatever band was playing with them that night.

Eager for the band to plug into a music community outside of Manhattan, Moore was coping with his own disappointments. "I wanted people to see us and like us," he says. "But I wasn't confident we were delivering the goods all the time." He was thrilled when the band pulled into Madison, Wisconsin, to play at a hardcore club—more of a rec room, in fact—he'd long heard about. But as much as he yearned for Sonic Youth to slip into that world, he also knew the band would never truly be accepted by the skinhead crowd. He'd first noticed it when they played a show with the Meat Puppets, then still in their hardcore period, at Folk City in Greenwich Village; the crowd kept shouting "Play faster!" at Moore.

In Madison, most of the audience was in the parking lot outside, another sign to Moore that his fantasies of Sonic Youth connecting with hardcore kids were likely to remain just that—wishful thinking. "I wanted Sonic Youth to be part of a community," he says. "I wanted to make a real impression on people and I had a real anxiety that we weren't really able to do it. I felt we needed to work on the same level as Black Flag or the Dead Kennedys, and I felt we were a little too outside that system."

Still, they arrived back in the city in early September feeling relatively content. "We had enough money to live for a few months," Ranaldo says, "and suddenly things started to look up." Another sign of change came in the fall, when they returned to Europe for another tour. Hatching a scheme to garner media attention, Paul Smith came up with what amounted to the band's version of the Beatles' *Magical Mystery Tour*. Hiring a bus, he filled it with the band and journalists and drove south of London to Brighton, where the band played on the city's expansive beach. (Adding to the ersatz '60s experience, a few members of the caravan took mushrooms as the bus set off.) Since it was early November, the weather was cold and rainy; Gordon, accustomed to warmer California beaches, was particularly unhappy to be there. But at the beach, Smith and Pat Naylor, whom he'd hired to handle publicity for Blast First, noticed something: a handful of fans who'd followed them to each stop on the tour. It looked like the start of what could be an actual following.

COMMERCIALLY, *Bad Moon Rising* did not rise swiftly. Since most of the major media outlets, from *Rolling Stone* through the indie-rock-oriented *College Media Journal*, ignored it, sales crawled along during the first few months after its March release. Even though Moore was disappointed by Sonic Youth's lack of connection with the hardcore crowd, another, broader community was nevertheless in sight. The days when the band had to settle for Neutral Records because no other independent company existed in New York were no more. Homestead was merely one of many homespun indie labels across the country—Twin/Tone in Minneapolis, Dischord in Washington, D.C., Enigma in southern California among them—that was releasing one vital album or single or EP after another, on a monthly basis.

The people who ran the labels and played in the bands were a young, collegiate (or just postcollegiate) crowd that had grown up with both the mainstream rock of the '70s and the punk that followed. The music they were creating—whether by the Meat Puppets or the Replacements in Minneapolis, who alternated Paul Westerberg's tortured-teen songs with Bachman-Turner Overdrive and Kiss covers—reflected that diverse input. The music was dubbed postpunk, but whatever it was, it was neither traditional punk nor middle-of-the-road rock (nor the techno-pop that so dominated MTV). Like the first punk movement before it, it was simply trying to make rock & roll mean something again, to strip it of a new sheen of arena-rock bloat that had settled over the music by the early '80s. Lording over it all, in terms of its credibility and integrity, was SST. By 1985, the label was known for far more than Black Flag or, for that matter, hardcore. Much like Def Jam, the leading hip-hop label at the time, SST had a distinctive logo and personality; the name alone promised a set of standards the label almost always delivered on during its early years.

As Ray Farrell discovered when he began working at the label in 1985, SST's digs were as low-down as their releases. A New Jersey native who'd initially relocated to San Francisco, Farrell, a shaggy-haired, levelheaded kid in his twenties, had worked at record stores and slowly became involved in booking bands and shows. Cosloy had recruited him to help with Sonic Youth's first California shows early that year, and Farrell found that as people, Sonic Youth weren't nearly as dark as he imagined they'd be. In the process of working within the California indie music scene, Farrell befriended Joe Carducci, who handled art layouts and record mastering for SST. When Carducci told Farrell the label needed a promotion department, Farrell signed up.

As he quickly discovered when he moved to southern California, SST was then run out of a small storefront in Hawthorne, its windows covered up with record boxes. Farrell's office—and, at first, home— was a closet; at night, he stacked a bunch of record crates (containing Minutemen LPs) around him to prevent rats from running across his chest in the dark. But Farrell's new position as promotion man bespoke the label's ambitions. Before, SST hadn't bothered to send records to college radio, since they didn't count on either its support or that of the press; hiring Farrell for such a job was another sign of how seriously SST was beginning to take itself as a business.

146

From working with Sonic Youth, Farrell was familiar with the band, and by late 1985, they were more than aware of SST. The label's hardcore roster had long fascinated Moore, and when the band was in search of a full-time booking agency, they turned to Global Network Booking, SST's in-house agency, which arranged tours for Black Flag, the Minutemen, the Meat Puppets, and other bands on the label. During its trip to California, the group had dinner with former Black Flag bass player Chuck Dukowski (aka Gary McDaniel), who ran Global.

Initially, it seemed unlikely that Sonic Youth and SST would join forces. SST gravitated toward bands in its part of the country, and Sonic Youth considered Cosloy a good friend. But SST was in search of what Dukowski calls "a nationwide vibe," and having Sonic Youth on the roster would facilitate that: "I thought it would help us to have a group, local to New York, working with us by giving us an inside angle with the New York scene and venues that could be used to help the West Coast groups that were going there on tour."

For the band, the lure of SST was equally enticing. *Bad Moon Rising* would eventually sell nearly ten thousand copies during its first year of release—"pretty astonishing numbers at the time," Cosloy recalls. During the next few years, it would sell another twenty thousand. But the band was not entirely confident in the label. "Gerard was fine, but there always seemed something suspect about Homestead," Moore says. To Moore, SST was "the ultimate label," and SST's Ginn knew they felt that way: "They were looking for the best opportunity at the time," he recalls. (Mike Watt also claims he lobbied hard for Sonic Youth on SST: "We used to have these long-ass pow-wows, seven or eight hours on the phone, and I remember talking about the Sonics and Greg said, 'They're nice people.' Carducci was begrudging. And of course, Greg called the shots, so they were signed.") SST not only had a more formidable lineup and more underground cred than Homestead but better financial resources, its own booking agency, and better national distribution. When Ginn called the Eldridge Street apartment to see if Sonic Youth wanted to make a record for the label, it was love at first call. "It was like a lottery ticket," says Moore.

"I was like, you had me at hello. There was no way I was going to deny doing records for SST."

The prospect of snatching the band from another indie label didn't seem to bother SST, either. "Sonic Youth were confident that the label change would be no big deal," recalls Dukowski, "and it wasn't." Yet it was a major change, a catastrophic one, for Cosloy. Whether it was Moore who called Cosloy and told him the bad news (as Moore recalls) or whether Ranaldo mentioned the switch to SST in a cab ride with Cosloy (as Cosloy remembers it), the news came as a blood-draining shock to their friend. Cosloy, who himself idolized SST, understood: "SST was my favorite label. Which label would *you* rather be on? Fuck, that's an easy question to answer."

But according to Hysen, Cosloy was also devastated that a band he'd supported and nurtured was leaving him so soon. Cosloy had hoped to transform Homestead into an SST rival, and he knew his label would never stand a chance if his few quality acts, like Sonic Youth, departed. "In retrospect, I don't think that would have happened under *any* circumstances," he says of Homestead's viability. "Homestead was a good and occasionally great label that was understaffed, underfunded, and owned and operated by a company that didn't like it and didn't like the musicians very much. Chances are it *never* would have been successful the way SST was, because SST had something you can't quantify— it was being run by people who believed in it."

When Sonic Youth convinced their friends in Dinosaur—the Massachusetts trio motorized by the guitar screech and blissfully melodic songs of J. Mascis—to also leave Homestead for SST, Cosloy's hurt doubled. Cosloy had been an early and vocal supporter of Deep Wound, the hardcore band that included Mascis and future Dinosaur bass player Lou Barlow. "That was hard, really hard," Gordon says of that period. "We loved Gerard. But we weren't sure about Homestead. We thought, well, Gerard could leave, and then what would happen?" They couldn't afford the risk, and by early 1986, they received one of SST's standard one-page contracts in the mail. With no hesitation, they signed it and mailed it back.

As PAUL SMITH was beginning to learn, a business meeting with Sonic Youth was unlike any he took with other Blast First acts. When Smith made one of his periodic trips to the States, he would generally meet up with the band at a restaurant, and one of his immediate tasks was to make everyone stop focusing on the menu long enough to concentrate on the financial and career-strategizing matters at hand. The food rendezvous were enlightening in other ways as well. During one discussion at an Indian spot, Smith noticed a couple at a nearby table pointing to the band and whispering—another sign that Sonic Youth, while hardly pop stars, were developing both a fan base and an image.

Whether in person or by way of transatlantic phone calls, they and Smith always seemed to have something to work out or work their way around. One of their first collective hurdles came in the fall of 1985, when the band presented Homestead and Smith with a new single, "Flower." The song had been cut in Los Angeles during their breaking-ground trip there early in the year; a local producer, Ethan James, had overseen it and another track, "Halloween," a masterpiece of sustained tension with Gordon talk-singing like a road-weary hitchhiker over creepily strummed guitars and a muted drum beat. One of Bert's last recordings with them, "Flower" was a feminist call to arms featuring Gordon, in more exhortative voice than usual, singing, "Support the power of women/Use the word . . . *fuck*." Musically, "Flower" was a throbbing lurk of a track, one long verse that never quite built to a chorus and thereby created a palpable sense of anxiety.

As with *Bad Moon Rising*, Smith received the completed artwork in the mail: a nude frontal shot of a woman, alongside a few snippets of the song's lyrics. Smith liked it—and more or less understood the way it used pornography to make a feminist point—but wasn't sure whether it would fly at Rough Trade. Neither did several company employees to whom Smith showed the cover. After a late October meeting, one worker circulated a petition against the art: "I propose to refuse to manufacture it. Can anyone give me a single good reason to use it?"

"They have a right to express their 'art' . . . somewhere else," wrote another. Beneath that comment were the signatures of nineteen other employees who agreed to prevent its release. ("Use the word no," scrawled one.) As a result of the staff revolt, Rough Trade refused to distribute the single. Miffed, Smith and the band released it themselves on an ad hoc label that, to Smith's bafflement, was then distributed by Rough Trade.

When meetings in the States didn't take place over dinner, they would often be held at the Eldridge Street apartment, the hub of Sonic Youth life, especially since the band still had no manager or lawyer. Such was the case one day in March. As usual, the band was spread around the tiny home—Shelley lying on the bed, Moore wandering around—and Smith, aware that a few earlier discussions with the band had led to later misunderstandings, decided to tape-record it with the band's knowledge. Ever the gear aficionado, Ranaldo grilled Smith on the make and model of the recorder ("I'm dying for one of these," he said).

In the course of the nearly two-hour meeting, Smith and the band mulled over a wide range of topics. In many ways, Sonic Youth could be very informal, but Smith realized soon enough that beneath the casual exterior was a band that knew exactly what it wanted, how it wanted to be presented, and how it expected to be compensated. On the table were the possibility of the band playing at a festival in France (and the band's concern that it would look as if they were merely an opening act for the Jesus and Mary Chain, who were also on the bill), their desire for a telex machine (Smith said he could look into it), a potential Scandinavian release for seven hundred copies of their next album ("He seems possibly disreputable," Ranaldo noted of the label owner), and the chance that their friends the Butthole Surfers would coheadline a show with them. (Moore was concerned that the media would debate "who's the better American band," which would, in turn, "put a strain on us hanging out.") Gordon watched and listened, taking it all in and interjecting cut-to-the-chase comments or questions; Shelley, still absorbing his surroundings, mostly let the others do the talking and haggling.

Just like a Sonic Youth song, the meeting veered off on tangents, the band members referencing Pat Benatar songs or making cracks about each other. When the non-business-savvy Moore inquired about how much money they'd make for a particular show, Ranaldo joked, in a clear dig, "It's amazing Thurston asked that!" To steer matters back on track, Smith would say, in mock military voice, "Okay, I require your *full* attention" or, at one point, *"Listen!"*

When an upcoming British tour was brought up, Ranaldo said, sharply, "When we get on the boat or whatever on the twenty-third [the last show of the tour], will we have money in our pockets?"

"I can't see why not," Smith responded. "I would certainly aim for a situation where you *do* have money."

As that exchange foreshadowed, financial matters—and the band's concern about what funds were coming in and going out—were a recurring cause of concern, especially since they were all still working day jobs. "At this point, I feel it's almost demeaning for us to not come away with money in addition to whatever critical plaudits we get or whatever," Ranaldo told Smith. "It would suck if we played for fifty pounds a night, or some shit." Smith responded that he would aim for between three hundred and fifty and five hundred pounds a night.

Ranaldo also grilled Smith on who would pay for a one-third-page ad in *Melody Maker*, royalties for *Bad Moon Rising* (Smith had already sent them one thousand British pounds and said another six thousand dollars were on the way), and why the "Death Valley '69" single hadn't made money in the U.K.

"We made money off Gerard's copy of it," Ranaldo said. "Do you have any figures for what we sold? Out of curiosity?" Not for the first time, Smith made a note to himself to check and get back to the band.

Discussing an overseas record deal, Smith mentioned the label would "pay seventy-five percent of everything that comes into their artists."

But, Ranaldo snapped back, "We're losing twenty-five percent of our money to *you*."

After explaining how Rough Trade worked, Smith admitted, "You could say you're losing that."

"Why are we paying *both* of you to license our record?" Ranaldo said.

"Because the record wouldn't have come out," Smith said, calmly.

"If we were informed of this, we would have said you had to split it," Ranaldo countered.

Smith went on to explain that the standard royalty was one pound five pence per record, with Rough Trade taking 75 percent, meaning Sonic Youth would, he explained, receive seventy-five pence per record.

"Of which *you're* taking twenty-five percent," Ranaldo said.

"Wait a minute," Smith shot back, adding that he would "have to argue with Rough Trade about that. Because that means I'm not making any money off the record."

"Make a copy of all that shit," Ranaldo said.

The meeting began to wind down, especially once Ranaldo found a joint in a coat pocket. "Yeah!" said Moore, excitedly.

At one point, Ranaldo also mentioned he was in possession of a cassette containing rough versions and mixes of every song the band had recorded to that point. "Wow," Moore responded.

"Like the second version of 'World Looks Red,'" Ranaldo went on. "'Shaking Hell' with the original vocal. It's the greatest tape. I have it *all*. Someday, twenty years from now. . . ." At the time, the thought that anyone would care two decades later seemed impossibly quaint.

LYLE HYSEN AND SUSANNE SASIC would also drop by Eldridge Street, and the two couples would eat out, see movies like *Mad Max Beyond Thunderdome*, or engage in long, involved conversations on music, art, and pop culture. During one visit, Moore and Gordon were eager to play Hysen a song the band had just recorded. Hysen didn't know what to expect, and he certainly didn't anticipate *this*: the guitars playing thick, crusty chords, Shelley's drums loud and thwacking, and Gordon singing, relatively straightforwardly, about young women who fantasized about bands, inspired by an L.A. magazine devoted to groupies. Hysen never thought his friends could create anything more normal-sounding than "Death Valley '69." Yet here was an uncomplicated, unfettered rock song called "Star Power." Moore and Gordon were noticeably thrilled with the track, as was Hysen: "It was a super-exciting time. You thought, 'Wow, they might be as big as the Meat Puppets.'"

"Star Power" was one of a number of tracks put on tape at Martin Bisi's studio in February and March of 1986, all to comprise the band's first album for SST. "Those songs seemed to come together effortlessly," says Shelley. "I don't remember *working* on any of it. It was like meeting someone and getting along and the conversation goes somewhere." Their new label was largely footing the bill for the sessions, which turned out to be another example of the inadvertent good timing that continued to follow the band. Nicolas Ceresole and Catherine Bachmann, who by then had married, were eager to recoup their financial investment in *Bad Moon Rising*. But due to the snailspace economics of the indie label system ("It's hard to get paid back in a few weeks, never mind a couple of years," says Cosloy), no money was forthcoming. "We needed it back," says Catherine Ceresole. "We were young and it was not our money." She admits there was "a hard time for a while" between the couple and the band, and the two parties didn't speak for a number of years afterward.

The second round of Bisi sessions continued the textural tinkering of *Bad Moon Rising*, sometimes literally. Another piano piece Moore had recorded at his family's house became the basis for "Secret Girl," Gordon's oblique rumination on being repeatedly asked (especially in the U.K.) about being the only woman in a band. "The male journalists there were almost afraid of women," she says. "If you were just portraying yourself as a girl, that was more threatening. It made me feel invisible there." "Marilyn Moore," which grew out of Moore's reading of Norman Mailer's book on Marilyn Monroe, was his attempt to personalize her story by making Monroe his sister; it opened with screams he and Ranaldo had taped in an old metal silo in Europe.

Ranaldo brought in pieces of several different songs he'd been working on—a driving rock & roll pattern and a sludgier, more metal portion—and chopped them up to form "In the Kingdom #19," adding multiple overdubs and sound effects. The lyrics, a vivid, blood-and-gas-soaked description of a car crash, derived from one of his on-the-road journals and his obsession with Beat poets. Given the lyric—a car "screeching along the guardrail," the driver "covered in blood"—Moore thought it would be funny to add a little something extra to the take. So, as Ranaldo was reciting the lyrics in Bisi's closet-size vocal booth, Moore tossed in a lit firecracker. Momentarily scared out of his mind, Ranaldo shrieked and leapt out of the booth, and, as everyone watched, began berating Moore, who sat silently. It wasn't merely the close-range firecracker that irked Ranaldo; given the song marked the first time he performed a solo vocal on a Sonic Youth record, he was bothered by what he felt was Moore's attitude. "I felt he was being a little too irreverent about it," he says. "So I got upset about it for a minute." But the scream ultimately sounded so good—so realistic—that it stayed in. "It was a bad decision," Moore admits, "but, hey, whatever it takes to make a song happen."

At the end of the song, Moore whispered "Never gave a damn about the meter man/until I was the man who had to read the meters, man," a line written by their new friend Mike Watt, who once had a job reading meters. With the release of *3-Way Tie (For Last)*, a record both layered and approachable yet true to their funky-punk roots, the Minutemen were at the dawn of a new creative era, and the hyperactive, garrulous Watt couldn't have been happier. But a few months before the Bisi sessions, Watt's world was decimated when D. Boon was suddenly, horrifically, killed after being thrown from the back of their van during a car accident. After Watt called her with the news, Gordon was so upset she began crying.

Devastated by the death of his close friend and unsure whether he wanted to play music again, Watt was at loose ends but agreed to drive East to drop off his girlfriend, Black Flag bass player Kira Roessler, at her new school in Connecticut. On the way back to California, he took a detour to Manhattan. One night he called the Eldridge Street apartment from a nearby bar, where he was seriously drunk and about to be kicked out; Moore and Gordon invited him to stay the night and talk about his situation. "I said, 'I don't want to play without D. Boon,' and they said, 'No, you have to—and use Kim's big ol' bass,'" Watt recalls. Dragged along to Bisi's studio,

Watt ended up playing Gordon's bass on "In the Kingdom #19" as well as a B-side, a cover of "Bubblegum." With its psychedelic-blues lead guitar from Ranaldo—the first time it was possible to hear the influence of Jorma Kaukonen and other freak-flag-flying guitar players in his work—"Bubblegum" didn't sound remotely like a Sonic Youth song, because it wasn't. Written by underground-pop Svengali Kim Fowley in the '70s and rediscovered by Moore on an old LP, "Bubblegum" was notable for its rare Gordon-Ranaldo harmony vocal and for the method in which it was recorded (the band played along with the original record, then wiped out everything except their own instruments). But it also stood out in the way it grooved in an old FM-radio way: proof they could, if so inclined, make regular rock and do it astonishingly well.

The time at Bisi's studio also found the band both tightening up and widening their sound. Shelley's roots in new-wave pop, even the discipline he'd gleaned from his high-school marching band, brought a more grounded sense of rhythm to "Green Light" and "Star Power," and his playing held together an instrumental called "Death to Our Friends." (Given its interlocking sections, Shelley says the title was a cheeky reference to Elton John's similarly structured "Funeral for a Friend," although Moore claims it was inspired by Boon's death: "It was a way of trying to be celebratory about the fact that you die. It had a double meaning.") Shelley broke out his mallets, another holdover from his marching-band days, for "Tom Violence," the title a play on Tom Verlaine's name.

In terms of new directions, though, few of the tracks were as conspicuous as "Expressway to Yr Skull," also called "Madonna, Sean and Me" on the back of the album and "The Crucifixion of Sean Penn" on the inside. "We're gonna kill the California girls," Moore sang, his voice a mixture of disgust and lazy-day slacker. The sentiments were an extension of "Death Valley '69"; the music was anything but. Moore had brought in the initial chord progression, and during the early stages of the song's construction, Gordon told him it was the best thing he'd ever written. The finished version started almost laconically, with unhurried chords and Moore's nonchalant voice, the violence of the initial image giving way to a more positive message: "We're gonna find the meaning of feeling good/And we're gonna stay there as long as we think we should." The first section then shifted to a more pounding, purposefully frazzled midsection, which then slid back into a languid, extended instrumental reverie. Listening to it was like standing waist-deep in the ocean and feeling waves break and recede around you. Five minutes in, the drums dropped out altogether, with Gordon's deep bass line and the guitars creating a cosmic soundscape that soon dribbled to a close. At seven minutes, it was not only the longest piece of music they'd recorded but the most elastic and spacious, and it suggested that any "noise band" connotation that still hovered around the band would soon be passé.

Right before the sessions had begun, the band dropped off a truckload of guitars at Bisi's studio. Looking at the jumble of half-broken, beaten-down instruments—some in cases, some not, some fully strung, some not—Bisi marveled at the sight. But the image came back to haunt him during the making of the record. As they were mixing "Expressway to Yr Skull," Bisi asked Moore if he was happy with the finished track. "And Thurston was kind of shaking his head—'Sounds too *good*,'" Bisi recalls. "Then there was this silence. I was like, 'Problem? No problem?' Nothing." Bisi felt the band wanted their music "to sound junky," just like their instruments— "They wanted to make things sound shitty or not quite right somehow"—but felt unable to accommodate that impulse. He wanted to make the most pro-sounding record he could, even dousing the tracks in reverb, a technique he'd later regret. But did the band have the same goal in mind? He was never sure. "I felt good about the album—we were developing our moves," says Moore. But there were, Shelley admits, "some growing pains" during its making.

For the cover, the band chose an intentionally jarring image: a stark, black-and-white Richard Kern photo of Lung Leg (taken from his film *Submit to Me*) that captured everything squalid about downtown New York, not to mention the country itself as the seeds of the Reagan revolution became to make themselves known in their neighborhood. (The new influx of homeless in and around the East

Village was a clear indication that the medical system was under attack.) Yet the music inside the jacket was more controlled and less chaotic—more introspective, even—than ever before. Set to Shelley's gently tumbling rhythm, "Tom Violence" was an especially calm, restrained way to open a Sonic Youth album; even Moore's singing, with its references to "my violence . . . find it in the father, find it in the girl," felt contained. Shortly into it, the song broke down, climbed to an electrical storm of guitar freneticism, and swung back to the original motif with a seamlessness they'd rarely demonstrated before.

Their off-center, unusually tuned guitars were still their own, and Moore and Ranaldo continued to pull new sounds out of them: rain-patter tones in "Shadow of a Doubt" (another example of Gordon's collage-style approach to lyric writing—the lyrics were taken from Alfred Hitchcock's *Strangers on a Train*) and metallic chime in "Green Light." Yet the sound was airier and more spacious; for once, the music suggested hope, a way out of the darkness. Gordon's voice on "Secret Girl" and "Shadow of a Doubt" was surprisingly seductive, and not even Moore's deadpan, emotionally restrained delivery could remove the sense of possibility lurking behind the chords of a semi-love song like "Green Light."

When SST and Blast First released the album in their respective countries in June, it was called *EVOL:* "love" backward but also the name of a film by video artist Tony Oursler. (A New York–born but California-schooled artist, Oursler specialized in video installations—projecting faces onto inanimate objects to beguiling and often creepy effect—and he and Gordon, whom he met at the dawn of Sonic Youth, had collaborated on several early projects, including "Making the Nature Scene" about architecture in Manhattan rock clubs.) In Los Angeles, SST's Dukowski jammed an early dub of the record into his car's tape deck and drove to his girlfriend's house in Silverlake. Captivated by its sound, he sat parked in front of her apartment building as *EVOL* played through. It didn't sound like anything else in the SST stable, but, Dukowski realized, for once, that was a good thing.

SEEING THEM ON THE STREET outside CBGB, she wanted to dislike them; she really did. Why shouldn't she? Diminutive and dark-haired, Julie Cafritz prided herself on being a brat, especially when it came to music. Growing up in Washington, D.C., she and her younger sister Daisy had been so tormented by all the Jimi Hendrix and Jeff Beck records that their older brothers played that she grew to hate rock & roll and the guitar. At Brown University, she met Jon Spencer, a fellow disillusioned anti-rock type; when both wound up back in D.C. after college, he told her he was starting a band, and even though she didn't know how to play guitar, she joined up anyway. The band, Pussy Galore, featuring Spencer, Cafritz, and drummer John Hammill, wanted nothing more than to dismantle rock completely, tossing aside all pretense of steady rhythm and melody; their live shows and records, like 1986's *Groovy Hate Fuck*, were gleefully deranged musical splatterfests.

A month after moving to Manhattan, Cafritz, then twenty-one, ran into Moore and Gordon on the Bowery, down the block from where she, Spencer, and their respective mates shared a sublet. She'd already made up her musical mind about them. Much like the previous generation had chosen between the Beatles and the Stones, Cafritz had to decide whether to support Sonic Youth or Swans; for the moment, she had opted for the latter's aural brutality. Besides, Sonic Youth seemed too *normal* to her. Already familiar with Pussy Galore, Moore and Gordon, who were playing with Sonic Youth at CBGB that night, were pleasant and helpful, even recommending Bob Bert for the newly vacant drum slot in Pussy Galore. "In my mind, I was thinking, 'Thank you, chumps,'" Cafritz recalls. "Sometimes I gave them their due, but most of the time I made fun of them." Sonic Youth seemed almost too successful and tuneful to support; they were the easiest of targets.

Yet in spite of herself, Cafritz, like many others in the indie community, found herself pulled into their orbit. She watched and read as they name-dropped new bands in interviews. Unlike her band and so many others she knew, Sonic Youth were actually releasing albums on a real record label, SST at that. Moore and Gordon recommended a booking agent for Pussy Galore and invited them to open for them in D.C. as part of the upcoming *EVOL* tour. They even inspired their successor: In interviews, Sonic Youth began talking up the idea—fully formed or not—of recording a complete remake of the Beatles' "White Album." When they finally began working on it in earnest, they learned "Back in the U.S.S.R." but, realizing how much work would be involved, decided to stop there. In the end, Pussy Galore beat them to the punch with their own complete remake of the Rolling Stones' *Exile on Main St.*: the symbolic passing of the irreverent torch.

Even Cafritz had to admit that, in relation to the scuzz-inclined musicians who populated her scene, Gordon and Moore were a relatively glamorous couple; Cafritz thought Gordon was so downtown-cool that she called her "the Fonz." At one point, they asked Cafritz to house-sit at Eldridge Street and look after their dog. While there, Cafritz couldn't help but rummage through their belongings, especially searching for passports to determine exactly how old they were.

By the summer of 1986, Sonic Youth did seem like kingpins on the developing market dubbed "college rock." SST initially pressed five thousand copies of *EVOL*, yet demand was such that the album went on to sell roughly forty thousand copies its first year out. Their status was also confirmed when they left New York in the middle of June to start the *EVOL* national tour, which would last until the beginning of August. For the first time, they left with what amounted to a crew. Terry Pearson, a native Texan who met the band when they played at his club, the Continental, in Austin, was hired for $225 a week to be their sound man, and Carlos van Hijfte, their Holland-based European booking agent, came along to work the lights, man their T-shirt stand, and savor his first extended taste of America.

The tour had been set up by Global Network, yet, much like the into-the-wild aspects of the *Bad Moon Rising* tour, the conditions were not always what they hoped they would be (especially for van Hijfte, who was accustomed to subsidized, relatively plush European clubs). Once they pulled up to whatever space they were booked into, Pearson would routinely have to cajole the club owners into letting him rewire the sound system, which always seemed to be humming or buzzing. Once the band began playing, the technicians would regularly scowl and tell Pearson this wasn't music, it was noise—and then leave altogether.

During the shows, the band's irregular tunings would create such a drony wall of sound that making each instrument sound clear became a nightly challenge for Pearson; when Ranaldo and Moore would pull a new guitar out of the drum box and retune onstage, Pearson especially had to scramble. (The musical squall was particularly challenging for Gordon, who would have to find the root note on her bass amidst the audio hurricane around her.) "When it was off, it didn't have the same power," Pearson says. "But when everything locked in, it was the most intense experience you could have. The music was truly going somewhere on its own, and you just let it go there." In Milwaukee on July 26, they met up with Dinosaur, who'd already released their self-titled first album; in his journal, Moore wrote they were "one of the best coolest bands in the U.S." Sometimes, Dinosaur seemed even louder than Sonic Youth.

Thanks to Global, the band was guaranteed between $500 and $1,100 per show, their best overall earnings. One typical contract, for a booking in Philadelphia at the Kennel Club on June 21 ("three floors of drunken Fillyfolk shelling out 12 bux to get in," Moore wrote in his journal), called for a $900 guarantee with the band receiving 75 percent of any gross over $2,200. (At the Roxy in Los Angeles, they were guaranteed $1,600, but such high figures were extremely rare.) But as van Hijfte learned, a guarantee in writing was no assurance of cash in hand. After a gig in Tucson, Arizona, on July 1, the club owner refused to pay the $500. When van Hijfte, whose English was limited, tried to be forceful, the club owner muttered something about having "other tools" at his disposal; to emphasize the point, his bodyguard flashed a gun. (In retaliation, Pearson stuck glue into the club's front door after they left: "If he wasn't gong to pay us, then I'd make sure he'd at least have to pay for a locksmith.") At the end of a show in Detroit, the promoter was nowhere to be found and his assistant claimed to know nothing, and the band—and the other acts on the bill, Dinosaur and L.A.'s Leaving Trains, also on

SST—were paid only a fraction of the $1,750 they'd been promised. "I never got more late-night calls about troubles with the promoter than I did from any other group on tour," recalls Dukowski.

Yet as with the record sales, attendance was slowly creeping up. Now as many as two hundred people would pay for a ticket—the West Coast shows, starting in San Diego, drew some of the largest crowds—and many of them stayed for the entire set, which included most of *EVOL* as well as new and unrecorded songs like "White Kross." (Onstage, Moore, not Gordon, ended up singing "Star Power," since the song's standard pitch was throwing her off.) No matter what material they were playing, Shelley's crucial function in the band became apparent. More so than any of their previous drummers, he became their onstage anchor: the one always on the beat, the one they looked to when it became time to return to the song after a particularly long and frenetic freeform section. Moore and Ranaldo felt especially freer to push the music to previously unheard areas, knowing the regimented kid with the Midwestern work ethic would always be there to bring them back to earth.

As Pearson and van Hijfte observed, their new employers were far from traditional rock stars in more than their music. As the *Miami Vice* soundtrack and *Exile on Main St.* blared from the boom box in the van, they visited Pine Apple, Alabama, to visit Doc and Dorothy Adams, Moore's grandparents. Pearson noticed that upon arriving in whatever city they were playing, the band would instantly head for record stores, book stores, and thrift shops, jamming their new purchases into whatever space they could find in the van. Backstage, hangers-on and anything approaching groupies were rarely an issue. ("We had a married couple, a married guitar player, and a drummer who looked like he was fourteen," Shelley says. "So that was *not* happening.") In Columbus, a bunch of them took mushrooms, with mixed results: "Bad idea, very bad gig," recalls van Hijfte. ("I'm not into it," wrote Moore in his journal. "It gets too fucking in the way of how I really want to feel.")

During their show in Boston on August 2, someone gave the band cocaine and, eager for a small, outsider's taste of the rock & roll lifestyle, they decided to use it in the van. As Ranaldo filmed the scene for an *EVOL* tour film, one of the entourage laid it out—and, as if remaking the classic scene from *Annie Hall*, sneezed, sending the drug flying out the window. In the long run, maybe they *all* weren't typical rock types.

THEY WERE HOME in the city only a few months when it was time to squish back into the van for another trek around the heartland and the south. The tour, dubbed Flaming Telepath, lasted only three weeks, but it solidified their bond with Watt. After his role in the *EVOL* sessions, Watt was so encouraged to resume life in a band that he and Minutemen drummer George Hurley formed another, fIREHOSE; an untested newcomer, Ed Crawford, was in the unenviable position of essentially replacing D. Boon. The tour reached an apogee of sorts when, during one show, everyone piled on Watt and blew out his knee in the process. (Watt contends they couldn't have known he had a bum knee to begin with.) As with the *EVOL* tour—during which they also shared stages with not just Dinosaur and Leaving Trains but Kentucky hardcore pop bashers Squirrel Bait—the tour was another sign that they were finally tapping into a larger, national indie music community. And Sonic Youth, a band all of five years old, were already being seen as its founding parents.

On the road, Moore and Gordon continued to maintain their decorum, even sharing a room with Sasic. (Shelley, Ranaldo, and Pearson split a room, taking turns sleeping on the floor or the bed.) Moore was also getting his first sense that Gordon was attracting her share of attention from the crowd. "I always knew there was lust involved with the audience," he says. "And I could certainly accept that. We were very loyal to each other. I never got the sense that there was anything to worry about with deceit. We knew each other enough." In rare instances, he was forced into a more proactive stance. During a show on an early European tour, an Italian fan reached out and grabbed Gordon's butt during "Early American." Seeing what had happened, Moore grabbed the stick and metal pipe he'd been using on his guitar and slammed the fan's hand. "He came backstage with a friend and acted like he was going to kill me or something," he recalls. "And I said, 'Before you do anything: If you were playing music with your friend or wife onstage, and someone did that, what would you do?'" The tension defused, the man skulked away.

Shortly before the Flaming Telepath shows began, the band took a decisive step toward straightening out its loose-limbed business affairs. Through the Manhattan club circuit, they'd become acquainted with Richard Grabel, who, as the American correspondent for England's *New Musical Express*, reviewed albums and concerts. Aware that his career as a rock critic had a built-in obsolescence, Grabel, a redhaired, raspy-voiced New Yorker, began attending law school; upon graduating in 1984, he took a job at Cowan and Bodine, a general-interest law firm. It was there, in August 1986, that he received a call from Gordon. She told him the band was about to start recording its second album for SST but felt the time had come for someone other than a band member to look over the contract. Perhaps they were wary of SST; perhaps they were still reeling from having signed away their publishing rights in Europe, a decision that would haunt them for years. After the call ended, Grabel ran out of his office and into the hallway, yelling, "Sonic Youth just called me!" Everyone just looked at him: No one in the firm knew who he was talking about.

The meeting with Grabel, at his firm's Madison Avenue offices, went well enough that they decided to retain him as their attorney. Like many, Grabel was struck by their unusual (for rock & roll) democracy—how there seemed to be no band leader and how, during meetings, different matters were handled by different people at different times. Problems would ensue only if he ran something by Moore and Gordon exclusively; Shelley and Ranaldo wanted their voices to be heard as well.

On the matter of SST, Grabel saw no reason for them not to sign what he called the benign paperwork, and all four agreed there was no reason not to continue with the label for the time being—although they decided to make at least one musical change. Their dissatisfaction with Bisi's final mix of *EVOL* led them to seek out another space,

163

and in their Lower East Side circles, they began hearing about Sear Sound. Squeezed into the middle of Times Square, the studio was an unlikely choice. Its heyday over, Sear Sound had been reduced to a home for jingles and soundtracks for the softcore horror films produced by Walter and Roberta Sear, the older couple who ran the studio. (Once, Gordon looked out into the hallway and saw a long line of scruffy oddballs auditioning for the Sears' next movie.) Yet by Manhattan standards, the studio was affordable and, more importantly, home to the old-school tube amplifiers and recording gear that newly intrigued the band.

Walking past one of the recording rooms after the sessions had begun, Sear heard Bill Titus, Sear Sound's in-house engineer, stop a take and tell the band they needed to tune their guitars. Sear ran in, telling Titus they were *supposed* to sound that way. The story was symbolic of Titus' early interaction with the band. An old-school engineer who regularly regaled the band with stories of working on Billy Joel records ("We'd be sticking our fingers down our throat while he was telling us," says Ranaldo), Titus was "doing it by the book," says Sear, and those rules dictated that musicians steer clear of studio gear. "Bill thought we were just kids," says Moore, "and, 'I'm the engineer, you're the musicians, you go in and play. Don't even *think* about touching the board.' And we were like, 'You've got to be kidding.' As soon as Lee started touching the faders, he was like, '*Do not touch the board.*'" Ranaldo handled them so many times, in fact, that heated arguments ensued; thanks to Sear, who acted as an intermediary, the situation was resolved, and the band was allowed to be somewhat hands-on. Titus did, though, insist they call out the number of each take as they recorded, and the sound of he and Moore each yelling out "seven!" would eventually preface "Stereo Sanctity." By the end, Moore and Titus were even joking about it.

Despite the tension, they managed to cut the record in a little less than two weeks in early spring, helped in part by new songs laboriously worked out and rehearsed at ex-Teenage Jesus member Bradley Fields' elevator-shaft-size basement rehearsal space on the Lower East Side. Many of the familiar elements of the Sonic Youth sound were in evidence: the way certain songs would seemingly crumble to a close or the manner in which a track would halt halfway through, transform into a series of overlapping guitar flutters, and then be thrust back to its original refrain. Both Gordon and Ranaldo again talk-sang their way through the songs for which they wrote lyrics.

Yet the record, called *Sister* after the band rejected Moore's push to name it *Sol-Fuc* (other early, discarded titles were *Kitty Magic* and *Humpy Pumpy*), had a sharpness and rhythmic drive that reinvigorated those now-established practices. Part of the album's strength was indeed attributed to those songs. "We were getting more seriously into song structure," says Moore. "It's not something we intended to do. It just became something we were getting more proficient at." "Schizophrenia" was one of two songs that took its cue from the work of Philip K. Dick, the celebrated but underground sci-fi writer. (*Sister* was also an oblique reference to Dick's obsession with his twin sister, who'd died at a month old.) The song opened the album with the most melodic chords they'd ever played; during Gordon's spoken-word midsection, the guitars snaked and wormed around her with a new clarity. "(I Got a) Catholic Block," Moore's coded musing on his religious upbringing and subsequent sense of Catholic guilt, was set to an unusually mattress-springy riff.

During those songs, Moore's singing was more naturalistic, less intentionally harsh. "Kotton Krown" began casually, with leisurely strummed guitars, before building to one of their most beautiful, lulling melodies; it also featured a rare Gordon and Moore vocal harmony that tied in with the song's devotional lyrics. (In concert, Moore would sing the song alone, since the pairing of their voices onstage never sounded as compatible as in the studio.) A cover of "Hot-wire My Heart" by San Francisco punkers Crime, suggested by Moore, wasn't an offhand joke but a jolt of old-school punk.

They still pushed their secondhand guitars to the limits, building to a frenetic tempest in the midst of "(I Got a) Catholic Block" or "White Kross" or throughout the coiled-up "Stereo Sanctity," another song based on the work of Dick (as well as Lucius Shepard's 1984 zombie sci-fi novel *Green Eyes*). But they also explored a new exquisiteness in the instruments. The tapestry-like wash of strummed acoustic and electric guitars in "Beauty Lies in the Eye," based on a series of Ranaldo chord progressions, meshed beautifully with Gordon's conversational delivery. One minute into "Pacific Coast Highway," the aggressively industrial grind of the song's central riff abruptly shifted to a slower portion, Ranaldo's lead guitar taking on the soaring clarity of a '70s arena-rock band. (The part was actually inspired by the melody of the Beach Boys' "Let's Go Away for a While.") Despite the adroit use of Sear Sound's wall-sized Moog synthesizer on "Pipeline/Kill Time," played by Shelley, the album felt organic: fewer effects than in the past (like samples or retrieved piano tapes), more emphasis on the band dynamic of guitars and drums. Although Shelley wasn't pleased with how thin his drums sounded, his work in particular was clearly the glue that gave the songs a new cohesion; as onstage, he both reined them in and set them free.

When it came to the lyrics grafted onto the melodies, the band remained deliberately enigmatic. "There was never a vote on lyrics," Shelley says. "That was the one thing that was kind of odd. You'd all work on putting the music together, and the vocalist had carte blanche: 'Here, I've finished this.' And you're like, 'That song's about *what?*'" Moore cut up different lines from record and concert reviews he'd written for his fanzine *Killer* to form the words for "Tuff Gnarl." (In issue number one, Moore extolled a Virginia hardcore band called Iron Cross, calling them "truly a tuff gnarl. . . . Surely to offend all douchebags.")

Ranaldo's lyrics were increasingly the most personal; "Pipeline/Kill Time" was based on a poem about his longtime friend Thom DeJesu's marital problems at the time. (A spoken-word part at the end of the song was deleted in order for the song to wind down with a lengthy instrumental fade-out.) As "Pacific Coast Highway" showed ("Come get in the car/Let's go for a ride somewhere/I won't hurt you"), Gordon employed fictional scenarios to hint at personal experience without giving too much away (in her case, the times the teenaged Gordon would hitch a ride to Malibu and hear about other hitchhikers vanishing or turning up dead). In lyrics as in personality, she remained reserved and guarded. Moore's words were becoming the most intentionally oblique. Much like the earlier "I Love Her All the Time," the lyrics to "Kotton Krown," with its suggestions of a "carnal spirit" and how "love has come to stay," referred to Gordon and Moore's relationship, albeit cryptically. "I wanted to write songs like that without being too blatantly obvious," says Moore. "It's a fine line between sensuous and sleazy."

"Schizophrenia," according to Moore, was also an indirect reference to his ailing brother-in-law Keller. "The lyrics always mean something to me," Moore says. "They're always referencing something personal, something I'm interested in or inspired by. But they're very much encoded for myself. I'm into that kind of linguistic play and surrealistic poetry; it creates a more open reading." Similarly, "Stereo Sanctity" embodied what he saw as the concept of "language as music" and not language as confessional expression, as so many rock songwriters before him had done.

Playing "Schizophrenia" for Paul Smith on Eldridge Street, Moore was taken aback when Smith said, "I can't believe you made a record like this." Moore didn't know what to make of the remark; maybe Smith was disappointed it wasn't noisy enough. No, Smith said; he loved it because it reminded him of New Order. Moore never would have thought of the connection. The British new-wave and synthpop scene so turned him off that, had he taken the remark the wrong way, he says, "I would have stopped writing songs."

WHEN SST RELEASED THE ALBUM in June 1987 (with Blast First issuing it in the U.K. the same month), the label ran ads featuring a half-naked, anorexic woman sprawled on a floor, a look of helpless fatigue on her face: "Have you ever seen your sister naked?" read the ad copy. Coming on the heels of the EVOL cover of Lung Leg and the splatter-movie effects in the "Death Valley '69" video, the photo, again courtesy of the mind and camera of Richard Kern, was a typical Sonic Youth graphic: disturbing, unsettling, a little lurid, a little extreme.

But it was also the type of image they were beginning to leave behind. Shortly after he began working with them, Smith saw the band's unwillingness to smile during photo shoots; their unfettered camaraderie and inside jokes would disappear as soon as a camera began clicking. But by the time of *Sister*, they were starting to loosen up. The humor, irony, sarcasm, and pop culture obsessiveness that had lurked beneath the surface began to reveal itself and, in many ways, subsume their earlier, more imposing image.

At one shoot, Smith saw them wearing Madonna and Bruce Springsteen T-shirts; he suggested they don something else so as not to confuse people, but they ignored him. To amuse the audience while they switched or retuned guitars onstage, they began playing tapes (on a large boom box they'd bought before the tour) of Madonna and Carpenters hits, and even more unlikely period kitsch like Glenn Frey's "You Belong to the City." (During the *Sister* shows, they also began including their own Ramones medley: "We were getting pegged as a serious New York band," says Shelley, "and we wanted to say, 'We like the Ramones like everybody else.'") "We were interested in negating a lot of the overly serious gestures with inanity," Moore says. "No wave had such a nihilist vibe to it, and even though we found it really attractive, again it was not really a part of our makeup. We wanted to take the piss out of things, to defuse them."

To Homestead's Cosloy, the emergence of the band's collective, absurdist wit was a defining moment in their career. "When they started doing interviews, kidding around and talking about rock music, that totally changed the picture," he says. "Up until that point, people were very skeptical or very wary of them. And over time, people began to figure out that maybe they're not that weird or fucked-up. There was nothing contrived about it. That was all stuff they really loved. They were into pop culture and rock and roll. But they were perceived as being more 'down with the kids,' even if they were a lot older than the kids." As Bisi observed during the time he worked with them, "They were like Warhol. They had a Warhol-esque fascination with celebrity. They thought about packaging and spin, and how to present things."

At the moment, no bigger or more fascinating pop celebrity existed than Madonna. Early on, the group appeared less than entranced with her. "Here's someone who was at one point sitting on Mike Gira's lap at Danceteria, hanging out and smoking cigarettes," recalls Moore. "And then I was selling food at this wagon in midtown and having to look at the cover of *Time* magazine with her on it. And I'm thinking, 'What the hell is *happening* here?' I'd never given any value to what she did musically; she'd play and we'd run out of Danceteria as soon as she was announced. It was so corny." But Moore himself had to admit that "Into the Groove," her ebullient, wonderfully pushy 1985 hit, was "a completely infectious song not unlike a great Beach Boys song." (Again, Lydia Lunch disagreed; thinking Madonna's music worthless, she began berating Moore for his championing of Madonna.) Ranaldo and Shelley connected with her songs as pop (in one of his Flaming Telepath tour journals, Ranaldo wrote about hearing the Ronettes' "Baby I Love You" on the radio and how "there's almost nothing in the world like a great song"). Not surprisingly, Gordon admired Madonna's use of sexuality as power. Mike Watt also sensed the influence of Roessler, a Madonna obsessive at the time.

Their Madonna phase crystallized during the *EVOL* sessions. Watt had recorded a one-man version of "Burnin' Up" for a single on SST's New Alliance label; for the flip side, Sonic Youth contributed their own take on "Into the Groove." Calling it "Into the Groovey," they played over the original Madonna recording, adding layers of sonic grime and Moore's own disaffected vocal. Although the single, credited to Ciccone Youth, was never meant to be anything but an entertaining side project, Smith realized he had something—his hippest band doing a cover version of a known pop hit. Since the original Madonna track was never legally sampled, Smith managed to get a copy to Seymour Stein, head of Madonna's label, Sire; in turn, Stein supposedly played it for her and received a verbal nod of approval. Although the single didn't make a large dent in the States, Smith pressed up eight thousand copies in the U.K., which sold out within a matter of weeks and made the British charts, thanks to exposure in dance clubs. Whether the people listening got the joke was another

matter, but in an unpredictable turn of events, an offhand cover became one of their best-known songs.

The packaging of *Sister* was another indication of the group's evolving image and aesthetic. They'd first featured German artist Gerhard
Richter's work on the original Iridescence single of "Death Valley
'69." For their new album, Moore wanted to use a Richter painting of
a young girl. The rest of the band was less enthused, but what
emerged was a new title, *Sister*, that played off that photo and the lyric
to "Schizophrenia." Ranaldo devised the idea of a cross on the cover,
and as with their collaborative songwriting, everyone added his or her
own art around it. Shelley contributed a postcard of the Madonna Hotel. Ranaldo chose a shot of his then nearly two-year-old son Cody in
the buff. (Cody had been born at the end of the day of the "Death Valley '69" video shoot in Kern's apartment; throughout the day,
Ranaldo was continually being handed a phone and told that his wife
Amanda was about to give birth—and also being told by Kern he
couldn't leave yet. Finally, when filming was done, Ranaldo ran home,
cleaned the fake gore from his chest, and dashed to the hospital; his
son arrived several hours later.) Ranaldo also supplied a Richard Avedon shot he'd cut out of a magazine, while Moore contributed, among
other images, a photo of Mickey and Minnie Mouse in front of Dis-
neyworld. In the liner notes, all the artwork was credited to "public
domain," but both Avedon and Disney begged to differ, leading to
cease-and-desist letters from both parties (SST was not considered
prosperous enough to sue) and a new printing of the cover with both
pieces of art blacked out.

From "Into the Groovey" to the irreverent use of Disney characters, even the way the back cover of *EVOL* listed the songs in an in-
correct order, the air around the band was suddenly thick with
irreverence. Part of the change could be attributed to California.
During their regular visits to Los Angeles to visit Gordon's parents,
Moore and Gordon had become friendly with Steven and Jeffrey Mc-
Donald of Redd Kross. Originally a teen hardcore band, Redd Kross
came to embody the burgeoning fascination with all things '70s
kitsch; they began making more old-fangled power pop and dressing

like extras on *Charlie's Angels*. David Markey, who'd seen Sonic Youth at the Anti-Club in 1985 and was part of Redd Kross' circle, also became a close friend. A native Angeleno who'd been making home movies since his preteen years, the goateed, curly-haired Markey became, with his movie obsession and low-budget underground film-making style, a natural ally. He and Moore shared a love of punk and, as it turned out, losses in their families: Their fathers had died the same year. Markey's first major film, 1984's *Desperate Teenage Lovedolls*, was cinematic punk rock. The tale of the rise and fall of an all-girl rock band comprised of runaways, it was crude in its cinematography and nihilistic in its plot: trash culture elevated to art.

In California, Gordon and Moore began spending more time with Markey, and inevitably Markey began using the couple in his short films. The most revealing of their new sensibility was *Lou Believers*, starring the couple and Joe Cole, a lanky, long-haired buddy of Markey's and former Black Flag frontman Henry Rollins. To the outside world, Cole was the son of TV actor Dennis Cole (who, in turn, was the ex-husband of Jaclyn Smith); in indie circles, though, Cole was beloved as a member of Black Flag's road crew and all-around hang-out pal. In the film, Moore—obsessed with finding James Woods, then starring in the film *True Believer*—went on a manic expedition around Hollywood. As Markey's camera rolled, Moore asked anyone he saw—people at theaters, in other cars, on a movie set—if they'd seen the actor. Although Moore's on-camera antics had their roots in his school-play days, it was still unimaginable that the dour-faced Sonic Youth of 1981 would have ever been part of such a project.

For all its outside influence, their punk-humor sensibility also had clear roots in downtown New York of the late '70s and early '80s. Much like conceptual art or hip-hop sampling, the recontexturalizing of pop culture was a way of investing found objects with a new, darker meaning. By that point, David Letterman had been pushing the ironic button for half a decade, but that approach was still fairly new to rock & roll. Sonic Youth were both sincere and sardonic, dour and droll, sometimes at the same time. Just like certain major pop stars, they could be anything to anyone.

At least once, they attempted to fit it all into one piece of music. Toward the end of the *Sister* sessions, they began working on "Master=Dik," their equivalent of collage art: a mishmash recording that blended together Moore's tongue-in-cheek rapping, tape loops using snippets of old Kiss songs (*"Ah know!. . . "* from "Strutter"), layers of effects, and Shelley's drumming. Starting with its title—an inside-joke reference to Masterdisk, the Manhattan studio where albums were mastered for release (and where Moore had briefly worked shortly before Sonic Youth had begun)—the recording was at heart a goofy throwaway. But it also felt true to their longtime interests: their fascination with experimental sound, nonlinear song structures, hip-hop, appropriation, arena rock, and the art of sound.

When "Master=Dik" arrived on a 12-inch single early in 1988, one of the B-sides was a tape of a European show in which the band gave one of its most chaotic performances—and knew it. Ranaldo and Moore made fun of their ineptitude; Shelley, typically determined to be professional, was the most embarrassed. When he heard it, SST's Farrell chuckled to himself. If they could come up with something like that and be so willing to puncture their own image, he thought they were ready for just about anything.

Chapter 6

ROCK BANDS RARELY WANDERED into Greene Street, the basement-level studio on Mercer Street in SoHo. At least, Nicholas Sansano wasn't accustomed to seeing them there. Ever since he'd begun working at Greene Street as one of its in-house engineers, Sansano—a jovial, flat-topped New Jersey kid with wire-rim glasses and a degree from the Berklee College of Music in Boston—often felt he was the only white guy in the room. The studio was a quick walk from the offices of Rush, the hip-hop management company run by Russell Simmons, and many of the firm's clients, including Public Enemy and Run-D.M.C., recorded their layered, sampled, beat-fueled records at Greene Street. As much as any place in the city, the studio was a rap clubhouse.

Then again, the rock band that visited Greene Street to meet with Sansano in the spring of 1988 didn't seem all that typical. As they gathered in an office at the studio, Sansano thought they looked fairly ordinary, far from flamboyant. The guitar player was uncommonly tall, the drummer unusually youthful-looking. In talking with Sansano about the possibility of making an album there, all four seemed to agree on several things: that their previous records hadn't sufficiently captured their dynamics; that they liked to hear and look at each other while recording; and that they preferred to record together and not piece together their records instrument by instrument, as was becoming prevalent.

Yet Sansano also noted how each had a precise, clearly delineated personality. With her unwavering gaze and woman-of-few-words demeanor, Gordon had, he felt, the grand vision of the band, the overall philosophy of what they wanted to do; she also had very particular preferences about how she wanted to record her voice. Inquisitive and questioning, Ranaldo began picking Sansano's brain about the studio's compressors and microphones; he wanted to know how the gear would hold up if they did, in his words, "something crazy." Shelley pointed out that the drums should sound like ones on old Television and Big Star records—and later brought Sansano copies of each to make sure he understood. Moore was harder to pin down; he made off-hand jokes about rock bands, but he was clearly the one, in Sansano's words, "keeping the spirit alive." Sansano had heard of Sonic Youth and had heard *Sister*, which had garnered the warmest reviews of the band's career and was the first of their records reviewed in *Rolling Stone*. But he was far from an expert on college-radio rock and rarely had anything to do with it.

If Sansano knew anything about Sonic Youth, though, it was that they had a fierce, aggressive sound. To give them a taste of what he'd done, he pulled out a vinyl 12-inch single of Public Enemy's "Black Steel in the House of Chaos" and cued it up. After that, he played "It Takes Two," a pumping, frenetically danceable Rob Base and DJ E-Z Rock single he'd mixed. Sansano wasn't sure how they would react, since there was nothing at all hip-hop about Sonic Youth. But as it turned out, they embraced the records. Everyone Sansano spoke with, even rock bands, cited hip-hop as the most musically progressive and forward-thinking genre of the day; compared with the dense, chaotic cluster of a Public Enemy track, even the pioneering hip-hop singles of earlier that decade sounded primitive. During this time, Ranaldo and Moore had also taken a lunch meeting with Rick Rubin, who, during his Def Jam days, had pioneered that very sound. But after telling them he was bored with rap and had grown more interested in pop melodies, Rubin essentially nixed his chances of working with Sonic Youth. Moore understood what the producer was saying but had no interest in going there, at least at that time.

Ultimately, the band decided Greene Street would be home to its next—and most ambitious—record. At $1,000 a day, the studio was costlier than any other place they'd worked, but it had its advantages, including its location, a short walk from where Gordon, Moore, and Ranaldo all lived. (After living in Manhattan and then Brooklyn, Shelley had moved to Hoboken the year before; the last straw arrived when he was mugged in Brooklyn, his glasses knocked off his face and broken.) The fact that Greene Street had once been home to experimental music—Philip Glass had once owned the space—held some mystical appeal as well. The band booked three weeks at Studio A starting in the middle of July, blocking out the room so no one would disrupt the sessions.

To Ray Farrell, the matchup of studio and engineer was encouraging. "The fact that they were using Nick Sansano, and not even *thinking* of using Wharton or their friends to do the same thing all over again, was a major step," he says. "They had a sense of wanting to do something more cohesive and bigger." In typical fashion, they drove up to the studio one day and began dragging out a pile of motley-crew guitars from the back of the van. Then they set everything up in the small, rectangular room, the guitars and amps in a half-circle around Shelley's drums. Sansano immediately noticed that each guitar had a piece of masking tape stuck to its back; the tape listed the name of a particular song and its tuning. The instruments, he says, "looked like a complete pile of junk. It looked like some of them were held together with duct tape—and some of them were." At the same time, he sensed they were very much in control of those instruments.

As Sansano gleaned not long after the meeting, Sonic Youth had a slew of new songs ready to be laid down; the work ethic established years before was still very much in effect. They'd undertaken their most extensive tour yet to promote *Sister*, playing in Europe and the States throughout the summer and fall of 1987. But by early in 1988, they'd already reconvened at their new rehearsal space in Hoboken to begin the arduous process of banging out material for the next project. As usual, Moore brought in a handful of ideas and chord changes, and as per their method, they spent the better part of several months laboring over them, contributing ideas and trying to fashion Moore's starting points into finalized songs. One was what Shelley calls "us trying to do a no-wave song with a half-learned ZZ Top riff," hence the title, "Eliminator Jr.," that played off the name of a Top album. "'Cross the Breeze" and "The Sprawl" were directly inspired by the big, fuzzy guitar sounds J. Mascis was discovering in Dinosaur Jr. (the "Jr." added after a band of San Francisco summer-of-love veterans, called the Dinosaurs, sued the younger musicians).

In the past, the large compositional lumps would be whittled down and sculpted like raw clay, but this time, the paring-down process was actually resulting in *longer* songs. The jams not only expanded (some to almost a half hour) but nearly stayed that way. As if taking a cue from the "Intro" to *Bad Moon Rising*, many of them had casual, lengthy preambles during which the guitars were gracefully picked or strummed. As usual, the band allotted space in the midst of each tune for noise breakdowns. Yet the material had a wide-open, panoramic feel, as if the songs were taking their time to get to where they wanted to go and then revving to full power once they arrived. Friends and fans alike, including former Black Flag frontman Henry Rollins, had been telling the band for years how much they loved hearing them let it fly on stage and that their records never quite captured that wild, roaming aspect of their music. This time, no one would be disappointed. With Moore on a writing spree, it soon became apparent what had to be done: Make a double album.

Although it had thrived during the '60s and '70s, the peak of the classic rock era, the double LP had became a symbol of all that was overstuffed and ponderous about rock: the land of conceptual themes and painfully over-inflated guitar or synthesizer solos. Four years before, the format had been partially redeemed by postpunk; the Minutemen's *Double Nickels on the Dime* and Hüsker Dü's *Zen Arcade*—double records both—had shown how two trios, one from San Pedro and the other from Minneapolis, could take the basics of hardcore and expand on its possibilities with an acoustic ballad here, a Creedence Clearwater Revival cover there. Yet those bands still wrote relatively concise songs and adhered to their punk roots; doing what

Sonic Youth was thinking of attempting was another matter. "The idea of stretching out on songs was kind of a radical thing to do," says Moore. "You didn't *do* a double album. So we decided to just let it flow." They would fashion a punk gesture from an anti-punk one.

Starting with their first EP, the idea of being fully prepared before recording had become a Sonic Youth point of pride; there was work to do and they were ready to do it. But they would also be routinely disappointed with the finished records; they would start playing the songs on tour and realize how much better—harder, tighter, tougher—they sounded onstage. So, once the bulk of these new songs had been worked up, they decided to perform them live and work out the kinks in public.

They did just that starting on June 9 and 10 at Maxwell's in Hoboken, ending with two nights at CBGB on June 23 and 24. The move proved a smart one. At Maxwell's the first night, the initial public performance of the new material, the singing wasn't always in tune, a few of the songs seemed on the verge of collapsing, and the band sounded tentative at times. At CBGB two weeks later, some of the songs still didn't have lyrics (or completed ones), and some didn't have titles; at various sets, Moore randomly introduced songs as "Steve's Sister" and "Waking Up on the Wrong Side of the Bed." But two of the new, interlocking songs, "The Wonder" and "Hyperstation," roared with a new ferocity, the guitars thicker and tighter, the screeching wilder.

Given the amount of preparation, the sessions at Greene Street were largely efficient—what Sansano calls "planned spontaneity." The completed "Teen Age Riot," for instance, was only about ten seconds shorter than the version they'd played during the first show at Maxwell's. Thanks to multiple layers of guitar overdubs (mostly by Ranaldo, still the last to leave every night), the songs grew even more monolithic at times, and many elements were refined. Ranaldo's delivery of a new song called "Hey Joni" was less harried and tense-sounding than at CBGB. At the last minute, Ranaldo brought in a home demo of "Eric's Trip," based on a drug-fueled monologue spouted by actor Eric Emerson in Andy Warhol's film *The Chelsea Girls*. The band learned it quickly, adding a flock-of-seagulls guitar prelude when they realized the song began too abruptly. Over the PA at the last CBGB set, they played a tape of an answering machine message left by Mike Watt, in which Watt chewed out Moore for accidentally tossing a bag of newly purchased cables in a trash can. ("You gotta watch the *mota*!" Watt barks, using slang for pot.) Set to a Moore piano track blanketed by the sound of his guitar amp overloading—such a beautiful and spooky sound when it happened that the band felt it had to be preserved on tape—it became a collage piece called "Providence," the city Watt had been calling from. (Watt wouldn't know about the incorporation of his message into their music until he heard the final album.) Pushing his own gear to the limits, Ranaldo asked Sansano to make sure his guitar was so loud that the needle of the console would be in the red the entire time.

With timing that couldn't have been worse, Greene Street's air conditioning system broke down as a wave of stifling, humid August heat clamped down on the city. Because the studio was a basement with no windows, Sansano asked everyone if they wanted to take a break. (When studio employees brought a bunch of Panasonic fans into the room, Moore playfully scrawled "Youth" next to the brand name.) But no, they wanted to keep working. One of the songs Moore had been singing onstage, "'Cross the Breeze," was ultimately given to Gordon to sing and provide lyrics. To lend the tracks an ambient sound, Sansano would often put microphones in the hallway outside the recording room.

The last few days were the craziest, because Paul Smith had already set up an album mastering date of August 18. Gordon wasn't happy with some of her vocal tracks, but they had no choice but to press on. In a rush to finish, they spent all night at the studio doing a final mix for what became "Trilogy"; Sansano showered at the studio, and the next morning, they all headed directly to Masterdisk in midtown. For what seemed like an astronomical sum—$30,000, what Moore calls "our first non-econo record"—they left the studio with fourteen completed tracks, enough for the double album they craved. Although they were pleased with it, they didn't see it as "our best work or a milestone, or whatever," says Gordon. For Ranaldo, *Sister* felt more groundbreaking. But it was done, and on schedule.

SMITH'S DEADLINE had not been chosen arbitrarily. By the time the sessions had begun, the band's initial infatuation with SST Records had turned to abject disillusionment. "After *Sister*, we felt like we'd made this really great record, and we'd be touring here and Europe and find out that nobody could get it," Ranaldo says. "We were really disappointed; we felt it was going to be more available than it was." (SST's Chuck Dukowski feels differently: "We were able to capitalize on the goodwill generated by *EVOL* to get *Sister* stocked deeper at retail, and we got it on the radio at many more stations.") Further aggravating the relationship between the two parties, the band would receive SST royalty statements but no subsequent checks. It often fell on Shelley to phone the label's so-called accountants—young indie kids who worked for the company—to ask for money. Since he was the only one in the band who still had to hold down a day job, often at restaurants, Shelley was particularly driven to make such calls.

Part of SST's trouble lay with the deluge of product that owner Greg Ginn was dropping on the public. By then, the label was releasing eighty or ninety albums a year, many indulgent and undistinguished and diluting the high standards the label had set for itself years before. SST still had a countercultural looseness about it; one Christmas, Farrell was given the choice of either a cash bonus or a pound of pot, and had to decide which was worth more.

Unfortunately, that unconventional approach could also extend to the label's business side; a cash-flow problem and rickety indie distributors led to a backlog in royalty payments. "The best label just eating *shit* right in front of you," says David Markey, who felt "a lot of creative accounting was going on because the numbers weren't matching up." One of the few times Smith saw Moore drop his guard and sound utterly despairing was when he spoke about the problems with SST; it was as if a dream had been shattered. "SST owes us money,"

Moore ad-libbed at CBGB during one of the new songs, "Hyperstation," adding, "it's really something real funny."

When the band made it clear they didn't want their next album to be handled by SST, Smith sensed a new opportunity. He'd been eager to open an American office for Blast First and, in January 1988, did just that, setting up makeshift digs in Tribeca, near an apartment he'd rented for himself. All Smith had to do was find an American distributor. Enigma wasn't the hippest, most underground-oriented company—it had the Smithereens, the New Jersey power-pop bar band, but it was also home to Stryper, the Christian rock hair-metal act. Still, Enigma worked with the highly regarded British label Mute, was more financially sound than SST, and shared distribution with a major, Capitol. In some strange way, Sonic Youth would be linked with Duran Duran, one of Capitol's star bands.

For the double album they'd just wrapped up, the band agreed to sign only a one-album deal with Enigma. The label wasn't thrilled with the arrangement, since companies preferred to tie up an act for a few records, but the label acquiesced. When Farrell was fired from SST, Smith immediately offered him a job at Blast First, which also added to the appeal of signing up with Blast First in the U.S.; having worked with Farrell for several years, the band had come to trust him.

In October, the finished album, called *Daydream Nation* after a line from "Hyperstation," was released in twenty-two territories, the largest distribution setup to date for a Sonic Youth album. By then, prerelease orders in the U.S. were already at nineteen thousand copies. In a gesture both cheeky and revealing of their deep-seated reverence for rock traditions past, each of the four sides of vinyl had a different symbol on it, a conscious imitation of the quasi-Celtic ones on *Led Zeppelin IV*. The last three songs, "The Wonder," "Hyperstation," and "Eliminator Jr.," were connected via feedback segues to form "Trilogy," the sort of endearingly pretentious gesture associated with prog-rock double LPs from a decade or two before.

Much like an old grand-gesture prog record, something about *Daydream Nation* was big, mysterious, inscrutable. Its austere cover— "Kerze," a Gerhard Richter painting of a candle—also brought to mind the mysterioso monolith incorporated into the artwork of Led Zeppelin's *Presence*. The lyrics were either cryptic or based on obscure references known only to them. "The Sprawl" (title courtesy William Gibson's *Neuromancer*) emerged when Gordon jotted down mumblings of quarreling junkies and hookers around Eldridge Street. ("Fuck you/Are you for sale?/Is 'fuck you' simple enough?") The stories Gordon had heard growing up around Hollywood provided the basis for the leering, casting-couch narrator of "Kissability"; Moore's daily walk from Eldridge to the studio was sketched out in "Hyperstation." The title of "Hey Joni," Ranaldo's lyric about the hardened life of a fictional female character, emerged when Moore made a reference to "Hey Joe," the garage-band standard recorded by Jimi Hendrix, the Byrds, and others; Ranaldo had also become immersed in old Joni Mitchell records.

As in the past, though, the music roared louder than the actual words. The album opened almost quietly, with the sound of Gordon's overlapping voices astride wafting guitars, but when the frenzied riffing of "Teen Age Riot" kicked in, firing up the music, the album never looked back. *Daydream Nation* rarely let up: from the gnashing power chords of "Silver Rocket" and the four-to-the-floor battering of "Eric's Trip" through the chugging muscle of "Total Trash" and the BB-gun beats driving "Kissability," through the last crashing chords in "Trilogy." The music only took a breather during "Providence" (and the moment in "Total Trash" when the guitars turned into hammers).

Moore sang his songs with the straightest voice he'd yet mustered; Gordon delivered her three—"Kissability," "The Sprawl," and "'Cross the Breeze"—in her most authoritative, demanding intonations, grabbing the listeners by the lapels of their shirts. Ranaldo's three vocals revealed the way his interest in melody and singing had evolved; even though "Eric's Trip" had morphed from a quiet solo demo to an unrelenting rocker, it was still relatively straightforward. ("Rain King," over which Ranaldo recited one of his mysterious poems, was one of the only moments when double-album lugubriousness set in.)

The continued use of nonstandard guitar tunings made everything sound a little off, but the album gloriously revealed the way the band was rewiring the rules of rock guitar in other, less obvious ways. As always, the music could veer from the prettiest of idle-strum introductions to the most feverish of freakouts, heard this time in "Candle." During "Silver Rocket," everything stopped and the guitars mutated into an avalanche in disturbingly slow motion: thick staccato riffs bumped up against noise tornadoes. The moment crystallized the way Moore and Ranaldo were revising the way two guitars played off one another in a band: Instead of trading solos back and forth—the way, say, Duane Allman and Dickey Betts had in the early Allman Brothers Band—they were swapping sounds and textures. With those guitars in uncommon unison on almost every track, the album felt like one very long song: an incessantly twisting, turning, mutating vortex.

Although "Teen Age Riot" never mentioned J. Mascis by name, Moore would often say the song was his call for Mascis to run for president in that election year. The song's reference to "stormy weather," though, was more direct, implying the clouds gathering around the country as the Republican Party looked to hold on to the White House in 1988. *Daydream Nation* captured a moment when decay seemed as if it were a permanent part of the national fabric. The characters who populated the songs were either dead or dying, corrupted or stripped of youthful idealism. (Gordon's lyric for "Eliminator Jr." was a veiled retelling of Robert Chambers' so-called "preppy murder" of Jennifer Levin, which exposed the underbelly of the city's yuppie culture of the '80s.) Yet the album was far from despairing; if anything, it was energizing, a call to arms. "It made a statement," Moore says, "that we were ready to take the music where it needs to go."

ONSTAGE, they'd grown accustomed to hearing and seeing many unususal things: someone yelling "Play some fucking noise!" or hurling a broken drumstick back at them, on one occasion hitting Gordon in the forehead. They'd grown to expect rapturous responses when they were good and exasperated faces when they weren't. But as they began playing most of *Daydream Nation* at the Ritz in New York on October

28, they heard something they hadn't quite heard before: a female voice yelling, several times, "I love you, Thurston!"

By then, the *Daydream Nation* world tour was about a month old. To rehearse for it, they'd decamped for Holland, playing the first show there on September 29 before warming up with a series of European dates, including two nights at the Astoria in London. Then they returned to America, where the buzz around the album was building, thanks in part to Enigma's extensive mailing of advance copies to the press. The American tour proper began in Boston, followed by the show at the Ritz, a spacious dance and rock club on East 11th Street in the Village. It was by far the biggest venue they'd played in the city, and by show time all of the 1,400 tickets were gone. The audience was dotted with overly excited aficionados, like the young women professing their love for Moore, and newcomers curious to see what all the fuss was about. But in the roped-off area in the upstairs balcony sat a new type of onlooker: two executives from Atlantic Records, Peter Koepke and Osman Eralp, and another from Geffen, Mark Kates. Steve Ralbovsky, head of A&R at A&M, also may have dropped by.

Shortly after the release of *Bad Moon Rising*, someone at Warner Brothers had called Homestead's Gerard Cosloy and asked for a copy of the album, then called back to say that Cosloy must have mailed the wrong record. In the years since, however, the major (or, at least, larger) labels had gradually begun looking more in the band's direction. During the *EVOL* tour in 1986, the band had met with Daniel Miller, then interested in signing them to his label, Mute, which had a penchant for British electronic and club bands like Erasure and Depeche Mode. In January 1987, Smith and a partner had been approached by EMI with the idea of starting a boutique label that would include Sonic Youth, but the deal eventually fell apart after a change of personnel at EMI.

During that period, Smith would ask the band if they were interested in signing with a corporation, and the notion was so unthinkable they would laugh. They were also more than aware that two of the major stars of the American indie scene of the '80s, Hüsker Dü and the

Replacements, had left their respective indies for Warner-connected labels and the latter had imploded soon after. But Smith also detected a note of genuine interest from Sonic Youth, as if they were also intrigued by the possibility and wanted him to explore any and all options.

By the fall of 1988, the interest was far more tangible. Despite the mass public's frustrating indifference toward a muscularly produced album like the Replacements' *Pleased to Meet Me*, the audience for college-radio rock was clearly expanding; R.E.M., who'd grown more popular with each year, were on the verge of starting their first-ever arena tour. If the genre wasn't the music of the moment, it was, to some, the music of the eventual future. "It was, 'I love this, the people I work with love this, let's just do it and hope there are enough people to buy these records someday,'" says Ralbovsky, who had already signed Soundgarden, a roaring, alt-Zeppelin Seattle band also once on SST, and was on the verge of nabbing Minneapolis' Soul Asylum. "We thought those kind of bands were the future. We didn't have a predetermined ceiling of what this could achieve in terms of commercial success. It was like, 'This is amazing—we have to sign this.'"

Certainly the initial sales reports were promising. On November 15, *Daydream Nation* was No. 1 on the *Rockpool* retail chart of indie record stores; the following day, it was the fourth most-added title on the Gavin radio alternative chart. When it eventually reached No. 1, Farrell called Moore to tell him the news; typically deadpan, Moore replied, "Oh, but it didn't get to zero yet." ("He was embarrassed by that kind of information," Farrell feels.) But the rapturous reviews that greeted the album also made executives sit up and take notice of a band many had ignored for years. *Daydream Nation*, wrote *Rolling Stone*, was "the sound of the New Rock Nation rising"; the album tied for third place in the magazine's annual critics' poll. To *Billboard*, it represented "the supreme fulfillment of Sonic Youth's fullbore technique in rock-song terms." In the U.K., *Q* called it "enthralling noise," *NME* gave it a 10 rating ("the most radical and political album of the year"), and *Record Mirror* called them "the best band in the universe." Whether it was the relative accessibility of *Daydream Nation* or the fact that so many of their peers from the early

'80s had bitten the dust, Sonic Youth were now standing taller than ever in their community.

A media milestone was reached when *Rolling Stone* published a feature on the band, written by esteemed writer Robert Palmer. The morning after the piece hit the newsstands, the phone rang in Smith's New York apartment. On the line was Ahmet Ertegun, the venerable and highly regarded chairman of Atlantic Records, the man who'd worked with everyone from Ray Charles to the Rolling Stones. Smith had no idea how Ertegun had tracked down his number, but he stopped wondering when Ertegun asked if Sonic Youth would be interested in meeting with him.

Neither Smith nor the band dismissed the call out of hand, especially since Enigma wasn't proving to be a substantial improvement over SST. The label's radio department was excited by "Teen Age Riot"—Ranaldo and Moore even made their own video for it, a montage of heroes from Patti Smith to Neil Young, all the clips taken from videos in their home collections—but the executives didn't know how to push it. The label also deemed a nebulous video for "Candle" too alternative. (So did Ray Farrell's dad; when they watched it at home together, he told his son the shot of an upside-down flame didn't make any sense.) Enigma's distribution seemed spottier than SST's as well. Farrell took a meeting with Capitol president Hale Milgrim but left with the sense that the label wasn't interested in applying the same kind of muscle behind the band that it had to the high-flying Smithereens.

In one regard, Milgrim's position was understandable: Sonic Youth's best-selling record to date, *Daydream Nation* sold between fifty thousand and seventy-five thousand copies in its first year, yet that figure was paltry for a corporate label. But the meeting left a bad taste in Farrell's— and the band's—mouths. Two months after the release of *Daydream Nation*, Smith received a memo from Mute, also distributed in the States by Capitol/Enigma, saying there were "problems" with Enigma and that he should "sign nothing without checking with us first."

A telling moment arrived in the fall, when the band was prepping the release of *The Whitey Album*, a full album of sound experimentation and hip-hop beats that had grown out of the Ciccone Youth "Into the Groovey" single. Craving a break from making traditional (for them) records, the band retreated to Wharton Tiers' studio immediately after they arrived home from the *Sister* tour. Excited by hip-hop, they brought along a sampling device and began concocting tracks and sounds right in the studio. What resulted weren't melodies but idiosyncratic drum programs, spatial effects, and layers of samples (everything from a Janet Jackson single to '70s disco hits). "After 'Into the Groovey,'" says Ranaldo, "we thought we would make our *License to Ill*."

Other than some brief, declaratory Moore rhyming on "Tuff Titty Rap" and a hip-hop overhaul of "Making the Nature Scene," the finished *Whitey Album* wasn't, in fact, a Beastie Boys–style record. It was more like sonic collage art: a grab bag of percussive effects tracks, ironic pop-culture jokes (Gordon's deadpan cover version of the Robert Palmer hit "Addicted to Love," set to an intentionally low-rent synth-pop track and filmed for a video at a Macy's make-your-own-video booth), and self-conscious cutesiness (the track "[silence]" was one minute of just that, a tribute to John Cage). "Two Cool Rock Chicks Listening to Neu" featured Gordon and Susanne Sasic, the band's lighting director and good friend, semi-seriously debating whether Gordon should try to manage Dinosaur Jr. or Redd Kross. In structure, length, and seriousness of intent, it couldn't have been more removed from *Daydream Nation*. The only hint of Sonic Youth guitar came halfway through, during a bit of "Third Fig," and the best track—an alluring piano and drum track soundscape called "Macbeth"—sounded nothing like them at all. (If anything, it predated what Moby would do in the following decade.)

The band wanted to release *The Whitey Album* simultaneously with *Daydream Nation*, but Smith and Farrell thought it best to wait a few extra months for the Ciccone Youth side project. They prevailed, but when it came to the cover art, the band's wishes still ruled. They wanted to use a photo of Madonna's face, albeit one so enlarged that only her nose, lips, and telltale facial mole would be seen. Given that Madonna had supposedly given her blessing to "Into the Groovey," the partial use of her image didn't strike them as any kind of issue.

But after the band finished giving an interview at the Blast First offices, label publicist Pat Naylor called them over to her desk. Holding up the artwork, she told them Enigma heads were concerned about copyright infringement and might want to change it.

"They're kidding, right?" Ranaldo said, incredulous.

"Fuck *them*," Gordon snapped. In the end, the cover was not altered.

HAVING BEEN LET DOWN BY SST and now Enigma, Sonic Youth were starting to see the major labels in a very different light. Except for Shelley, who was twenty-seven, they were now in their early to mid thirties. A major label promised not only larger cash advances and far better global distribution but, says Moore, "real straightforward publishing and accounting and a medical plan. It was like working with a really good banking operation in a way."

For his part, Smith liked the idea of finding a corporate home for Blast First; in his mind, Sonic Youth would remain with his label, which, in turn, would be distributed by a major. One night in New York, Smith bought a bottle of wine, went to his apartment, and examined the band's combined worldwide sales figures. He then inflated each one, ending up with an illusory figure of 225,000—the kind of number, he thought, that would make Sonic Youth's record-buying fan base appear larger than it was. An electronic tallying system for the record business had yet to be implemented, so Smith could essentially concoct whatever figure he wanted.

Curious as to which labels would want them and what they could get out of a deal, the band made themselves available to any who came courting. The first were Koepke and Eralp of Atlantic, both working at the label's fledgling "alternative music" subdivision. The department was, in Koepke's words, "a ghetto for all the new breed of artists who didn't sound like Led Zeppelin"—one of the best-selling bands in the label's history—and Sonic Youth fit the bill. By the late '80s, Atlantic was mostly associated with the likes of Genesis, Debbie Gibson, and innumerable hair-metal bands, and while Koepke was more overwhelmed by Sonic Youth's Ritz show than by *Daydream Nation*, he knew what the band could bring to the label: namely, "how groovy we could look by association."

The two men took the band out to dinner and saw four different personalities at work. Moore was, to Koepke, "slightly aloof" and mostly scanned the restaurant; Ranaldo and Shelley were happy to talk about music and record-making. To Koepke, Gordon was the most distant, yet the power center of the band, the one who'd have to be convinced. Koepke felt their self-confidence and their desire for "a big push and perhaps a big check." At the same time, he realized they weren't remotely interested in changing themselves to attain such goals. "It was very clear they weren't going to turn around and start writing hits," Koepke says. "You couldn't have even broached that. They would have looked at you like you were from Mars. They would have known you didn't have a fucking *clue* as to what they were all about."

The band then met Ertegun, happily eating up his oft-told but endlessly entertaining stories about partying with the Stones and driving Billie Holiday home. A&M's Ralbovsky was similarly intrigued; having already signed a distribution deal with Twin/Tone that landed him the Feelies and the Mekons, Ralbovsky was in the process of overhauling a label best known for Peter Frampton, the Carpenters, and the label's cofounder, Herb Alpert. Despite the controlled chaos of Sonic Youth's music and live shows, Ralbovsky, like others in the business, was taken with how adult and centered they seemed. But he too sensed they weren't in any rush to hook up with a major; in fact, the band informed Grabel that if no worthwhile deal was forthcoming, they'd consider making their next record for Enigma.

Other meetings were far more surreal experiences. One day they found themselves in an office at the Sony building facing Tommy Mottola, the label's imposing, slicked-hair president. After marching in with his posse—"these East Coast gangster guys," Gordon recalls—Mottola informed them he was prepared to press a special "star-making" button beneath his desk that would instantly make them famous. The band was quiet during the ensuing conversation, although Smith brought up the issue of creative control when he asked about a Columbia act whose new release had been remixed without his input. On the street in front of the building afterward, Moore turned to Smith—who accompanied them to a few preliminary meetings, even though they were still on his indie label—and, peering down with his bangs falling in his face, said, "At least I know what the devil looks like now."

Equally comical was a dinner at an Italian restaurant in Greenwich Village at which the band and Atlantic reps were joined by Bob Lawton, their new road-work agent. When the band left SST, they also lost the services of the label's tour booking agency. In need of a replacement, they turned to Lawton, a wry, long-haired member of Boston's music scene who moved to New York in the late '80s to start his own agency, the Labor Board.

The label employees schmoozed the band and talked of large sums of money. When one asked if Sonic Youth had a manager, Moore casually gestured toward Lawton and said, "Yeah—*him.*"

Lawton was hoping he would eventually land that job—he was eager to work with the band in a bigger capacity—but it hadn't happened yet; in effect, Sonic Youth still had no one officially overseeing that aspect of their career. But the executives, thinking Lawton was their man, instantly turned to face him—extending their hands, smiling, chatting him up. "No one had so much as mentioned I was at the table," Lawton says. "I don't think anyone had even passed me *bread.*"

The incident was revealing of the curious but alert way the band was welcoming the majors. "They were really cynical about signing with a major label," says Markey. "Thurston even said, 'Oh, we're the next Replacements and Hüsker Dü. We're going to get signed and then get dropped and it's just going to be a mess, but here we go—we're going to go for it and step up.' They were very curious about working within that structure, doing what they do but bringing it into a different arena. They were also cynical about anything happening." To Sansano, they'd wonder if any of these record people had actually heard their records.

Despite the band's wariness toward the scenario—Shelley in particular was the most averse to leaving the world of independent labels—the

189

move to a major seemed increasingly inevitable. In February 1989, the *Village Voice* published its annual Pazz and Jop critics' poll. First place went to Public Enemy's *It Takes a Nation of Millions to Hold Us Back*, followed by *Daydream Nation*. In his A&M office, Ralbovsky saw the *Voice* poll and realized all the publicity wouldn't help his chances; everyone in his business would now know who Sonic Youth were.

One night at Greene Street, Sansano encountered Arif Mardin, then vice president of Atlantic and a revered pop and R&B producer. To Sansano's surprise, Mardin congratulated Sansano on the success of *Daydream Nation*. "It was so odd," Sansano says. "It was, 'Wait a minute—*Arif Mardin* is coming in to congratulate *me* on my work with a band he has *no* musical connection with whatsoever.' It was one of those moments where you're thinking, 'Man, this is a screwy business.'" On a legal pad on his desk, Grabel began jotting down the names of interested parties, a list that grew to twenty record companies. Grabel didn't know there *were* twenty record companies.

As CRITICAL ACCEPTANCE and industry interest began swirling around them, the *Daydream Nation* tour continued into the spring. With Lawton booking the shows, they made the jump to larger clubs and occasional theaters, their per-show guarantee leaping to $2,000 a night, sometimes double. "I thought, 'Holy shit, I didn't know you could *make* that much money playing music on the underground circuit,'" says Mark Arm, whose new, post–Green River band, Mudhoney, was one of Sonic Youth's opening acts. Mudhoney was supposed to be paid $200 a show, but on nights when they made only half that amount, Sonic Youth regularly chipped in the rest.

Other than the offices of people like Ertegun and Mottola, *Daydream Nation* was taking the band to places they'd never ventured, including the Soviet Union. With the help of the country's ministry of culture, they'd been invited to play a series of shows in February in Leningrad, Moscow, Vilnius, and Kiev. No one, including the band and Ray Farrell, knew what to expect when they flew into Moscow on

February 4, and the performances were indeed an odd lot: The gigs were in hotel basements or college dorms, the sound systems often not much more than a rigged-up stereo system. The crowds were euphoric, jaded, or perplexed; at one show, sound man Terry Pearson watched a group of Soviet dignitaries and KGB agents arrive in their suits and then, as the show progressed, recede further back in the hall and then outside. The band traveled by way of rackety, chugging trains and, when they found someplace to eat, would wait hours for some "weird mystery meat," Gordon recalls, to eventually be placed before them. ("We felt like we were being held captive," she says.) They felt like they were in a third-world country, complete with bootleg copies of *Daydream Nation* (and homemade photos of candles for makeshift covers).

Yet even there, they left an impression. Eugene Hütz, a sixteen-year-old student in Kiev, Russia, had never heard of Sonic Youth, but he and his friends routinely went to the dorm at the Institute of Aviation to see whatever local or national band was performing there. One day, they heard an American "metal" band called Sonic Youth would be playing. Attending the show, they saw a pile of guitars on the stage that looked like "a pile of chopped wood," Hütz recalls. When the band came out, they blasted through the *Daydream Nation* songs so loudly that the bones in Hütz's body rattled. Every five minutes he had to walk out to restore his "sense of well being," he recalls. "I couldn't take it, but it was so amazing." Afterward, he tracked down a bootleg of the *Sonic Youth* EP.

When they returned to New York in April, following another round of British and European shows, they had to grapple with not only the major-label decision but their arrangement with Smith. By the late spring of 1989, the band's relationship with their British and now American label head—in Grabel's terms, "a trusted advisor but never a manager"—was growing increasingly sour. The first serious crack in the association had occurred nearly three years before when, at the Eldridge Street apartment, Moore received a call from a friend congratulating him on Sonic Youth's new album. Since *EVOL* had been recorded but not yet released, Moore was confused. The friend went on to describe a two-LP live set called *The Walls Have Ears*: one side of concert recordings featuring Bob Bert on drums, the other with Shelley. Moore—and the rest of the band soon after—was even more baffled when they heard it was distributed by Rough Trade, home to Blast First.

According to Smith, the idea for a live Sonic Youth album came in part from the band; they'd discussed releasing a collection of concert recordings but had never found the time to compile it. Like many of their fans—and sometimes the band itself—Smith was astonished by how much brawnier and more potent the songs sounded live (particularly "Expressway to Yr Skull") and felt those moments should be preserved. In what he saw as a gift to the band—they made so little money on the road and often returned to the States without much to show for it beyond a thicker press kit—Smith took it upon himself to fashion two records' worth of live tapes. He gave it a title, pressed up two thousand limited-edition copies for Rough Trade to distribute, and planned to send the band a bunch of copies and a small wad of money.

Never known for relinquishing involvement in their work, fiercely protective of their image and recordings, Sonic Youth did not quite see *The Walls Have Ears* as any sort of gift or blessing. "Our creative-control thing was put on the spot by this guy," says Moore. "We were kinda livid. Maybe it was a British-label thing: 'We'll do what's best for you.' But how could he not know the band would be upset by that?" Shelley, who had joined the band only the year before, immediately asked why they were trusting Smith, especially since SST was equally put off by a "new" album arriving right before the launch of *EVOL*. "Sonic Youth weren't about sitting back and letting someone dictate what they should do," says Pat Naylor. "They wanted to be involved in every aspect and Paul likes to be creative. It was a roller-coaster relationship."

In retrospect, Smith admits he "overstepped my boundaries" by releasing the record. But even after apologies and lessening of tensions, and even after the album received a laudatory plug in *Rolling Stone*, relations between the two parties continued to fray. When Blast First published a *Whitey Album* ad in the U.K. with the tagline "gives good head," Ranaldo sent a fax to the Blast First office with a sharp riposte:

"We don't want our band used for your little in-jokes, band consensus." Always the band member who kept the most track of finances, Ranaldo in particular was concerned with what he calls "a lot of shoddiness to the accounting that would leave us scratching our heads. Maybe it was justified and maybe it wasn't."

For Smith, dealing with the band became something of a high-wire act. He often felt they wanted to be left alone, yet sensed they were offended if he ignored them too much. Smith and Gordon had an especially complex rapport: His brash personality and her inward one refused to mesh. Yet by his own admission, Smith was not always in the habit of being in constant communication with his acts: "If I don't have any useful information for them, or anything to say, then I can't do anything until I have something useful for them. All through my life I've gotten into tangles with people for this very reason." For a band that wanted regular updates, Smith's absences were glaring. There was, Gordon says, an "inconsistency about Paul. He was either in the picture or out of the picture."

During the long *Daydream Nation* tour, the situation only worsened. Smith flew to Charlotte, North Carolina, for a meeting, the band sullen and uncommunicative. "They had some good times together, but it became more difficult with Paul and the band," says Naylor. "The fallings-out got more frequent." During initial talks with the major labels, Smith often took an aggressive, blustery stance with the interested parties. For Smith, it was all about his confidence in the band: "I thought a major would be *lucky* to have the Youth. They had the feeling they were lucky if a major signed *them*. If that's arrogance on my part, then I suppose I was guilty of it." To the band, though, his stance had the potential of turning off potential suitors, another sign of their conflicted feelings about crossing over to the big leagues.

Something had to give, and it finally did on June 2, 1989, when the band went to Smith's apartment, ostensibly to discuss another video for *Daydream Nation*. To Smith's surprise, the four of them were accompanied by Lawton. After awkward small talk about the major-label get-togethers to date, the band grew quiet until Lawton was forced to state the real intention: The band didn't want to continue working with Smith. "It just went 'round and 'round and I thought, 'Okay, we could be here all day, and he's not getting it,'" recalls Lawton. "So I had to be the guy, because none of them could say to Paul, 'It's over.' Kinda bad scene."

Smith looked over and the four of them were, he recalls, "looking at every corner of the room" except in his direction. In another indication of the way in which he tended to avoid conflict, Moore was either asleep on one side of the couch or pretending to be. ("If Thurston really doesn't want to talk to you, he pretends to be falling asleep," Farrell says he learned.) Since the band didn't have a contract with him and the Blast First deal was album to album, Smith had no choice—legal or otherwise—but to accept the situation. Devastated, he told his staff he was leaving for a lost weekend.

In the end, Moore, Gordon, and Shelley were the least sentimental about the break with Smith, Ranaldo the most. ("He did more than anyone to bring us to that point, and then right at the point of the payoff, he got the boot," Ranaldo says. "It was kind of a sad situation.") But the group democratic approach ruled. After the meeting, Ranaldo, always the closest in the band to Smith, called to say he was sorry things had gone down that way. With a corporate home a real possibility and so many of the leading independent labels beginning to wither, the firing was another sign that the first phase of the band's career was coming to an end.

THE BAND HAVING DIVESTED ITSELF of Paul Smith, it was left to Grabel to field offers from the majors and negotiate on their behalf. As in the past, timing worked in their favor. By 1989, Grabel had moved on to a larger and more dominant law firm, Grubman, Indursky & Schindler, which finagled lucrative contracts for the likes of Billy Joel and Bruce Springsteen. By summer, the once-long list of labels on Grabel's desk had shrunk to three: A&M at the top (even though Ralbovsky hadn't made an actual offer), followed by Atlantic and, a distant third, Mute.

Unexpectedly, another interested party came to the table. After catching the band's show at the Ritz, Geffen college-radio promotion man Mark Kates saw the band's music—and individual personalities—at work. Growing up in the Boston area, Kates had been drawn to singer-songwriter bands like the Eagles and had seen every show he could by local heroes J. Geils. But after hearing the Clash and, mostly, Mission of Burma, Kates had no further use for what he called "hippie-type shit" and became a postpunk enthusiast. Genial and ebullient, he'd gone on to work at his college radio station and two indie labels before moving on to Geffen. Through Lawton, an acquaintance from their mutual time in Boston, Kates heard the band was considering the upgrade to a major label. If he wanted to lure any act to his label, Sonic Youth was the one, and he alerted Geffen A&R executive Gary Gersh, who already seemed aware of them as well. Flying to New York, Gersh—a polished industry veteran—walked into Grabel's office and announced he was going to be the person to sign Sonic Youth to Geffen Records.

Thanks to his role in launching the careers of everyone from Laura Nyro and Crosby, Stills & Nash to the Eagles and Jackson Browne, David Geffen was both a rock kingmaker and one of its most cunning and savviest businessmen. In 1980, after he'd sold his Asylum label and went into a temporary retirement following a cancer scare, Geffen returned, launching a new company named after himself. After a bumpy start, Geffen Records had established itself by decade's end as the home of Guns N' Roses, Whitesnake, Aerosmith, and Cher, whose careers had either been launched or reignited by the label. Few of those records were played in the respective homes of Sonic Youth, but as people captivated by pop culture and rock legends, the band saw Geffen himself an object of fascination. Here was someone who'd signed Tom Waits, dated Cher, and dealt with Neil Young's musical lurches. Geffen Records also had a unique business structure: Although it was distributed and part owned by Warner Brothers, it was essentially autonomous, with a small roster and a hip-boutique image. "It seemed like completely the *wrong* thing to do," says Moore. "But the reality of Geffen was, 'Wait a minute—they have no affiliations with any of these corporations at all.' I felt we'd be much more autonomous there and do our thing and utilize their distribution."

Ready to make a move, A&M offered to fly the band to L.A. to see a Dinosaur Jr. and Redd Kross show and take additional meetings. During a tour of the label's famous studios, A&M cofounder (and recording act himself) Herb Alpert popped in, said hello, and, in another unreal moment, pulled out his trumpet and played a cappella for them. Although no one at A&M knew, Grabel also suggested the band visit Geffen headquarters, essentially on A&M's tab. At the company's informal offices on Sunset Boulevard, they even wound up in a conversation with David Geffen himself. "He didn't pretend to know our music really well," says Ranaldo, "but as the president, he knew he had to put in an appearance." During the conversation, the band brought up one of Geffen's most controversial moves: suing Neil Young for releasing what Geffen deemed commercially unviable records. If anyone would do that, Shelley thought, it would be Sonic Youth. Geffen tut-tutted, saying he and Young were still close. As a Tom Waits fan, Shelley was also taken aback by Geffen's dismissive attitude toward the low-selling albums Waits had made for Geffen's Asylum label in the '70s.

"It was a double-edged sword," Gordon says. "There was history, but at the same time, not *good* history."

The band also had concerns about Gersh, particularly his reputation for spending considerable amounts of money making albums, which clashed with Sonic Youth's frugal approach. Yet the band liked Gersh personally, and Gersh seemed to admire their music. Even one of his previous associations, helping run the Grateful Dead's self-run label in the '70s, intrigued them, since they were newly respectful of the Dead's business model: modest record sales but a loyal fan base, creative autonomy, and longevity. Gersh smoothed over many of their concerns about David Geffen, and they learned that Kates, who was practically drooling at the idea of the band signing to the label, would also work closely with them. "Somehow we thought Geffen had a little more realistic take on who we were and what might happen with us," says Ranaldo. "Some of the others, we didn't feel like they had *any* inkling of what we were about."

With Grabel's encouragement ("He said, 'you need to be on a label that's hot,'" says Gordon), the band gave the go-ahead for negotiations to begin, which they did in the summer of 1989. (It didn't hurt that Grabel's law firm had also worked with Geffen in the past.) Although Geffen executives weren't aware of it at the time, neither Atlantic nor A&M had actually placed any money on the table. At staff meetings, Atlantic president Doug Morris appeared apathetic about signing the band. When A&M's Ralbovsky heard Geffen was in the picture, he assumed his rival would win out. Nonetheless, Grabel implied to Gersh and Kates that other deals were in the works and that Geffen should step up to the plate. Desperate to convince the band to move to Geffen, and fully aware of their Madonna jones, the garrulous Kates cobbled together a box of Madonna promotional posters and goodies and sent them to the band: "We turned on all the burners."

The gambit paid off. The first draft of a Geffen contract flew back and forth between Grabel and the label, with various paragraphs added and deleted, until all agreed upon the final version: a deal for five albums, estimated at roughly $300,000. Standard for such a deal, the label would own the master tapes of the records, but the band would retain control over the music and artwork. (According to Grabel, Gersh initially said the label wouldn't be able to accommodate creative control, but acquiesced after Grabel implied the band would back out if they didn't get it.) The records were grouped together: If the label accepted the first, they would have to release the second; if they released the third, the fourth would be put out with no questions, and so on. For all the band's concerns, Grabel recalls "a lot of happy faces" with the final contract. To make the move even more comforting, Geffen also hired Farrell, with whom the band had worked at both SST and Blast First, to help with promotion and marketing.

Along with many of their friends in their community, Pussy Galore's Julie Cafritz—who, despite her initial qualms, had become one of Gordon's closest friends—watched the negotiations unfold. Although they ended with Sonic Youth sharing a record company with Steven Tyler, Axl Rose, and Cher, the news made a certain amount of sense. "If you were going to sign a band from that scene, it made sense they would be the ones," she says. Hanging out with some of the band at CBGB that fall, Cafritz saw Grabel rush in with the latest version of the contract for the band to read over. "I was just thinking, 'Wow, now there are managers and entertainment lawyers and big contracts you had to negotiate,'" she recalls. "And with real money attached to them and consequences and things you couldn't get out of."

Were they being welcomed by a new, more accepting world, or was the world moving in their direction? At that moment, it was hard to tell. When the deal was finalized, Gordon called Kates and, in an even-toned voice, gave him the news. She also told him the next band the label had to sign was a group from Seattle called Nirvana; she and Moore were listening to their Sub Pop debut, *Bleach*, all the time. "We've a new larger more uneducated audience to attend to," Ranaldo wrote in his journal on July 4, 1989. "Who knows what will happen but it'll be different than playing for your friends."

PART 2

INFILTRATION

Chapter 7

THE CALLS BEGAN ARRIVING early on Eldridge Street, rousing them from their mattress on the floor in the back room. During Moore's childhood trips to the fallow Alabama plantation where his grandparents lived, Doc Adams had nicknamed him Slug, since the kid didn't move very fast, especially in the morning. Little had changed in the two decades since, but the voice on the other end of the line didn't know; there was work to do, and decisions to be made. The voice was asking them to consider touring with a superstar band, raising the ticket prices for their shows, or any number of other proposals intended to move Sonic Youth, a band now signed to Geffen Records, forward in the marketplace.

The voice belonged to Jim Grant, who, with his partner, a lawyer named Roger Cramer, had become the band's first official managers. With the Geffen deal wrapped up, a professional business organization was now in order; Ranaldo couldn't continue collecting cash and keeping track of receipts at the end of their shows. "We felt like we had to have a manager," says Gordon, "because who wants to deal with all that bureaucracy?" During the major-label meetings during the spring and summer of 1989, Bob Lawton thought he might be taking on that role; certainly he was willing to, although the band hadn't made up its collective mind on the matter. Lawton himself mentioned the possibility to one Geffen executive, who told him Lawton stood to make a good deal of money if he took the job. But the executive mustn't have been overly impressed with Lawton, or was perhaps concerned about his lack of a managerial background. Soon after, the label strongly suggested the band hire an experienced handler.

Either through Gersh or their lawyer, Richard Grabel (or both), Grant and Cramer entered the picture. In theory, the combination seemed logical. Their most prominent client at the time, Living Colour, had graduated from downtown Manhattan clubs to an opening-act slot on the Rolling Stones' *Steel Wheels* tour in 1989, and its debut album was on its way to platinum. Living Colour had made that transition with a brand of headbangers-ball pop-metal that made Sonic Youth's music seem even artier than it was, but the band was initially game. "We didn't have much sense of what we needed in a manager," says Ranaldo. "But they seemed like they knew how to interface with a label, since they were doing a lot of that with Living Colour."

To complicate matters, even the label wasn't the one they thought they'd signed with. As the band soon discovered, they wouldn't be on Geffen proper but a newly launched sibling company. David Geffen had wanted to call it Asylum, resurrecting the name of his old '70s company, but legalities prevented him from doing so; at the last minute, the label was instead called DGC, for David Geffen Company. Not everyone was wild about the clunky name or the toppling-letter logo; some Geffen employees began belittling the offshoot, saying the initials stood instead for "Dumping Ground Company." ("We thought, people are going to laugh at us," says Kates. "We were bummed.") DGC even had its own offices, a bungalow behind the main Geffen building on Sunset Boulevard.

In the midst of hiring a manager and getting their first dose of major-label politics, the band also found time to start prepping for its Geffen debut. Several factors distinguished the nearly dozen songs that emerged from woodshedding in their Hoboken rehearsal space. The new compositions had far more pointed pop culture references. Along with his usual slew of basic ideas, Moore brought in a previously unrecorded instrumental from the band's early quasi-hardcore phase; it was later retitled "Mildred Pierce" after the Joan Crawford movie. (The song was resurrected when Moore joined his friend David Markey in a series of one-off shows with Markey's jokey punk cover band Tusk, and the band needed something to play.)

One particularly long and curving instrumental piece became the basis for "Tunic (Song for Karen)," Gordon's eulogy for Karen Carpenter. As was the vogue, Gordon came to hear in Carpenter's voice more soul and sorrow than most people first thought. Just as important, she came to see Carpenter, who'd died of anorexia six years before, as a "victim of society, and how a lot of women feel that the only control they have over their lives is their body. In her case it was not feeling good about her body and wanting to disappear. It seemed to go against sensuality, or being a woman." Carpenter was a perfect vehicle for Gordon's take on feminism and dominant males, of which Karen's brother Richard was clearly one. In a small way, Gordon also related to Carpenter's use of food to express herself: Since cooking was an important part of the Gordon family in Los Angeles, Gordon would express dissatisfaction at dinnertime by refusing to eat her father's well-prepared meals.

"Tunic (Song for Karen)" wasn't the only song they wrote about celebrity and the people who navigated their way through it. Moore's lyric to "Dirty Boots" referred to the taxing touring life. The previous year, Gordon had interviewed LL Cool J for *Spin*, only to discover that the object of her fascination wasn't as hip as she thought; his favorite rock bands were the less chic likes of Bon Jovi, he was a fan of misogynistic comic Andrew Dice Clay, and he'd never heard of hardcore or Iggy Pop. (When she filled him in on the Stooges, the rapper just replied, "I like Bon Jovi.") The encounter became the basis for "DV2," later renamed "Kool Thing," in which Gordon alluded to the interview by making reference to "walking like a panther" (an LL album title). Sonic Youth weren't stars and perhaps never would be, but the new songs suggested they were already thinking about the way in which fame could undo and corrupt pop stars and rappers alike.

Unlike those on *Daydream*, the new songs were even more precisely worked out (almost all had finished lyrics), and a few were shorter, in part as a reaction to the unremitting touring behind that album. "It actually *wasn't* as much fun playing the songs live," says Gordon of the *Daydream* performances, which consisted largely of the songs from that album. "By the end of the tour, I was so sick of those songs. It felt like Led Zeppelin during their last period—just overblown and *too long*." Once the material was in more or less completed form—they also made room for experiments like the instrumental "Tuff Boyz," in which the guitars sounded as if they were sawing into steel beams—they began recording demos at Waterworks, a studio on 14th Street.

The fact that the band was laying down early versions of the songs was also significant. In contracts, some labels would demand to hear demos as a way of keeping tabs on an album's progress; certain contracts even specified that a label had approval over a producer. Sonic Youth's Geffen contact had no such stipulation, but the band cut the rough tracks anyway. They wanted the people at DGC to know what they would be working with, and they wanted to have a firm handle on the material once they began finalizing it in a larger, even more high-end studio.

When it came to deciding who would oversee the album, Gary Gersh, their A&R man, had several ideas. With his Rolodex full of industry connections, Gersh began presenting the band with names of high-profile producers, focusing especially on Daniel Lanois. Best known at the time for his work on U2's *The Joshua Tree* and *The Unforgettable Fire* and Peter Gabriel's *So*, Lanois had also collaborated with another close Gersh friend, the Band's Robbie Robertson. The Lanois sound was panoramic, airy and spacious—as Gordon says, "a little too soft for us." Lanois' real test came, though, when the band traveled uptown to Rockefeller Center to tape an appearance on NBC's new series, *Night Music*. Hosted by jazz saxophonist David Sanborn and organized by Hal Willner, the eclectic record producer and *Saturday Night Live* music coordinator, *Night Music* was willfully diverse: Anyone tuning in might see Leonard Cohen, Nick Cave, the Residents, Conway Twitty, and other far-from-prime-time players. One episode of the show's second season continued that legacy. In addition to Sonic Youth, whom Willner had discovered with *Daydream Nation*, the show featured Lanois (then promoting his first solo album), the Indigo Girls, and shrieky experimental artist Diamanda Galas.

The lineup was *too* wide-ranging for some staffers, who, in a meeting, demanded the Indigo Girls receive more screen time than the others. During Sonic Youth's rehearsals, it was the camera crew's turn to object: The music was so amplified they threatened to film from the back of the theater unless the volume was lowered. After adjustments were made, the taping began. For what amounted to their network television, debut, Sonic Youth performed a jittery, jumpy "Silver Rocket," Ranaldo and Moore almost colliding during the song's midsong explosion.

For the episode's finale, everyone except Galas gathered onstage to stomp out "I Wanna Be Your Dog." The old Stooges song had become a regular part of Sonic Youth's live repertoire, especially during encores, when they would invite anyone from Mudhoney's Mark Arm to Iggy Pop himself onstage to sing it with them. But this assemblage was the most bizarre of the bunch. It was hard to imagine a more unusual sight than Sonic Youth flanked by Sanborn, the Indigo Girls, and Hiram Bullock, the series' house-band guitar player (best known as the original guitarist on David Letterman's NBC show).

Also joining in was Don Fleming, a Georgia-born guitarist and singer who'd befriended Moore and Gordon after he'd moved to New York and was playing in bands like BALL and the Velvet Monkeys. With his height and laconic demeanor, Fleming could have easily passed for Moore's brother, and the two became comrades in mayhem. Fleming was one of many friends who had long, involved conversations with the couple about the move to Geffen or a similar company. "They weren't too sure if it was a great idea or not," says Fleming, "and they were really worried about selling out. But they didn't have a great record deal [with Enigma] and they were struggling. They were frustrated on various levels. They weren't sure how to take it to the next stage. But this was their attempt."

Obsessed with wreaking a bit of havoc at the taping, Fleming brought along a toy plastic whistle for the "I Wanna Be Your Dog" jam. During Sanborn's sax solo, Fleming ran over and began playing in unison. If that wasn't a strange enough spectacle, Fleming then decided to see if woodwinds could feed back and began smashing the whistle into an amplifier. "I was like, 'What the fuck?'" Sanborn recalls. "But it was kind of funny. Weird theater."

To Moore, the moment was "fucking beautiful." The last gesture, though, would be saved for Lanois. As the closing credits rolled, Moore grabbed a hedge clipper, ran over to Lanois, and cut the strings on his guitar. To Moore, the reason was simple—"I thought it would look fucking cool on TV"—but in some ways it was a test, as Moore admits: "I think we were looking to see if he could actually ride out something like that." ("The group version of us can be mean sometimes," Shelley says.) Whether Lanois knew the stunt was in the works remains unclear. Lanois, eager to work with the band because he felt "when feedback is musical, it's fantastic," says Moore warned him beforehand that the hedge clippers would appear during the jam. Yet few at Geffen recall Lanois' name coming up again. The band insisted on producing the album themselves, again with Nicholas Sansano on board as their engineer, and the label—for the moment—approved.

FOR ONCE, they had a sizable budget at their disposal, and despite their fiscally conservative instincts, they weren't averse to using some of it. At Sansano's recommendation, they began recording their Geffen debut at Sorcerer Sound, a downtown studio favored by Television's Tom Verlaine. After working on *Daydream Nation*, Sansano knew very well that the band, Ranaldo in particular, loved to pile on guitar and effects overdubs. At Sorcerer, which had a ceiling so high it had a catwalk, Sansano linked together two 24-track recording machines, which would allow for as many layers and instruments as the band desired. J. Mascis, who'd been enlisted by Moore and Gordon to help out with the demos and then the actual recording, convinced a wary Shelley to buy a larger, more expensive drum kit.

As a way to vary his own contributions, Shelley had begun incorporating maracas into his playing. ("They're doing all these weird things to their guitars," he says. "Not a whole lot you can do to drums! I wish I had electricity and ampage. It's hard to compete with some of those things.") One day, Shelley and Sansano visited an instrument store in Times Square to rent additional percussion devices, ultimately choosing a tympani. But when the large drum arrived at Sorcerer, it was so bulky they weren't able to take it out of the freight elevator. Having no choice, they left it where it was, Shelley banging on the drum in the large, dank service elevator.

As amusing as the story was, it was also revealing of the way matters in the studio quickly grew out of hand during the first few months of 1990. Although the songs were well mapped out, structurally and lyrically, Sansano and the band tried all manner of different, more elaborate techniques: hanging microphones from the catwalk, isolating Shelley in a drum booth. "All of a sudden, you're in a big room and you want to get that big sound," says Shelley, "and you want to do what Jimmy Page did with ambient mics." Adds Moore, "It was like a fantasy. Imagine bands like this making records with that sound. Imagine this kind of music being produced like an Aerosmith record. What would it sound like?"

Yet little seemed to be going right: Guitar strings would break, wrong chords would be struck. "It took us forever to get final takes," Ranaldo says. "Something would inevitably go wrong for *somebody* and we'd have to start again. I remember getting fairly frustrated with it." Before the sessions began, David Markey was told the band might want him to film them for a making-of-the-album documentary; Markey thought he had the ingredients for a film not unlike Jean-Luc Godard's *One Plus One*, which chronicled the creation of the Stones' "Sympathy for the Devil." But when the recording proved more troublesome than imagined, the idea was scotched before Markey even had a chance to buy a plane ticket from Los Angeles.

Once the basic tracks were finally completed, Sansano and the band returned to Greene Street, Sansano's home base, to continue work on the songs and begin the all-important process of mixing the record. What should have been the final lap, though, proved to be an endurance run. Layers upon layers of additional guitars were piled on; vocals were tricked up with megaphones and other distortion devices, particularly on "Mary-Christ." As with the earlier "Hey Joni," another Ranaldo song, "Mote," seemed to begin too abruptly, so the band cut up a bunch of tapes, spliced them back together, and created an audio collage to open the song. At one point, Moore's amp began overheating, heaving, and finally blowing up, and what Sansano calls "an ungodly sound" began emitting from it—a sound nonetheless so fascinating that, as with "Providence," they decided to record it. The result was "Scooter + Jinx," as well as a blown fuse that crashed the building's electrical circuits.

Also ensconced at Greene Street were Public Enemy, working on what would become *Fear of a Black Planet*. It would have been hard to imagine two hipper New York acts of the moment, and it was even harder to imagine all of them, complete with Public Enemy's large posse, sharing space in the small lobby shared by both of Greene Street's recording rooms. But each party was well aware of the other, and the mutual respect was apparent when Gordon and Moore came up with the idea of having Chuck D., Public Enemy's brimstone-voiced frontman, add a part to "Kool Thing." After they broached the subject to him and he seemed amenable, Sansano made it happen. Sitting down with his pad, Chuck D. knocked out a few lines—mostly declaratory comments like "Word up!" and "Fear, baby!"—and recorded his part in five minutes.

For additional support, Moore and Gordon asked not only Mascis but Fleming to help out: Mascis, who'd started his career as a drummer, would consult on the percussion sounds, and Fleming, who had an ear for harmonies and tuneful singing, would aid Moore and Gordon in laying down their vocal parts. "Everyone was nervous," Fleming says. "They were delivering this thing to a major label. So they wanted to have a certain buffer around them, people they knew well who they could turn to and say, 'Is this working?'"

Yet even the buffer created unwanted stress. Starting with the way the label tried to steer the band away from using him, Sansano felt pressure to prove himself, and the fact that Sansano found himself dealing with new, hands-on managers Grant and Cramer (rather than calling the band directly, as he was used to doing) didn't calm his nerves. "All of a sudden, everything had to be codified and formalized," Sansano says. "It went cold turkey from this seat-of-the-pants, grass-roots operation that was really quite efficient to this mega-formalized situation that was a bit unnecessarily confrontational. I felt a distance from the band."

The presence of Mascis and Fleming confounded him as well. Sansano loved Mascis' dry, deadpan wit, but he couldn't figure out exactly what the two extra hands were supposed to be doing. Ranaldo and Shelley were equally unnerved; they weren't accustomed to anyone other than the four band members having input. "It was the first time we were bringing in people other than engineers," says Ranaldo. "And it was bound to bring up certain levels of discomfort."

Sansano himself wasn't sure on the final direction of the album: He felt some band members wanted it to sound radio-friendly and polished but others didn't, and it was often hard to tell who wanted what on any given day. "It was arduous," says Gordon. "It was hard to tell what the record sounded like." At times, Fleming would look toward the control room and see the four of them circling Sansano, each offering a different take on how a song should sound. "I always felt, 'My God, what a position to be in,' because there's no one perfect answer," Fleming recalls. "I felt really bad for Nick. He'd be sitting there and have four completely different opinions being thrown at him, almost all the time, every step of the way."

Flying in from Los Angeles, Gersh popped into the sessions now and then, listening to the rough tapes (and, to Sansano's dissatisfaction, not saying much) and taking the band out to dinner. It was becoming apparent to everyone that the album was veering out of control. "They were using people they trusted," says Ray Farrell, who heard reports filter back to his L.A. office, "but it was getting perhaps a little brighter and more embellished than they'd imagined. By the time it was finished, they were going, 'What did we just *do*?'" Finally, Gersh had a solution: Hire Ron Saint Germain, who helped put a sonic-rush gloss over records by everyone from metal bands to the Bad Brains. Feeling he no longer had the band's confidence, Sansano agreed to leave the project, but was so hurt by his firing that he didn't speak with the band for several years.

As demonstrated by the running suit he wore to the studio, Saint Germain wasn't the band's breed of coworker, but they went along with the decision. By the time the album was done, costs had risen to over $150,000, five times the price tag of *Daydream Nation*. For such a cost-conscious band, the figure was particularly galling. "It was our fault," Shelley says. "It just got out of hand. We should have just released the demos. It would have saved us a lot of money." Talking about the record later with her friend Tony Oursler, Gordon seemed particularly dejected. "That's not us, that's not Sonic Youth," she told him. Later, she told a friend that when she heard the final mixes, she started crying.

THEY WERE FAIRLY SURE they hadn't sold their souls—even with Saint Germain's mixes, the finished album hardly sounded like any of the leading mainstream rock bands of the time, like Poison or Mötley Crüe—but they couldn't be certain. Everything was coming at them from all sides. In early 1990, David Geffen sold his company to MCA; suddenly, Geffen Records was not quite the boutique mini-major it had been but part of an engulf-and-devour corporation. With a release date for the record in sight, Gordon began mocking up a cover. Taking its cue from "Mildred Pierce," it would be based around a black-and-white drawing of Joan Crawford by Raymond Pettibon. The younger brother of SST founder Gregg Ginn, Pettibon specialized in black-ink drawings that felt like cells taken randomly from comic strips, yet worked on their own. In an article for *Artforum* in 1985, Gordon praised Pettibon's work as "statements unto themselves" that "feed off the simplistic morals of made-for-TV movies, which center around 'contemporary' questions."

To road-test the creative-control aspect of their contract, they wanted to call the album *Blowjob?* To the disappointment of Ranaldo in particular, the title was changed to *Goo*, from one of the songs ("My Friend Goo"). Instead of the Crawford shot, the band chose another Pettibon drawing: an illustration of two sunglass-sporting British mods, based on an actual photograph connected to the "Moor Murders" in '60s England, which involved the grisly killings of five children. Very much in his comic-panel style, Pettibon wrote, alongside the piece: "I stole my sister's boyfriend. It was all whirlwind, heat, and flash. Within a week, we killed my parents and hit the road."

Whichever Pettibon painting was used, the decision to feature his work was largely aesthetic: Pettibon came from their world and reflected their sensibility. He'd drawn early album covers for Black Flag, had his work published by SST's book division, and even went through his own Charles Manson phase. Like them, he was drawn to the banality of pop culture for the twisted messages that lay beneath it. He even inspired two of the new songs. "My Friend Goo" took its cue from *Sir Drone*, an hour-long video Pettibon wrote and directed starring Mike Watt and fellow artist Mike Kelley (another old friend of Gordon's) as L.A. teenagers starting a punk band; Scooter and Jinx were characters in that same film. But the use of Pettibon's painting was also a self-conscious move meant to assure fans Sonic Youth was still the same Sonic Youth of the previous decade. "That was so important at the time, to point back and say, 'We may be *here*, but this is where we really are,'" says Ranaldo. "That, in a way, we were still in that world of SST and music that our 'scene' had been making. I don't know if in so many words we would have admitted that at the time, but it was something like that."

Yet they no longer were in the world of SST, which became immediately apparent when Gersh, at a dinner with the band, saw a rough draft of the cover and placed his hand over the lettering—particularly the "killed my parents" part—and asked if they needed it. In light of the mushrooming record censorship movement instigated by groups like the Parents' Music Resource Center, which had managed to convince record companies to place warning stickers on albums, anything remotely graphic or explicit was carefully monitored. (In a particularly chilling example of the self-censorship then seeping into the industry, one major label—MCA, Geffen's new parent company—hired an executive to scrutinize lyrics before they were recorded; that way, the company would ward off potential stickers.) The cover would ultimately be released as per the band's wishes, but, as Ranaldo recalls, "The fact that they would even ask us was pretty mind-boggling."

The management situation was proving to be a far greater stumbling block. The band had never before had to cope with anyone guiding their career so closely, and Grant and Cramer were unaccustomed to working with musicians so headstrong and so anxious about their credibility. "The label wanted them to make better-sounding records," Grant says, "and I kind of carried the label's water. It was upsetting to them." Grant, thirty at the time, met with major resistance to ideas that Ranaldo, for one, dubbed distasteful and had "nothing to do with aesthetics or creative potential." One after another, each suggestion, such as higher ticket prices, was vetoed by the band. "We'll do a certain amount of things," says Gordon, "but we're not going to jump through hoops."

Among other things, Grant pushed for the band to "mainstream its business," in his words, starting with its touring operation. With Sonic Youth having graduated from the indie ranks, Grant and Cramer felt, logically enough, that the band should begin working with more prominent agencies. The band itself was not opposed to the upgrade, and after Grant and Cramer received their go-ahead, the next casualty of Sonic Youth's revamped business infrastructure became Carlos van Hijfte, then still handling many of their European shows. Out of the blue, van Hijfte received a services-no-longer-required fax from management; when he called Grant, he was told in no uncertain terms he was fired. "That was ugly," van Hijfte recalls. "It was a horrible conversation. It was the big-time manager going, 'We don't want to know you; we want to get rid of you.' I was like, 'Oh, my God, what is this? I give them ten years of my life—what are they doing to me?' I guess they were fed up with small indie record companies and they were also fed up with small indie booking agents."

Not everyone in the band was willing to have Grant and Cramer fire Lawton, who in many ways symbolized Sonic Youth's ongoing connection with the American indie underground. But that process began as well. When Grant broke the news to Lawton over lunch, the booking agent was put out and angered (even though Grant says he offered Lawton a monetary settlement). Unlike the situation with van Hijfte, though, this time the band seemed to have second thoughts:

They wanted to keep Lawton after all, which confounded Grant even more. "I really miscalculated," Grant admits. "I was just trying to be expeditious. I thought they could be served by working with people who would take them to the next level. I wanted to take a cottage business and branch it out." After a while, the calls to Eldridge Street became more exasperating, especially to Gordon: "I just couldn't take it anymore," she says.

Grant and Cramer also realized that the differences between them and the band went beyond who would set up which concert tours. Taking a meeting with Gordon and Moore at 84 Eldridge, Grant listened as the couple slagged major labels. Why were they so wary? he thought. Did they intend to alienate people they were working with? As someone who hadn't come from the indie circuit, Grant didn't understand that particular take, the inherent conflicts underground musicians were facing as they began signing with larger companies. "Their music was so free and so different, and I didn't really understand what I was in the middle of," Grant admits. "I didn't realize that their goals and perspectives were going to have some relationship with where they were musically. It shouldn't have been a surprise to me, but it was."

Ultimately, the situation proved as stressful for the managers as for the band. Cramer would groan when the phone rang and a secretary would announce that someone from Sonic Youth was on the line. Loyal to Cramer, Grant realized he wasn't up to the task. After only a few months on the job, both men decided the band simply wasn't worth the aggravation and resigned.

BY THE TIME *Goo* was set for release on June 23, 1990, a new manager was already in place. The band had been hearing about a kid named John Silva from their friends Steven and Jeffrey McDonald of Redd Kross, whom Silva managed (as best he could, anyway, given their rowdiness and tendencies toward excessive behavior). Silva had several other factors in his favor. He was a few years younger than Grant and came from indie rock. His girlfriend, Lisa Fancher, had started Frontier, the L.A. indie that released albums by the Three O'-Clock, the Long Ryders, and others in the so-called paisley underground. Smooth and ingratiating, Silva was a record nerd at heart—his visits to record swap meets in the L.A. area impressed Moore—and he had a better grasp on how to help bands navigate their way from the underground to the above ground. "He was just this guy," says Ranaldo. "We were like, 'Well, Redd Kross seems pretty happy with this guy—maybe we should try him.' So we took him on, and we got along with him."

"John got the art *and* the commerce," says Janet Billig, a publicist who worked for Silva. "And he was more of a peer for them. He was in the community, and they appreciated that."

Silva was also part of a power team. By 1990, he'd joined Gold Mountain, a management company headed by Danny Goldberg. Like David Geffen, Goldberg was a music business veteran but with an even more varied background: He'd been everything from a journalist and ACLU official to an employee of Led Zeppelin's Swan Song label, and later a president of both Atlantic and Warner Brothers. His own management firm, formed in the early '80s, had a roster that included Bonnie Raitt and the Allman Brothers Band. By signing with Gold Mountain, Sonic Youth would have it both ways: a day-to-day handler with indie credibility (Silva) and a firm run by an industry player (Goldberg).

Launching a Sonic Youth record, especially one with a DGC logo on the back, would have to be done the right way, of course. As Kates more than knew, "You couldn't have a Sonic Youth pizza and bowling party, which ninety percent of bands would do." But there were other, more clever ways to draw attention to *Goo*, like sending journalists advance cassettes wrapped in cellophane and placed in plastic Ziploc bags filled with a gooey substance. The label, Kates and Farrell in particular, was also concerned that the group's base—college radio and independent, mom-and-pop record stores—not be alienated by the band's move to a major. To smooth over that transition, Kates arranged for the band to visit college radio stations in the weeks leading up to *Goo*'s release. From his days at SST, Farrell knew the band was particularly adept at working a room; he would watch as they would stroll into a station or store and immediately begin chatting people up, especially compared to other SST acts at the time. "J. Mascis was so shy he couldn't *speak*," Farrell says. "One day the Meat Puppets would be friendly, and the other day they'd be too stoned and you wouldn't be able to relate to them." By comparison, Sonic Youth were easy; they knew the importance of being sociable and making the right connections in any situation.

The station visits allayed most of their fears. In Boston, a female DJ was so overcome by the sight of Ranaldo and Shelley that she began crying. With Kates accompanying them, Gordon and Moore visited college outlets in the South, like Duke University's station, where the young staff laid out a guitar and bass for Moore and Gordon when they arrived, and the two improvised live on the air. Yet Kates was also reminded they weren't stars yet. When the three of them arrived at the Ritz-Carlton in Atlanta, sweaty and exhausted from driving in a van all day, hotel employees asked them to step out of the lobby as soon as possible; they had a dress code to enforce.

They needn't have been worried about a backlash: *Goo* was very much a Sonic Youth record. Songs began with spurts of feedback or intentionally slothful guitar figures; sometimes a noise meltdown emerged right after a chorus. "Dirty Boots," the album's second single, included all of those. The album continually messed with the conventions of a standard pop record. Shelley's drumstick-click count-off at the start of "Mary-Christ" (Moore's song about, in his words, "what punk-rock Catholic girls would be like") was the sort of thing heard on demos, not polished major-label releases. Songs also weren't supposed to end by launching into the riff of the following track and then abruptly stopping, which was the case with "Mary-Christ": Moore began playing the "Kool Thing" chords during the fade-out. (The bit emerged from the way they would play both songs back to back in rehearsal.) "Scooter + Jinx," one minute of instrumental guitar savagery, and "Mildred Pierce," whittled down to a little past two minutes from the eight-minute-plus demo version, were overtly self-conscious moves, as if the band was going out of its way to prove it could still make obnoxious instrumental chaos while collecting David Geffen's paychecks.

Fortunately, the music felt not just emboldened but bold; for all the difficulties in completing the record, *Goo* had, ironically, a cocksure swagger. The forty-eight tracks of recording space may have been burdensome, but they also made for guitars that, with their piled-on chords and noise tangents, sounded as if they'd been bench-pressed. With Shelley's drums more prominent in the mix than before, the rhythms swung and shook. From the rubbery punk groove of "Mary-Christ" to the multipart pummel of "Cinderella's Big Score" to the way the stuttering guitars introducing "Kool Thing" gave way to snarling thrash and whiplash drums, the band had never before packed such aural wallop. Chuck D.'s fleeting cameo in "Kool Thing" didn't make for the historic rap-rock merger the song portended, but the track was a miracle nevertheless: Both wailing and seductive, it merged the brawniest hook of the band's career with some of their most wild-eyed, runaway-train playing.

Goo lacked the fluid consistency of *Daydream Nation* or *Sister*, yet its songs were strong enough to support all the production heavy lifting. The serrated unison guitars that opened "Tunic (Song for Karen)" gave way to a supernatural, unrelenting track with one of Gordon's most controlled and focused vocals; true to its subject, the song felt ghostly. (During the interlude of guitar waves, Gordon and J. Mascis could be heard in the background, singing Carpenter hits.) Taking its lyrical cue from Sylvia Plath's poem "The Eye Mote" and an Anthony Burgess sci-fi novel, "Mote," sung by Ranaldo, had lyrics that read like an acid trip; they tried to capture the sensation of something getting stuck in someone's eye and how the experience can alter one's vision. Yet like most of the songs that featured Ranaldo's voice, it had a straightforward, melodic drive. Although Gordon was never happy with the way "Titanium Exposé" came out, the song was epic: an elephant-caught-in-a-trap intro, followed by monolithic slabs of guitar, then trade-off vocals between Moore and Gordon that harked back to "Schizophrenia." The song slammed the album to a confident close. Like everything that had come before, it was music not connected to blues, country, folk, or jazz—music unhampered by history and free to do as it pleased.

As Gordon's bratty-kid vocal on "My Friend Goo" ("my friend Goo goes . . . p-u!") showed, *Goo* was not without its sense of humor. The jesting extended to photographer Michael Lavine's splash of band portraits on the inside packaging. The sight of Sonic Youth dolled up as retro, fur-wearing, '70s-style rock stars (their idea, their clothes) was clearly an inside gag, another indication that *Goo* was the world as seen through a winking, art-boho looking glass. (The photos were also a marked contrast to Lavine's starker, black-and-white band portrait inside *Daydream Nation*, taken on an East Village block at night.) But *Goo* was also the sound of a band extending its hand, firmly but cautiously, to the large, unknown world outside its door.

BEFITTING THEIR UPGRADED STATUS, the band was booked into bigger venues for the *Goo* tour, which would last through the end of 1990. To prepare for four straight months of roadwork, they played a handful of warmup shows in out-of-the-way venues. To a country bar a short drive from downtown Las Vegas, they brought along two opening acts: STP, an all-woman punk band featuring Julie Cafritz, who'd had a less-than-amicable split with Pussy Galore, and a group of relative upstarts from Seattle called Nirvana.

Sonic Youth's awareness of Nirvana predated their conversation with Kates. They'd heard a copy of *Bleach*, released the previous year, and had become instant admirers; Moore and Gordon loved the album's blend of bristling audio and pop melody. Moore even played it for Ron Saint Germain during the *Goo* mixing sessions, telling him he wanted their album to sound that way, but Saint Germain was less than open to the idea. Although they saw Nirvana give a calamitous performance at the Pyramid Club in New York City around that time, they also picked up on the star power of Kurt Cobain. "You should get this record *Bleach*, because our friend Kurt is going to be *really* famous," they told Jim Grant during their brief working relationship. At the video shoot for "Dirty Boots," Moore brought along a bag of

T-shirts to wear, one of which sported a Nirvana logo. ("No one had ever *heard* of Nirvana," says director Tamra Davis. "We all said, 'What's *that* shirt?'") Beyond Cobain's riveting anti-star persona, the band seemed to genuinely like him and consider him a kindred punk spirit. When Shelley walked into the Vegas venue during soundcheck, he was taken aback by the sound of Cobain playing a Crucifucks song. "He was wild and could unleash this primal energy," says Gordon. "And he was soft-spoken, but not *too* soft-spoken."

Nirvana was also in the midst of a career-changing moment. Shortly before the start of the tour, they'd recorded rough versions of songs that would end up released a year later on *Nevermind* and had given copies of the tape, *Sheep*, to Sonic Youth. At the time, Nirvana was recording for Sub Pop, the Seattle indie, but out of frustration with the label and his own growing (and conflicted) attraction to fame, Cobain was already thinking about major labels and big-wheel management. Since he had an awestruck reverence for Sonic Youth and the way they managed to retain their identity and integrity over the course of a decade, Cobain began asking the band about Geffen. In turn, the band suggested they consider their newly hired managers at Gold Mountain. Eventually, Nirvana would sign up with both companies.

Soon, Nirvana was drawn into the Sonic Youth solar system, a vast network of independent and underground musicians they'd cultivated for nearly ten years. It was a world to which many at Geffen, with the notable exceptions of Kates and Farrell, were not accustomed, and in order to have Sonic Youth's respect, many of those employees felt the need to brush up on their alternative nation. "I had to get up to speed in this vocabulary very quickly," says John Rosenfelder, Kates' assistant in the radio department of DGC. "I had to raise my own sensibility about music, art, and everything else. I had to increase the level of my game in order to represent them intelligently and speak about them in a smart way. I had to go to Sonic Youth college." Like many, Rosenfelder was worried that not knowing the names of the right bands—or admitting admiration for a pop act not considered legit— could hurt his credibility. When he, Kates, Gordon, and Moore went to a Metallica concert in Los Angeles, a clearly excited Rosenfelder turned around to see Gordon, arms folded and a frown on her face. Rosenfelder instantly felt he'd lost points with the band. "It was so easy to soil yourself," Rosenfelder says. "You wouldn't want to be the guy who said the wrong thing at the wrong time."

By now, "Sonic Youth college" was a largely well-attended place. Photographers, visual and conceptual artists, cartoonists, underground filmmakers, and musicians all seemed to gravitate toward them (or vice versa). Using Pettibon's work on the cover of *Goo* was the first step in moving this network into the mainstream. The second phase arrived when the band decided to commission a video for each song on *Goo*. As per standard record contracts, Geffen and the band together footed the bill for the relatively high-cost clips for the official singles "Kool Thing," "Dirty Boots," and "Disappearer." But for the other seven tracks, the band approached their filmmaker friends, offering each $500 to make a clip for a song of their choosing. Dating back to their SST days, when they allowed a young filmmaker named Kevin Kerslake to direct low-budget but visually inventive clips for "Shadow of a Doubt" and "Beauty Lies in the Eye," they sensed the way in which even cheaply made videos could enhance their image and add to their mystique.

Although none of the homemade *Goo* clips would be shown on MTV, the crazy-quilt assemblage amounted to a tour of indie and underground film techniques at the dawn of the '90s. Newly clean from heroin addiction, Richard Kern chose "Scooter + Jinx," partly because it was the album's shortest song. Hiring two strippers and filming them in his apartment, he turned his video into an homage to his own, earlier work. The clip cost so little that Kern had money left over. Tony Oursler, then teaching in Boston, chose "Tunic (Song for Karen)" and opted for a similarly low-tech approach: The childlike set was designed by his students. The resulting clip was both kitschy (clips of the Carpenters, including Karen romping with Mickey Mouse at Disneyland) and creepy (Oursler incorporated his technique of projecting faces onto inanimate objects, by way of Gordon's face transforming into a skull). Unfortunately, the Carpenters footage had to be blocked out at the last minute when Silva's office called Oursler to see if he'd received permission to use it. Since Oursler hadn't—in part because he claims he was told by the band it wouldn't be a hurdle—Karen and Richard were ultimately excised. For the label-funded clip for "Disappearer," filmed in Canada with the band in drag, the band hired a twenty-nine-year-old indie filmmaker named Todd Haynes. Haynes spoke their pop-culture language as well: They all knew about *Superstar: The Karen Carpenter Story*, a film "bio" of the late singer that used dolls to tell the story (and was never officially released thanks to music licensing problems).

Once Markey picked "Cinderella's Big Score," Gordon suggested he take a cue from *Mala Noche*, the first work of a new filmmaker named Gus Van Sant. In a move that would somewhat predate Van Sant's later *My Own Private Idaho*, Markey turned the song into the tale of a male teen runaway turning tricks. For his second *Goo* video, for "Mildred Pierce," Markey called upon a new friend, Sofia Coppola. Still largely unknown to the public—her big-screen debut, in her father's *The Godfather: Part III*, was still months away—Coppola was little more than a nineteen-year-old art student who'd just relocated from the Bay Area to Los Angeles. Unsure of what she wanted to do at that point in her life, Coppola was leading an unfocused life, dabbling in art, fashion, and acting. Markey met her through Redd Kross—Coppola and Steven McDonald had become a couple—and flashed upon Coppola's striking, near-Mediterranean looks when it came time to cast a young Joan Crawford for the video. Made up to look like Crawford, complete with wire hangers for that extra *Mommie Dearest* touch, Coppola jabbed and lunged at the camera, acting the part as best she could ("If you can call that acting," she says).

An even younger and more novice filmmaker was asked to contribute. Several years before, Phil Morrison, a North Carolina native and music and film buff, had moved to New York to attend NYU; he'd barely started classes when he went to CBGB and saw Sonic Youth, then performing *Bad Moon Rising*. Standing in front of the stage, Morrison was particularly captivated by Gordon. "She didn't look like a woman in a band," he recalls. "She looked like an intellectual. The guys were rocking the way guys rock. But Kim didn't seem to make any effort to perform for *me*. It was confusing." Later, Morrison got to know Moore and Gordon when he began working for Lawton's booking agency. Moore would often stop by the office on lower Broadway, showing off whatever records he'd just bought and taking Morrison shopping himself.

Morrison wound up directing "Titanium Exposé," which came to embody the pop-DayGlo theme that ran through *Goo*. The clip's opening credits took their cue from '70s television cop shows, and the way each segment focused on a different band member was inspired by Led Zeppelin's *The Song Remains the Same* film. In "Titanium Exposé," Morrison also heard "not only a love song, but a domestic love song" (particularly in Gordon's "sugar babe, do it to me" refrain). Therefore, Morrison decided to film Moore and Gordon at home on Eldridge Street, with at least one unexpected result. Viewing the finished video months later, friends and band members watched, jaws agape, as Moore and Gordon passionately made out for the camera. The suggestion was Morrison's, and initially Moore, for one, was reluctant: "It was a little embarrassing. We knew it was showing a side of us we weren't exhibiting that much publicly. But for the sake of art, we did it."

That was an understatement, of course. "I thought, 'Oh, my fucking God—these people *do* that?'" recalls Cafritz, who had seen the way the couple gingerly interacted on the road. "At that point, I knew them well enough that I *knew* they did. But it wasn't clear to me that they would ever make that clear to anybody else. Everyone who knew them was like, 'Wow.'" Even Shelley admits to feeling "a little uncomfortable" watching it. As with *Goo*, it was another indication they were both winking at—and embracing—the idea of a public identity.

USING THE STANDARD INDUSTRY FORMULA—the number of copies an act's previous album had sold—Geffen shipped seventy-five thousand copies of *Goo*. By the end of the year, sales had more than doubled that amount. By industry standards, roughly two hundred thousand copies was a relative flop, but in this case, it seemed like a victory. "In Gersh's vision, this was going to take a long time, and maybe it *never* takes," says Farrell. "But that's not what it was about. You're getting behind a band that does something different from everything else in the world. That was a very important part of the Geffen Records personality. It was very much an artist's label." The album's relative success was also an indication that an audience for this music was coalescing, albeit slowly: The Lemonheads' first album for Atlantic, released around the same time, sold a fraction of *Goo*.

Still, the label hoped for more. In an attempt to entice commercial radio, it released an edited version of "Dirty Boots," condensing its guitar-chaos section in the process. "They always wanted everything shorter, and it rubbed us the wrong way," Ranaldo says, yet the band knew certain compromises had to be made. The album's obvious focus single, though, was "Kool Thing," which reached an impressive No. 7 on the *Billboard* Modern Rock chart. ("Teen Age Riot" had only drifted as high as No. 20.) Crossing "Kool Thing" over to pop radio, however, was proving trickier. In an attempt to expose the song to large crowds, Kates included it on *Time Out*, a compilation of Geffen and DGC tracks given to sports arenas and stadiums. Then, at Gersh's suggestion, hip-hop DJ and rapper Daddy-O of Stetsasonic was hired to remix the song, but the band immediately spurned the track after hearing it. "It was the biggest piece of shit," Shelley says. "It was a waste of money and didn't represent the band." (The band was so mortified that the track was pointedly omitted from an expanded edition of the album released fifteen years later.)

Most auspiciously, Geffen spent $50,000 making a video for the song, helmed by Tamra Davis, a rising L.A. director whose résumé included such hip-hop clips as Tone-Loc's gritty, low-budget "Wild Thing." The budget for "Kool Thing" was far more than the cost of Davis' other video, for "Dirty Boots," a lip-synched performance clip set in a club with a mosh-pit *Romeo and Juliet* subplot. (Davis also reedited Haynes' original clip for "Disappearer" when label executives found it confusing.) But it was still relatively cheap compared with most videos, especially the absurd $1.7 million the label would spend on Guns N' Roses' "November Rain" the following year. For a homemade set, Davis and her crew covered her own production office in tin foil; to film the elusive, ever-busy Chuck D., Davis and Gordon were forced to track the rapper down at his label, filming him in a hallway as he emerged from a meeting.

The video's most striking visual element, though, was Gordon. Staring down the camera with formidable fake eyelashes and flashing more skin than ever before—even a hint of cleavage—Gordon was the clip's focal point. "That was another dramatic thing that happened," says Cafritz. "It was, 'Oh, they signed to a major label and now Kim's fucking sexy—what's *that* about?' I think it had to do with the fact that you're thirty-seven and you realize you can still be hot and you'd better take advantage of it." Gordon's transformation from withdrawn, bespectacled band member—the shy librarian—to fashion-conscious sexual icon had actually been gradual. With each passing year, she'd shed her inhibitions a bit more, reflected in her increasingly freer stage garb: The short hair, glasses, clunky boots, and occasional flannel shirt gradually gave way to shorter skirts and sleeveless tops. The ironically worn bell bottoms in the *Goo* photos could be traced to the band's friendship with Redd Kross, who'd been plumbing '70s fashion. But an equally key figure in Gordon's makeover was Susanne Sasic, who not only handled lighting and merchandise on the road but introduced Gordon to accessories like glittery jeans. The Gordon seen in the "Kool Thing" video and on the *Goo* tour (wearing, among other things, flared pants bedecked with stars) had become a formidable stage presence musically and visually: Pounding out bass lines in hot pants, she was both one of the boys and one of the girls.

Yet while "Kool Thing" made it onto MTV's *Buzz Bin*, it never became the hit single or video everyone had hoped. "'Kool Thing' was commercial for them, but it really wasn't a commercial song," says Robin Sloane, who, as Geffen's creative director, oversaw videos and album covers. "We worked really hard, and the band did make certain compromises. But MTV is based on radio airplay." As a reminder of the way things worked, the head of promotions told Sloane, "A good video is one that's in heavy rotation." Pop radio still didn't know what to make of music like "Kool Thing"; there were no obvious slots for it or songs by bands like them. Sloane also felt a video that focused entirely on Gordon and the band playing on the aluminum-foil set would have stood a better chance; the footage of black dancers, a Wall Street yuppie, and other literal representations of the lyrics was "common," she says. But in the end, the final cut was the band's call. "Ultimately, it was the artist's decision," she says, "and no one could ever overrule the artist."

Just as the *Goo* campaign was beginning to wind down late in the year, following several months of American and European tour dates, Silva contacted the band over Christmas break with an intriguing offer: Neil Young had asked if they would open for him and Crazy Horse on their Smell the Horse tour from late winter to early spring. Ranaldo and Shelley, rabid and longtime Young fans, were particularly thrilled at the idea (as a teenager, Ranaldo had learned to play every song on *After the Gold Rush*). Although not as much of a devotee, Gordon had written about the drug metaphors in Young's "The Old Laughing Lady" in *Artforum*. Geffen executives were keyed up, too; the idea of introducing the band to Young's classic-rock fan base, and in arenas at that, was too enticing to pass up. The musical connection seemed obvious as well: Young's love of volume, electricity, and feedback, especially when he teamed up with his long-suffering backup band Crazy Horse, seemed a compatible match for Sonic Youth. "We'd been asked to do big tours before, like Robert Plant and the Cure," Moore says. "And we always said, 'We're not interested—it's not what we do.' But Neil was somebody we were interested in.'"

The money was worth considering, too, as was the magnitude of it. They'd long heard about what it was like to embark on large-scale tours of huge venues with road crews and bus caravans; the idea was practically folklore. A decade earlier, they'd spurned such trappings—not hard to do, since they were inconceivable anyway. But starting with signing with David Geffen's company, sampling the big rock world was proving too hard to resist. They said yes to the Young tour and were told to show up at the Target Center arena in Minneapolis for the first show, on January 22, 1991.

THEY HAD A SENSE of what they would be up against. They knew they'd be playing shorter sets than usual, and in cavernous places with less precise PAs. They knew they would be performing to an audience that might not always grasp the connection between the crackling-thunder power and extended forays of Crazy Horse and their own. They knew they were entering the big-league world of a rock tour. "We knew it would be insane," Moore says.

But they didn't count on how insane. In many ways, the first show, in Minneapolis, set the stage. During the opening song, Gordon's amplifier blew out, and since Young's crew only worked for Young, the band ended up moving around amplifiers on their own. When they finished, playing a half-hour set heavy on *Goo* material, they were greeted with isolated pockets of applauses, scattered booing, and, mostly, blank looks.

So it went during the early weeks of the tour; the audiences didn't know what to make of them or their music. They knew what to make of Gordon; scattered screams of "take your top off!" punctuated the air. But Young's fans were not always as progressive as their hero; they wanted to hear Young's anthems, and they weren't tolerant of the racket that preceded him. If anything, they were far more charitable toward the band that preceded Sonic Youth, Social Distortion, the veteran Orange County punk band whose sound had grown more arena-friendly in recent years.

Yet the treatment on the part of Young's crew took them aback the most. In their world, Sonic Youth were just short of royalty. But in this setting, they were just another upstart band, the kind that didn't get soundchecks and wasn't allowed to sit out front and watch Young during his set. (They took to calling Young's tour manager "the Doberman" for the way he would chase them away while Young was playing.) Gordon was particularly put off by the "very macho" backstage vibe of Young's crew, which was just short of a motorcycle gang, and what she calls the "whole attitude toward women, like having strippers for birthday parties. It was real eye-opening as far as what big rock was like." They quickly bonded with Crazy Horse guitarist Frank "Poncho" Sampedro, but he was the exception. "They treated us like shit," says Ranaldo of the crew. "They were not into having to do the extra work."

After the tenth show of the tour, at New York's Madison Square Garden on February 10, their friend Tom Surgal told them they not only sounded terrible but that he could barely hear them. Afterward, their sound man, Terry Pearson, confirmed that starting with the show in Minneapolis, Young's crew had instructed Pearson to lower the band's volume from their standard 105 to 110 decibels to 90. The practice was standard for arena tours: Either because they don't want to be upstaged or simply want to be louder, headlining acts routinely make sure their openers are quieter. The Young camp would insist it wasn't specific to Sonic Youth. But the sound problems were a last insult. Not only were they being deprived of soundchecks before each show and then facing indifferent, sometimes hostile, responses—now hardly anyone could hear them anyway. (After a number of shows had taken place, Young's crew also told Pearson he couldn't play Carpenters music on the PA before Sonic Youth went on.) "It was ice-cold water in our faces," says Nic Close, who had just signed on as one of the band's guitar technicians. Everyone in the band witnessed the rare sight of Moore coming off-stage fuming.

During the tour, Young himself was a fleeting presence, popping into their dressing room only a few times. When he did, he was friendly and told them he played "Expressway to Yr Skull" in his dressing room before he took the stage each night. "Neil really liked what was going on with our guitars," Moore says. "He was saying, 'How do you do that?'" (Young even let Sasic cut his hair backstage as Sonic Youth stood around and watched.) But when Young visited them before the next show, in Philadelphia, they told him they were thinking of leaving the tour; if they couldn't get the volume they wanted on-stage, the whole experience was pointless. Lawton was also displeased when Sonic Youth were asked to take a pay cut for the Southern leg of the tour, since tickets in those venues weren't selling as well.

Unaware of the situation, Young told them he'd take care of it, and he did: Gathering his crew around, he told them to give Sonic Youth all the volume they desired. (In the dressing room, he also told the band not to worry about a scheduled appearance on David Letterman's show: "Tell Letterman I've taken you under my wing," he said in his deep, resonant voice.) The problem was fixed, although Pearson received more than a few dagger stares from Young's crew at the first show after the incident. Barely a week later, the crew was equally unamused when Moore gave an interview to a Canadian newspaper in which he complained about the amplification and made cracks about Young's crew: Peter van der Velde, their road manager, was called into the office of Young's crew and given a scolding.

The response at some shows, like at the Hartford Civic Center in Connecticut, was respectable: Moore acknowledged his mother in the audience and dedicated "White Kross" to his brother Gene. When the tour arrived in Detroit, Julia and Ivan Shelley were finally able to see their son play in his band, nearly six years after he'd joined it, and Julia couldn't believe it. "He's such a calm, concerned kid, so thoughtful," she says. "And then when he plays behind the drums, he's all aggressive. He was—what do you call it, Dr. Jekyll and Mr. Hyde?"

Yet even with the volume back up—or perhaps because of it—the tour often felt like a public hazing. At Hershey Park in Pennsylvania on February 26, they found themselves confronted with such overwhelming booing they could barely hear themselves. "Who *are* these guys?" Pearson would regularly be asked as he stood at the soundboard in the middle of the arena, followed invariably by "They suck." ("Did they even play a *note?*" one audience member was overheard to say.) When the band realized that converting Young fans was futile, the sets grew even more outlandish. Using his cord, Moore took to dangling his guitar over the lip of the stage, resulting in even more gnarled sounds. "The more animosity we'd get from the audience, which was *common*, the more we would just crank it up and play our most blistering sets," Moore says. "The audience was like, 'No, stop!' We knew we weren't converting people to what we were doing. It was just like this journey, and it was so absurd that we enjoyed it."

In his mind, Moore must have flashed back to the days when, as a teenager, he'd trekked to arenas to sees the likes of Blue Öyster Cult and the J. Geils Band and had left unmoved: "Arenas just seemed vapid," he recalls. But he also remembered the time he saw Kiss and its opening act, the obscure '70s power-pop band Artful Dodger. The fact that few in the crowd paid the latter any mind stayed with him: "That made an impression on me. I thought, 'This is what it must be like to be in a rock band with a record out, and who knows who the fuck cares?'" Fifteen years later, Moore knew what it was like to be Artful Dodger.

To the chagrin of Shelley and Ranaldo—such diehard Young fans that they were awestruck by the oversized *Rust Never Sleeps* props resurrected for the Smell the Horse tour—Young invited only Moore and Gordon aboard his personal bus one evening. As Young fiddled with his prized collection of Lionel toy trains, adjusting the *"whoo-hoo!"* sounds on each, they talked, and Gordon offered to make dinner. Since there was no food on board, Young's driver pulled over at a Kentucky Fried Chicken to buy raw meat, and Gordon whipped up a stew. Still, she was nervous the whole time: Given where the meat came from, the last thing she wanted to do was give Neil Young food poisoning.

Mark Arm, who'd befriended them and become an occasional tour-mate, visited backstage when the tour arrived in Seattle in April. Seated next to him in the crowd was an older Neil Young fan not happy with Sonic Youth's set. "Don't you see the connection between the two?" Arm asked him.

"What are you *talking* about?" the man replied. Speaking with Moore backstage, Arm received the distinct impression that "he seemed like he was ready for it to be over."

A week later, it was, but not without an appropriately incongruous grace note. To help drive their gear from town to town, the band had hired Maurice Menares, a wired twenty-one-year-old New Jersey kid ever happy to play class clown. A hip-hop fan unaware of Sonic Youth before the tour, Menares became a backstage foil for Moore; the two would wander around empty arenas before shows, reeling off parodies of hip-hop patter and jargon. Markey filmed one such escapade for a short film, *Rap Damage*, Moore shouting into microphones in and around Los Angeles. Driving the equipment truck back from the Midwest, Menares was stopped for speeding. As local police—and the band—soon discovered, Menares didn't have a license. To make sure their equipment made it safely back to New York, the band had to hire another driver to fly out west and retrieve it.

Chapter 8

RECORDS—THEY NEEDED RECORDS, as many as possible. In the early days, when the band would stay with friends or friends *of* friends, it wasn't uncommon for Moore to flip through someone's home LP collection and stumble across an obscure album he was desperate to own; inevitably, the person would just give it to him. They were no longer crashing in strangers' homes, but the on-the-road routine didn't change. Whether it was during the tours for *Goo* or with Neil Young, anyone who worked for Sonic Youth noticed the same daily ritual. The van or bus would arrive somewhere, the band would check into wherever they were staying, and Moore would immediately pull out the Yellow Pages in his and Gordon's hotel room. Quickly finding the listings for the nearest record stores, he'd rip out the page and hit as many as possible by foot or taxi. Ranaldo and Shelley (and Terry Pearson) were avid record shoppers as well, but reflecting an obvious gene passed along from his scholarly father, Moore had become the band's most obsessive collector. He even traveled with a small notebook listing the names and serial numbers of rare vinyl he needed for his archives.

Eventually, the music library grew so sizeable, and took up so much space, that Moore and Gordon rented a second, equally compact apartment at 84 Eldridge to house them all, as well as piles of books and clothes. But even those additional quarters weren't enough, and, besides, the incoming Chinese gangs in the neighborhood were resorting to guns to settle their disputes. With an extra advance from

Geffen, as well as money their landlord paid them to leave the building once it was sold to a new owner, the moment came to leave behind their first home and, along with indie labels and certain business associates, relegate it to their past.

In search of an ample-size loft, they found a large, raw space on Lafayette Street, in the far trendier and more bustling SoHo. A quarter of a million dollars later, it was theirs. With the help of an architect, the space was remodeled and restructured; walls were added, as was an office surrounded by LP shelves. As a reminder of the factory building it had once been, water pipes snaked across the ceiling, and the gas station up the street had a snack stand so unappetizing that even former Lower East Side residents hesitated before entering it. Moore had a few apprehensions: Writing to a teenage fan a few years later, he called SoHo and Tribeca "bourgeois to the max, but beyond that, there's a historical vibe I dig." Taking out the garbage one night, in fact, he was struck by how much the building's back alley reminded him of the cover of the first Ramones album—the same album he'd bought after his father's death. But with its price and location, the apartment was also a sign of both changes in the city and the band's economic standing. "They were totally *The Jeffersons*," says Julie Cafritz, one of many friends who dropped by and marveled at the new space.

Another indication of their newfound position in the cultural universe arrived months later, when they set off for a European tour. Invited to play outdoor festivals, they decided to bring with them a caravan of bands who arose in their wake and saw Sonic Youth as pioneers and godfathers. One was Nirvana, who by then had also signed with Geffen/ DGC and were awaiting the release of their just-completed *Nevermind*. In late August, the troupe, which also included filmmaker and friend David Markey, Dinosaur Jr. (who also left SST, but to sign with Sire, home of Madonna), the Minneapolis all-woman grunge band Babes in Toyland—even the Ramones—arrived in Ireland for the start of what came to be known as the Year Punk Broke tour.

To compensate for the canceled *Goo* movie, Markey had been invited along to film the shows for a documentary Moore jokingly referred to as *Tooth or Hair*, a pun on Madonna's backstage tour film from earlier that year. The revised name came when Markey and the band were watching MTV Europe and, to their surprise and disgust, saw a video of Mötley Crüe butchering the Sex Pistols' "Anarchy in the U.K." The sight was both amusing and appalling; despite the Crüe's neo–New York Dolls look during their early days, it was hard to imagine any band further removed from punk than the L.A. hair-metal party boys. Someone, Markey perhaps, made a crack about how 1991 was the year punk would break into the mainstream. The joke became the official name for the two-week tour, which began in late August in Cork, Ireland, and wound its way through England and Germany before wrapping up in Holland.

For Sonic Youth, the shows were a welcome relief from the often exasperating Smell the Horse tour that had ended months before. They were now among their friends and peers, performing for large, generally enthusiastic audiences who, as in their earliest European performances, appeared open to them and their music. Onstage, they played songs from various periods in their career but also debuted several new ones, like a coiled-up rocker called "Chapel Hill." Nirvana, playing to their largest European crowds, were sometimes upstaging Sonic Youth, as Cobain hurled himself into walls of amplifiers and the trio debuted some of the *Nevermind* songs for the first time outside the States.

True to the film's original intention, Markey caught on film a number of Madonna-related skits that captured both the band's sense of humor and its loose, affectionate relationship with Cobain. ("Nirvana were like Sonic Youth's children on that tour," says Markey. "They were coming in under their wing.") Gordon and Cobain improvised a parody of the infamous *Truth or Dare* scene in which Madonna pretended to vomit after Kevin Costner visited her dressing room. Gordon had become a maternal figure to indie rock boys, always interested in hearing what troubled them and listening as they opened up about their music and lives. She even made fun of her own tendencies; in one scene, she earnestly asked J. Mascis how he was doing and if he and "Uma" had broken up. Markey's camera also caught moments when

233

Cobain and bandmates Krist Novoselic and Dave Grohl were more than willing to act like rock stars even though they weren't ones yet: getting plastered before and after each show and wrecking dressing rooms. Markey also noticed that Sonic Youth were the happiest he'd ever seen them, especially compared to the Young shows. Markey had joined their tour bus for a few of the Young dates and noticed how the audience response in Reno and San Francisco had caught everyone involved off guard.

During at least one moment on the tour, though, the camaraderie backstage may have become a bit too loose. Wandering into Nirvana's dressing room at one of the German shows, Gordon saw a note from the local Geffen-Universal label rep: "Welcome to Germany and good luck on your tour!" it read. Keeping punk alive in her own way, Gordon wrote "fuck you!" beneath it. Unfortunately, the same Geffen executive saw the message and thought Nirvana themselves had scrawled it, resulting in a "fuck you too!" written under Gordon's scribble. John Silva, who managed both bands, was then put in the position of smoothing things over with the ruffled Universal employees.

On one hand, the fallout of the botched gag (which Markey didn't include in his eventual film, *1991: The Year Punk Broke*) was amusing. "Whenever I try a practical joke, it always backfires on me," Gordon says. "I felt bad." Yet it was a signal they were no longer a purely indie band and that their actions would sometimes have repercussions. "Everything after that would be under a microscope," observes Markey. "That tour was the last moment of innocence for everyone involved."

THE HANDFUL OF CASSETTES that arrived at Bryan "Butch" Vig's home in Madison, Wisconsin, in the fall of 1991 was a daunting batch. Each seemed to consist of complex, drawn-out instrumental pieces that stretched out to as many as fifteen minutes. Mostly Vig was thrilled—the tapes contained the raw material for the next Sonic Youth album, which he would be producing—but he was also utterly vexed. Whenever he would start a project, Vig hoped to get a sense of where a band was going and where the song structures lay. He couldn't get a handle on either as he made his way through the piles of tapes; it was even hard to tell what the individual sections of the songs were.

Vig knew the tapes were coming, since he'd just returned from New York, where he'd met Moore, Gordon, Ranaldo, and Shelley to discuss the record. On several levels, Vig was a comfortable and comforting choice for producer. Like the band, the young producer with the droopy swoops of hair falling around his face had risen up from indie rock of the '80s, having been a drummer (in Spooner) and, most notably, a producer of local hardcore bands at Smart, his low-budget studio in Madison. At thirty-four, Vig was exactly in between Ranaldo and Moore in age and was, in Ranaldo's words, "not someone from the corporate world. He was this punk-rock kid, and we could relate to him." After graduating to producer, Vig worked with several Sub Pop bands followed by the Smashing Pumpkins on *Gish* and L7 on *Bricks Are Heavy*.

While visiting Moore and Gordon's apartment, Moore had pulled out a copy of "Acceptance," a single Vig had produced for the Wisconsin skinhead band Mecht Mensch. Vig was taken aback when Moore said he wanted the next Sonic Youth album to sound like the scratchy, underproduced 45. Then again, Vig was equally stunned that Moore even owned it; the band had only pressed up a few hundred copies, so it was unfathomable to Vig that one had found its way into *anyone's* New York apartment.

Since Vig had just wrapped up work on Nirvana's *Nevermind*, the hire also made sense to Geffen. With the help of Andy Wallace, a producer and engineer who'd earned industry respect by applying a smooth lacquer to even the harshest metal records, *Nevermind* was both brutalizing and radio-friendly. That it was an immediate sensation wasn't lost on anyone either; on January 11, 1992, shortly after the Sonic Youth sessions had begun, *Nevermind* managed to oust Michael Jackson's *Dangerous* (which admittedly had less buzz than a dead bee) from the number-one position on the *Billboard* chart. "Sonic Youth are always zeitgeisty," says Cafritz, "so it sounded really appealing at that moment. And everything was so crazy that it was actually possible they might have a hit. You write the same songs but oddly enough, they might go over in a much bigger way. And you can facilitate that by using someone like Butch. You had to seize that moment and not walk away from it."

During his first talk with the band in New York, Vig was initially intimidated but realized they were more approachable—and more amenable to suggestions—than he imagined. He told them he wanted to tighten up their arrangements, make them sound "larger than life," in his words, and spend time on their guitar sounds. The band didn't voice any major objections, even when Geffen insisted that Wallace mix the album after Vig wrapped up the basic tracks, surely due to the success of *Nevermind*. In fact, Gordon, who was both their sonic police and a fan of low-end sound, admired the records Wallace had mixed for the thrash metal band Slayer. In very little time, Vig landed the job.

Vig could tell they were game when the next batch of tapes arrived at his home; given how much punchier the songs sounded, it was clear the band had done a good deal of self-editing. Vig booked time at the Magic Shop, a studio very close to the new Moore-Gordon household. He then moved to New York for three months in early 1992 to start the process of making a Sonic Youth album that would be both true to the band yet land them the sales and airplay everyone thought were actually conceivable.

When Vig asked Geffen's Gary Gersh for advice on how to work with the band, Gersh told him to try to get into Gordon's psyche; Gersh considered her the hub of the band. Figuring out Moore wasn't always easy, either. "He seemed kind of aloof, like he wasn't inter-ested," says Vig. "And he came across as multitasking; there was something else always going on. But we could be working on some-thing and you'd think he wouldn't be paying attention and then whatever it was—the guitar sound, a transition part—he was totally into it."

Vig felt a certain amount of pressure, some self-imposed and some not. Whenever he would mention the project to friends, they'd say,

"Wow, it's going to be amazing!" ("Those kinds of comments sneak into your psyche," he says.) To him, the band didn't seem in the least fazed or stressed, but he did realize early on he had his work cut out for him. Not only were their preferred Fender Jazzmaster guitars cheap and hard to tune, but each had its own tuning; like many before him, Vig was confounded when he saw the swatches of tape on the back of the instruments, each with a hand-written jumbled alphabet signaling a specific tuning.

Vig realized that approach was essential: "Because the notes go off, they create these harmonics and make it sound much bigger. If everything was in tune, it wouldn't sound that full. It would sound like a normal band." Yet he also realized it would be a struggle to figure out exactly how those unusual tunings should sound, and he forced the band to be more precise than it had ever been. "It was real task-oriented working with Butch," says Moore. "You had to sit there with a strobe tuner and really incrementally tune. I thought, 'Okay, this'll be interesting.' In a way I appreciated it. We were using these unorthodox tunings, and he really zoned in on that aspect of the music."

In addition to putting them through guitar-tech paces, Vig worked them in ways few had in the studio; in search of the sharpest, most precise performances, he made them do multiple takes of most of the songs. "They didn't always *like* doing that," Vig says, "but they did it." Some of the tracks—a simple, stout rocker called "100%," a grinding, gnashing one called "Youth Against Fascism"—came fairly quickly. Others, like a floaty, intricately structured piece called "Theresa's Sound-world," were harder to pin down. In order to achieve the right balance between its wafty verses and tenser, more frenetic bridges, Vig made the band redo it innumerable times before a magic performance finally occurred, late on the evening of April 9, all the studio lights off. "That really hit the mark," Moore says. "If anything really was one hundred percent successful in our relationship with Butch, it was pretty much that."

The sessions were a learning experience but one the band was willing to entertain, at least at the time. "We were usually impatient with that stuff, but at that moment in time we were willing to give Butch free rein," says Ranaldo. "He worked in certain ways we wouldn't have necessarily been drawn to, but at that point we were just like, 'Okay, let's see what these guys can do.'"

What they could also do, in postproduction, was contour the sound of the band. To make Gordon's voice smoother and more radio-ready, Vig ran it through a harmonizer. During the mixing process, Wallace blended in prerecorded drum sounds—a snare here, a kick drum there—to augment Shelley's kit and make the drums sound more prominent. ("There are things we did I wish we hadn't," says Shelley. "I was saying to Andy, 'Yeah, that's cool, but let's take the samples down a bit.' I was cautious.") Among the friends visiting the Magic Shop to hear the results was Bob Lawton, who saw the band spending more time than ever fine-tuning its music. "Again, it was 'how far are you gonna go, how many rough edges are you gonna take off?'" he says. "Where they used to go in and cut songs, now they were working for a long time on one thing."

Thanks to their bond with Vig and the trust they invested in him, the sessions were still far more enjoyable than those for *Goo*. An especially friendly, laid-back presence, Vig was a subtle taskmaster. There were still plenty of very Sonic Youth moments, as when Ian MacKaye of the fiercely indie D.C. band Fugazi was invited into the studio, handed a guitar, and told to improvise, on the spot, a part for "Youth Against Fascism." In an intentional nod to their indie years—or at least Moore's affinity for hardcore—the band also dashed off a cover of "Nic Fit," originally recorded by another D.C. hardcore unit, the Untouchables, led by MacKaye's brother Alex. Moore made up his own lyrics, with the idea of rerecording the vocal later. But the band felt the take was so spot-on they released it as it was, Moore singing "sonic tooth, sonic truth" (another reference to their earliest records) instead of MacKaye's own words.

When Vig and Wallace were mixing "Theresa's Sound-world," Shelley asked them to turn the drums down when the song arrived at its careening midsection. "I don't know *anybody* in a band who's ever said that," Vig recalls. "But they wanted the guitars to become literally this wall of sound and the bass and drums to be a pulse mixed behind it." Standard record-making practice dictated that such a mix would be the last way to ensure a song's commercial viability. But in the post-*Nevermind* world, nothing seemed standard anymore.

MARK KATES, the Geffen alternative radio promotion executive and ongoing Sonic Youth champion, couldn't quite believe what he was hearing. It was the spring of 1992, the sessions for the band's highly anticipated second DGC album had wrapped up, and there he was, at lunch at the Hamburger Hamlet across the street from the label's Sunset Boulevard offices, being told by Moore and Gordon that there was a chance Lee Ranaldo might no longer be in Sonic Youth.

From the start, the group dynamic had been complicated. Compared to many bands, they were a true democracy; everyone had a say, and even though they were married, Moore and Gordon seemed to agree as much as they didn't. (As with their lack of physical interplay on the road, it was another way of keeping things professional.) And yet the fact that Moore and Gordon were a couple, as well as the genesis of the band, was hard to avoid; the way Moore and Gordon used Fleming and Mascis on *Goo* was one example of the collective power they wielded. Even though he was far from the leader and would listen to everyone else's point of view, Moore in particular cast a shadow over the band with more than just his height. He had named it, he was the prime motivator, and many of their songs began with his ideas, even if they were then put through the group hammering-out process.

For years, the songs Ranaldo would sing or bring to the sessions always stood apart. Unlike Moore and Gordon, he wrote direct, comparatively accessible lyrics that harked back to the singer-songwriter records he'd absorbed as a Long Island teenager. The music sounded different, too: Some were composites of several ideas, while others, like "Eric's Trip" from *Daydream Nation*, were more clear-cut (and more traditionally sung) than most Sonic Youth songs. But as time went on, Ranaldo's contributions began fitting in even less. During the *Goo* sessions, he'd arrived with an unnamed ballad that came to be called "Lee #2." Like the earlier "Pipeline/Kill Time," it was another song—an open letter, really—inspired by the romantic travails of his friend Thom DeJesu. With its fluid folk-pop groove, the song was worked up by the band—one arrangement featured Nick Sansano on organ and piano, Moore on bass, and Gordon on guitar—but ultimately shelved. "Kim and Thurston had a hard time working on it because I think they felt it was a lightweight song," Ranaldo says, "which in a sense it is." Even Ranaldo had to admit to himself that "Lee #2" didn't know where it wanted to go, and a finished take was never nailed down. Also during those sessions, Ranaldo allowed a spoken-word part during the closing minutes of "Mote" to be deleted so the song could end with an extended instrumental fade.

During the sessions for the new album, Ranaldo showed up with "Genetic," which, like "Lee #2," was already fully formed by its author. With its interlocking sections—an impassioned rush at the start, followed by slower middle and end sections that never quite came around to the original chorus—the song had the structural feel of a Sonic Youth track. Yet with Ranaldo's clear tenor and its lyrics about a romantic connection and breakdown (and the lingering regret that followed), it felt very much like the work of its writer and less like that of the band.

When the album, which was nineteen tracks long, needed to be trimmed, Moore, Gordon, and Gersh all agreed: "Genetic" would have to go. "I wasn't willing to have that," Moore says about retaining "Genetic" and bumping another track. "It would have affected the sound of the album." This time, though, the decision did not go down as well as it had with "Lee #2." Even though two songs Gordon sang ("The Destroyed Room" and "Hendrix Necro") and one that featured Moore ("Stalker") were also dropped, Ranaldo was rattled by the decision. "I felt there were other songs that could have just as easily been left off as that one, in terms of the quality of the songs," he says. "Sometimes Thurston doesn't have the patience for something he doesn't understand right away. And I was bringing in stuff that added different kinds of elements to the group."

"He didn't take it well," Gordon says of Ranaldo. "He took it personally."

The situation wasn't merely about one song, though; it was the culmination of tensions that had been brewing within the band for several years. For his part, Ranaldo felt his songs weren't taken as seriously as the others': "It was the George Harrison syndrome. George's songs never got as much time and energy from the rest of the band. I was sort of feeling that sometimes. Thurston and Kim tend to favor the songs with their vocals on them." For their part, Moore and Gordon felt the true Sonic Youth sound could be achieved only when the four principals fashioned a song together, over time, and they wanted the band to adhere to that method. "Genetic," admits Gordon, "had a different vibe from all the other songs we worked on together."

Compounding matters, Ranaldo was experiencing his share of personal tumult. In 1989, he'd met a transplanted Canadian named Leah Singer at the downtown club the Knitting Factory, where Singer was curating a festival devoted to handmade instruments and electronic music. The two quickly hit it off personally and professionally: With her background in print journalism in Canada, radio and commercial voiceover work in Japan, and film (she'd received a degree from New York University the year before), Singer, six years Ranaldo's junior, shared his interests in visual arts and the printed word. She'd seen plenty of American punk and postpunk bands while living in Winnipeg, and during her year in Japan, she'd been exposed to local noise combos. If anyone seemed like a soul mate for Ranaldo, it was the slender woman with the dark hair and large eyes.

The following year, Ranaldo and Linn separated, and by 1992, he and Singer had become a couple, although given that Ranaldo and Linn had a child, the separation was not easy. "It was really hard," says Singer of that time. "There was a lot of soul searching." Although Ranaldo confided his inner turmoil to friends, he shared little of his personal troubles with the band. "There was a lot of heavy stuff going on for me in that period," Ranaldo says. "It was making me question a lot of what was going on around me at the time."

One of those matters, it appeared, was his status in the band. Although Vig never heard anyone yelling, he sensed the tension over the

"Genetic" debate and overheard some terse discussions. While he personally liked the song, Vig realized it was a matter for the band to work out. At a tense band meeting at the studio, Moore explained his overall philosophy toward the band. "'Genetic' was a song that was obviously based on some personal issues Lee was dealing with at the time," recalls Moore. "And I felt a little weird having the band being set up for him to voice those issues in. And he said, 'Well, it *should* be set up for me to voice those issues—why would I be in it otherwise?' And my argument was that the band really started out as a forum for something I wanted to express. And that obviously changed over time." Not surprisingly, the conversation—or the implication that directly emotional songs weren't the stuff of Sonic Youth—didn't especially placate Ranaldo.

Hearing about the situation over lunch with Moore and Gordon, Kates and a DGC coworker were taken aback. "I remember thinking, 'That's pretty intense, that that could happen over one song,'" Kates recalls. For a brief moment, the possibility of Sonic Youth being a trio hung in the air as Ranaldo pondered his options. Some feel he considered leaving the band, although Ranaldo says it "never got quite that extreme."

"We tried to make as much allowance for Lee, and it became a little tempestuous," Moore admits. "That was the most tempestuous era we had in our career. It was a bit of a showdown."

After a few difficult weeks, the matter died down, a compromise of sorts reached when "Genetic" became the B-side for the album's first single, "100%." In retrospect, Ranaldo had to concede that the Sonic Youth working method (and, in certain cases, Moore and Gordon's wishes) overruled everything. "People don't feel close to a song when it's not something they put a lot of time and energy into," he says. "There's something to the fact that we had this body of songs we worked on for months and months and then this other one pops up at the last minute and you can't help but feel a little less close to it." The wound would heal, although it would take several more years for a complete mend.

FOR ALL THE "GENETIC" TURMOIL, the band still felt better about the new album—to be called *Dirty*—than they had about *Goo*, and Geffen felt even more confident. *Dirty* was penciled in on DGC's release schedule for July 21, timing that, for the label, couldn't have been better. In the wake of Nirvana's success, a market for such bands— now dubbed "alternative" rock—suddenly existed in greater numbers than anyone had thought possible. On the heels of *Nevermind*, Pearl Jam had scraped the top of the charts with its debut, *Ten*, and Soundgarden's *Badmotorfinger* broke into the Top 40. Only a dozen commercial alternative stations existed when *Goo* was released; now, over one hundred had sprouted up around the country, all featuring DJs more than happy to scream out "Temple of the *Dog*!" or "Eddie *Vedder*!" as they played records by the types of bands they'd dismissed a year before.

Across the country, A&R scouts for major labels stopped searching for the next Axl Rose or Bret Michaels and went looking for the new Cobain or Vedder—the next angst-ridden child of a broken home who screamed out his pain in song. A grunge movie—Cameron Crowe's *Singles*—was in the theaters, grunge clothing was soon in Macy's, and, most laughably, products like "grunge pencils" were sold in school supply stores. The flannel shirts that the stage-diving teens (and Moore) wore in the "Dirty Boots" video two years earlier were now in vogue. If it were ever conceivable for a Sonic Youth album to go gold or platinum—sales of either half a million or a million, respectively— the moment seemed to have arrived.

Beginning with the almost intentionally primitive avant-garage pounding of "100%," *Dirty* sounded primed to enter those leagues. Although the final bill for its creation was roughly the same as that of *Goo*, *Dirty* was as monstrous and jumbo-sized as Vig had wanted it. The songs didn't sound radically different from anything the band had come up with before, but they were buffed, chrome-shiny. Even when the songs stretched out to five or six minutes, everything sounded under control. The tracks sported easily identifiable choruses and more scrubbed and form-fitting arrangements. Ranaldo's lead guitar lines coiled around the songs like octopus legs; thanks to the integration of samples, Shelley's drums sounded more strapping. Gordon's voice was at times almost unnaturally tuneful; "Orange Rolls, Angel's Spit" featured the most varied singing of her career in the way it leapt from phlegmy to orgasmic to girl-group creamy.

The album still had a few lengthy, rangy instrumental breaks, and a truly extended noise guitar spurt erupted halfway through "On the Strip." There was even a hint of Glenn Branca influence: The car-engine-turning-over segment of "Swimsuit Issue" recalled the beginning of the fourth movement of Branca's *Symphony No. 1*. But the songs didn't fall apart as they had in the past. Moore and Ranaldo both flailed wildly on their frets during the ferocious interlude of "Theresa's Sound-world," but the arrangement then gently wafted back to its quieter, moodier refrain.

The sound of an unrestricted band trying to prove to the world (and themselves) it could balance art and commerce, *Dirty* was often thrilling as a result; it was also a testament to the way Vig and Wallace finessed the band's transition to pop. "Sugar Kane" (another result of Moore's curiosity about Marilyn Monroe, named after her character in *Some Like It Hot*) commenced with a whopping, sludgy riff that gave way to a springy bounce and, with Ranaldo's lead guitar snaking around and brightening it, a chorus hook. "Chapel Hill" galloped, "Purr" careened—but each in ways that recalled classic rock more than anything the band had cut pre-Geffen. "Drunken Butterfly" had typically mischievous origins. Originally called "Barracuda" in demo form since it felt like something Heart would have recorded, it became a tongue-in-cheek homage to the band when Gordon, singing in a particularly guttural tone, based its lyrics on Heart song titles ("tell it like it is," "even it up," and so forth). As the quartet pounced on its bludgeoningly basic riff, they sounded like the most arch metal band on the planet.

"Drunken Butterfly" aside, *Dirty* was the band's least emotionally guarded record. A handful of its songs, like those of the almost love song "Sugar Kane," were still riddles, but they were in the minority. The mood-swinging, soft-to-hard "Wish Fulfillment," the one Ranaldo-sung track that did make the cut, was a typically emotive song about a still unnamed, semi-famous friend and, in his words, "friendships and how they change once fame enters the picture." Moore was surprisingly blunt. With record censors, the Clarence Thomas hearings, and a presidential election all in the air, Moore threw vague caution to the wind and declared his support for Anita Hill (and his dislike of George H. Bush, "a war-pig fuck") on "Youth Against Fascism." The unsolved murder of Bob Sheldon, owner of the left-leaning Internationalist bookstore in North Carolina, brought out a typically encoded, but clearly agitated, lyric for "Chapel Hill."

"There was a lot happening around us at the time," Moore says. "And I think we were into making a sort of charged record. It was a heavy record." The heaviness only increased in December 1991, when random horrific violence hit even closer to home. Moore and Gordon still kept in touch with their L.A. friend Joe Cole; he and Gordon had lip-synched together in an intentionally crude, homemade video for "My Friend Goo." But their friendship was cut short not long after. After being robbed at gunpoint on the street near the Venice apartment they shared, Cole and Henry Rollins were led back to the apartment by the muggers. Once inside, Rollins managed to escape out a back door, but Cole was shot in the head. Gordon gasped when Rollins called to tell her the news; the murder made no sense. Moore's lyrics to "100%" were written in Cole's honor ("It's hard to believe you took off," Moore sang, as straightforwardly as he ever had), as were Gordon's to "JC," a set of free-verse, largely spoken reminiscences of her times with Cole ("That wasn't how it's supposed to be/Clear blue eyes, justice tries," she sang, ending with the fairly forthright, "You're walking through my heart once more"). The fluttery, jittery guitars behind her felt like an angry eulogy.

"JC" aside, Gordon didn't use her newfound higher-visibility platform to write sentimental, personal lyrics or love songs to her husband. Still more interested in inhabiting the lives of others than revealing much about herself, she used the songs she'd given on *Dirty* to further her ongoing theme, the lives of oppressed women. The narrator of "Shoot" was a prostitute abused by her john; the sinister, lurking music behind her felt like a visit to the seediest side of town. (By the song's end, Gordon sang as if she were vomiting.) In "Swimsuit Issue," Gordon slipped into the character of a real-life DGC secretary who sued the company after she claimed she was sexually harassed by the label's former general manager (about a year before the *Dirty* sessions). According to the suit, the executive pulled out his penis in front of the woman and made her watch him masturbate, among other supposed offenses. (The case was settled out of court for a reported half-million dollars, although the executive admitted no guilt.) The song, which named neither the company nor the executive, was also inspired by Gordon observing the way Geffen secretaries received flowers (but rarely a promotion) on Secretary's Day. "It was a corporation that was just as conservative as any other business or corporation," she says, "yet people think it's so cool because it's the record industry. But it's not very liberated."

"Male white corporate oppression," as Gordon taunted in "Kool Thing," had been a recurring theme in her songs; in some ways, "Swimsuit Issue" and "Shoot" were more polished updates of "Shaking Hell" a decade before, as well as *Daydream Nation*'s "Kissability." The roots of Gordon's mind-set predated the band by years—back to when, as a twelve-year-old living in Hong Kong, she'd endured the sexual taunts of American sailors who thought she was several years older. As a teenager in Los Angeles, she'd heard all about the strange men who offered to take girls' pictures or cast them in dubious movies; she'd even been approached herself. "It's weird to grow up and feel all the time that you have to be aware and have a wall around you," she says. The feelings didn't evaporate when she became a musician. During Sonic Youth's early days, she'd encountered more than a few club owners who told her "good show" after a gig and then pinched her butt. In her songs, if not in her guarded persona, she was finally letting it all out. The fact that she was doing so on the album many thought would make Sonic Youth stars was one sign of how little they ultimately wanted to compromise.

Although some at DGC were uncomfortable with the way "Swimsuit Issue" reminded people of one of the label's low points, everyone at the company, and at Gold Mountain management, could practically taste the album's potential success. The expectations, according to DGC's John Rosenfelder, were *"huge."* Cobain was repeatedly name-dropping them (and other precursors, like the Melvins) as influences. The company printed up T-shirts that read "Sonic Summer '92." The radio promotion staff was given strict orders to do whatever it took to get "100%" as much airplay as possible. (A radio edit of the song was commissioned, although calling it that was almost a joke: All the label did was delete the few seconds of bristling feedback that opened the song.) "In the process of Nirvana blowing up, everyone got a promotion," says Rosenfelder, who, along with most of the company, knew how influential Sonic Youth had been in Nirvana joining Geffen. "Sonic Youth got a big recording budget, nice posters, Butch Vig. The Sonic Youth bump was: 'We're really going to throw down for *Dirty*.'"

As far back as *Sister*, even possibly to "Death Valley '69," the band had been hearing they were on the verge of a mass-audience break-through. They'd grown jaded about such comments, but the expectations suddenly didn't seem so absurd. "I don't think *we* were that positive something was going to happen," says Ranaldo. "But given the times, we thought that if it was ever going to happen, it would happen then." For once, the band seemed more than happy to play along. When Geffen's East and West Coast divisions were pitted against each other in a company baseball tournament, Moore helped make special shirts for the occasion, scribbling "Western Stars" on their Ts over a crude star drawing.

UNLIKE PREVIOUS ROAD TREKS, which began as soon as the accompanying album was in stores, the *Dirty* tour commenced a few months later, at the dawn of fall. It was preceded by a few warm-up shows, including a free performance in New York's Central Park (with avant-jazz band leader Sun Ra opening) that was so thunderous, residents of nearby buildings on Fifth Avenue filed noise complaints against the city. The idea behind delaying the official *Dirty* tour came from the major leagues: This time, Sonic Youth would release an album, let it build in sales and momentum, then hit the road, "because that was the way *big* bands did it," says Lawton. "You build *up* to a tour." In arranging the itinerary, Lawton and Silva focused on even larger theaters than on the *Goo* tour, itself a sign that expectations were building.

Hal Willner, the record producer who'd first met the band when they appeared on *Night Music* three years earlier, witnessed the upgrade up close. Showing up for their appearance at the Warfield Theater in San Francisco on Sept. 24—the sixth show of a planned nearly yearlong tour—Willner beheld tour buses, a full crew with technicians, and roadies. The days of dilapidated guitars stashed in a drum case by the side of the stage were gone. It was, Willner thought, a long way from the sight of Ranaldo showing up for the *Night Music* taping with guitar cases tucked under each arm, a free hand carrying an amplifier. Unfortunately, Willner wasn't able to go backstage and say hello, since he couldn't find anyone at the venue who knew him.

As unpredictable and volatile as their stage show could be, their individual moves and personae were more or less cemented: the way Moore flailed his head back and forth, eyes closed, the way Gordon seemed to be kneeing her bass with her right leg, the way Ranaldo would thrust his guitar in the air. There would never be anything close to a standard Sonic Youth performance; a good night could devolve into an off one, and vice versa. Yet the band's show that evening, at the 2,500-seat Warfield, revealed how they were conforming to larger halls and ticket holders hearing them for the first time—while, at the same time, toying with that scenario. The *Dirty* material— "100%," "Shoot," "Sugar Kane" (dedicated to Hillary Clinton), even a rare performance of "Genetic"—adhered closely to the recorded versions; guitar mania and noise tangents were kept to a minimum. "Totally pro!" Ranaldo cracked at one point.

"Next year, the stadium!" Moore shot back.

Before "Teen Age Riot," Moore addressed the crowd with robotic sincerity: "I would like to thank everybody for not going to see Guns N' Roses tonight and coming to see Pavement and Sonic Youth instead." The audience cheered. In a slower, even more deliberate voice, he added, "Please don't lose control of your emotions when it comes to spoiled rock star narcissism. You know what I mean?"

Did they? Did they know what to make of those kind of comments or Gordon's own sarcastic references to Guns N' Roses (she dedicated "Swimsuit Issue" to Axl Rose)? (It wasn't the band's first dig at the biggest star on their label: A long-haired, baseball-capped dunce hitting on a girl in the "Dirty Boots" video was intended to resemble him.) Did they grasp the inside jokes in the between-song tape collage, which blared hip-hop records, Spanish voices, and a preacher? Was the voice over the PA announcing "You should go on tour with Alice in Chains" a joke? Were Sonic Youth making fun of the latest "grunge" buzz-band? (Most likely.) Before "Nic Fit," how many in the audience recognized the snippet Moore sang of the decade-old "Confusion Is Next"? What did the crowd make of the fourteen-minute "Expressway to Yr Skull" that closed the show?

In the past, the band knew the type of people who went to their shows. "They were just like us," says Shelley, "the weirdoes interested in something different. And they were all our age, from my age to Kim's age. Back then, it was all our peers." Now they weren't so sure. As they discovered, some of the kids who bought tickets knew little, if anything, of the records that preceded *Dirty*. Some were there because they'd seen Cobain sporting a Sonic Youth T-shirt or read an interview in which he touted his predecessors. "It was the beginning of a whole time when people came to the show because they heard about you on MTV," says Ranaldo. "It was a whole different thing from the SST days, where people found out about things through word of mouth or a fanzine. All of a sudden, there were people at our shows who maybe didn't know our history or what we were really about." Maurice Menares, who was promoted from equipment driver to tour merchandise seller, took note of the fresh-scrubbed teenagers buying shirts, particularly the girls who thought Moore was "this cool music boy" and revered Gordon.

The band mostly laughed or chuckled about the situation. They found it amusing when kids at the shows would start moshing and stage diving during songs that didn't call for it. But the moshing could also be a problem, especially when the stage divers would accidentally step on Gordon's array of pedals—she was, as always, at stage center—and the show would have to stop while technicians reconnected the gear. On more than one occasion, Ray Farrell of Geffen would watch as Moore asked the crowd, "So, is Nirvana really popular here?" The crowd would inevitably erupt, and Farrell couldn't figure out the motivation: Was Moore doing it to goose the crowd? Ultimately, Farrell sensed that wasn't the case. "It was more a preoccupation with trying to understand what was going on," he says. "A band they helped bring in was changing everything, and they were in the middle of this phenomenon." In fact, the band's feelings toward Nirvana's left-field breakthrough were conflicted: At various times, they felt proud, amused, envious, and frustrated. "It was," says one of their business associates at the time, "like having your baby brother suddenly become president."

Backstage, matters grew even more curious. They'd long been fascinated with stars and starlets. Now, thanks to the way in which alt-rock was in vogue, some of those people were showing up in *their* dressing rooms. At a stage-dive-heavy show at the Santa Monica Civic Auditorium on March 3, during the final leg of the American tour, Oliver Stone dropped by the T-shirt booth. "It was as if the band just came on Hollywood's radar and this was the 'new wave' of rock and they needed to understand it," says Bill Mooney of Tannis Root, the North Carolina–based merchandising company the band had begun working with in 1988. (Given the unauthorized Xerox art used on the band's pre-Geffen T-shirts—for instance, a photo of Sean Penn punching out a photographer—Mooney also realized he and his company would have to be more careful now that actual stars were checking out the merchandise.) Michael Hutchence of INXS chatted up Gordon. Gene Simmons of Kiss dropped by, proclaiming them "hot!," making crude comments about the women at the show, and asking if they would contribute to a Kiss tribute album that Simmons himself, in typical self-promoting fashion, was organizing. "You've got Simmons over here, Hutchence over there," recalls Markey, who was also in the room and filming. "What are these people *doing* here? Sonic Youth weren't going gold or platinum. But these superstar people were attracted to them."

Keanu Reeves, a fledgling bass player who looked starstruck around the band (especially Gordon), showed up at more than one show. The following year, he would start his own band, Dogstar, supposedly named after a line in a Henry Miller book. But was it coincidence that the lyric "See a dogstar jivin' like he's magic snatchin'" appeared in "Candle"? At another event, Kates noticed a Los Angeles Raiders football player clearly taken with Gordon—and seemingly unaware that her husband was also the guitarist. Kates had to gently suggest it would be best not to hit on her. In L.A. and New York, various celebrities and industry people seemed to be everywhere. "A lot of people knew that music was changing and that these guys were at the forefront of that," Menares says. "There were a lot of people who were latching onto them. I could see people sucking the big dick."

In his office in New York, Lawton received a phone call from U2's management, asking if Sonic Youth would consider an opening-act slot with them. Having worked with Sonic Youth for nearly five years, Lawton had a sense they wouldn't be interested, especially after the Neil Young experience. Instead of saying no immediately, though, he threw out a figure of $25,000 a night: "If you want to buy credibility, it's gonna *cost* ya," he barked in his scratchy voice. The caller on the other end, flabbergasted by a figure easily ten times what an opening band might be offered, said he'd call back but never did. Instead, the next call Lawton received was from Silva, angrily asking what Lawton had done. But Lawton shrugged it off. Taking what he thought was his cue from the band, he knew there were limits.

AT SEVENTEEN, Chloë Sevigny was one of the alternative nation kids. With her skull-cropped hair and smoldering yet disaffected gaze, she looked like an especially troubled child of suburbia. She didn't have too many friends in her high school in Darien, Connecticut, but with the few she had, she'd listen to albums like *Goo* and *The Whitey Album* and take the train into Manhattan on a regular basis to hang out with the skateboard boys, buy cigarettes, and smoke. For her, the vogue toward "grunge" in the fashion industry was a blessing: She liked the fact that models were starting to look "a little weird" and that their body shapes weren't perfect in the usual sense of the word. For Sevigny and many other kids, grunge was proof that the mainstream was becoming more accepting of nonideal beauty.

Kids like her were cropping up around the country, buying not only Nirvana and Alice in Chains but discovering, for the first time, bands like Dinosaur Jr. and Sonic Youth that had come before. Sevigny avidly devoured every issue of *Sassy*, the comparatively edgy, real-world teen magazine that had made celebrities (and sometimes pinups) of so many of the new alt-rock stars. (Delivering fan mail to Moore and Gordon, band publicist Dennis Dennehy watched as they opened one that read, "Hope to see you in *Sassy* magazine soon, you fucked up assholes." To Dennehy's surprise, Moore burst out laughing: "Most bands would be horrified to get a letter like that. But Sonic Youth knew why it was cool to be in *Sassy* and also knew why it was cool for one of their fans to get mad about it.") Backstage at a Dinosaur Jr. show, Sevigny even met Moore, who asked her if she had an extra lollipop. Sevigny had developed a crush on Moore—"the shaggy hair, the height, the boyish charm"—and after the encounter, she ran over to a girlfriend and they squealed in delight.

During the summer of 1992, just before the start of her senior year in high school, Sevigny landed an internship at *Sassy* after one of the magazine's editors saw her on the street; realizing here was an authentically "edgy" teen with fashion sense, the editor asked her to be part of a photo shoot. Through the same contact, Sevigny heard Sonic Youth was preparing to make a video and that they might need someone who looked appropriately waifish. Sevigny expressed interest but was still unprepared when the phone in her parents' home rang and her mother yelled out, "Chloë! It's *Kim* calling!" Sevigny thought it was her friend Kim from school, but instead, it was Gordon, asking her if she wanted to star in the video for "Sugar Kane." As Gordon explained over the phone, the story line would involve, as Sevigny recalls, "this grunge girl who's discovered on the street and swept up in this high-fashion grunge world and becomes a model." The video would culminate with the actress showing up at a "grunge" fashion show and coming out nude "as some sort of protest."

Sevigny was taken aback: by the call, the conversation with a rock star she worshipped, and the thought of doing a nude scene as her first acting role. But she was already thinking of becoming an actress, so she said yes; it would be a good opportunity to test the waters.

Before long, Sevigny found herself being filmed in a Perry Ellis studio in the city, along with a bevy of models and Marc Jacobs, the young, street-conscious Ellis designer. More than just one of Gordon's close friends, Jacobs had introduced a line of Ellis high-priced flannel shirts and skull caps—grunge wear for the wealthy. For comfort, Sevigny had brought along some of her friends, including Harmony Korine, a skater and NYU dropout she'd met in the city, and Harold Hunter, one of the city's most celebrated skateboarders. Even with their support, she was still startled when she walked out, naked, to see not just Sonic Youth but members of another one of her favorite bands, Pavement, staring at her. During the filming, Sevigny was also able to meet and speak with Gordon and Moore; she was surprised to hear them talk about not only fashion but youth-cult touchstones: "I couldn't believe these underground icons were into all this pop culture."

Directed by Nick Egan, a young Brit mostly known for album covers and book jackets and designing a label for Jacobs' fashion line, the "Sugar Kane" video wasn't quite as direct as Sevigny (and Geffen's Robin Sloane) had thought; the quick, choppy editing made the plot hard to follow. But in the way it tapped into the corporate-grunge industry and vaguely mocked it, "Sugar Kane" demonstrated the way the band was able to plug into hot-button culture topics and yet glide above them. "It was kind of strange for a while there in the early nineties," says Bob Bert, taking it all in from behind the drum kit in Pussy Galore. "It's like they were trying to sell out and keep their street cred at the same time." By having Sevigny walk out naked (albeit with black bars over her breasts) instead of donning a thousand-dollar grunge dress, it also embodied the band's often conflicted feelings about the big-money alternative climate in which they found themselves. (Not everyone in their circle grasped the conflicts, though, with Mudhoney singer and Seattle resident Mark Arm particularly disheartened: "To tell you the truth, I thought that was bullshit. They embraced this designer who all of a sudden made really expensive grunge fashions, which seemed ridiculous to me.")

The video also embodied the way in which the band continued to ensure that Gersh (and Geffen overall) were living up to their promise of creative control. Using artist and longtime Gordon friend Mike Kelley's stuffed animals for the cover of *Dirty* was one part of this strategy; Kelley's incorporation of found art (like damaged-looking toy animals) fit the band's aesthetic just as Pettibon's illustration had on *Goo*. (Geffen executives hoped the puppets could be incorporated into videos or marketing campaigns, but at Kelley's insistence, they never were.) The same tactic would now extend to their videos: With some input from Sloane, the band—Gordon especially—would select directors, stars, and concepts. If they wanted a particular, even unproven director (Egan) or actress (Sevigny), so it would be.

As a result, they began cultivating a slew of rising talent drawn to work (and hang out) with Sonic Youth, and the band was equally drawn to them. Whether it was planned or not, the union had a dual purpose: It connected them to a new generation while helping the band avoid seeming dated. Another case study that summer was Adam Spiegel, a twenty-three-year-old from Maryland who, under the *nom de camera* Spike Jonze, edited *Dirt*, *Sassy*'s male counterpart. A skateboarder, the diminutive, goateed, and enigmatic Jonze also made short films, including *Video Days*, a twenty-four-minute film for the Blind skateboard company that reveled in the rising art of street skating. To songs by Hüsker Dü, Black Flag, and the Jackson 5, skaters Jason Lee (then a bleached-hair skatepunk) and Guy Mariano rode guerilla-style between cars and in empty parking garages; the sardonic ending found them all partying and dying in a car crash. Sold mostly in skate shops or by mail order, *Video Days* was a word-of-mouth phenomenon—making it all the more surprising to Jonze when he returned home to find a message on his answering machine.

It was Gordon, saying she was a fan of *Video Days*. "It was such a crazy phone call to get on my answering machine," he says. "Kim Gordon from Sonic Youth is calling about this skate video I'd made."

Jonze already knew Tamra Davis; he'd done a *Dirt* photo shoot with the Beastie Boys' Mike Diamond, Davis' boyfriend. As it turned out, the band and Davis were preparing a video for "100%" that would have an action-sport component—telling the stories of Joe Cole and Henry Rollins as if they were skaters. Jumping at the chance to get experience behind something other than his usual High 8 camera, Jonze was given a 16 mm—his first—and shot footage of Lee and Mariano. Lee also made his acting debut, such as it was, as a Cole-like character murdered in the video. In the process, Jonze learned what a location scout was— "which," he says with a laugh, "wasn't part of making skate videos." Davis even let him edit some of the clip himself. The video would mark his first foray into the world of semi-pro filmmaking; it would also mark the band's second encounter with the censorship jitters hovering over the music business. When Gordon showed up on the set in a T-shirt that read "Eat Me," Davis called a Geffen executive to warn her; as a result, Davis stuck a piece of tape over the "M."

The "100%" clip had another notable outcome. When Davis prepared to film the band lip-synching in a West Hollywood home, Gordon invited Sofia Coppola. In the two years since she'd become part of the Sonic Youth universe via David Markey and the "Mildred Pierce" video, Coppola was still finding her way. Whatever acting career she may have pondered after "Mildred Pierce" was destroyed with her much-mocked role in her father's *The Godfather: Part III;* instead, she turned to, among other things, launching her own fashion line, Milkfed. But Gordon had another plan in mind for her: On the set, she introduced Coppola to Jonze. "Kim was the one who fixed us up," says Coppola. "She was always pushing it. Kim was a matchmaker." The fact that Keanu Reeves was also there—he lent Gordon a bass guitar for the shoot—nearly crushed the potential romance: Reeves also seemed attracted to Coppola, and the shy, easily intimidated Jonze retreated. But before long, Jonze and Coppola had hooked up, attending Sonic Youth shows together and stage diving to "Teen Age Riot."

The way Coppola and Jonze took a cue from Gordon also revealed the way in which Sonic Youth were now viewed as the imposing older siblings of the new alternative arts world order—the coolest kids in the school cafeteria. "We didn't feel conventional enough to be a model for anyone," Gordon says. Yet their lack of convention was the key. The Sonic Youth stance—a seeming indifference toward fame and fortune, an arch take on pop culture, an air of unfazed detachment—was everywhere. They hadn't been the first to wear T-shirts ironically, but suddenly everyone seemed to be doing the same. They weren't the first to notice a Japanese alt-pop trio called Shonen Knife, but once Sonic Youth plugged them in interviews, that band's word of mouth soared; soon enough, they were recording for Virgin Records. Phil Morrison, the up-and-coming filmmaker who'd directed the "Titanium Exposé" video, started having dreams in which Gordon would suddenly appear, casting a judgmental eye on whatever he was doing. Talking with friends, he discovered he wasn't alone. "Lots of people dreamed about Kim," he says. "That was a real phenomenon. And it wasn't about sex. She was the person you would be most concerned about whether they think you're cool or not."

By the middle of 1993, many of Sonic Youth's longtime cohorts—Mike Watt (with his band fIREHOSE and then on his own); the Butthole Surfers; Don Fleming's own band, Gumball—were suddenly being offered contracts by conglomerates. When he began making his first album on his own, for Columbia, Watt called Gordon for advice. "She told me, 'You have to talk to them and control all the marketing,'" he recalls. "Kim was worried about me being misrepresented. I never had to deal with that before—all that phoniness." Watt wrote down everything Gordon told him and then relayed his demands in a phone call with Donnie Ienner, then the label's president. Ienner listened and, to Watt's astonishment, seemed to take note of Watt's requests.

As a way to sate Sonic Youth, Geffen offered to turn the band into a de facto A&R department; at their cue, DGC would sign (or seriously consider signing) any acts the band thought had artistic potential.

Soon enough, one band championed by all of them (Manhattan's Cell) and another by Moore (St. Johnny, from Connecticut) had DGC contracts, though neither had anything approaching a national fan base. "At the time," says Lawton, "everything seemed to be opening up more. The old guard was falling by the wayside." Suddenly, nearly anything seemed possible.

Chapter 9

As BUTCH VIG SENSED EARLY ON, the obstacles they faced in broadening their audience were there from the start. Upon his return to Madison after the bulk of work on *Dirty* had been completed, Vig proudly played the rough mixes for friends at Smart Studios. "I just don't get this," one of them said. "It sounds like a mess." Taken aback, Vig, after a few moments of awkward silence, said, somewhat defensively, "Sonic Youth is the sound of rock music being destroyed." His friend had no response.

On one hand, Sonic Youth had never infiltrated the pop world as much as they had with *Dirty*. By the time the touring and promotional campaign had run its course, in the summer of 1993, the album had sold just shy of three hundred thousand copies—over one hundred thousand more than *Goo*, never mind most of their indie records. Thanks to the hard sell of Mark Kates, John Rosenfelder, and other Geffen radio promotion men, "100%" rose as high as No. 4 on *Billboard*'s Modern Rock Chart, the band's highest-ranking single. Just before the album came out, Moore even wound up on the cover of the chops-minded *Guitar Player* magazine, part of an article on the new six-string heroes of alternative rock. All told, the entire year was a vindication for a band that, less than a decade before, had trouble finding a home for *Bad Moon Rising*, even in the indie ranks.

Yet in light of expectations, a sense of disappointment lingered over the album and the year. "100%" was no "Smells Like Teen Spirit," no destroy-all-monsters rock radio anthem. To many ears, the guitars, even with a layer of studio gloss, still sounded eccentric; the feverish squealing alone in the song's verses must have confounded outsiders. "'100%' was not a great radio song," Kates admits. "It wasn't a break-out song." MTV remained cool toward their videos; even some Geffen executives, like creative director Robin Sloane, thought the clips were intriguing but hard to follow, the story lines too murky and the quick cuts too quick even for MTV-reared eyes. The fact that none of the *Dirty* singles even approached Top 40 airplay also hindered any hopes of MTV exposure. "We had our shot with 'Kool Thing,'" says Peter Baron, then Geffen's video promotion executive. "And after that, we always strove to get to that point again and never did. The sound of Sonic Youth was not the sound of commercial radio. They were not down the middle."

The label's perhaps inflated hopes for *Dirty* were summed up when, at Kates' urging, "Youth Against Fascism" became one of the album's singles. The song's allusions to Anita Hill (and the upcoming presidential election) made it a rare instance of Sonic Youth making direct reference to the times; "I Believe Anita Hill" T-shirts, playing off a key line in the song, were printed up. But the plan proved a major miscalculation. It was, Kates says, "one of the biggest professional mistakes of all time. I had people at my own company telling me I was out of my mind." Sure enough, the song went nowhere in airplay or sales. "I don't think we ever thought of it as a single," Ranaldo says. "They thought it was topical. Record companies are often deluded about stuff like that." In an unintentional sign of how the single's success was not destined to be, the word "Fascism" was misspelled on bumper stickers and buttons printed up to promote it.

Yet as Vig sensed upon hearing his friends' reaction to the album, resistance from commercial radio and MTV was merely one barrier the band and label faced. Despite their affiliations with grunge and their interest in connecting to that audience, Sonic Youth were simply not flannel rock. "It was typical of the stupid way people think," Gordon says. "Nirvana's whole thing was obviously a fluke. But all the interviewers said, 'Don't you think it's going to happen for you?' Listen to the *music*.

Use your *ears*. Our songs weren't really that different than they ever were." Their younger peers—Nirvana, Pearl Jam, Soundgarden, Smashing Pumpkins—were not always the most pointed lyricists; their rage and turmoil seemed strangely nebulous, as if they were so pent-up they could barely articulate what was troubling them. Yet even blurred frustration was more accessible than topics like sexual harassment in the workplace, the murders of two unknown-to-the-masses people, and other subjects that permeated *Dirty*. Two years earlier, the band had recorded a cover of the New York Dolls' "Personality Crisis" as a give-away single for *Sassy*, but even with only two thousand copies to pass along, the magazine was left with several boxes of records when not enough readers wrote in. As Christina Kelly, then one of the magazine's editors, recalls, Sonic Youth weren't as big as the Lemonheads.

"They thought it would sell itself, in a way," Moore says of *Dirty*, "but it wasn't like that. We were a little too old at that time anyway." The band's ages—between twenty-nine and forty—were, in fact, outside the core MTV demographic. But birthday years weren't the only factor. Reflected in the sober way they ran their lives and business, Sonic Youth were adults. It served them as human beings but not as rock stars; anyone trolling the rock press or gossip columns for items about crazed, drug-snorting groupie-chasers wasn't likely to encounter any of their names. They were too mature and cerebral for an audience interested in exchanging one group of rock & roll animals for another.

The band seemed relatively unfazed when a platinum-sales award never showed up at their doorstep: "I don't think any of us had feelings of regret when it became apparent like, 'Oh, it didn't really *fly* like they thought it would,'" says Moore. But at the label and management offices, and even with friends who hoped their success portended the onset of a golden era in the culture, a feeling of disenchantment permeated the air. Gold Mountain's Janet Billig sensed it when she visited the Geffen offices; she could taste the letdown. "After *Goo* it seemed like the market was wide open, but it became quickly apparent that it was wide open only for this one certain thing," says Julie Cafritz. "They didn't sound like the other bands who were selling. It was more like, 'Oh, right—radio sucks, MTV sucks, and kids have shitty taste.' That was the *real* message." Of the "Sonic Summer '92" shirt, DGC's Rosenfelder says, "Boy, were people pissed at that shirt, because it sort of didn't come true."

The band itself was baffled by the situation, but the reasons for their lack of crossover were glaringly obvious. "The music was too difficult to be hugely popular," Ranaldo says. "I don't think any of us as singers are palatable to the mass market. I may have the best pure voice, but I hardly sing at all. I don't think Kim and Thurston's voices are that marketable; they're more idiosyncratic and personal. The music had twisted changes, noise, and dissonance. Nirvana was straightforward. They were on message with what they presented; the sound and the emotions were a total package. Our stuff was all over the map compared to that." Once the hubbub died down, Ranaldo says, "It was like, 'Well, whatever—that's what the business people told us, and they're wrong again.'" With that, they decided it was time to go about their business, their way.

IN THE MIDDLE OF 1993, Gary Gersh left Geffen to become the head of Capitol Records, and Geffen president Ed Rosenblatt gave Gersh's job to Kates, who was itching to leave radio promotion and become more involved in record making and signing bands. However, the change had no effect on Sonic Youth's system of delivering finished records to the label. Four years earlier, in the fall of 1989, they'd recorded demos of the songs that would become *Goo* and sent them to Geffen, but that modus operandi would not be repeated. Sonic Youth was obligated to tell their immediate Geffen supervisor when and where they'd be recording and with what producer or recording engineer. But the label's involvement ended there. The finished tapes would show up, and Geffen/DGC would put them out: That was the agreed-upon arrangement, and they continued to hold the label to it.

So it was, in the early months of 1994, that a completed master tape of their next record showed up on the desk of Ray Farrell. Still among the most avid supporters of the band at the label, Farrell was determined that Sonic Youth CDs—as well as the vinyl they insisted on printing up of each new release, even though the format was nearly deceased—wind up in as many record stores, big and small, as possible. Since stores ordered copies of new albums in advance, Farrell received early previews himself, and the tape that showed up on his desk had a title scrawled on it: *Experimental Jet Set, Trash and No Star*. He had no idea what it meant, but he sensed what it symbolized: "I remember looking at that title and thinking there was something else going on. It was a signal to the company that the band was going to do things on their terms. It was a return to their roots in the sense that no one knew what the title meant."

The album had begun taking shape the previous spring, right at the tail end of the last European shows to support *Dirty*. They had already rehearsed in their new practice space in the city; onstage in Portugal in July, they interspersed "Kotton Krown" and "Kool Thing" with a few of the in-progress compositions, which were largely lean and tight. One of them, "Tokyo Eye," had the crowd clapping along even though it was an instrumental. Studio time was booked for October and November at Sear Sound—the same studio where they'd recorded *Sister*, but in name only. In the years since, Walter and Roberta Sear's business had relocated around the corner from Times Square, and the sound in its main recording room promised more musical intimacy than the band had achieved on either *Goo* or *Dirty*.

Since they'd been happy with the *Dirty* sessions and still felt comfortable with Vig, they hired the producer again; once more, Vig was sent a cassette with rough versions of the material. But to his surprise, the tape was nothing like the ones he'd been sent in advance of *Dirty*. Instead of long, unedited jams, these songs were generally shorter and more concise, "almost like two- or three-minute pop songs," he recalls. Vig was equally surprised when the band announced upfront they didn't want to belabor the process the way they had with *Dirty*; they wanted to do as few takes as possible and be more spontaneous. "At the time, we were responding more to the sort of music we liked that was more experimental and internalized," says Moore. "It was underground in reaction to the mainstream co-opting of the punk rock world and Nirvana, which became this big thing. All of a sudden it was Green Day. But you started seeing this celebration of experimental ideas and turntablism. That to me was completely exciting."

"With *Goo* and *Dirty*, we had the promise from the label of 'This is gonna be your big record,' and we were sick of hearing it and playing that long in the studio and spending all that money," says Ranaldo. "Against our better judgment we said, 'We'll go along with this and see what happens. We did it our way for ten years. Let's try it *their* way.' We went along with it to see where it led us, and it didn't ultimately lead us anywhere that was interesting." Although the new approach was an obvious rebuke to everything Vig had accomplished on *Dirty*, the producer didn't mind; since the band wanted to spend less time and money on the record, he even took a pay cut in order to work with them again.

Once Vig and the band settled into Sear Sound, the producer realized the band was dead set on its intentions. Overdubs were kept to a minimum; if a track wasn't nailed in a few takes, the band would tell him (and engineer John Siket) they were moving on to another song. "They'd do one take and go, 'That was the most perfect we've ever played that,' and we'd all start laughing," Vig recalls. "But I could tell that they were serious, too." The phrase "good enough!"—usually emanating from Moore's mouth as much as anyone's—became both a running joke and a statement of purpose. "We didn't want to labor it so much," says Shelley. "In the past Butch asked the guys to tune up between every take, and we're like, 'We're just gonna play.' We just wanted to get into it and not be stopped every five minutes. We wanted it to be a more immediate record."

The interest in low tech manifested itself in any number of ways. At one point, they handed a guitar to the sixty-something Walter Sear, who didn't actually know how to play the instrument; he banged on it for a while, and the resulting noise was incorporated into the final take. Elsewhere, Moore liked the sound of a cassette demo so much he insisted on using that take instead.

"We can't do that—it's really muddy and hissy," Vig remarked.

"Yeah, but the vibe is cool," Moore replied, and the rawer rehearsal tape was indeed used. (Later, Vig had to admit Moore was right: "There was something in the mix that sounded great.")

During another take, the buzz emanating from Moore's Fender Jazzmaster was driving Vig nuts, especially during quiet passages. "That buzz isn't part of the sound," Vig said, to which Moore replied, "But it *is*." Vig convinced Moore to turn slightly while playing, eliminating some, but not all, of the hum.

Later, when Vig tried to surreptitiously use a buzz remover on some of the tracks, his assistant asked, "Well, should I patch this before or after the . . . ?"

"What do you mean—before or after *what*?" Ranaldo said, picking up on the conversation. Vig had to confess to his plans, and the machine was not used. "They were like, 'Take it off—let it be what it is,'" Vig says. "They felt that the initial idea of how a song was expressed and performed was one of the most important elements. If you start belaboring it, it will lose the character of what it was to begin with."

The bulk of the basic tracks were finished in less than a week, just like the early days. But when it came to readjusting to the new working method, Vig wasn't alone. As much as Shelley agreed with the basic idea, he also preferred to work on his drum parts as long as possible until they were just right. Such wouldn't be the case with *Dirty*'s successor. "I probably would have worked on that album more," says Shelley. "But when you're in a group and it's the singer or guitar player who was saying, 'Okay, that's it,' it's hard to keep it going. 'Good enough' wasn't my favorite phrase." The swiftness with which the album was made was evident not only in the abbreviated recording time and lower budget (at least $50,000 less than *Dirty*) but in the way the recordings were remarkably close to the versions the band had played onstage in Portugal months before.

At the very end of the sessions, as Vig was heading home to Wisconsin, the group slipped in one more recording: a ghostly, Moore-sung cover of "Superstar," the old Carpenters hit, for inclusion in a Karen and Richard tribute album. In another sign of how acceptable they'd become in certain circles (and how times had changed since their "Tunic" video), Richard Carpenter not only sanctioned the remake but allowed clips of him and his sister to be used in the song's video, directed by David Markey and featuring the band in rare formal wear. Markey himself sensed how big "alternative" rock had become when he was handed a $50,000 budget to accommodate a Hollywood soundstage, air-conditioned trailers, cranes, caterers, hair and makeup artists, and a full crew.

Conspicuously absent from the completed new album were any songs sung by Ranaldo. Still smarting from the way his numbers had been treated on *Dirty*, Ranaldo purposefully held back. "After the hassles of my songs on those last two records, I don't think I even strived to have a song on that record," he admits. "I just felt like, 'If you guys don't want my voice in the mix, then I won't bother singing.' The songs always get divvied out. And maybe I didn't volunteer to sing any on that record."

Indeed, the album was largely considered Moore's baby; he'd written a number of its songs during a Japanese tour of his own, along with Mosquito, the band comprised of Shelley, his high school friend Tim Foljahn, and indie rock man of mystery Jad Fair. Shelley recalls that one of its songs, "Bull in the Heather," was largely conceived by Moore and Shelley in the band's rehearsal space. "The songs were written to be played fairly minimally," says Moore. "It was less wide and more linear than *Dirty*, which was sort of against the grain of what the record company wanted to hear. They wanted to hear heavy chunk riffing, especially with the advent of stuff like Stone Temple Pilots. Those [*Experimental*] songs were anti-that. It was definitely not a good career move, but what are you going to do? That's what I had happening at the time."

As Moore almost predicted, Kates was less than enthused when he visited Sear Sound to sample the results. By then, Geffen's three top-gun A&R men—Gersh, John Kalodner, who oversaw Aerosmith and White Zombie, among others, and Tom Zutaut, whose erratic charges included Guns N' Roses—were all gone or on the way out. Having overseen acts who sold millions of CDs for the label, the three men were formidable, charismatic figures in the Geffen offices. With their departures, it was up to those replacing them, like Kates, to prove themselves—and Kates quickly realized that the first Sonic Youth album he'd be overseeing would be their least commercial for the label. "I wasn't particularly psyched about what I was hearing," he recalls. "I remember thinking that I didn't see how this could do as well as the last two." The band told him, somewhat jokingly, that *he* wanted them to be more successful than they did, and Kates felt that choosing "Bull in the Heather" as the album's first single would only seal that fate.

In typical Sonic Youth fashion, Moore's in particular, the band defused the tension with humor. "Compilation Blues," a song recorded during the sessions for a collection of DGC rare tracks, was a twisted toss-off that poked playful fun at Nirvana (the lyrical reference to a "mosquito," just like in "Smells Like Teen Spirit") and Kates ("This is for Kate-o, for his compilation"). Kates laughed along with it—especially since he had little to do with the record eventually called *DGC Rarities Vol. 1*—but he also felt stymied. "I wanted them to reach more people and be more commercial than they were comfortable with," Kates says. "Everyone at the company wanted them to do well. But I was more guilty than anyone else of not accepting who they *were*. And that means doing records like *Experimental*. There was a limit to what I could do." Grappling with anything that could get radio play, he asked Vig to remix one of the tracks; Vig tried but couldn't find a way to do it. The album would be released in its intended form.

REFLECTING THE WAY in which he was its guiding inspiration, Moore had given the album its name, *Experimental Jet Set, Trash and No Star*. Not surprisingly, the title had no single explanation. It was either a play on their alter egos—Ranaldo, Gordon, Moore, and Shelley, respectively—or, as Moore told writer Alec Foege, it was inspired by the time Yoshimi P-We, the drummer of Japanese noise-thrashers the Boredoms, was in the company of Moore and Gordon and approached by autograph-seeking kids. "No—no star!" she said, in broken English.

As Farrell had initially sensed, the record was an intentional reaction against *Goo* and *Dirty*, and not merely in its lengthy title. Compared to the two albums that came before, the songs, some barely three minutes long, were short and spurty, intentionally fragmentary. The arrangements were sparer, the blanketed layers of guitars stashed away. With Moore (and sometimes Gordon) playing unfussy guitar figures and Ranaldo winding simple guitar leads around them, the songs had the feel of glorified demos. The windswept noise shards, screams, and bursts of static-drenched noise often felt as important as the melodies themselves. "We wanted it to be less rock," Gordon says. "*Dirty* was pretty much the pinnacle of that. I guess we were really disappointed in the label that they didn't get MTV to play the record. Or we just felt, 'Well, we're just not that sort of band anyway.'" (Another sign of their disillusionment: the way backstage passes given to Geffen workers read "weasel." At least one Geffen executive was miffed by the intimation.)

Even Gordon admits *Experimental Jet Set, Trash and No Star* was "a *weird* record." On first listen, the album didn't portend any strangeness—just the opposite, in fact. At the end of the sessions, with only acoustic guitars and drums left in the studio, the band decided to knock out B-sides on the spot. Gordon's take, a merger of New York grit and Appalachian folksiness called "Razorblade," did end up on the flip side of a single, but Moore's crack, "Winner's Blues," became the album's first track. With its shaggy-dog voice and acoustic strums, the song was the most intimate and bare-boned opener for a Sonic Youth album. For a few minutes, at least, it was possible to think they were reaching out to an audience in a different way than they'd tried before.

The thirteen songs that followed put any of those hopes to rest. As embodied by "Bull in the Heather," the sound was disjointed and brittle, with a chilly, metallic edge and random splotches of guitar noise. The first minute of "Starfield Road" amounted to a wind tunnel with a beat. Then came an actual, charging melody and Moore's voice (singing nonsensical lines like "Aye ye butt cheeks are tamed/As I splooey m'name in flame"), but only for another minute before the song abruptly ended. Like portions of the album, it felt more like a tease than a finished number.

The same went for "Screaming Skull," a two-chord thumper that was one of the most rudimentary songs they'd ever recorded. Cowritten by Moore and David Markey, it took its cue from the night Markey drove Moore and Gordon to the Sunset Strip but wouldn't tell them where they were going. To their surprise, his car pulled up in front of SST Records' newly opened "Superstore." ("Oh, my God," Moore said as Markey filmed.) Moore and Gordon were both taken aback at the sight of their former label, the one they had to coerce to be paid royalties, reaping the rewards of the "alternative" gold rush. Later, in Markey's apartment, he and Moore banged out the song, complete with inside-joke references to Hüsker Dü, the Lemonheads, and former Germs guitarist Pat Smear, working at the store at the time. "Let's go there, *Sister*'s there," Moore sang, the sarcasm in the words bolstered by the way his voice was distorted by amplifier effects. "Self-Obsessed and Sexxee," Moore's take on all the new alt-rock women on the scene, was more structured and complex, but still felt almost unfinished.

As frustrating as parts of the album could be—like the way in which "Waist" kicked into a fluid groove that seemed to end just as it began—the minimalism paid off in other ways. The starker arrangements provided more snug settings for Gordon's voice, bringing out nuances that hadn't been heard before. During recording, Gordon wanted what Vig recalls was a "weird and bluesy quality, almost like you just discovered a rare track." The result was "Bone," a Gordon-written song that began with a hammer-of-the-gods power-shred before settling into a drowsy, low-down groove, Gordon's voice nestling into it. The title derived from a character in Dorothy Allison's novel *Bastard Out of Carolina*, which Gordon was reading during the sessions. The airier atmosphere of "Skink," its lyrics inspired by Carl Hiaasen's novels *Double Whammy* and *Native Tongue*, brought out the guttural, low-scraping quality in Gordon's voice. The concluding and longest number, "Sweet Shine," was indeed one of the sweetest melodies the band had ever devised, Gordon's voice floating above the melody. "I'm coming home to Swall Drive," she sang—a rare, if still cryptic, reference to the plot of land her family had owned in Los Angeles decades earlier.

Years later, the band would call *Experimental Jet Set, Trash and No Star* a transitional album; some in the band couldn't even remember many of its songs. A sense of ambivalence and impermanence hung over it, even down to the cover. For the first time since *Sonic Youth* in 1982, the artwork featured their faces instead of a piece of art. The design came about by default: They couldn't decide on any particular cover, so a Geffen designer threw one together at the last minute, inspired by the cover of a bootleg of *Goo* demos. (The label did fork over extra cash for jewel-box inserts that allowed fans to change the album cover at will.) Reflecting their own ambivalence about the point they'd reached in their career, the album would be indecisive to the end.

EVERYTHING THEY'D ONCE imagined for themselves—that combination of artistic integrity and substantial record sales—seemed to be coming true for everyone except them. But even for those who'd achieved that goal, the results weren't always pretty. Pearl Jam's Eddie Vedder was clearly grappling with his success. "I'm being honest when I say that sometimes when I see a picture of the band or a picture of my face taking up a whole page of a magazine, I hate that guy," he said at the time. Ever since the days when the Replacements signed with a major, grappled with possible success, and self-destructed, indie bands had agonized over whether or not they were selling their souls. But few seemed to wrestle with it as publicly and intensely as Kurt Cobain. By early 1994, Cobain was consumed by the conflicted career feelings that erupted after the mammoth success of *Nevermind*. No longer the comparatively carefree kid who'd opened for Sonic Youth in the late '80s, Cobain was moody, withdrawn, and addicted to heroin.

"There was a big divide between what he *thought* he wanted and what he could deal with," Gordon says. "You can have one romantic idea about what it's like to be famous and rich. But there's a lot of drudgery. Record companies are machines and they like to work people. There was a lot of stuff Kurt thought was bullshit that he couldn't reconcile with. He was depressed to begin with, but it filled him with anxiety."

The two parties still shared a handful of lighthearted moments. Talking with Gordon before Nirvana began recording *In Utero*, the band's knotty, twisty follow-up to *Nevermind*, Cobain enthused that he wanted to make a clanky, noisy album—"just like Sonic Youth!" Gordon advised him against it; she knew that songs, not feedback, were his strength. But there were more telling signs of his struggles as well. When Nirvana played the New York Coliseum in November 1993, Ranaldo popped into Cobain's dressing room so that his son Cody, then eight, could meet the band. What Ranaldo encountered was a distracted, barely articulate Cobain who managed to perk up while speaking with Cody but otherwise seemed deeply unhappy and in the grips of something.

The two bands shared the same manager, John Silva of Gold Mountain, so they heard all the inside dirt, knew what was happening, saw the unraveling. They knew all about Courtney Love, whom Cobain had married two years earlier. Love had first entered the Sonic Youth universe around 1990, when she'd begun badgering their mutual friend David Markey to pass along a package to Gordon: "practice tapes, photos, articles of clothing—bizarre teenage-girl stuff," Markey recalls. She and Markey had known each other for several years, having met as extras in a Hollywood movie, where they both played punk rockers. Later, Love put together a band, Hole, but given her scattered ways and demeanor, few knew whether to take it seriously. When she announced to Markey that she was going to make an album and that Kim Gordon would produce it, Markey could only roll his eyes in disbelief at such exaggerated claims.

But Love was nothing if not relentless and focused, and after she continued nudging, Markey finally acquiesced and sent the package to

Gordon. At first, Gordon declined the offer: She'd never produced a record before, and, she says, "My first thought was, 'She's quite a character, and I think I'll keep my distance.' Some people you just know are trouble." Yet Love wouldn't take no for an answer. To *Bad Moon Rising* and *EVOL* producer Martin Bisi, whom Love also approached, she referred to Gordon as a "foxcore goddess." After Love asked again, Gordon agreed, but only if her friend Don Fleming lent a hand in the control room. Despite Love's obvious mania, Gordon still thought she was, at heart, "a really good singer and entertainer and front person," and the idea of helping a band led by such a magnetic, strong-willed woman appealed to Gordon as well.

As it turned out, Gordon had some free time in Los Angeles in the late spring of 1991. In the midst of the Smell the Horse tour, Neil Young had become sick and had to cancel the Los Angeles dates. (To Moore, the cancellations were final proof that the tour was "a bust," since it meant Sonic Youth wouldn't be playing an arena in the music-industry town that was L.A.) With the last-minute downtime, Gordon and Fleming were able to record the first Hole album, *Pretty on the Inside*, in a week. In the studio, Gordon gave the band general direction (Fleming handled the studio technology), as Love hung on her every word. "The rest of the band would look to me," says Fleming, "and Courtney just keyed in on Kim."

Fleming was impressed with Love's focus and intensity: While they were recording vocals for one song, Love literally ripped her clothes off while she sang. Like many at the time, Fleming sensed her drive but also her talent. Gordon had more mixed feelings. "Against my better judgment I got involved," she says. "She was either charming and nice or screaming at her band. She can be charming when she wants to get something out of somebody. It's pretty extreme." Later that year, Gordon would express her ambivalence toward Love in the lyrics of *Dirty*'s "On the Strip," the story of the "smartest girl on the Strip" who's "talkin' stories about your crazy trips/Messin' with stars and dumb tricks." She and Fleming also caught a glimpse of her intense world when one of Love's friends came by—a woman who cut up people's skin in patterns before stitching it back up. "It was like a designed scar," Fleming says. "But she had no training in it. I was like, 'Oh, my God.'"

In the years that followed, the band's interaction with Love remained friendly or cordial. She hung out with them during a portion of the 1991 Year Punk Broke tour, and during a backstage interview with MTV, Moore pointed to Love and called her, with equal degrees sincerity and wit, "the biggest star in this room." But by early 1994, the band's interaction with Cobain and Love grew more sporadic, due partly to their hectic touring schedules and partly, Gordon feels, to Love's influence. "Courtney really kept everyone at bay," she says. "Occasionally we'd see them when we were playing in Seattle. But the fact that he was with someone who alienated everyone around him was proof he was self-destructive." During one encounter, Gordon found it odd that Cobain, whom she rarely saw anymore, began asking her for advice, as if he had no one else to talk to.

Early in the afternoon of April 8, Gordon was in the apartment of her friend Daisy von Furth, the married younger sister of Julie Cafritz, when the phone rang. The two women were friends as well as business partners: They'd been asked by the owners of X Large, the Beastie Boys' clothing line, to start a comparable line for women, X Girl, which would focus on form-fitting jeans and tops. Gordon's interest in fashion was an obvious throwback to her mother's clothes-making skill; she remained the sole fashion-conscious member of the band. (At one point during his working relationship with them, Paul Smith had suggested to the men in the band they wear something other than work shirts. "Looking down at me through his fringe of hair, Thurston said, 'If I had money, maybe I'd spend it on those kinds of things,'" Smith recalls. "But he didn't want to go there.") "Kim spent so much time working on a look," says von Furth. "So it was a clotheshorse's dream. She realized she could be *paid* for her taste." The following day, X Girl was scheduled to put on a guerilla-style street catwalk show, which Sofia Coppola and her boyfriend Spike Jonze were helping to produce; Francis Ford Coppola, model Linda Evangelista, and actor Kyle McLachlan would be among those in attendance. (Moore would even plug X Girl in the lyric in *Experimental Jet Set, Trash and No Star*'s "Waist.")

The call put a momentary damper on things. It was Moore, telling his wife that Cobain had shot himself in his home earlier that day. Before Cobain's name was even mentioned, Gordon assumed the news was about Mudhoney's Mark Arm, who was going through his own period of self-indulgence. When she heard it was Cobain, Gordon was, she says, "relieved" it wasn't Arm: "Kurt's death was incredibly shocking and upsetting. It was a surprise that he *shot* himself, but it wasn't a total surprise." For his part, Moore, stunned as well, left their loft and went for a long walk, winding up at Kim's, a record store in the East Village, where he soon heard one of the store's employees telling someone on the phone about Cobain's death; Moore had to leave.

That night, Shelley was performing in town with the Raincoats, the British all-woman punk band who'd just reunited; both Cobain and Gordon had written liner notes for reissues of their old albums. Not surprisingly, the mood backstage was dour. Gordon reiterated to Farrell that the news of Cobain's death wasn't, in many ways, incredibly startling. "Anybody who can throw himself into a drum kit at the end of a show has got to be a little nuts," she told him. But it was still upsetting and unsettling, a sign that the dark side of pop culture was darker than they'd imagined.

IN THE MIDST of all the disturbing word out of the Nirvana camp, culminating with the suicide, at least one piece of positive news made the rounds. In the Moore-Gordon household, a baby was on the way. To many around them, the news was genuinely astonishing. It wasn't merely the couple's ongoing decorum, especially on the road. Ranaldo and Shelley had never heard Moore or Gordon talk about children; the same went with their longtime sound man, Terry Pearson, who noticed how maternal Gordon was toward young male musicians but never heard her talk of having her own child. During the *Daydream Nation* sessions, Ranaldo's friend Thom DeJesu had dropped by with his newborn daughter, and Moore instantly ran over, telling him how beautiful she was. DeJesu was pleasantly surprised; he hadn't expected such a reaction. When Vig heard the news, he flashed back to the night during the *Experimental Jet Set, Trash and No Star* sessions when Gordon passed on having a beer with dinner: It suddenly dawned on him that she must have been pregnant at the time, although he didn't get the news until later.

They had actually been trying for a while, but, Gordon says, "It was never the right time. Then you just sort of have to do it." During a marketing meeting for *Experimental Jet Set, Trash and No Star* in their Lafayette Street loft, with Kates in attendance, a doctor called to say they would be having a girl. A baby shower for Gordon's female friends took place shortly thereafter, complete with baby gifts and finger sandwiches. ("It was very girly," Cafritz recalls.) The shower was another sign that their domestic lives and their musical and creative weirdness were often two very separate worlds.

Because she was forty-one, Gordon faced certain obstacles; she and Moore eventually turned to a surgeon who specialized in high-risk pregnancies, and Gordon had no choice but to have a Caesarian section. The baby, with her blond hair and deep, probing gaze, was born (two weeks late) on July 1, 1994. In search of a name that was both playful and didn't have any "bad associations," in Gordon's words, they flashed on Coco Chanel. "We weren't really into Coco Chanel," Gordon says. "We just thought it was a cool name." The middle name derived from child actress Hayley Mills, star of the early-'60s Disney hit *The Parent Trap* and Gordon's first idol; Mills' teen pop hit, "Let's Get Together," was the first 45 rpm single in Gordon's collection. So it would be: Coco Hayley Gordon Moore. From their room, which faced the East River, Moore watched the Fourth of July fireworks illuminating the city sky before they checked out.

Soon enough, a rocker, a crib, and all the other accoutrements of parenting were sharing space with the records, coffee-table art books, and Jessica Wood ceramic art in the apartment. A copy of *Your Baby and Child*, a long-standing parenting guide, took up space on a shelf next to Moore's tattered paperback of a biography of art-rocker Rick Wakeman. Among Coco's early babysitters was Chloë Sevigny, who'd moved to the city after graduating high school and was an early model for Gordon and von Furth's initial X Girl clothing ideas. Trying on prototypes in von Furth's apartment, Sevigny would listen intently as the women gossiped endlessly about indie rock boys.

When Gordon and Moore were out one night and Sevigny babysat, Coco began crying as soon as her parents left. Usually she would calm down soon after, but not that night. Despite her years babysitting in Connecticut, Sevigny didn't know what to do. Thinking it would be comforting for the infant to hear her parents' voices, she stuck a Sonic Youth album in the stereo. But it didn't work—the music just made the baby wail harder.

ONCE THE NEWS of Gordon's pregnancy leaked out, any thought of touring behind *Experimental Jet Set, Trash and No Star*, which was released May 10, 1994, was tabled. Shortly before the birth, they managed to squeeze in an appearance on *The Late Show with David Letterman*, Gordon appearing very pregnant as they performed "Bull in the Heather," the album's first single. With Tamra Davis again directing, they also cobbled together a video for the song.

Much like the album, the video was done very much on their own esoteric terms. "With the first couple of videos, there was the possibility they could make you a pop star," Davis says. "Whereas by the time of 'Bull in the Heather,' it was like, 'Let's just make a really cool video, something we really love, and not have any of those expectations.'" A scene of young boys playing air guitar in a bedroom was inspired by a photo of Moore and his childhood friends used in the album's artwork; a re-creation of the '50s movie *Baby Doll* came from Gordon. Kathleen Hanna, then the raw-throated lead singer of the riot-grrl band Bikini Kill, danced around in front of them as they lip-synched to the track. As with many of their songs, the reference points made little sense to anyone except the band.

Still willing to maintain their media profile, the band promoted the record in whatever way they could. Moore went on *120 Minutes*, MTV's "alternative music" program, and hosted a show featuring Beck. A young, wide-eyed but observant Angeleno, Beck Hansen had himself spent time on New York's Lower East Side as a squatter-style folkie before returning to Los Angeles and reinventing himself a hip-hop-folkie musical collage artist. When his indie single "Loser" became the talk of that town in 1993, the major labels began circling. Immediately after a conversation about him with his bosses, Mark Kates, who was courting Beck, returned to his office and received a call from Moore asking him who this Beck kid was. (Like many, Kates couldn't believe the way in which Moore continued to keep track of every new underground band or musical trend.) Beck certainly knew who Sonic Youth were: When another major-label executive met with him, Beck told him he only wanted to sign with the label that had Sonic Youth. If they could get away with what they were doing in those confines, he thought, so could he. Soon enough, Beck too became part of the DGC roster.

In the label's offices, expectations for *Experimental Jet Set, Trash and No Star* were not quite as high as those for *Dirty*, but hope lingered nonetheless. Although Kates didn't agree, many at the company thought "Bull in the Heather" was the band's most approachable single. Their associations with of-the-moment musicians—riot grrls and Beck, whose debut album, *Mellow Gold*, was released a month earlier on DGC—couldn't hurt, either. Kates' gut feeling, however, proved to be correct. "Bull in the Heather" reached no higher than No. 13 on the *Billboard* Modern Rock chart. On May 28, the album debuted at No. 34 on the magazine's album chart—the first and only time they would crack the Top 40 on their own—but quickly plummeted.

More tellingly, "Bull in the Heather" wound up being the only video made for the album. Gordon's maternity leave was one reason, but Geffen was also becoming more conservative with its funds. Despite Cobain's death, 1994 would prove to be one of the company's most financially profitable years: Albums by Counting Crows, Beck, Hole, Aerosmith, and Nirvana (a posthumously released *MTV Unplugged in New York*) would boost revenue to half a billion dollars. By comparison, Sonic Youth's *Experimental* sales of barely 250,000 copies—a slight drop-off from the sales of *Dirty*—left many at the company unimpressed. Other, more popular bands were vying for the available video budgets. "Sonic Youth hadn't sold the way people had hoped," says Sloane, "so the label was becoming a little more hesitant with videos. If a video was only going to get three plays on *120 Minutes*, it was a waste of money."

They continued to appear in the pages of *Sassy*, continued to be the darlings of the rock press; *Experimental Jet Set* was received pretty warmly, as if it were the beginning of a return to their old, freeform days. Cobain's death was front-page news even in the *New York Times*, a sign (along with more depressing ones, like Ethan Hawke's unctuous slacker character in *Reality Bites*) that the alternative-nation world had made a major impact on the culture. But it was also hard to tell how well known any of them were. "Kim and Thurston were famous," says Phil Morrison. "But no one was *actually* famous. Suddenly it was the confusion of not being countercultural. It was about behaving counterculturally while being the culture."

At this particularly strange and confusing juncture, though, it wasn't too late to capitalize on their influence. Although the sales of *Experimental Jet Set, Trash and No Star* bore out Kates' concerns, the number didn't stop the band's lawyer, Richard Grabel, from flying to Los Angeles six months after the album's release to meet with Geffen president Ed Rosenblatt and David Berman, the company's head lawyer. "Nirvana blew up," Grabel says, "and we felt Geffen owed Sonic Youth for having introduced the two parties. And more than that, members of Sonic Youth talked to the guys in Nirvana and encouraged them to sign to Geffen: 'We'll be label mates and it'll be great.' And we believed that was very influential in getting Kurt and the other guys to go with Geffen. We all felt—me, the band, the manager—that it was time for Geffen to say thank you to Sonic Youth for making Geffen the artist-friendly label people thought it was."

With Rosenblatt sitting behind his desk and Berman and Grabel each taking a different couch, Grabel forthrightly announced that in light of Nirvana's record sales, Geffen needed to show its gratitude to Sonic Youth in tangible ways. As Rosenblatt and Berman listened silently, Grabel laid out his demands: He wanted the band's current contract scrapped in favor of a new seven-album deal, which would in-

clude more substantial cash advances for each record, and he wanted a
signing bonus in the seven-figure range. "I had no idea if they were
going to kiss my butt or throw me on my ass," Grabel says. "I didn't
know those guys well, either. I was still a relatively green lawyer."
Without saying much, Rosenblatt said the company would mull it
over and get back to him, and Grabel flew back to New York.

Within the ranks of the label, opinions on the demands were
fiercely divided. The A&R staff felt it wasn't worth debating: Even if
Sonic Youth were not moving truckloads of CDs, the band was owed
something. Their presence on the label had enticed not only Nirvana
but Hole, Beck, and promising bands like Scotland's Teenage Fan
Club; some even suspected Gersh initially signed Sonic Youth thinking they would be just that—a magnet for other, possibly more commercial underground bands. "Their mere presence on Geffen's roster
and their willingness to say to Nirvana, 'Hey, these guys are okay,' or
'This Gersh guy, he's okay'—that alone helped change the future of
that label just as much as Guns N' Roses and John Lennon being
shot," says Gerard Cosloy, who remained a fan, if an occasionally critical one, after they'd left Homestead. "So I would say Thurston Moore,
Mark David Chapman, and Axl Rose are the three most important
names in the history of Geffen Records."

The fact that Sonic Youth was a low-maintenance, low-cost unit,
one that didn't spend exorbitant amounts of money in the studio or on
videos, also played in the band's favor: They brought credibility *and*
thriftiness to the company. However, the lawyers were confounded.
Here was a band that had barely sold more than a quarter-million
records, and they were asking for all this? At meetings, a few Geffen
lawyers vehemently argued against the deal and for dropping the band
altogether. The timing was problematic as well: Coming so soon after
Cobain's suicide, the demands struck some as opportunistic. (Gordon
maintains, "It wasn't *our* idea.")

As it turned out, Rosenblatt was in their corner. Before he'd joined
Geffen Records in 1980, he'd been a vice president at Warner Brothers—the major label that stood by the likes of Randy Newman, Bonnie Raitt, and Van Morrison during their lean years, the label that

believed in long-term careers for its artists. Rosenblatt applied that same philosophy to Geffen, and Sonic Youth benefited from it as much as anyone. "I remember Eddie saying, 'We need to have it taken care of, and we're going to take care of it,'" recalls Kates of Grabel's offer. Within a few weeks, Rosenblatt called Grabel and told him it was a done deal. Sonic Youth's business team had managed to leverage their cool.

Celebrating the completion of *Daydream Nation*, summer 1988: engineer Nick Sansano (with champagne), Moore, Shelley, Ranaldo, and studio manager Dave Harrington hover over assistant engineer Matt Tritto and Gordon. *(Photo courtesy Nick Sansano)*

Gordon designing the cover of *Daydream Nation* at Greene Street studios. *(Photo by Nick Sansano)*

The big score: Moore pondering lyrics in the studio during the troubled *Goo* sessions. *(Photo by Nick Sansano)*

Two different types of hair metal: Gordon and Moore meet their new DGC/Geffen label-mates Nelson, 1990. *(Photo by Mark Kates)*

Preparing to take the stage for a free show in the parking lot of Tower Records, San Francisco, August 1990. *(Photo by Jay Blakesberg)*

Confronting the emerging alternative market at the Tower Records lot, August 1990. *(Photo by Jay Blakesberg)*

Taking a break in Rotterdam during the summer 1991 "Year Punk Broke" tour with Nirvana, Dinosaur Jr., and others. *(Photo by David Markey)*

Anarchy in the U.S.: Moore gives power (and strums) to the people, 1991. *(Photo by Ebet Roberts)*

In bloom: David Markey, Kurt Cobain, and Kim Gordon at the
Pukkelpop Festival, Belgium, August 1991.
(Photo by Thurston Moore/courtesy David Markey)

Before the fall: Courtney Love and Gordon at the Reading Festival, Berkshire,
England, August 1991. *(Photo by David Markey)*

Time to connect with the grunge crowd: Moore, Gordon, Shelley, and Ranaldo, outtake from *Dirty* photo session, 1992. *(Photo by Richard Kern)*

Rock and roll, all night: Gordon, Gene Simmons, unidentified friend, and Shelley, backstage at the Santa Monica Civic, 1993. *(Photo by David Markey)*

at scratch fever: Julie Cafritz and Gordon as Free Kitten, 1993. *(Photo by Jim pring and Jens Jurgensen)*

he art couple: Lee Ranaldo and Leah Singer, New York City, 1994. *Photo by Stefano Giovannini)*

Into a new groove: Moore (center) delving into freeform improvisation onstage with drummers Tom Surgal and William Winant, 1997. *(Photo by Catherine Ceresole)*

Sidetripping: Moore and baby Coco visiting William Burroughs at his home in Kansas during the R.E.M. tour, 1995. *(Photo by Lee Ranaldo)*

...othed lunch: Gordon, Michael Stipe, and Burroughs. *(Photo by Lee Ranaldo)*

...hortly before taking the stage at Lollapalooza, George, Washington, July 1995. *(Photo by Jay Blakesberg)*

A room of their own: pondering the future at their new studio, Echo Canyon, 1998. *(Photo by Stefano Giovannini)*

"A thousand edits": as Joni Mitchell keeps watch, Ranaldo gears up at Echo Canyon, 1998. *(Photo by Stefano Giovannini)*

Neither home nor alone: Moore and quasi-doppelganger Macaulay Culkin, on the set of the "Sunday" video, New York City, 1998. *(Photo by Lee Ranaldo)*

Moore, Gordon, and Jim O'Rourke during the *Goodbye 20th Century* recording sessions, Echo Canyon, 1999. *(Photo by Lee Ranaldo)*

Psychic hearts: Gordon comforting Moore during a migraine attack on the *NYC Ghosts & Flowers* tour, 2000. *(Photo by Stefano Giovannini)*

Last men standing: Ranaldo and O'Rourke wrapping up another long night of *Murray Street* sessions, Echo Canyon, 2002. *(Photo by Stefano Giovannini)*

New York City ghosts and flowers: Gordon and mentor Dan Graham at a Gordon gallery opening, circa 2002. *(Photo by Stefano Giovannini)*

Jam back at the house: Gordon and Moore at home in Northampton, Massachusetts, 2002. *(Photo by Stefano Giovannini)*

Sonic youth, the next generation: Moore instructs Coco in the ways of the piano, Northampton, 2002. *(Photo by Stefano Giovannini)*

Radical adults: O'Rourke, Ranaldo, Gordon, Moore and Shelley after wrapping up *Sonic Nurse*, New York, 2004. *(Photo by Richard Kern)*

Twenty-five years and counting: back to a quartet and taking a break during the *Rather Ripped* recording sessions, New York City, early 2006—almost a quarter century after the very first Sonic Youth shows. *(Photo by J. Scott Wynn/Retna)*

Coming around again: one final show at CBGB, June 2006, four months before the club closed. *(Photo by Jen Maler/Retna)*

Chapter 10

IN LATE SPRING, ED ROSENBLATT flew to New York to meet with the band and firm up their revised contract; in the process, he learned more about their next record, which was almost finished. The arrival of Coco had brought about a temporary pause in Sonic Youth activity; with no full-scale tour to back *Experimental Jet Set, Trash and No Star* and Gordon and Moore settling into lives as urban parents, the second half of 1994 was relatively quiet. Gradually, though, they began reconvening at their new rehearsal space on Mott Street, three flights down into the belly of the Lower East Side beast. Aside from a bodega on the block and a Mexican restaurant down the street, not much else was around to distract them. They were left to their own devices, which now included Moore and Ranaldo's newly purchased effects pedals—vintage, shoebox-size contraptions that lent a layer of shimmery textures to their guitars.

Even with Coco in the mix, they managed to find several hours a day to restart the diligent process of working up material. But little about the new project would repeat the way its predecessor had been constructed. The rough song sketches were longer, looser, and more spacious than those on *Experimental Jet Set, Trash and No Star*. To Ranaldo, that album, the one without any of his singing, didn't feel "group connected, but the next record felt like the old days again." Ranaldo himself was feeling in a better place. After five years, his divorce from his first wife, Amanda Linn, was almost finalized, and he and Leah Singer were now living together not far from his former loft on Duane Street, where Linn and their son Cody remained.

Gordon was also entering the project with a different perspective. As a way to nudge friend Julie Cafritz back into music making after her last band, STP, collapsed, Gordon coaxed Cafritz into forming an intentionally crude two-guitar duo, dubbed Free Kitten. Inspired by primitive indie bands like Royal Trux ("they made records with *two* people," says Gordon, "so it didn't have to be a band"), Free Kitten made its debut at a noise improv show in Manhattan; trying to prove women could make experimental noise as much as men, the two women flailed at their guitars. What started as a one-off goof, though, became a somewhat more serious undertaking, especially once Free Kitten recorded a few singles and then expanded to a full band with the addition of Pavement bass player Mark Ibold and Boredoms drummer Yoshimi P-We. "It was a band of second bananas," says Cafritz. "It was the better version of the roadies having a band." With this lineup, Free Kitten unleashed an entire album, *Nice Ass*, in 1994. The songs, written and sung by Gordon and Cafritz, were a bristling, mocking lot that brimmed with swipes at indie rock boys, the music business, and various unspecified targets; as with their first show, Free Kitten wanted to be as abrasive and offending as possible, and mostly succeeded.

Free Kitten gave Gordon both an outside-band showcase (an even more prominent one than Harry Crews, a short-lived, more conceptual band she'd formed with Lydia Lunch in the '80s) and a place to write her own songs and play more guitar. "In Sonic Youth, Kim wasn't starting the songs," says Cafritz. "But once she got on the guitar and did half the songwriting with me, she was hard-pressed to go back to bass." Gordon had played a six-string on several earlier Sonic Youth songs, including "The Good and the Bad" and "Crème Brûlée." But when the band reconvened, Gordon stuck with her relatively new instrument. "I knew that if I played guitar, it would immediately change the sound," she says, "and make it less rock and more open." She was right: The absence of a bass resulted in a subtly different group sound, all midrange and high-end and little low-end. "It changed the dynamic," Gordon admits, and in more ways than one: Shelley, who was simply told Gordon was sick of being the bass player, had to readjust his drumming to compensate for the lack of a deep-bottom anchor. (Later, sound man Terry Pearson bought a device that allowed him to drop Gordon's guitar one octave, making it sound more like a bass in concert.)

When time came to put the songs on tape, several other modifications were made. Unexpectedly, Mark Kates received a call from his DGC coworker Ray Farrell telling him he and Kates would be sharing A&R duties on the record. Kates says the conversation was "pretty devastating," but part of him had seen it coming: His dissatisfaction with *Experimental Jet Set, Trash and No Star* had surely set the changeover in motion. ("Maybe I wasn't deferential enough to their artistic needs," he says.) The fact that he was also doing A&R for Hole didn't help his cause; the band had lingering mixed feelings about Courtney Love. For the first time in its career, Sonic Youth also decided to make a record outside New York. Georgia was briefly considered, but the locale was switched to Memphis when they began hearing from friends like Pavement about a funky, lived-in studio called Easley, located far from the tourist-driven Beale Street and closer to the city's airport. With its large, rec-room space and comparatively low cost (about half the price per day of a Manhattan studio), Easley was appealing on several levels. The velvet Elvis paintings in its lobby also provided an appropriate layer of pop culture kitsch. In late winter, they loaded up a truck with their gear and headed south.

With its casual atmosphere and air of musical history, from R&B to Elvis, Memphis proved to be something of a healing place, especially after their last three stress-filled projects. With no Butch Vig or Ron Saint Germain in the room, they would produce the record themselves, using only the same engineer, John Siket, who'd worked with them on *Dirty* and *Experimental Jet Set, Trash and No Star*. "There was a stiffness to the way some of the songs are played on *Goo* and *Dirty*," says Gordon. "So this was the beginning of us finding a way to record our music more naturalistically. That record is loose. It sounds like *music*, and more organic."

Since much of the material had been worked up in Manhattan before the trip, the sessions were even less harried than they expected. If a particular song wasn't immediately falling into place, they took a break and indulged in one of the city's many charms: thrift shops, Shangri-La Records (Memphis' leading indie and underground record store), roadhouse clubs (in Mississippi, they caught a set by blues man Junior Kimbrough), and the famed duck march at the Peabody Hotel. On Easter Sunday, all of them, plus Coco and her on-the-road babysitter, Maurice Menares, attended the Reverend Al Green's church service. "It was fun being away from everything," Gordon says, "It was very relaxed. We went for so much barbeque I don't know how the record ever got made."

When they actually were recording, another, newer sensibility arose. When they listened back, the New York demo of a jarring, discordant track called "Panty Lies" sounded better than anything they'd cut in Memphis, so in a few cases, they either used the original work tape or integrated part of it into the finished Memphis performance. It was the beginning of a determinedly anti-polished approach to record making: the attitude, which represented further fallout from the early Geffen days, that a song would never sound as good as the first time it was put on tape. "That was the period of 'the demo had the best feel and we'll never make that better,'" Shelley says. "John Siket would make fun of it: 'It can't be better because it's not the demo!'" Shelley didn't always agree; like Ranaldo during overdubbing, he preferred to work over the material until it was the most fine-tuned it could be. But taking a cue from the rawer, post-grunge indie rock poking up around the country, Moore and Gordon preferred a more spontaneous approach.

Visiting the band in Memphis, Farrell, in his part-time role as A&R man, saw the constructive results of the change in locale. "There were no distractions," he recalls. "Even though they were in Memphis, it was like they were in a really small college town. They were very focused." The move was particularly evident in a track worked up in New York prior to the relocation. One day, Moore began playing a melodic chord change, his effects pedal lending the strums a glistening, watery sound; Ranaldo joined in with a single-note lead to accompany it. Over time, that rudimentary foundation expanded but with a twist: The finished song had a mellow, pretty verse and chorus, and Moore sang it as if he were concentrating hard not only on staying in tune but matching the exquisiteness of the music.

Even though Kates knew he wouldn't be as involved with the new album as its predecessor, he too made the trip to Memphis. Proudly, Ranaldo told him they'd finally done it: They'd written a hit—although, he added, it was twenty minutes long.

And it was: Over time, the song that had begun in New York, "The Diamond Sea," inflated to nearly a half hour in length. After the initial verse-chorus sections, the melody slowly dropped off entirely and intricate, overlapping guitars took over, each section meticulously worked out, almost sculpted. "We felt really alienated from the major-label industry at that point," says Ranaldo. "It seemed like everyone's head was up their ass, trying to shove all these bands on the public and do what Nirvana did, which was obviously never going to happen again. With 'The Diamond Sea,' we really got back to what we really did, which was noisy sound experiments. We were starting to flex those muscles again."

"Beginning with that song, nearly every record after that had that vibe," says Farrell. "The records become less concerned with rock music. They had more space in the songs. And they started to expand on the ways the guitars interact with each other."

Of Ranaldo's hit-single line, Kates recalls, "That was a very typical Sonic Youth thing to say and do. It was always a creative battle with a lot of humor." Yet Kates also sensed he could do something with the track; after all, it *was* strikingly tuneful, especially for them. Already pondering possible radio entry points, Kates thought length wouldn't be an issue; one way or another, the song could be made to work.

What Kates didn't hear at the time was that the band was also pondering a name change for the new album. The fact that they were no longer youthful may have been a factor, but their own past was also beginning to weigh on them. "We wondered, what would people's reactions be to a new record if they took us as a brand new band?" says

Ranaldo. "How would people react if they didn't have the jaded history of all our past records? By that point, every record was being judged in relationship with another record." The idea eventually receded, but the name they wanted to use—Washing Machine—would instead become the title of the album. It was a play on something Moore and Gordon once said about the band being a brand, like an appliance, although Ranaldo also feels it was a subtle dig at their pop era, as if they were cleansing themselves of being "dirty."

During his visit, Kates also mentioned a proposal they should consider: They'd been offered a slot on the summer 1995 Lollapalooza tour. If they were still interested in reaching out to the mass numbers of kids still taken with moshing and so-called alt-rock, here could be their latest, and perhaps best, opportunity.

SHOULD THEY SIGN ON FOR LOLLAPALOOZA? At first, they weren't sure. The tour—an annual music festival, traveling circus, and flea market cofounded by William Morris agent Marc Geiger and Jane's Addiction frontman Perry Farrell—had launched in 1991 with a lineup heavy on underground and indie rock: Jane's Addiction alongside Nine Inch Nails, the Butthole Surfers, and Body Count (rapper Ice-T's hard-rock band), among others. In what would amount to the first sign that the new youth market had money to burn, the tour made $10 million, and the success of *Nevermind* later that year only made Lollapalooza more appealing to both the music business and kids who'd begun worshipping Kurt Cobain and Eddie Vedder. With each subsequent year, the tour grew grander in scale and profit, attracting large, mostly white crowds happy to pump their fists to Pearl Jam, Soundgarden, Smashing Pumpkins, Red Hot Chili Peppers, and Ice Cube; they could also buy ethnic fast food and T-shirts (and, perhaps, investigate the festival's voter-registration and animal-rights booths). Lollapalooza even made money in 1993, when the headliners were Primus, the Bay Area smarty-pants trio with the squirmy, borderline-novelty funk-pop songs.

Due to their ambivalence toward Farrell and the increasingly commercialized, corporate-alternative world Lollapalooza had come to symbolize, Sonic Youth had resisted the tour in the past. "It never represented where we were coming from," Shelley says. (Earlier, Moore described the festival as "a tacky thing" to the *New York Times*.) In 1993, though, Free Kitten had played on a few of Lollapalooza's smaller, fringier second stages. Even though Gordon and Cafritz were continually fighting to be heard over the din of Tool on the main stage, Gordon and Moore (who also served as their van driver) found the festival vibe mostly satisfying. On the sidelines, they were also shielded from the politics of the main stage—who went on first or last, who got paid what amount of money, and other wheeling and dealing. Maybe being a part of the festival one day wouldn't be such a bad idea.

By 1995, Lollapalooza's very triumph in the marketplace began working in the band's favor. Farrell and Geiger were acutely aware of the criticism that the festival had strayed from its underground roots and had too much of an eye on the pop charts, so they decided to reverse course and go "indie college radio core," as Geiger says. In its own way, the festival had become a metaphor for the ascent of the new music, the way it was struggling with its own integrity and credibility issues. "We were looking at keeping the programming as fresh as you can keep it under the death and overcommercialization of the underground, which happened right around that time," Geiger says. "Right then was Matchbox 20, Better Than Ezra, and Third Eye Blind. If we wanted to be big, we would have put on *those* fucking bands. But we wanted nothing to do with that."

In that scenario, according to Geiger, Sonic Youth were immediately approached as the headliners: They were, he says, "the godfathers" of the scene. (According to one source, the band would only participate if they were the headliners; others say any number of bigger-name bands backed out, leaving the organizers without many options.) But before the lineup was set, an amusing game of musical phone tag ensued when some of the bands contacted—Sonic Youth,

Pavement, Hole, the Jesus Lizard—began feeling each other out, wondering if the other would take the Lollapalooza plunge. Sonic Youth ultimately agreed, partly because of the other acts on the bill and partly because the paycheck promised by the tour would help them achieve their next goal: the financing of their own studio. If successful, the tour would give them the monetary ammunition to truly do things their own way, at their leisure, and in their own creative playground.

In the end, Lollapalooza 1995 would round up the largest number of fringe or indie acts since its inception. Technically, Sonic Youth, Hole, and California hemp-rappers Cypress Hill would be the headliners, each paid equally. They would be sharing the main stage with indie rock pals like the Jesus Lizard and Pavement, as well as Sinéad O'Connor, the ska-pop band Mighty Mighty Bosstones, and Beck. (One beneficiary would clearly be Gold Mountain, which managed not only Sonic Youth but Hole and Beck.) The second stage would include bands Sonic Youth suggested (Mike Watt, Pork Queen, Thomas Jefferson Slave Apartments) and an impressive lineup that, depending on the city, would include the Roots, Yo La Tengo, Built to Spill, Coolio, the Dirty 3, Superchunk, and Moby, then in his hardcore-band period. The organizers had a feeling such an eccentric lineup wouldn't do as well as the previous year's Lollapalooza, fronted by the Beastie Boys and Smashing Pumpkins. And they were right: Ticket sales, especially in Midwestern cities like Kansas City, were slower than in 1994. "It was absurd in a way that we were the headliner," Gordon says. "We weren't going to draw. It was like letting the inmates rule."

Before they embarked on Lollapalooza, however, they had another road obligation to fulfill. Even though the Neil Young experience had left them wary of being an opening act, this offer was difficult to turn down: R.E.M. were beginning their first American tour in six years and had asked Sonic Youth to come along for several weeks of West Coast and Midwest shows. (The first week or so of U.S. dates were ultimately scrapped when drummer Bill Berry had an aneurysm burst onstage in Europe.) The money wasn't as much as they'd received on the Young tour, but they'd been friendly with R.E.M. for a long time. Both bands had played the Music for Millions concert in New York back in 1981, albeit on separate nights, and Moore had contributed a guest vocal to the band's latest album, *Monster*, intoning on the glam throwback "Crush with Eyeliner." Geffen executives were strongly in favor of the tour—it would be good exposure for Sonic Youth—and since Lollapalooza had been booked into some of the same outdoor sheds and venues, the R.E.M. shows would also serve as a warm-up for working the larger stages.

But as with the Young tour, the actual experience proved to be less rousing than expected. R.E.M. fans were more tolerant of twisty alt rock than Young loyalists, but they were equally apathetic to Sonic Youth and the still-unreleased Memphis songs the band was playing. Many concertgoers didn't even bother entering the venue until R.E.M. appeared. From behind his drum kit, Shelley would look out each late afternoon and see nothing but empty orange seats; "This is thankless," he would think to himself. Due to concerns about the strain put on Michael Stipe's voice—and R.E.M.'s decision to extend the time between songs in order to rest Stipe's throat, or so Sonic Youth were told—Sonic Youth's set was sometimes cut back from forty-five to thirty minutes; "The Diamond Sea" alone would eat up most of that time. "I'm like, 'Who cares about Stipe's voice—you got a drummer who almost lost his *head*!'" says booking agent Bob Lawton. "But everything around R.E.M. was so uptight and scary then."

The tour also gave them a glimpse into the type of career they still didn't have. Fourteen years earlier, both R.E.M. and Sonic Youth were new, marginal bands recording for small labels in their respective cities. In the years since, both had made the leap from indies to major labels, and both took pride in their uncompromising positions when it came to their art. Yet the turns each had taken were dramatic. R.E.M. were now an arena band with hit singles and traveling tour chefs; later in the tour, after Sonic Youth's stint, they would headline Madison Square Garden. If "Kool Thing" had taken off, perhaps Sonic Youth would have been in the same position. But it hadn't, and they weren't. "I remember feeling that here we were, two bands, peers and contemporaries," Ranaldo says. "Yet they were through the roof in terms of public recognition. They had such a big operation around them." By comparison, Sonic Youth were, Ranaldo says, "just this opening band."

THEY'D JUST FINISHED their first set on the first Lollapalooza when the initial incident happened. Jim Merlis, an easygoing, bespectacled publicist for Geffen Records, was sitting in a tent backstage at the Gorge, a spectacular outdoor venue in George, Washington. As the publicity person in charge of monitoring Hole, Merlis always knew to expect the exasperatingly unexpected when it came to his notorious client, but he wasn't anticipating this: Gordon rushing up to him with a clearly shaken Kathleen Hanna of Bikini Kill. "This is Hole's publicist," Gordon told Hanna, by way of introduction, before saying to Merlis, "She has a story to tell you."

Hanna had been standing by the side of the stage during Sonic Youth's set; Moore had even dedicated "Bull in the Heather" to her. But as the band played, oblivious to what was happening behind them, Hanna and Courtney Love had exchanged words and then, apparently, fists, with Love throwing the first blow. Even knowing Love as he did, Merlis didn't know what to do; neither did Mark Kates, who was in Sonic Youth's trailer after their set when Hanna came in to tell them what had gone down. Writing about the incident in an online Lollapalooza journal for *Spin* magazine that went up that day, Moore wrote that "everyone is disgusted and grossed out," while Ranaldo, in one of his own entries, called it "an incredibly unfortunate move which I truly hope is not the first of many across a long summer." As Gordon says, "It set the tone."

They knew it would be something of a circus, this Lollapalooza. Their own entourage had expanded: Ranaldo brought along his son Cody, then ten, and Moore and Gordon came armed with Coco, who was almost one and just learning to walk. The baby had plenty of her own gear as well: a folding crib, an inflatable pool for the hot outdoor shows, and, of course, her manny, Menares. After being situated in the back of a noisy tour bus, Coco would become an especially deep sleeper. At first, the haul seemed worth the trouble. On the first day, they sound-checked for six hours, even resurrecting early songs like "Confusion Is Next." The sound system was one of the best they'd used, and lighting director Susanne Sasic bathed them in elegant blue lights and strobes; the performances promised to be among the finest-looking and -sounding of their career.

Compared with the R.E.M. and Young tours, they felt comparatively at home. Lollapalooza 1995 was, as Pavement bassist Mark Ibold says, "more of a social thing. We were friends with all these bands, in one way or another." From the start, everyone shared dressing rooms, popped into each other's backstage areas (Love would be constantly storming into Pavement's space and telling them she'd finished the *New York Times* crossword puzzle ahead of them), and mutually wondered how it had come to this. "We were being paid more than we'd ever been paid," Ibold recalls. "It all seemed kind of unreal—that we would be doing *our* music in this kind of venue and with that crowd."

As the tour continued, though, everyone realized that the alternative rock nation around them wasn't quite the same as the one they'd envisioned. Each venue inevitably featured a booth manned by a DJ from the local "commercial alternative" radio station, who would crank hits from bands who weren't even on the bill, like Stone Temple Pilots and Pearl Jam. On at least one occasion, Ranaldo and Love approached the booths and complained. Sometimes the musicians weren't even sure who those ten or twenty thousand kids standing around in the sun were—how much they knew about the bands or whether they were coming simply for the now-established Lollapalooza brand name. Walking through the crowd unrecognized one day, watching kids singing along with the new Beastie Boys album on the P.A., Ranaldo wondered how familiar the crowd was with his own band. His suspicions were confirmed when, onstage in St. Louis, he made a reference to their connection to the "New York school of minimalism" and heard no response whatsoever from the crowd.

Of them all, Moore seemed to struggling the most, especially in the early tour dates. "Our show was pretty wack," he wrote in his journal on July 8. "Each show is worse than the last. It was harsh and unflowing. I was totally unfocused and discombobulated"—to the point of forgetting his own lyrics onstage. The crew had already taken to writing out the words on large cue cards in case that happened—the year before, Moore had had two operations for a detached retina and was unable to wear his contact lenses onstage—but the situation proved more problematic. Ever the most determined to be prepared and professional, Shelley was growing especially exasperated with Moore's onstage forgetfulness. ("They're *your* songs! You *wrote* them!" he yelled at Moore backstage once.) Chronicling another Lollapalooza set in his journal, Moore admitted to "babbling on stage" to the point where Shelley was "getting pissed behind the drums," yelling, "Let's start the fucking song!" Afterward, Moore was, by his own admission, mortified.

Lollapalooza 1995 summed up the crazy quilt that was modern rock by the mid decade. Pavement's droll-slacker rambles contrasted with the Bosstones' party-ready ska-pop, which in turn seemed miles removed from the pent-up aggro-punk of the Jesus Lizard. (In one of the tour's few scandalous moments, Jesus Lizard singer David Yow was arrested in Cincinnati for exposing himself onstage.) Beck's performances were notably chaotic. Still in the midst of making the transition from slacker folk-rapper to song-and-dance geek, he gave borderline-amateurish performances; more than a few in the crowd acknowledged his missteps by hurling bottles in his direction. O'Connor exited the tour early, claiming her pregnancy was taking a toll on her, and was replaced quickly with another Geffen act, the buzzed-about British band Elastica. Then there was Hole. When the tour was being organized, the band's *Live Through This* album hadn't yet caught fire (according to Geiger, this accounted for why the band wasn't the headliner). But by that summer, the album had become a hit and Love a full-on distressed celebrity. Propping up one leg up on a guitar amp with her baby-doll garb, roaring into the microphone, and often stage-diving into the crowd or excoriating them for one reason or an-other, Love was her own miniature onstage drama every day.

For Sonic Youth, closing the show each night had its advantages (they were able to have the first soundcheck, thereby ensuring the best acoustics possible). But since Hole preceded them each evening, the arrangement also had its drawbacks. From the first show, Moore had wondered, in his journal, whether "the multitude would split after pogoing to the celebrity punk [Love] but they stuck around." As the tour continued on, though, he saw that wasn't always the case: In-evitably, after Love left the stage, some portion of the crowd would leave, either from festival exhaustion or not being predisposed toward Sonic Youth. (In one of his journals, Ranaldo memorably referred to it as playing to "the jingle of car keys.") As he played, Moore would watch as an exodus made its way toward the exits. "There were a lot of people who were into us," he says, "but there was also this influx of people who came to see Courtney do her thing—Kurt's widow freak-ing out onstage. For them, that was the show. And there was a large part of the audience that pretty much had no interest in anything other than moshing, and we didn't really do that."

Even offstage, the hurricane that was Courtney Love would have an impact on them: On the days when Love would arrive late at the venue or her limo would get lost on the way, Sonic Youth's set would have to be curtailed to meet union cutoff times. From the sidelines, Lawton watched anxiously as the clock ticked—hoping, praying, the band wouldn't do its traditional set closer, "The Diamond Sea," and go over its allotted stage time. (Usually, Lawton lucked out: "Accord-ing to the official clock, we have seventeen minutes left," Moore an-nounced at the first show in Washington. "So we're gonna play one more song and we're going to play it for exactly seventeen minutes.")

To complicate matters, Sonic Youth didn't play most of their recog-nizable songs: The crowd would hear no "Kool Thing" or little if any-thing from Goo or Dirty, the albums that newcomers would most likely be familiar with. Instead, the set dipped back to "Tom Vio-lence," "Pacific Coast Highway," "Expressway to Yr Skull," even "The

World Looks Red" from *Confusion Is Sex*. Performed for the first extended periods of time onstage, the *Experimental Jet Set, Trash and No Star* material loosened up: The fat riffs and relative brevity of "Self-Obsessed and Sexxee" and "Starfield Road" were ideal for restless festival crowds. The audience would also hear material from an album that was finished but not scheduled for release until a month after the tour was over.

With Sonic Youth facing a few thousand empty seats on many nights, Lawton and tour manager Peter van der Velde took to approaching fans in the cheap seats and asking them to move down front. Sometimes they were successful; other times, they had to talk security guards into the idea. "Sometimes it looked bad," Lawton says. "You look out at the lawn and there's all these Sonic Youth fans a mile away. But we got everyone up front over time." At first rattled, the band came to accept the situation. "For us," Shelley says, "it was like the lunkheads left and the people who cared about music were there. So we played for twelve thousand instead of twenty thousand—that was okay. We could do our thing."

"People said it was the worst place to be after Courtney," says Lawton. "And it was and it wasn't."

Their ambivalence toward Love was, at times, only matched by hers toward Lollapalooza. (In one of her online journals, Love derided the festival: "Its [sic] boring sexless and elitist as it was always going to be.") Privately, she would tell friends that Sonic Youth seemed too middle class, too much like an art project and less like blue-collar, underdog musicians (like, for instance, Cobain). In theory, Sonic Youth admired her band ("She was doing good shows behind a great record," acknowledges Ranaldo), and Moore in particular, who'd been talking up Hole since their first indie single, maintained fond feelings for Love and worked the hardest at bonding with her. On July 25, she cajoled a crowd in Boston into singing happy birthday to him. ("An eerie Marilyn singing to Mr. President vibe and I was indeed 'touched,'" he wrote in his journal.) A few days after the Hanna incident (which stemmed from Love's admitted jealousy toward those who'd been close to Cobain before Love entered the picture), Love and

Moore had a one-on-one talk and cleared the air. "Everything's gonna be ok," he noted in his journal, "but you never know."

Early on, Menares had looked forward to arranging backstage get-togethers with one-year-old Coco and Love's daughter, Frances Bean, who would turn three during the tour. But the play dates rarely happened; Love's unpredictable behavior made for an especially tumultuous backstage area. Visiting her son, Eleanor Moore was startled to see Love throw open a backstage door and hurl a loading case down a hallway. "We were trying to hang out, but it was a lot more work than I was interested in doing," Menares recalls. "I didn't really want Coco in that kind of environment. I was there to protect her. And being around [Love's] kind of personality, it was explosive at times. It was, 'Wow, that's a crazy camp over there.'"

Gordon, already dismayed that riot-grrl supporter Love had been in a fight with Hanna, decided to keep her distance; in some ways, Love reminded her of her brother Keller, living in the grips of paranoid schizophrenia. "Someone like that, you just have to remove yourself," she says of Love. "You can't really engage. If you open yourself up, they'll just screw you. I couldn't deal with her without wanting to punch her." Toward the end of the tour, Moore and Gordon also discovered why it was so hard to find backstage parking: Love's people had instructed security that only members of Hole (and their entourage) be allowed in the area. Moore, who managed to bypass security once by fooling a guard into believing that Gordon was Love, was infuriated, as was Beck. By the end, Moore wrote, they barely even saw Love, whose white limousine would drop her off and pick her up right before and after her set.

As the tour worked its way across the country, toward its final shows at the Shoreline in Mountain View, California, near San Francisco, the atmosphere backstage was thick with bonding and fatigue. Celebrities came and went: Nancy Sinatra in Los Angeles, Drew Barrymore (then dating Hole guitarist Eric Erlandson) at others. Ranaldo felt disconsolate when Cody was sent back to New York to be with his mother. ("He's not going to be 'little' much longer now," he wrote wistfully.)

When it was finally over, they left with more money than they'd ever made—a low seven figures—and a sense of accomplishment. As Shelley says, "It showed we could *do* it—transfer our thing to a bigger environment." Yet the image of concertgoers heading toward the exit signs during their set would linger with them, confirming some of their worst fears about a possible larger audience for their work. The way the media lapped up Love's behavior (articles on Lollapalooza in local newspapers would sometimes only mention her) confirmed that the mainstream press didn't understand their world. Their chance of attaining some degree of stardom seemed to grow dimmer with each passing month, but maybe it wasn't worth it after all. Writing again about Love in his journal, Moore wrote that the experience "only reinforced to the rest of us that rock stardom is puerile, tacky, and very outdated."

THIS HAS TO BE THE ONE, Mark Kates had been telling himself the entire year. Even though he was only partly involved with its creation (yet received full A&R credit in the liner notes), Kates felt *Washing Machine* was their best and most accessible work since *Goo*. "The Diamond Sea" had been edited down to a five-minute single, an ideal length for a commercial-alternative station playlist. Lollapalooza had exposed them to over a million concertgoers. The band had even trimmed the length of the first track, the Gordon-sung "Becuz." (The three cut-off minutes of instrumental drift would be dubbed "Untitled" and turned into an album cut all its own.) With the release of *Washing Machine* on September 26, Kates says, "everything seemed to be perfectly in line."

On the heels of the chilly, snappish *Experimental Jet Set, Trash and No Star* and the coiled-up, purebred rock of *Dirty*, the new album felt like an exhale after a long period of stress. Whether or not it was the result of the Memphis atmosphere, the best songs breathed more, even expanding to lengths previously never reached in a studio: nearly twenty minutes for "The Diamond Sea," just about ten for "Washing Machine." With the exception of the New York-rooted "Panty Lies," the songs stretched out like arms extending after a long nap. Tracks that began melodically would invariably shift tempos halfway through and make U-turns into extended instrumental passages, yet even those passages would rarely be as savage as in the past. Ranaldo's lead parts, especially on "No Queen Blues," nodded to the rock past, sounding as if they'd been lifted from the stage of the Fillmore East in 1968. In general, texture—from the lapping waves of guitar feedback in "The Diamond Sea" to a rare, serene vocal harmony between Moore and Ranaldo on "Unwind"—prevailed.

As Gordon's far less confrontational lyrics also revealed, *Washing Machine* was their most human-scaled record to that point. Taking a cue from her new role as parent, she mused on young girls and motherhood (although, again, by way of characters rather than first-person perspectives). What she calls Memphis' "great stuck-in-time quality" allowed her to tap into her fascination with '60s girl groups, most clearly on "Little Trouble Girl," narrated by a girl who has a heated fling with a boy and yet still strives for her mother's approval. ("It's about the idea that girls in general have this genetic need for approval and to be perfect," she says, "and that's what causes the rifts between teenage daughters and mothers.") Gordon had befriended Kim Deal, of the Pixies and then the Breeders, and Gordon and Spike Jonze had codirected the Breeders' "Cannonball" video. Deal returned the favor by adding intentionally old-school "sha-la-la" vocals that served as counterpoints to Gordon's recited delivery. Lorette Velvette, the singer and guitarist for the Memphis indie band the Hellcats, and Melissa Dunn, a local artist, also added harmonies, resulting in the closest thing to nostalgic pop (albeit of the off-kilter kind) the band had ever made.

With its references to "soda pop" and the way in which Gordon sang the come-on lyrics as if she were a hair-twirling '50s greaser kid, the album's title track invoked the past—even as the fuzzy guitars behind her remained rooted in the present. Also tapping into girlish associations, "Panty Lies" contained images of a newborn ("Little girl playing in the closet/First comes walking, then comes talking") and a series of Gordon grunts that sounded like imitations of baby talk.

For his part, Moore sounded reflective and unhurried in both singing and playing. Swaying and languid, "Unwind" implied a new life with a child. Although Moore denies Cobain is the subject of "Junkie's Promise," their late friend's spirit nonetheless hung over the song (particularly the chorus line, "I heard you say, 'You know I hate myself,'" which seemed to reference Cobain's "I Hate Myself and I Want to Die"). Yet even though it had an angry, resigned undertone, the song felt contemplative.

Washing Machine also marked the vocal return of Ranaldo, whose voice turned up on two tracks. Set to a poem inspired by a walk around New York, "Saucer-Like" hummed and jangled. The reference to 2015, twenty years later, made "Skip Tracer" recall a similar time-travel reference in "Hey Joni," although the new song was a jumble of imagery. The title, lingo for private eyes who track those who've gone missing, came from William S. Burroughs' novel *Queer*, and part of the lyric derived from the night Ranaldo saw a show by Mecca Normal, the Canadian indie duo, and was less than impressed. (His reference to "the poetic truths of high school journal keepers" reportedly upset the band.) With their freer, more open structures, both songs were more reminiscent of Sonic Youth group compositions than the homemade tunes Ranaldo had brought in during past sessions, another sign that the earlier rift in the band had healed.

The climactic "The Diamond Sea" rolled out casually, the lilting melody and Moore's phrasing subtle and delicate; he even sang about how "love is running wild." At the eight-minute mark, though, it shifted to a long, intertwining instrumental passage. Structurally, it recalled "Expressway to Yr Skull," but reflecting adulthood and confidence, the feel was drastically different: muted and mature rather than intentionally raucous. The guitars massaged and circled each other; eventually, the squeals grew more untamed, but only during the closing minutes of the song's nineteen minutes and thirty-five seconds. "During those Geffen years, they did start making a lot more money, but their obsession with fucking things up never went away," says Tim Foljahn, Shelley's high school friend (and participant in some of Moore's side projects). "They like to take something and turn it over and over until they see what falls out. It's a big art project. But it's more in their nature than anything else. I don't think it's conscious. It's their nature to keep mixing it up."

Did they mix it up enough, though, or too much? *Washing Machine* felt natural to them, but what was organic for Sonic Youth was, as always, not necessarily in sync with the times. When the first week's sales figures arrived, Kates was stunned to see that, for all the buildup, the album had only motivated fifteen thousand to buy it. At a staff meeting the next day, one of the label's head executives looked at Kates and said, "Explain this. How come it wasn't bigger?"

Kates himself didn't have much of an answer: Perhaps if it had come out during Lollapalooza, instead of a month later. (For his part, Shelley called it "the worst piece of shit we've done. Well, I'm exaggerating. I loved the *experience* of it, but it doesn't stand up for me." His two favorite tracks, "The Diamond Sea" and "Little Trouble Girl," were also the only ones on which Gordon played bass.) Although "The Diamond Sea" ended up garnering airplay on a few major alternative stations, the song never spread to smaller outlets. Its video—a compendium of split-screen concert footage shot by, among others, Spike Jonze and David Markey—was intended to pay homage to concert films of the '60s and '70s. But the video's inside joke—fake venue names beneath each clip, all made up by the whimsical Jonze—probably went over most people's heads.

"People at the company were sick of hearing about how important the band was," Kates says. The band, meanwhile, was sick of hearing about how *this* new record would be the one. "Playing Lollapalooza was a bit of a compromise," says Shelley, "but it was also like, 'Okay, we want you guys [at Geffen] to really hit it. Do what you do.' The tour was a pretty good fit and we made it work for ourselves. But one of the motives was to get your record to the people, and we failed there."

Certainly the musical winds were starting to shift. As the softer ticket sales of Lollapalooza 1995 showed—it only grossed $12.8 million, compared to the previous year's $26 million—the festival no longer felt fresh, and audience for the music had peaked. In a sense, it had probably crested the year before, with Cobain's death. It was no coincidence that the biggest American band after his suicide was Hootie and the Blowfish, the anti-Cobains: easygoing, thrilled to be onstage, happy to perform on whatever television program would have them. Unlike most of the grunge crowd, they radiated friendliness and warmth; their only angst seemed to stem from whether they would have enough time before each concert to get in a few rounds of golf. "It was a real youthquake moment," says Cafritz of the so-called grunge years. "For whatever reason, the mainstream is receptive to the little stream, which would normally never flow into the mainstream. And then of course, it ebbs away."

"I was more naïve that this was going to open up this secret world of ours," says Shelley. "Kurt being interested in Half Japanese or the Raincoats, I was like, 'Wow, people are going to buy these records.' But it didn't happen, for the most part."

Still, there would be one last push. Mark Romanek had made a name for himself directing lavish, expensive, and visually arresting videos for Madonna, R.E.M., Lenny Kravitz, and the Red Hot Chili Peppers, among others. Having just spent $7 million on a sci-fi-themed clip for Michael and Janet Jackson's "Scream," though, he yearned to work with bands more to his taste. "I was worried I would lose my 'street cred' with the more 'alternative' artists," he says, "worried they might boycott me, as if I had cooties or something, and that I wouldn't get to work for these bands and artists who were so important to me." Romanek reached out to labels to hook up with some of those bands, one being Sonic Youth. The offer was impossible to resist: Romanek videos were almost guaranteed to be taken seriously by the MTV staff, and he was willing to charge less.

Given he was known for being extremely hands-on, both the band and the label knew the group would have to give up control. "If you want Mark Romanek," says Geffen creative director Robin Sloane, "you say, 'Okay, whatever you want.' Everyone really wanted to try this one last shot, and try and make something that was popular." Even for a band insistent on having a hand in all its visuals, the chance was worth taking.

The video would be for "Little Trouble Girl." In a phone conversation with Gordon, Romanek laid out his concept: a childlike alien creature with long, suction-cup fingers wandering around a futuristic home, office, board room, and other corporate settings. "I felt a little alien girl might be a nice metaphor for the song's sense of alienation, though no pun was intended," Romanek says. "A little alien girl in a male domain seemed more visual and more obliquely feminist, without being propagandistic." Gordon told him she liked the idea, but it was still hard to let go; Sloane fielded more concerned calls from Gordon than she had during her previous five years working with the band.

Reluctantly leaving Moore and her new baby, Gordon decamped to Los Angeles for the filming. In the end, only she and Kim Deal would be featured in the video. Romanek was concerned that the men in the band would object, but no one did; by then, the novelty of making videos had worn off even for them. Filming on digital video and spending over $100,000—low budget for him, costly for the band— Romanek did indeed emerge with the most eye-popping, beguiling clip in the band's history, complete with glammed-out Gordon and Deal. Everyone seemed happy; Sloane thought it was "a cool little film with images you could hook into."

But, again, without the support of pop radio, which ignored the single, the video was invisible on MTV and other outlets. Ultimately, *Washing Machine* only sold about 160,000 copies, about half the number of its predecessor. Something was clearly over, and not just for them; even their most stalwart supporters at the label seemed to realize what they were up against. "I thought, 'If this is as far as it gets, headlining venues and one radio song, 'Kool Thing,' then they got their due,'" says Kates. He wasn't alone in that thinking.

FOR THOSE WHO WORKED with them, it was sometimes hard to tell if the band even wanted mass recognition. "As it turned out, they weren't really up for it," Kates admits. "I don't know if that was necessarily important to them. Or all four of them at one time, let's put it that way." Geffen's Sloane felt they were conflicted about who they wanted to be and what audience they wanted to reach. "Did they want to have a big hit pop record?" she says. "They sort of did, but in order to do that, you really have to want it. You can't have one foot in here and one foot there. You have to say, 'I want to be a rock star.' But I don't think they wanted the huge celebrity or really cared about the money. I don't think they really wanted to do what you have to do, which is shake a lot of hands and talk to a lot of people. They made certain concessions musically, but they always wanted to do what they wanted to do."

As the dawn of 1996 arrived, they could look back on the previous six years and make an impressive list of accomplishments. Even without chart hits and MTV support, they'd made more money than they had in the previous decade. More people had been exposed to their music than before. Whether those people liked it or not was another matter, but at least the records were readily available thanks to Geffen's global distribution and promotional dollars. Guitar manufacturers were giving them free strings in exchange for endorsements. Moore and Gordon weren't the only ones with a new home: Just before the start of Lollapalooza, Ranaldo and Singer purchased a multi-tiered loft near New York's City Hall. The place had high ceilings and stairs that led to a balcony overhang containing bedrooms and office space; as in the Moore-Gordon home, books, records, and instruments took up a good chunk of space.

As pop-culture aficionados, they could easily make another list of all the celebrities with whom they'd hobnobbed. The stars weren't just backstage but at the same MTV music and movie awards ceremonies to which Sonic Youth was now invited. At one, the 1994 MTV Movie Awards, Moore performed Beatles covers with an alt-rock supergroup that included Don Fleming, Dave Grohl, Soul Asylum's Dave Pirner, the Afghan Whigs' Greg Dulli, and R.E.M.'s Mike Mills. Since they'd played on the soundtrack to *Backbeat*, a shockingly non-tacky docu-drama about the early days of the Beatles, the ad-hoc band was billed as the "Backbeat Band." When Moore flew to Los Angeles for the ceremony, MTV put him up at the infamous rock & roll hotel the Chateau

Marmont, and Markey, one of his guests, looked around one afternoon to see Quentin Tarantino, Wynona Rider (then dating Pirner), and Drew Barrymore. In the limo ride to the awards, the musicians made caustic comments about the warm cans of soda and beer. Before they went on, their dressing room was buzzing with the stars of the youth-culture entertainment galaxy: Rider, Phoebe Cates, Michael Stipe, Courtney Love, MTV VJ Kennedy, and actor Donal Logue (then the toast of MTV thanks to his "Jimmy the Cabdriver" character). Near the backstage entrance, Moore, Don Fleming, and the others found themselves staring with a combination of awe and bemusement as Robin Williams, John Mellencamp, and Janet Jackson strolled by. "All of a sudden," Markey recalls, "you find yourself in this other reality, so surreal and bizarre."

"During *Experimental* and *Washing Machine* was the period when people had the most perceptions of us having some kind of interesting presence in the culture," Moore says. In terms of that zeitgeist moment, though, no one could have guessed what happened next: the day in October 1995 when a Geffen publicist was contacted by the producers of *The Simpsons*. In the works was a Lollapalooza-inspired episode in which Homer Simpson, desperate to appear hip to Bart, became a sideshow attraction at "Hullapalooza," an alt-rock festival. Cartoon versions of Lollapalooza bands were therefore needed. The show's producers gathered a list of everyone who'd appeared at Lolla-paloozas, and the name "Sonic Youth" jumped out early; series creator Matt Groening had been a longtime fan.

Despite the agreed-upon $1,000-a-day paycheck for recording their voices in a New York studio, the band nearly backed out when they heard Love had been offered a cameo as well. (The confrontation was another indication of how Lollapalooza had strained relations between her and the band.) When Love and Hole proved hard to pin down, the matter resolved itself, and the episode, which also featured animated versions of the Smashing Pumpkins and Cypress Hill, was filmed in February 1996. The cartoon Moore was made to look the same height as the rest of the band, but otherwise, they had few complaints; the cameo solidified their place in the culture at that moment. From

Homer walking by a "Bungee Jump Against Racism" sign to the animated Gordon dryly cracking that the festival was about "music and advertising and youth-oriented product positioning," the show's barbed digs at "alternative" music—namely its mix of corporate sponsorship and Gen X slackerdom—were in line with Sonic Youth's own skepticism toward Lollapalooza. For years afterward, they'd be approached by strangers and asked if they were that band from *The Simpsons*. In addition to lending their voices and images, they also recorded their own, noise-screech deconstruction of the show's theme song: a piece of music that, by six-degrees-of-Sonic-Youth coincidence, had been written by Danny Elfman, Gordon's long-ago boyfriend. After years in the L.A. punk band Oingo Boingo, Elfman had by then established himself as a successful movie scorer.

In various ways, their own past haunted them. In the press, *Daydream Nation* was still regarded, for better or worse, as a benchmark. "Critically, it was, 'It'll never be like it was with *Daydream Nation*,'" Moore recalls, "which was really weird, because *Experimental* and *Washing Machine* were going even further out in a weird way. But there were all these responses critically that were like, 'We lost track of our inventiveness,' which I found strange." *Rolling Stone*'s *Alt-Rock-a-Rama* book praised *EVOL* as one of the "50 Most Significant Indie Records" and one of the "100 Most Influential Alternative Releases of All Time" ("Kool Thing" was cited as one of the "20 Most Influential Alt-Rock Videos"). Reflecting the dangers of mass media infiltration, it also snidely listed X Girl under "Not Alternative," and Gordon had raised more than a few eyebrows when she had earlier appeared in Gap ads.

Yet the pressures of playing the game to whatever level they did took their toll at different points. Moore had had his onstage meltdowns during the Neil Young tour. Ranaldo had been the most rattled when early business associates like Paul Smith and Carlos van Hijfte were let go. "I didn't like that period at all," he says. "It wasn't a normal modus operandi for Sonic Youth. I wasn't very happy about that. If we ever second-guessed what was going on in our career, it was probably right around that time, when we were making *Goo* and *Dirty*. We were having huge black clouds of troubled moments." In addition to being rattled herself during the creation of *Goo*, Gordon was perturbed when the band made the move to even bigger theaters and halls for its *Washing Machine* tour starting in late 1995. In October, they played before 2,800 at the Orpheum in Boston, up from 1,500 the previous time, at the Avalon Club. But the larger, classier venues, most with seats, meant quieter crowds and more distance from them. Touring on buses, which happened not long after they'd signed with Geffen, also meant less interesting highway drives about the country; the days of stopping into funky eateries or discovering America seemed further away than ever.

For Shelley, the eruption point arrived during a photo session to promote *Experimental Jet Set, Trash and No Star*. By then, his ninth year in the band, Shelley was no longer the "new guy"; he'd grown more assertive in his opinions and was often frustrated when outsiders assumed Gordon and Moore *were* Sonic Youth. During the increasingly awkward shoot, intended for *Rolling Stone*, the photographer kept trying to place Gordon front and center. When an assistant asked her three bandmates to take off their shirts, Shelley had had enough. "I thought that was ridiculous and I didn't want to be a part of it," he says. "Not everyone had the same take on the group that you did. Sometimes they just dealt with Kim and Thurston, and sometimes that was difficult." To the dismay of a Geffen publicist in attendance, Shelley stormed out.

But a more indicative episode, for better or worse, came when longtime Sonic Youth aficionado Keanu Reeves threw a party celebrating his thirtieth birthday. (Dogstar even opened for Sonic Youth several times, and Reeves continued to pop up at their shows, eventually confessing to Tamra Davis he had a longtime crush on Gordon.) For his party, Reeves rented out the Pickwick Ice Center, a skating rink in Burbank; for entertainment, he hired Moore, who put together an ad hoc trio with Mike Watt on bass and David Markey on drums.

On the night of the event, the trio found themselves in the middle of the rink, standing on blankets that covered the ice. Moore was in the midst of preparing his first solo album, *Psychic Hearts*, and wanted to play songs from it, but neither Watt nor Markey were familiar with the material and had to fumble their way through the set. "It was just absurd," says Moore. "A complete and utter mess, but kind of funny." At one point, Reeves skated over to Moore and dropped an ice cube down his back as he was playing. (Perhaps he was slyly getting back at Moore for the time Gordon and Moore called Reeves to see if he would star in the "Dirty Boots" video. After the call, conducted by speaker phone from the Eldridge Street apartment, Moore and Gordon hung up and began talking about how nice but spaced-out Reeves seemed—only to be told later, by Reeves, that they hadn't fully disconnected the call and that he'd heard every word they'd said about him.)

As they tried to learn Moore's new numbers on the spot, the musicians would glance up from their instruments and see Reeves and his guests—Brad Pitt, Sofia Coppola, Spike Jonze—gliding past them on skates. As Markey recalls, "It was a David Byrne 'you may find yourself . . . in the middle of a large skating rink playing for Keanu Reeves' party' moment. It was totally bizarre." To add to the strangeness of the evening, Moore and Markey were driven back to Markey's apartment by Reeves, since Coppola, who'd given them a ride to the rink, ended up leaving with Jonze.

On the way out of the rink, Moore looked down at the slightly shorter Markey. "That," he said, in his pokerfaced voice, "was the single most fucked-up gig I've ever played in my life." It seemed to sum up one particular aspect of the previous last six years, except it wasn't always so amusing anymore.

PART 3

REFUGE

Chapter 11

THE HOUSE HAD BEEN ON THE MARKET for over a year when its owner, the Clarke School for the Deaf, received word that a "family from New York," as they were described, was interested. Neither the Clarke staff nor David Murphy, the local real estate agent in Northampton, Massachusetts, recognized the names of the potential buyers, Thurston Moore and Kim Gordon. But it made sense that parents with a child would want to have a look at the three-story, center-hallway colonial on the leafy street near the center of town. The first floor had a sizable eat-in kitchen, a living room, and a back patio; next to the dining area was a space ideal for a study. All told, several bedrooms and six fireplaces were scattered throughout the house's six thousand square feet. The front yard wasn't large—just enough space for a circular driveway, a wooden porch, and a cluster of trees, one of which would drape the lawn with bright, golden-mustard leaves in the fall. But the woodsier backyard, large enough for a garden, would compensate. All told, the house was bigger than any home Gordon or Moore had ever lived in.

The western part of Massachusetts was stuffed with colleges and universities; Northampton itself was home to Smith College, and many of the twenty-eight thousand who lived in town worked for area schools. The professorial air extended to the nearly ninety-year-old house: With its white pillars and its ivy that had begun crawling up the faded-brick façade, the house emitted a funky-bookish ambience.

Not surprisingly, the previous owner had been the headmaster of the Clarke school. "When Thurston saw that house, that was it," says friend Don Fleming. "He was convinced they had to get it."

By the early summer of 1997, Gordon and Moore had been hearing about Northampton for over a decade. Byron Coley, the feisty, opinionated writer and critic who'd interviewed them for his *Forced Exposure* zine in 1985 and had become a very close friend, was living in the area with his family. Free Kitten had recorded there. Starting in the late '80s, Moore and Gordon had spent a few summers in that part of the state with friends like Coley, taking the 150-mile drive up from Manhattan.

They'd never seriously entertained the notion of leaving downtown, but the arrival of Coco had altered those plans. Neither Moore nor Gordon had grown up in the city, and they weren't sure whether they wanted their child to, either. "We didn't want to raise a kid in Manhattan and constantly have to hover over her," Gordon says. "We didn't want to move to Brooklyn or a commuter town. I wanted to feel like I was living in a different place. New York is a very selfish city in a way. It's very distracting. As a parent, it's hard to have focus." The competitiveness of the school system, even for preschools, concerned them, as did the ever-climbing cost of private education, which was beginning to approach $25,000 a year. Moore told Chloë Sevigny that having Coco grow up in the East Village or SoHo was a concern, since, he told her, "the sidewalks are like catwalks." Their minds turned to Northampton, as well as the equally collegiate Raleigh and Chapel Hill, North Carolina, regions.

Although the Clarke staff had never heard of Sonic Youth, the school found the match compatible: "I have always felt that the people who would best understand what deafness was all about would be people who depend most on their hearing," a school spokesman told the *Daily Hampshire Gazette*. At $500,000, the house was priced higher than most homes in town, but Northampton had begun trumpeting its "sophisticated rural lifestyle" in its promotional literature. The transformation was apparent not only in its country-home landscape but in the quaint and increasingly upscale shops sprouting up on the town's main drag. In another sign of how good Sonic Youth had been to them, Moore and Gordon put down $150,000 toward the house's purchase and, in August 1997, filed a "declaration of homestead" with the town's chamber of commerce. With that, they began the gradual process of remodeling the house and commuting between there and Manhattan, preparing for their eventual move when their daughter would begin school.

By then, downtown Manhattan was no longer home base for Sonic Youth. Moore and Gordon would keep the apartment on Lafayette Street, using it as their base of operations when they made the three-hour commute into the city for band rehearsals, gallery openings, and business meetings. Shelley remained in Hoboken, where he'd moved in 1987, and had settled into a side-street walk-up apartment that was eventually renovated and remodeled. (By coincidence, the town was also home to Bob Bert, his predecessor, as well as Lyle Hysen, the Moore and Gordon friend and Das Damen drummer who'd hoped he would have been asked to take Bert's place but, to his disappointment, never was.) Only Ranaldo and Singer would be living full-time in the city.

Given how their music and lifestyles had been defined by the area below 14th Street, the news that Moore and Gordon were fleeing the city was jarring, even for friends; everyone had grown accustomed to seeing them out at clubs or events on a seemingly nightly basis. Yet the move was actually far from unexpected; both the town and the home had a scholarly air about them. In time, the study would be dominated by floor-to-ceiling stacks of Moore's collection of Beat-generation poetry journals and crates of vintage LPs; an antiwar placard signed by Allen Ginsberg would come to hang over the fireplace. A piano and various stringed instruments and exotic percussive toys would be strewn around the hardwood floors and throw rugs in the living room; bookshelves would be crammed with stacks of oversize art books. With their traditional (for rock) lifestyles and middle-class upbringings, they'd never felt completely at home in the scummy Lower East Side anyway. In a way, they had come full circle: A move to Northampton was akin to a homecoming.

311

The immediate impact of the uprooting wasn't felt by the band, especially since Moore and Gordon took their time moving up to Northampton. But hints of their new lifestyle began to creep into their music. When a second and somewhat more sophisticated Free Kitten album, *Sentimental Education*, arrived in 1997, its most striking track was "Noise Doll," Gordon's straightforward song about her new life (and arguably her most direct and personal song ever). Accompanied by her own coarsely strummed garage rock chords, Gordon sang about her daughter, then three, wanting to watch a video instead of sleep. "We read some books, she shook her head/Sang some songs, turned down the light," Gordon sang, like any other parent trying to get her child to go down for the night.

"It doesn't matter about what you do as far as success goes," Gordon told her friend Tony Oursler in a videotaped interview for his archives. "It all comes down to . . ." she said with an abashed smile, "diapers."

WHO WAS THE "ROCK GUY," they wondered, and what was he doing here? The Festival International Musique Actuelle Victoriaville in Quebec City, Canada, had never been the province of rock bands; the annual festival presented only the most audacious in improvisational freeform jazz and avant-garde music. Even if people knew that Sonic Youth was far from a conventional rock band, it was still surprising for some to see the name Thurston Moore listed in the lineup on May 17, 1996.

It was equally unusual to Moore and his two collaborators—Tom Surgal, his pal and experimental percussionist, and William Winant, Gordon's long-ago high-school classmate, who'd gone on to play with John Cage and other modern composers—when they faced a cadre of local jazz critics and writers before their performance. "They were all *over* us," recalls Surgal, a watchful, dry-witted New Yorker. "It was, 'What are you rock and roll people doing?' They were very defensive." From speaking with skeptical writers at the festival, Winant sensed they knew Sonic Youth but didn't know much about Moore and his particular tastes.

In a way, the media wasn't alone; the performance puzzled not only the writers but more than a few in the crowd. With no prior rehearsal or practice, the three men went onstage and played two half-hour-long pieces of nonstop improvised music for electric guitar and percussion. There were no Sonic Youth songs nor, for that matter, singing. The two drum kits played sometimes in the same tempo but just as often not; when he wasn't scraping his fretboard, Moore made his guitar imitate chiming bells or, at its most extreme, a moose humping a wolf. Using an effects board, he also conjured the sound of a ham radio, complete with attendant static. When the drums took over for one especially long stretch of improvised ambient rhythms, the music recalled not the freeform moments of Sonic Youth but, of all people, the "Space" jams of the Grateful Dead.

Although the Victoriaville crowd may have been taken aback by what they saw and heard (one girl did scream "I love you!" halfway through), the performance was far from a shock to anyone who had talked music with Moore during the first half of the '90s. Early that decade, a young New Jersey native and fledgling experimental guitarist and sound-shaper named Alan Licht had run into Moore on a PATH train to Hoboken; to Licht's surprise, Moore gabbed about nothing but free jazz. Licht had grown up immersed in indie rock of the '80s but, after discovering the minimalist compositions of Steve Reich, had begun playing far more untethered music built around waves of feedback and structures that were more jazz than rock. "At the time, the Cold War had ended, and there was this real feeling of freedom," Licht says. "After ten years of worrying about nuclear war, all of a sudden that wasn't an issue. Free jazz was a musical expression of that freedom." In 1991, he and Moore wound up onstage together as part of the Blue Humans, led by one of the scene's elder noise-guitar statesmen, Rudolph Grey. Wearing a backward baseball cap, Moore stood still on stage right, keeping a vigilant eye on Grey and the other musicians. He was clearly tentative about playing this new form of music—music that, even more so than Sonic Youth's, was built entirely around improvisation.

Gordon, a jazz buff since high school (John Knight, her boyfriend prior to arriving in New York, had furthered her interest in the music as well), had tried introducing Moore to free jazz years before but to no avail; it was still too alien to him. John Erskine, the first Sonic Youth sound man, attempted as well: He'd shown Moore his collection of Sun Ra albums, but Moore seemed more puzzled than eager to hear them. As the next decade arrived, though, Moore's all-encompassing fascination with improvisation burst wide open. When Anya Strzemien, a sixteen-year-old Connecticut high-school student, mailed a list of questions to Moore in October 1995 (and was shocked to receive hand-written responses not long after), she asked him to name his "best show." His response was telling: not a Sonic Youth concert but "the other night in D.C.—me and Tom Surgal did a duo gig that totally connected to the cosmos." Moore's immersion in the new music reflected several overlapping stages: his scholarly interest in music, especially anything close to the fringe (and a batch of free-jazz tapes Coley had given him); his desire for an outlet for his own music during the Geffen period; and the band's first extended break in nearly fifteen years.

Relative to the steady flow of recording, rehearsing, and touring that had begun in 1981, the months leading up to the purchase of the Northampton home had been relatively calm ones for the band. The period from the fall of 1995 through the middle of 1997 passed without any new group music. The only album to arrive in stores during that time was *Screaming Fields of Sonic Love*, an anthology of pre-Geffen indie recordings. The compilation was tied to an extensive Geffen reissue program of the band's back catalogue, every record from *Confusion Is Sex* to *The Whitey Album*. When SST still hadn't forked over its unpaid royalties to the band by 1991, Richard Grabel, Sonic Youth's lawyer, began sending threatening letters to the label. (One was reproduced in the first issue of *Sonic Death*, a typically cheeky, do-it-themselves fanzine the band published in the '90s: an update of sorts of Moore's *Killer*, but focusing primarily on Sonic Youth.) As a way to lessen some of the debt, SST agreed to return the rights to the recordings to the band and Geffen, paving the way for the reissues. Since Josh Baer at Neutral had sold the rights of the first two records to SST for $9,000 when Neutral folded, the arrangement meant Geffen owned *Sonic Youth* and *Confusion Is Sex* as well.

During the extended downtime, the moment came to indulge in a venerable rock tradition: solo and side projects. But as attested by Moore's Victoriaville performance (released on record as *Piece for Jetsun Dolma*, named after the female Buddhist deity), the offshoots were as unconventional as anything the group was producing. Ranaldo was the first to venture outside the band, and his 1987 album *From Here to Infinity*—released at the urging of Paul Smith and comprised entirely of instrumental tape loops—set the tone for what would come from each of them: Anyone expecting anything close to "Eric's Trip" or "Mote" was instead confronted with something else entirely. By the middle of the '90s, Ranaldo's love of Beat poetry and guitar-amp surges came to the fore, sometimes intertwining: Solo records like *East Jesus* and *Amarillo Ramp* set his spoken-word pieces to overpowering waves of feedback and loops. He also began publishing books of poetry and notebooks; one, *Jrnls80s*, would provide the first peek into the band's life on the road during that decade.

For reasons that puzzled some at Geffen, Ranaldo never released an album devoted to the type of straightforward songs he'd contributed to Sonic Youth. He traced part of the reason back to the "Genetic" controversy: "I don't know if those kind of events, not feeling that kind of encouragement from the others for those songs, maybe contributed to my lack of being prolific in the future. I'm sure if those songs had been embraced, it would have motivated me to write more." For all his outward confidence, Ranaldo was, according to Singer, plagued with self-doubt about his songs (and about showing them to the band). On his own, though, Ranaldo was able to express emotions and feelings—even recall erotic moments involving former girlfriends—with a freedom he didn't always have in the band. That side of his work spewed out on his own records of the period: "The Bridge," from 1995's *East Jesus*, recalled a car drive with his father, while the sensuous "A Bit of Memory" and the soul-searching "Bloomington, Indiana: Autumn," both from the later *Dirty Windows*, were more directly personal than anything heard on a Sonic Youth album.

315

Moore, however, had no reservations about writing material on his own. In the months following his daughter's birth, he brought Shelley and Shelley's friend Tim Foljahn into Sear Sound for several days, emerging with one of the few rock-oriented side projects from within the Sonic Youth camp. (Another was *Dim Stars*, a gritty 1990 collaboration between Moore, Shelley, Don Fleming, and one of Moore's heroes, Richard Hell, that effectively recreated the waning days of New York punk sound.) Of course, Moore's were still not predictable songs: Instead of picking up where "The Diamond Sea" left off, the tracks on *Psychic Hearts*—the stretched-tight title track, the trippy modern psychedelia of "Ono Soul," the clanking stomp of "Cindy (Rotten Tanx)"—were intentionally primitive. "Thurston wanted to explore a minimalist thing," says Foljahn. "He would literally say, 'You gotta play it dumber.'" Certainly, it was easy to detect the influence of his childhood favorite Kiss in "Patti Smith Math Scratch," whose art-damaged boogie beat would never have found its way into Sonic Youth. In what amounted to Moore's equivalent of "Drunken Butterfly," "Cindy (Rotten Tanx)" worked titles of '70s Kiss and Sweet records into its lyrics.

DGC commissioned a video for "Ono Soul," directed by David Markey and styled by Chloë Sevigny, and the album arrived in stores in May 1995, just before the start of Lollapalooza. Calling themselves Male Slut, Moore, Shelley, and Foljahn played some of the songs on one of the festival's occasional side stages. When *Psychic Hearts* sold less than any Sonic Youth album of the Geffen era, few were surprised; if anything, it seemed an anomaly even for Moore. On his own, he was increasingly drawn to quickly made, volume-driven improvisational work, onstage and in studios. The approach played into both his intrigue with sound and his lack of interest in spending inordinate amounts of time in studios; he could quickly move from one project to another. With guitarist Nels Cline and White Out (the improvisational band consisting of Surgal and his wife Lin Culbertson), among many others, Moore began venturing into free jazz at clubs and music festivals. And as with Ranaldo, the work resulted in an explosion of explicitly noncommercial albums distributed by small labels.

In the early '80s, Moore had started his own label, Ecstatic Peace!, out of the Eldridge Street apartment; the company, such as it was, released a series of LPs and singles, including one by Das Damen. Yet it was Shelley who waded deepest into the world—and business—of independent labels. Inspired by the mix tapes he would make for friends, and eager to release a single by ex-Dinosaur Jr. bassist and songwriter Lou Barlow, Shelley founded Smells Like Records in 1992. (The name, a joke playing off the then-huge "Smells Like Teen Spirit," was one Shelley came to loathe.) The label reflected both Shelley's industriousness and taste. (A few years later, he would also become a part-owner of Maxwell's, the Hoboken club near his apartment.) Dating back to his mother's love of country singers, he tended toward stark singer-songwriters and their troubled-life ballads; it wasn't surprising, then, that he was drawn to Chan Marshall, a mood-swinging, Southern-born indie rock balladeer who performed under the name Cat Power. After seeing her open for Liz Phair at a Raincoats concert in New York, Shelley brought her to Sonic Youth's Mott Street rehearsal space in late 1994 and recorded *Dear Sir* and *Myra Lee*, albums released on Smells Like. Two Dollar Guitar, built around Foljahn's own grippingly stark songs, was also a Smells Like act.

A year after he'd begun working with the volatile, temperamental, often despondent Cat Power, Shelley found himself embroiled in an even more dramatic scenario. Killing time in an airport after missing a flight during Lollapalooza, Shelley placed a call to Townes Van Zandt, the revered, bony country-folk singer-songwriter responsible for sadly haunted songs like "Pancho and Lefty" and "If I Needed You." Having become obsessed with Van Zandt's music after discovering it on a compilation, Shelley had an idea: to use Sonic Youth's quasi-A&R arrangement with Geffen to oversee a Van Zandt comeback. On the phone, Van Zandt was polite but brief—and unaware of a band called Sonic Youth—but his wife Jeanene also spoke with Shelley. With her help, a plan was hatched to make a stripped-down Van Zandt album, much like the ones Rick Rubin had begun making with Johnny Cash.

Shelley had actually been carrying Van Zandt's number in his wallet for a while but had been too nervous to call; like many in the industry, he'd heard the stories of Van Zandt's self-destructive ways, his binges, his reckless behavior. As Shelley discovered firsthand, the tales were far from exaggerations. Geffen paid to have Van Zandt flown from Nashville to Memphis, where Shelley was making an album with Two Dollar Guitar. As Shelley watched while trying to retain his awe for the older musician, Van Zandt went on a major bender, drinking continuously and telling Shelley he wanted to "be a band, like the Rolling Stones!" The weirdness only continued when Two Dollar Guitar backed Van Zandt for a few very rough shows in the Carolinas. Later, in a Nashville studio to record demos for the possible album, Van Zandt was surly, shooting Shelley nasty looks but managing to make his way through a few songs, one of them an improvised swipe at his young semi-producer.

Although the demos were "okay, not great," Shelley says Geffen was still intrigued enough to fund studio time at Easley, the Memphis studio where Sonic Youth had cut *Washing Machine*, during the week after Christmas 1996. Shelley remained hopeful: "I wanted to do this so badly and his music meant so much to me that I really thought I could pull something together. The goody-two-shoes part of me said, 'I said we're going to do this and we're going to finish it! When there's a will, there's a way!'"

But his sense of optimism collapsed when Van Zandt showed up at the studio in a wheelchair; he'd fallen out of bed and, unbeknownst to everyone, including himself, had broken his hip. For a few hours, everyone attempted to get Van Zandt to finish a few numbers, but between his physical pain and the vodka he was downing to kill it, the sessions were slowly expiring. Fully realizing an album was not to be, at least at that point—"it wasn't working, it was just sad"—Shelley sent Van Zandt back to his hotel. "It was a train wreck," adds Foljahn, who was pitching in on the sessions, "We couldn't get through a song. His trip was the old blues guys, and he had sort of turned himself into one."

In Van Zandt's hotel room, Shelley broke the news to the singer; it wasn't the time, and he sensed Van Zandt realized it too. Van Zandt gave each of the musicians an odd gift almost as a farewell gesture; Shelley's was an envelope with a Marilyn Monroe stamp on it. A few days later, Shelley and Foljahn returned home to Hoboken, and no sooner had Shelley fallen into bed when the phone rang; it was Jeanene Van Zandt, telling him her husband was dead, apparently of a heart attack. According to Foljahn, who received his own call about it from Shelley, Shelley sounded like he'd been hit on the head with a baseball bat.

Gordon's own side project, X Girl, ran into troubles of its own. By 1997, the company was adrift. "It was sometimes painful walking past the store and seeing a rack of clothes that came out wrong," recalls Daisy von Furth. "Also, we ran out of ideas. We weren't real designers." When a Japanese company offered to buy them out—the clothes were still popular in Asia—Gordon, von Furth, and their partners were more than ready to cash in. Each walked away with close to $500,000, which, for Gordon, represented more than she'd ever made in Sonic Youth.

THE NEW HOMES and side projects added to their peace of mind and reinforced their un-rock & roll inclinations toward stability. But they needed another refuge, something far more concrete, and they found it a few blocks from Ranaldo's loft. They tired of bouncing from one rehearsal space to another, and now they were able to do something about it. With the money they'd made at Lollapalooza, as well as the higher cash advances extracted from Geffen as a result of Grabel's canny renegotiation of their contract, they had the funds to fulfill their dream of having their own fairly permanent studio.

Through a newspaper ad, they learned of available space at 47 Murray Street, two streets north of the World Trade Center. Like many of the blocks surrounding it, Murray Street was grimy and raucous— a bustle of activity during the day that gave way to near desolation at night when the Wall Street crowd went home. Midtown Manhattan, the heart of the city's music business, felt even more remote.

The space was unvarnished but workable. The elevator opened onto a small foyer; to the left was a boxy room with wood panel walls, dark tan carpet, and an air-duct shaft running across the ceiling—a room

319

ideal for a console. Around the corner but out of eyeshot was a large room suitable for practice and recording. Beyond that space was a hallway flanked on either side by small rooms (and a bathroom and shower) perfect for storing guitars, drums, and years of tapes culled from rehearsals and concerts. Above the studio was Off Wall Street Jam, where stockbroker types would form ad hoc bands to kick out their own rock-star-dream jams; Sonic Youth could often hear them through the walls, banging out rough versions of classic rock. Amusingly, a strip bar up the street—the New York Dolls Gentlemen's Club—shared a name with one of the favorite bands of Moore's teen years.

The cost of recording *Goo* and *Dirty* still unnerved them, so here was the solution: a place where they could record whatever and whenever they wanted and without continually eyeing the clock, as they had while working in higher-priced rooms. The rent was relatively affordable—$2,500 a month—so starting in the middle of 1996, they took it. Renaming it Echo Canyon (Ranaldo's idea, taken from a line in an episode of the '50s TV series *The Adventures of Superman*), they hired recording engineer Wharton Tiers, with whom they'd worked intermittently since *Confusion Is Sex*, to hook up the $75,000 worth of recording equipment they'd purchased. "It was sort of like a clubhouse," says Ranaldo. "It was a further indication of our moving off the grid, in a way."

As a sizable but not overwhelming investment, Echo Canyon fit squarely with the Sonic Youth business model set in place by the middle of the '90s. From the start, they'd agreed to credit all songs to the band and share the publishing and record royalties equally. (To their surprise, former drummers Bert and Sclavunos would continue to receive royalty checks for their contributions to the early records.) During their years on indies, the band had learned to be thrifty and hold on to whatever cash they'd earned. Frugality had been ingrained in them by their families, such as the way in which Gordon's mother made her family's clothes. In terms of major-label contracts, they knew well that most of the money an artist spent— for recording, touring, promotion, making videos, having records placed in upfront displays in stores, and on and on—came out of the act's pocket. Only when a record sold enough to equal those costs would an artist begin making royalties, but those costs could add up to millions of dollars.

In that context, thriftiness became more crucial than ever, manifesting itself in any number of ways. Throughout most of the Geffen years, they'd declined to take tour-support cash from the label. Prior to a road trip, they would instead book a handful of college concerts to raise the necessary money for road expenses; such was the case in the spring of 1995, before the *Washing Machine* tour, when a string of campus gigs netted them about $50,000. They often requested a little whiskey and wine in their dressing room but declined lavish backstage buffets; they knew they'd ultimately have to foot that bill as well. They told Bob Lawton, who continued to book their concerts, that something wasn't worth doing if it meant taking a loan against their own money.

Other than buying tape, cash was not a huge issue with Echo Canyon. They could practice, improvise, and jam as much as they wanted without fear of a huge bill at the end of the day, which they began doing as soon as the studio was operational. They started by recording three tracks for Richard Linklater's film version of Eric Bogosian's play *Suburbia*, including a Gordon-sung bossa nova, "Bee-Bee's Song." But they also began making shapeless, languid instrumental pieces, clearly not the kind of music Geffen wanted or expected. One day, Moore had an idea: release some of these recordings on their own label and call the company SYR, for Sonic Youth Recordings. They'd made eight-track demo recordings of previous woodshedding sessions, but now they had tons of them, and on better-quality recording machines. Besides, the odds of Geffen wanting any of this type of music were slim.

When a new Sonic Youth album finally appeared, in May 1997, almost two years after *Washing Machine*, it neither looked nor sounded like anything that had come before. The record was credited to Sonic Youth, but from its cardboard packaging to its minimalist red-checkered cover art (inspired by a French experimental label), *SYR 1* was clearly not aimed at anyone who still remembered "Kool Thing" or "The Diamond Sea" and was hoping for another. The four nonvocal tracks grew out of jams at Echo Canyon. Stretching out over nine minutes, "Anagrama" wallowed in the interplay between languorous guitar strumming and spatial effects; Shelley's drumming was among his most experimental, veering from metronomic beats to percolating rhythms toward the end. Alien spaceships sounded as if they were finally landing on earth in "Improvisation Ajoutee." The most grating and droning piece, "Mieux: De Corrosion," was encased in hissy feedback and gradually, after a snarling punk midsection, deteriorated into crunchy noise crashes. *SYR 1* returned Sonic Youth to their obsession with pure sound and beyond-rock composition, as if most of the previous fifteen years had barely existed; the music was made to please no one but themselves.

In the Geffen and DGC offices, the arrival of *SYR 1* (which, like subsequent releases, was distributed by way of Shelley's Smells Like label) was greeted with only mild concern. The label did make it known that should any of the SYR projects take off commercially, the company would step in and, in some manner, take over. But given the style of music, everyone knew the chances of that were unlikely. "It wouldn't have made sense for Geffen to be associated with it," says Ray Farrell. "We didn't really give a shit. If the standard studio output coming out on Geffen was going to be difficult to sell and get in stores, why would you want to be involved in something like this?"

But as Farrell also saw, the initial SYR release helped the band's credibility in the world of indie labels and mom-and-popish record stores: "Part of it was a perceived 'going against the grain' by putting out something your record company doesn't know about. A kid sees it and thinks, 'Oh, man, Geffen probably doesn't even know.'" The following year, the band also released *Hold That Tiger*, recorded in Chicago during the *Sister* tour. The cover photo of Bert, who'd left the band by the time the show was originally taped, reaffirmed the band's insouciant sense of humor—as did the fake label name, Goofin', a pun on Geffen. The bogus record company logo was, Farrell felt, another sly swipe at their corporate bosses. "I don't know if it was a funny pun or a signal that they wanted to look cool to certain people or about a certain amount of frustration with being on a major label and not selling as many records as somebody else," he says, admitting it was "hard to get a feel for the band's collective sense."

Their increasingly indifferent attitude toward Geffen was apparent in other ways. Just as the SYR projects were gearing up, Kates approached the band about an electronic remix album. In 1997, the media was abuzz with the notion that techno and its various offshoots would be the new rock & roll. The idea was misdirected—in terms of star power and rock hooks, techno would never be grunge—but it wasn't without merit: Head-spinning singles from the Chemical Brothers and the Prodigy were more exciting and stimulating than most of the mainstream rock of the time. For Geffen's *Infinite Beat* discs, Kates wanted to commission a drum-and-bass remix of a Sonic Youth song.

"That was the hot thing that was happening," says Moore. "And they were saying, 'It would be such a cool thing for you guys to do.' Yeah, but it would *really* be wrong. You'd be like an old lady in a miniskirt. Not something people would want to hear." Even though electronica was all the industry rage, the band rejected the idea.

IN THE NEARLY FIFTEEN YEARS since Sonic Youth had recorded *Confusion Is Sex* at his basement studio, Wharton Tiers had remained in touch with the band. He'd worked with them on and off, on *The Whitey Album* and various B-sides and cover versions. (One of the latter, a remake of Alice Cooper's "Is It My Body," would remain Gordon's favorite of all her vocal parts on a Sonic Youth record.) Working with them on a daily basis to set up Echo Canyon, Tiers found the band seemingly comfortable with each other, as did other friends who'd known them through the years. "I remember Steve saying to me, 'It's just our fate—Sonic Youth are the bridesmaids, never the bride,'" recalls David Markey. "Once they figured that out, that that was their place, they sort of adjusted. It wasn't going to happen for them on that level. They wanted it on their own terms, and their own terms are completely askew from what pop music is."

With nearly two years having passed since the completion of their last Geffen album proper, *Washing Machine*, a new record needed to be created. Having been such an integral part of setting up Echo Canyon, Tiers was the natural choice for coproducer and engineer on the next project. Yet as Tiers quickly learned, the Sonic Youth method of album construction would be radically different this time. In the previous years he'd worked with them, the band would craft its new material in practice or onstage to make for efficient, money-saving sessions.

With Echo Canyon at their disposal, that approach would be relegated to history. As always, the new songs began as instrumentals, but the band threw a new wrench into the proceedings. Starting in the spring and extending into the fall, they began playing the vocal-free material onstage, working it out bit by bit. Concurrently, they began putting the slowly evolving tracks onto tape at the new studio. Even though it was taped over and over, one of the first tracks they finished was "Hits of Sunshine (for Allen Ginsberg)," Moore's lyrical ode to the Beat poet who died in April, shortly before the sessions began. Reflecting the post-rock bands they were now listening to, the song stretched out, broke down, and slowly, minimally, came back together. "It was long and very mellow," says Tiers, "and it became the blueprint song for the record."

The rest of the album, however, came together far more arduously. With plenty of hours at their disposal and no firm deadline, the band recorded take after take. "You could imagine making *Sgt. Pepper* was like that," Ranaldo says. "They had all the time in the world and explored every limb until they got where they wanted to go with it." The band had woodshedded like this for years, of course, but never with a recording engineer around. "They wanted it to be loose and free," Tiers says, although for him, the process was "slightly torturous. You had to imagine a lot."

Other tribulations both inside and outside the band contributed to the prolonged, occasionally exasperating environment. Halfway through the sessions, Gordon had to cope with the death of her father Wayne, who succumbed to the Parkinson's that had been eating away at him for several years. Meanwhile, as the band continued to tinker with the song fragments they were batting around, they grew less concerned with note-perfect performances and more with "vibe," in Ranaldo's term. The tactic, which had its roots in the *Washing Machine* sessions, still did not sit well with Shelley, who preferred to hone his parts to as close to perfection as possible, especially since drums could rarely be re-recorded once a final take was determined. "Most of the other players can go and fix *their* parts," he says. "I'm the person who has to live with what's there. Sometimes the drums suffered for spontaneity."

The new, hardly glitch-free studio in which the band was working added a fresh, frustrating wrinkle to the situation. Far more vocal in his opinions than he'd been a decade before, Shelley would sometimes insist a particular track not be released, and the band would oblige; other times, according to Ranaldo, "We'd say, 'This is it, and that's all there is to it.' It was pretty much one against three." ("What Steve didn't realize is that sometimes his parts were better before he evolved them," Gordon says, adding, "He's a different kind of player than we are.") The debate was typical of the give-and-take involved in any collaborative effort (Ranaldo and Shelley would take as many of the same sides as not), yet it was also a reminder of the ongoing, frontline bond between Moore, Gordon, and Ranaldo, even nearly two decades after the band's formation.

During the drawn-out sessions, they were booked onto *Sessions at West 54th Street*, a PBS music series that was the network's equivalent to the long-cancelled *Night Music*—a showcase for nonmainstream music. During the taping, they performed instrumentals of several of the new songs, including a jabbing, bumpy track called "Static Overview." At Echo Canyon, though, the song became so hard to nail down that Tiers went to the TV studio, borrowed the recording from the telecast, and incorporated parts of it into the finished version, later renamed "Female Mechanic Now on Duty." (It may have been the ultimate example of "the demo" being better than anything that came after.)

Just when the record seemed finally finished, the band made its debut at Lincoln Center's tony Avery Fisher Hall in November 1997, playing instrumentals of most of the new songs. (At the show, Frank Olinsky, an album cover designer hired by Geffen to work with the band, glanced around and saw ushers at the upscale concert hall trying to restrain audience members from dancing in their seats.) Feeling the performances at the theater were stronger than some in the can, Tiers suggested that the band return to Echo Canyon and take another crack at the songs—to, in his words, "inject more vitality" into them. Increasingly antsy over the recording process, Moore would have been happy to release the instrumental Lincoln Center tapes as an album, although even he realized the idea was unrealistic. In the end, Tiers spliced together different takes of songs for finished versions; he would later refer to the album as *A Thousand Edits*.

WHEN IT WAS FINALLY DONE, they initially called it *Mille Feuille*, with a cover photo of Moore holding a pastry. But the title was changed to the English translation, *A Thousand Leaves*, a line that popped up in two of Gordon's lyrics, and the cover was given over to "Hamster Girl," a piece by Los Angeles artist Marnie Weber. In keeping with Weber's disturbing cut-and-paste montages, "Hamster Girl" juxtaposed a small rodent with a young girl (Weber herself, modeling blankets at age ten) who was sporting animal horns. "It was obviously not something they put together to sell a lot of records," recalls Farrell, who by then had taken over as the band's label liaison after Mark Kates exited Geffen in late 1997. "And the more you look at it, the less sense it makes." Olinsky, who was given the artwork by Gordon for the cover, found the image "strange and creepy, but awesome."

As someone with a lengthy résumé of album covers under his belt, Olinsky knew well how record companies could interfere with the best-laid cover-design plans. But he sensed those rules didn't apply to Sonic Youth: He never heard a single word from anyone at Geffen about either that cover or any of the subsequent ones he would lay out for them. Whether the label respected the band too much or felt creative squabbles weren't worth the effort at that point was hard to determine.

In keeping with the cover, the music was among their most demanding. The monster-squashing-city static that opened the record, paving the way for the first track, "Contre Le Sexisme," was itself a statement: What would follow would be far less concerned with pleasing anyone at a record company than the four Geffen discs that preceded it. "Contre Le Sexisme" was less a song than what amounted to a spoken-word piece, Gordon reciting in a variety of tones, soothing to angry, as if she were auditioning for a part in a film. (Not surprisingly, Gordon had had a longtime interest in acting, going back to her appearances in early Markey short films, and later she'd also taken acting lessons.) Halfway through the track, the crackling electro textures gave way to a muted industrial clatter, like a war between robots and machines that was breaking out in the distance.

The editing and splicing that had gone into "Female Mechanic Now on Duty" was evident. A song of aggressive, almost violent love, it began with their crudest, most prodding metal riffing, then decelerated to a languid midsection before turning gentler and dronier for its finale. Gordon's delivery shifted with it: Her tight-throated seething in the first portion gave way to a more singsongy delivery by the end, like someone working through conflicting emotions. In the way it tried to encapsulate the range of a woman's feelings and self-images, the song was unintentionally inspired by Meredith Brooks' pop hit "Bitch." Hearing Brooks sing "I'm a bitch, I'm a lover/I'm a child, I'm a mother" on the radio one day made Gordon want to write what amounted to a retort. One of Gordon's other vocals, for the bile attack "The Ineffable Me," mined a similar, even more sexual vein, although the actual lyrics were penned by Moore.

Mostly, though, *A Thousand Leaves* possessed a pastoral spaciousness rarely heard on a Sonic Youth record. The band had never before sounded so relaxed: Some of the tracks extended to over eleven minutes but in an almost casual way, and the repeated lyrical references to children (especially "Snare, Girl," with the gentlest vocal Moore had ever sung) lent the album an unruffled ambience. "French Tickler" also explored the place where sexuality and antagonism meet: "Your neck is my favorite," Gordon sang, to a floaty, dreamlike melody. Moore's lyric for "Hits of Sunshine (for Allen Ginsberg)" had enough references to dreams, gardens, hues, and a "goddess lover" to qualify for something penned during the Summer of Love; its references to Ginsberg were, at best, roundabout.

Far more revealing was what arrived three minutes into the song: a subtle, drawn-out passage of Morse code guitar lines and lazy-afternoon wah-wah pedal licks—bliss in slow motion. They'd indulged in guitar jams before, of course, but in another clear break from the past, the song had more in common with minimalist composers like Steve Reich than it did with any of Sonic Youth's punk or no-wave antecedents. Moore's serene "Wild Flower Soul" opened with sweet, roomy chords, followed by a prolonged, intricate guitar jam that worked itself into a delirious swirl and, finally, a hell-hounds-unleashed frenzy before revisiting its mellow refrain. The songs were little journeys unto themselves.

The album's relatively hopeful, borderline-idyllic atmosphere continued with "Sunday." The band had originally cut the song for the *Suburbia* soundtrack, but the version on *A Thousand Leaves*, with Moore's bristling strums pushing it along, was smoother and more cohesive than the earlier take. Optimism also ran through a slower, darker piece that, in rehearsals, had been dubbed "Woodland Ode" but was eventually retitled "Hoarfrost." Sung by Ranaldo, its lyrics were inspired by a visit he and Singer made to her parents in Winnipeg, during which the couple went for a walk in the snow, following in each other's footsteps. Its slow, meditative crawl, all sustained delicacy, had the feel of a lost Velvet Underground song. (Ranaldo also tackled "Karen Koltrane," about a lover from his college days who he learned had "a far less extraordinary adulthood" than he'd first imagined.)

By the time the album was released, on May 12, 1998, their North American tour had already begun. *A Thousand Leaves* and the first two SYR releases demonstrated their desire to continue pushing forward into uncharted territory rather than become an oldies act, and the concerts that supported the new album took the same approach. The main set of each show consisted of the new album in its entirety—no old songs whatsoever until the encore, when they resurrected "Death Valley '69" and "Shadow of a Doubt." Anyone buying a ticket and expecting to hear flashbacks to the grunge-era Sonic Youth most likely left wanting more.

The trek, barely a month long, also reflected the changes in their lifestyles and the new realities (and lowered expectations) of the business around them. Instead of taking in numerous cities, the tour concentrated on multiple nights in San Francisco, New York, Los Angeles, Seattle, and Washington, D.C. "Why go play Sacramento?" Bob Lawton says. "Why bother? They really are a city band. The real fans would go. Everyone else—*whatever*. It didn't matter. It was obvious that whatever commercial prospects remained were somewhat less than they had been. That music was just going to appeal to the number of people it had previously appealed to." Other efforts were made to save money: Instead of running a full-page ad in the *Village Voice* announcing their three-night stand at Irving Plaza, they bought space for one line—"Sonic Youth on sale now"—in the Irving ad that alone saved them thousands of dollars. In their dressing rooms, Markey noticed a noticeable drop-off in celebrities.

With its punchy melody and largely optimistic lyric (about "a perfect day for a perfect friend"), "Sunday" was, to Farrell and others at Geffen and DGC, a natural single and radio focus track. In what would be the last big-money video the label would finance, Harmony Korine was hired to direct a clip for the song. In the years since he'd met the band on the set of "Sugar Kane" with his girlfriend, Chloë Sevigny, Korine had gone on to fulfill his dreams of becoming a screenwriter and filmmaker of the *enfant terrible* sort. He'd written the script for Larry Clark's hot-button verité film *Kids* (which also starred Sevigny) and made his directorial debut two years later with the even more controversial *Gummo*. In a dementedly inspired move, Korine cast Macaulay Culkin—the aging teen star who'd grown to resemble a younger Thurston Moore—in the video, which juxtaposed footage of Culkin face-sucking his new bride, Rachel Miner, with artier, enigmatic imagery of ballerinas. Culkin, Sevigny recalls, was "game—he hadn't really done anything in a while, and he's a very subversive, twisted kid, a real eccentric." (When she and Korine visited Culkin and Miner at their hotel suite the night before the shoot, they were surprised to see stuffed animals and a baby blanket on their bed.)

Relative to the band's previous few singles, "Sunday" had a rhythmic groove and a video with a publicity hook. But the musical landscape around them was changing. Other than Radiohead, whose *OK Computer* had come out the previous summer, mainstream rock had begun settling into a dreary, post-grunge funk. The most vibrant, energized music, starting the previous summer, came from the worlds of pop, hip-hop, and electronica. Plenty of adventurous rock existed, but mostly on indie labels and from bands exploring the subtler, quirkier, post-rock sounds that *A Thousand Leaves* tapped into. In this new world—and with Gersh long gone and neither Kates nor Farrell having the same degree of clout within the Geffen compound—the single, video, and album never stood a chance. The label may have been perplexed by the "Sunday" clip too: "That video was a mess," grouses one former Geffen executive.

A Thousand Leaves, Ranaldo says, was "a real reflection of where we were at the time. We weren't into making anything concise. We were just playing what we felt like playing. We really didn't feel like what we needed to be doing was producing another record like *Goo*. The climate for it was not really there anyway." That fact became apparent when the album sold only sixty thousand copies; *Dirty* had sold five times that number only six years earlier.

ERIC BAECHT, an employee of San Francisco's Fillmore auditorium who'd taken a side job as one of the band's guitar techs, immediately sensed something was wrong. It was the morning of July 4, 1999, and Baecht was helping the Boredoms prepare for their set at This Ain't No Picnic, an all-day, multiband festival at the Oak Canyon Ranch in Orange County. With Sonic Youth scheduled to play later that day, Baecht began keeping his eye out for their equipment truck. But it never arrived, and Baecht began to wonder where it was.

By then, everyone else already knew. Since their gear needed to be at the venue before they did, driver Bill Ryan pulled into a Ramada Inn in Orange, close to the festival grounds, on the night of July 3. He parked the rental truck, housing all the band's touring instruments and equipment, in the hotel's parking lot. After checking that he could see the van from his window, he went to sleep.

When Ryan awoke early the next morning and opened his curtains, all he saw was an empty space where the truck had been. At first, he was confused: Had he parked it somewhere else and simply forgotten? But no—the truck was simply gone. At some point between 1 A.M. and 7 A.M., thieves had hotwired it and driven off.

By 8:30 A.M., the band, manager John Silva, and Lawton, all encamped around Los Angeles, had heard the dispiriting news. The list of the stolen goods was depressingly long: twenty-seven guitars, twenty amplifiers and speaker cabinets, twelve microphones, twenty-nine effects pedals, and a drum kit, as well as a guitar tuner, a drill charger, circulator fans, guitar strings, and 998 Sonic Youth T-shirts to be sold at shows. "It was a crazy thing to have somebody tell you over the phone," Ranaldo recalls. "It was a violation, an awful thing." Guitars that had been gutted and retrofited to play certain songs were now history; Shelley's green Gretsch kit, courtesy of a drum collector in Germany, was no more.

"We are fucked," Ranaldo wrote in an e-mail sent out that day. The note, widely disseminated through the media, pleaded for any information on the stolen goods and offered an unspecified reward for their return. (Shelley maintains he was most sanguine about it: "We're really fortunate that that was our problem—we lost a truck of rock and roll gear. It sucked, but I've been in enough places to know there are a lot of other problems.") After the shock and outrage wore off, the day became a frantic scramble for equipment: "It was kind of a panic," Moore recalls. Calls went out, and friends like Steven McDonald of Redd Kross and Smokey Hormel, Beck's guitar player, loaned them guitars. Even though it was a Sunday, Lawton convinced one music store owner to open up his business so the band could quickly buy replacement gear.

The frenetic activity continued at the show grounds. The festival lineup was filled with friends and acquaintances, including Sleater-Kinney, Mike Watt, Superchunk, and Guided by Voices. Before the show, Baecht and Nic Close, the band's other guitar tech, canvassed each band's gear, asking for a loan for the day. As each band finished its set and walked offstage, Close and Baecht were then handed an instrument or two. Frantically, the men ran backstage, clipped off the strings, restrung them, and tuned each for a particular song. ("It almost brought tears to my eyes," recalls Shelley of watching the process.) Moore himself had to adjust to shorter guitar straps rather than the elongated ones he was using to accommodate his long arms and height. Between the loaned guitars and their lack of interest in canceling the show altogether, they were able to cobble together a set. The show became both a rescue operation and, given the contributions of the mostly younger bands, a referendum on Sonic Youth's status in the world it helped create. Even with their increasingly different personalities, the group itself was forced to band together as one and pull through. "That afternoon," Shelley says, "was one of the most beautiful afternoons we had together as a band."

The truck was eventually found, abandoned, outside of L.A.; not surprisingly, it was empty. They would later laugh that the joke was on the thieves: How much cash would anyone get for an army of gutted, refurbished instruments that looked like candidates for the trash bin? "It was a drag, and I felt very cynical about it," Moore says. "But there was something almost funny about it getting ripped off. It was usable only for us."

Their management filed an insurance claim estimating the total value of the stolen instruments, gear, and records at $71,698; the band would eventually be reimbursed for a third of that amount.

Plenty of other guitars and amps were awaiting them back in New York, and in time, they would retrofit other instruments to play songs like "Eric's Trip"; thanks to Internet tips, a couple of the guitars were ultimately retrieved as well. But what was lost was a portion of their own history. One of the purloined guitars was the Drifter, the four-stringed, no-fret guitar Moore had discovered in Gordon's apartment almost two decades earlier—a tangible and nostalgic reminder of their origins. The theft signaled the end of a tumultuous decade and the start of a new, hazier one in terms of their work and identity.

Chapter 12

THE MUSIC DISCHARGING from the car stereo was brutal and aggressive, all jackhammer intensity with little—make that no—interest in traditional melody. By the summer of 1999, the move to Northampton was almost complete; Coco, who was five, was on the verge of entering kindergarten, and Moore and Gordon became more or less full-time residents of Northampton. Whether tooling around town or taking one of his frequent three-hour drives into Manhattan, Moore began hearing a new, assaultive type of music on the radio and in the air. During one drive, he popped in a CD by Slipknot, a band that wore masks and didn't so much sing as belch; the accompanying music battered away unrelentingly.

The genre had been dubbed nu-metal, and along with its sibling style rap-metal, it merged the rivet-gun blasts of thrash metal with the rhythmic propulsion (and sometimes rapping itself) of hip-hop. Sonic Youth had tried their hand at a rap-rock fusion post-"Kool Thing": They'd recorded a track with Cypress Hill for the largely ineffectual soundtrack for the 1993 action movie *Judgment Night*, which featured collaborations between rockers and hip-hop acts. But this was something new, something that made not just Sonic Youth but early Glenn Branca sound downright soft. On the level of pure intensity, Moore related to what he heard. "They were like the end of the world, really out there," he says. "It was impressive, in a way." But in general, the new genres left him unmoved: "All of it was, 'We're dudes, and we're heavy, and we're bummed.' It was all these guys with baseball caps, emoting. I'm sure it was very genuine for a lot of those guys, but I found it really corny. There was musically nothing interesting to me. It was just so juvenile."

Yet as one decade wound down and another one started up, bands like Slipnot, Korn, and Limp Bizkit—or rage-propelled rappers like Eminem, whose first album arrived that year as well—were not fringe acts making an ungodly din on the sidelines; they were the sound of mainstream rock culture. Their ascendance was just one illustration of the ways in which the pop climate around Sonic Youth had once again mutated. Beck was now a pop star, albeit one with a restless musical imagination and a purposefully opaque personality (credited, in part, to his enrollment in Scientology). Former Nirvana drummer Dave Grohl was now fronting his own band, Foo Fighters, and Grohl, also managed by John Silva, had made the transition from backup player to media-beloved rock star. But the world over which Sonic Youth had once lorded was largely in tatters. Courtney Love was as much an actress as a musician; many of their peers were no longer on major labels. The moment when indie rock crossed over had passed, with Lollapalooza having run its course; thanks to flagging ticket sales and a muddled identity, its days as a touring festival ended after 1997.

It wasn't simply rock that had changed, though; it was the culture at large. Everything—even worlds like pro wrestling and talk radio that had been around for years—felt more amped up and in everyone's faces. The word *extreme* was everywhere, used to promote sports, snack foods, even deodorant. Sonic Youth had once been extreme themselves, but now they were, by comparison, subtle, and nowhere more so than on *A Thousand Leaves*. They were suddenly elder statesmen for a movement that didn't seem to exist anymore.

As to where they would fit in, the answer was unclear. They could give in to prevailing trends, although exactly how was anyone's guess; several years before, they'd shown no interest in cashing in on the techno boom. In a strange way, they'd become stubborn traditionalists; when Moore and Ranaldo had the idea to record an album with the two men playing pianos rather than guitars, Gordon rejected it. But perhaps the road to the future lay in the past. At a crossroads for their kind of music, maybe they could tap into the long-ago bohemian culture that gave birth to the musical avant-garde, iconoclastic literature, and Beat verse. The plan was far from intentional or thought out, but maybe they could transcend pop charts and trends and position themselves as part of an ongoing cultural heritage. They would go back underground, since what was aboveground no longer seemed amenable to what they were doing.

The process had more or less begun in May 1998, when the band, joined by percussionist William Winant, played an in-store show at Amoeba Music, the weird music–friendly record store in San Francisco. Rather than playing songs, they jammed on the sort of material they had begun releasing on the SYR albums. From that moment, an idea for a thematic SYR album evolved: an entire disc devoted to interpretations of new-music composers. By offering their takes on works by John Cage, Steve Reich, and composers associated with the Fluxus art scene of the '60s, they would pay homage to the musical avant-garde that preceded them. (As critic John Rockwell wrote, Cage was defined by a "questing spirit of adventure" and a "determination to seem fresh and even outrageous," qualities that surely appealed to Sonic Youth and some of their peers.) Along the way, they could also make a case for the connections between classical and certain strains of modern rock and, by implication, present themselves as heirs to those composers.

With Ranaldo and Winant initially leading the charge (Winant particularly lobbied for pieces he'd played or ones written by composers he'd worked with), the band settled on about a dozen works. Ranaldo, Gordon, and Moore selected pieces by Yoko Ono and another Fluxus-associated composer, George Maciunas. Composer Pauline Oliveros wrote one especially for the project. In March 1999, almost a year after the Winant collaboration that inspired it, the sessions began at Echo Canyon. The band—joined by Winant, engineer Wharton Tiers, and sound-collage composer and longtime friend and collaborator Christian Marclay, among others—filled the studio not just with guitars but tympani and sundry percussion instruments. As they huddled over scores and sheet music, or faxed them back and forth to him in the Bay Area, Winant saw how serious they were about the project. For a twelve-second interpretation of Ono's pre–John Lennon work from 1961, "Voice Piece for Soprano," Coco was instructed to stand on the building's fire escape and scream several times.

By the time they'd finished overdubbing and mixing, in the fall, they emerged with not one but two discs, a double CD called *Goodbye 20th Century* released on SYR in November 1998. Although the band's name was featured prominently on the cover, the album was a Sonic Youth project in name only. The compositions—and the band's interpretations—were an esoteric, spacious, celestial bunch. At moments it was possible to hear Sonic Youth amidst the nonconformist, anti-symphonic clatter: when the guitars imitated a slowly approaching tidal wave in a rendition of James Tenney's 1971 piece "Having Never Written a Note for Percussion," or when Gordon's muted whisper made cameo appearances in two pieces by American composer Christian Wolff. With its almost entirely instrumental tracks filled with windshield-wiper guitars, snow-crunching rhythmic accents, sound effects, and instruments that sounded like various mammals, *Goodbye 20th Century* was the farthest thing from rock of any type. It was sound as music, and vice versa.

The underground-culture aspect of *Goodbye 20th Century*—compositions that dismantled the idea of a "song" and instead explored the outer limits of sound—carried over to the album of original material Sonic Youth began sifting through during the same period. In both their arrangements and lyrical references, the new songs would pay homage to the city's enduring bohemian arts community: "a record dedicated to New York and the Beat poets from the twenties to the fifties," says Ranaldo. "It had as much to do with our vision of poetry through that period as it was a rock record." That same year, in line with this delving into the literary past, Ranaldo coproduced an unearthed recording of Jack Kerouac reading *On the Road*.

As with *Goodbye 20th Century*, the new project was intended to place the band's work in a much larger and more steadfast cultural context. Gordon referenced the late Jean-Michel Basquiat, whom she'd seen hanging around Todd's Copy Shop long before, in "Never-mind (What Was It Anyway)" (starting with the title, the lyric, Gordon's comment on the dangerous allure of fame, also alluded to Cobain). Moore name-checked the equally late underground poet d. a. levy in "Small Flowers Crack Concrete," whose terse, free-verse lyrics recalled levy's work. "In a lot of ways, it was about teaching," says Moore. "It was about this whole collection of literature and music history we try to employ in our work. We know that we exist as a hybrid of that. That's what that album was about—feeling part of this lineage, being aware of the history of it, and being excited by it."

With Tiers again hired as coproducer and engineer, the band put at least two of the songs on tape before the equipment theft. When they regrouped in August to continue working on the album, "it was pretty much back to zero and starting again," recalls Tiers. Forced to utilize a backline collection of guitars and basses, such as a Gibson Les Paul that Moore found lying around the studio and had never played before, the band had no choice but to rethink its own approach. The melodies and sounds that emerged were even bumpier and less linear than the ones on *A Thousand Leaves*; nothing would approach the rush of "Sunday." Several numbers would be built around spoken-word recitations, not just by Ranaldo but Moore as well. Even Shelley would play in a less conventional manner, avoiding kick-snare-hi-hat combinations for more intentionally irregular rhythms. "At that point, we were really becoming like one of those classic old FM album-oriented bands," says Ranaldo. "We were making records that were conceptual or were going where we thought we had to go with our music at the time."

The songs, including one that would eventually be called "Renegade Princess," were a tricky, sometimes awkward lot to learn. But that was merely the first of several hurdles. Echo Canyon still had plenty of technical bugs to work out; the console had to be reset constantly.

Listening to the band rehearse in the studio, Tiers grew increasingly baffled by what he was hearing. "They were making a record for a commercial record company and this wasn't commercial music at all," he says. "As a producer, I was going, 'Guys, where are the songs?' I had a whole vision of what that album would sound like. I wanted to make a rawer and more dangerous-sounding record than *A Thousand Leaves*. But it wasn't really pretty *or* dangerous."

Over time, tensions grew between the band and Tiers—not merely over music but money and work schedules. "Maybe Wharton was losing interest a bit," Shelley says, "and maybe the way we work is a little difficult or boring to someone." In the fall, the band took a break and, in a meeting, decided to bring in an outsider to finish it. Although they already had someone in mind, the tapes would sit in the studio, unfinished, for several months.

As RANALDO SAYS, there were also "other distractions." One was the birth of his and Singer's first child, Sage, in August 1999, four months after Ranaldo and Singer married. Another diversion most likely emanated from the business side. A year prior to the start of the new album's sessions, the Seagram Company, which already owned Universal Music (Geffen's corporate parent), consolidated its hold on the industry by buying another music behemoth, PolyGram. Geffen was suddenly a small part of an even larger conglomerate. In the aftermath of the mergers, hundreds of bands on various labels were dropped, although Sonic Youth, along with Beck, Counting Crows, and Hole, among others, were retained at Geffen.

Although their contract with the label could have easily been broken, Sonic Youth's self-sufficiency aided them. "They weren't a huge cash drain," says one executive at the label. "People liked them, the press liked them, they had a steady fan base. Why not have them around?" Others feel the label wanted to avoid embarrassment. ("No one wanted to be known as the person who dropped Sonic Youth," says one former colleague.) Perhaps someone at the company remembered how damaged Warner Brothers Records' reputation had been during the '80s, when it unexpectedly rid itself of legends like Van Morrison and Bonnie Raitt, both in sales slumps at the time.

By the time of the merger, Geffen, once a proud and profitable label, was increasingly vulnerable. (Even David Geffen was gone.) Although the success of Guns N' Roses and Aerosmith had resulted in plenty of bonuses for its executives, the label's stylistic limitations were beginning to be a liability. "We, up to this point, are a rock and roll record company," Ed Rosenblatt, who was promoted from president to chairman of Geffen in 1994, told *Billboard* at the time. "We are not in the urban business. We are not in the country business. We're not in the classical music business. We are in the rock and roll business." But by 1999, that wouldn't be enough. The label had no hip-hop acts, no boy bands, no teen pop divas. Recent signings like Lisa Loeb weren't turning into the stars the label had hoped; despite a lacquered production, Hole's 1998 *Celebrity Skin* album was a disappointment. The label's biggest seller of the period was a Rob Zombie album that fell clearly in the nu-metal camp.

"We fought for our generation of bands to dominate the roster, and we won," says Mark Kates, "and that ultimately led to the undoing of the company." In a symbolic move during the corporate merger, DGC, the label's alternative rock home base, was shut down, its artists absorbed into Geffen. By then, Sonic Youth's visits to the company's L.A. offices had grown sporadic at best.

In one regard, the way in which DGC (and Geffen overall) had been subsumed aided Sonic Youth; executives at the label were so distracted they didn't seem to care that the band continued to release records on SYR, including two in 1999 (one of them *Goodbye 20th Century*). But that was the only positive news on the business side. During a round of job eliminations in January 1999, Ray Farrell, the last person with whom the band had a strong personal bond at the label, was laid off. Geffen was effectively no longer a functioning record company, just an imprint with a tiny staff. In conversations with Farrell right before his dismissal, the band told him they would stick with the label. "It was better, financially, to ride out the deal than to say, 'Let us out and we'll go indie,'" Farrell recalls. "They had a couple more records, so they were better off just going along."

As they were wrapping up the album that came to be called *NYC Ghosts & Flowers*, the band found itself face-to-face with the executive turnover. They still hadn't met Jimmy Iovine, the former record producer now in charge of Interscope, Geffen's corporate parent (nor would they for several more years). Instead, Geffen's newly promoted president, Jordan Schur, came by Echo Canyon. Years before, Schur had signed a young rap-metal band called Limp Bizkit to his Flip label. When Flip came under Interscope's wing, and when Limp Bizkit went on to sell four million copies of its *Significant Other* album, Schur's standing at the company zoomed up. At thirty-five, he became head of Geffen in 1999, the same year Rosenblatt retired.

From the start, the rapport between the band and Schur was awkward. As everyone gathered in the console room at the studio, Schur began chatting them up, talking about how big a fan he was. But whether out of nervousness or lack of knowledge, he raised eyebrows by referring to *Dirty* as *Sugar Kane* and then listing the bands that were important to him: "you, the Pixies, Sonic Youth. . . ."

Who was this guy, they wondered? Did he even know who they were? (Schur maintains that *Dirty*, along with Jane Addiction's *Nothing Shocking* and Weezer's debut, "pushed me into the business after I'd been alienated after all the hair bands." His first release as Geffen president, the soundtrack for the Arnold Schwarzenegger horror film *End of Days*, included "Sugar Kane.") To herself, Gordon grimaced every time he inserted the word "fucking" into words, as in "un-fucking-believable" or how he would "guaran-fucking-tee" something for the band. The fact that Schur had been associated with the likes of Limp Bizkit frontman Fred Durst didn't help his standing, either.

Schur attempted to be deferential and encouraging, but also found himself confronting a different type of client. "I was in *awe* of them," he says. "But I made it clear: 'Look, I see something building with you guys. You guys are moving toward something and I don't know if you want to go there, I don't know if you want any *help* getting there.

But I want you to know you're one of my favorite bands and I'm here for you in any regard.'"

To Schur's surprise, he was met not with approving smiles—the way most musicians would have reacted to such a pitch from the head of their label—but with dead air. "Nobody *said* anything to me," he says. "Nobody responded." To break the uncomfortable silence, Moore blurted out, "Yeah—all *right*." At that moment, Schur realized he would have to adapt himself to them, not the other way around.

Within band circles, the meeting would become renowned, recalled with chuckles, groans, and eye rolling. But it was also a glimpse into the revised playing field on which they found themselves. While he was there, Schur didn't ask to hear any of their in-progress music; in light of what *NYC Ghosts & Flowers* was becoming, it was probably best for everyone.

A FRESH PAIR OF EARS was needed to listen to the incomplete tapes and help turn them into a cohesive album. As was often the case, they didn't have to look far; someone they already knew was standing by. At Gordon's suggestion, they turned to Jim O'Rourke, a musician and producer who'd been circling around the band for several years. O'Rourke had just finished mixing *SYR 5*, a collaboration between Gordon, turntablist and sound mixer DJ Olive, and former DNA drummer Ikue Mori. Based around Gordon's voice, guitar strums, and deliberately skeletal songs and lyrics, the record amounted to her de facto solo debut, albeit one in which she was encircled by Olive's rattling, outer-limits rhythmic soundscapes. Gordon liked the way O'Rourke worked and the sound of the records he helped engineer or remix for bands like Smog. Perhaps here was the answer: someone who knew them and their history and could make sense of the jumble they'd recorded.

As musicians go, O'Rourke cut a nondescript figure. He was short in height and impish in demeanor; thanks to the bags that often hung beneath his large eyes, he tended to look more tired than he actually was, and his wardrobe veered toward the rumpled and thrift store. But in indie and experimental music circles, O'Rourke, at thirty, was already something of an underground legend. The product of blue-collar immigrant America—the son of an Irish gas-company employee and a maid—O'Rourke, born in Chicago, had been inhaling music since childhood. His parents would listen to Irish music on the radio, and when he was six, they bought him his first guitar. But their son wasn't destined to sing Celtic ballads; instead, the hypnotic fiddles and accordions of Irish music instilled in him a love for drones. In fourth grade, he and some friends made a rumbling noise by shaking a friend's guitar amplifier; putting it on tape, they called it "War."

His musical tastes also took on a wildly eclectic quality. The first album he bought with his own money was Paul McCartney's *Band on the Run*; he later became enamored of the low-fi pop of *McCartney* and *Ram*, the first two, mostly handmade albums McCartney made after he left the Beatles. (As O'Rourke would later declare, the early '70s was "the best time for music.") He loved albums, not singles; the broad palette (and orchestrated lushness) of LPs like Van Dyke Parks' *Song Cycle* spoke to him. At thirteen, he developed a crush on Cyndi Lauper; many years later, after he'd moved to New York, a poster of her would decorate his apartment. He played guitar and bass in his high school jazz band and became enamored of fusion (Chick Corea's Return to Forever and Weather Report) and prog (King Crimson and Rush). The latter interest was helpful when he had to deal with his school's menacing stoners: "We'd do Rush's 'YYZ' at the basketball games, and that bought me a week of no beat-ups. Rush saved my life in high school."

But thanks in part to the first edition of the *Rolling Stone Record Guide*, as well as a priest in his Catholic high school, the teenaged O'Rourke became intrigued by John Cage, which in turn introduced him to a world of avant-garde composition he'd never known before. Years later he would use the same phrase—"ass-kicking"—to describe both Rush's *Moving Pictures* and Steve Reich's *Desert Music*. At the suggestion of friends who knew he liked dissonance, O'Rourke had heard *Confusion Is Sex* and the *Kill Yr Idols* EP but was underwhelmed. "People said, 'Well, gee, if you're really into this people-beating-up-guitars things, you'll love Sonic Youth,'" he recalls. "And I heard 'Lee Is Free' and said, 'That's not improvised music!' At the time, I wanted my rock to sound like *rock*, and I wanted my noise really noisy." Although he admired *EVOL*, he stopped listening to most indie rock by the end of the '80s, preferring either classical or, for what he calls "straight music," Sparks and 10cc.

After recording indie records on his own, O'Rourke joined Gastr Del Sol, the Chicago band led by David Grubbs. In some ways, the band almost seemed to have been invented for O'Rourke. His first album with them, 1994's *Crookt, Crackt or Fly*, ambled from twelve-minute electronic music explorations to the woodsiest and most atmospheric of instrumental acoustic guitar pieces: John Cage bumping into John Fahey. Gastr Del Sol were a particularly bright example of the uncategorizable post-grunge indie, dubbed post-rock by the rock press. "When Tortoise came out, everyone was like, 'Oh, the avant-garde is moving back into rock,'" he says. "But as far as I was concerned, Gastr was the only band that *did* have avant-garde elements."

Shortly before and during this period, O'Rourke ran into Ranaldo and Moore at experimental music festivals like the Table of the Elements gathering in Atlanta in 1994. At one such event, Moore gave him a copy of the band's just-finished *Experimental Jet Set, Trash and No Star*. But, O'Rourke recalls, "I wasn't really interested in that kind of music. I was like, 'Whatever.' I listened to it, but I was listening to other music at that point." An early festival collaboration with Ranaldo, and one listen to Moore's *Piece for Jetsun Dolma*, made him rethink the band; O'Rourke realized Sonic Youth weren't just dabblers in freeform and avant-garde music but students of it.

O'Rourke left Gastr Del Sol in 1997 to make more of his own idiosyncratic records. Yet he soon decided it was best to "get a job," in his words; that way, he wouldn't have to rely on the meager sales of his own albums, like 1995's avant-folk *Bad Timing*. Becoming a producer for hire, O'Rourke began shuttling back and forth between Chicago and New York. During one Manhattan session to which he'd invited Moore, he wound up back at the Lafayette Street apartment, having dinner with Moore, Gordon, and Alan Licht. At one point, Sparks came up, and as Gordon and Licht sat listening, O'Rourke and Moore had an impassioned half-hour conversation about the defiantly oddball '70s art-pop duo. Later, Licht would be convinced that O'Rourke's eventual membership in Sonic Youth started that night, with that conversation.

Seemingly month by month, O'Rourke gradually became a part of the Sonic Youth solar system. Temperamentally, it was easy to see why: Droll and mild-mannered, often overly apologetic and deferential, O'Rourke was able to slip into any number of situations (including a nearly two-decade-old band whose members each had strongly held viewpoints and opinions). But the musical connections ran deeper. O'Rourke, who was so indie he preferred vinyl over compact discs, was moving closer to pop, especially on his 1999 album *Eureka*, which featured broader, lusher arrangements than *Bad Timing*; folky guitars coexisted with Beach Boy harmonies, horn sections, and pop craft reminiscent of Burt Bacharach. Sonic Youth, meanwhile, had begun heading in a more underground direction. O'Rourke and Sonic Youth would complement each other, add to each other's understanding of that alternate universe.

Memories differ on which member of Sonic Youth O'Rourke met first; it may have been Ranaldo. Yet it was Moore with whom O'Rourke eventually bonded most intensely. Both were proud record-collector geeks who shared passions for everything from '70s boogie slobs (Black Oak Arkansas for Moore, Groundhog for O'Rourke) to the musical avant-garde. When O'Rourke flew into New York for recording sessions, Moore would take his new friend record shopping or invite him to improv gigs at the Cooler, a club in the Chelsea area, with the likes of Licht and Tom Surgal. In O'Rourke, Moore found someone equally willing to spend hours ensconced in dark, musty used-record stores; it was as if he'd finally found a replacement for his high-school music soul mate Harold Paris. Once, O'Rourke joined Moore as he walked infant Coco in her stroller. As they passed a record store, excitedly comparing notes on the vinyl they'd bought, a gust of wind blew a piece of plastic shrink-wrap into the baby's face, and

Coco began crying. Bizarrely enough, the shrink wrap came from one of O'Rourke's own albums.

By October 1997, O'Rourke had grown so comfortable with Moore (and so supportive of his free-jazz side) that he enlisted Moore to play in the orchestra for dance and choreography innovator Merce Cunningham's "Forward & Reverse" piece at the Brooklyn Academy of Music. O'Rourke played his Powerbook, while Moore played guitar table-top style. Before rehearsals, the two men stopped by Echo Canyon. The rest of the band was already there, and soon enough, Ranaldo announced they should jam and handed O'Rourke a guitar. All together, with O'Rourke also working various effects pedals, they played an hour's worth of freeform improvisation: a long, intentionally shapeless noise-squirm (eventually called "Invito Al Cielo") with Gordon reciting over bleepy soundscapes, and another, in time called "Radio-Amatoroj," that had the percussive bang and clatter of a Cage work. The session, O'Rourke's first with the full band, gave him a peek into how they were evolving and making use of their own studio. It also gave him a sense of the kind of records they were making when, a few months later, Ranaldo called to say the jam was being prepared as the third release on SYR. O'Rourke had no idea he was part of anything close to an actual record.

O'Rourke had wanted to relocate to New York ever since high school, when he came across vintage photos of La Monte Young, Tony Conrad, and Philip Glass playing in downtown lofts in the '70s. In 1999, he finally made the move, and thanks to his new friendship with Sonic Youth, became a regular visitor to Echo Canyon, hanging out and fiddling around with guitars and amps. He became an integral part of the *Goodbye 20th Century* project, helping select some of the pieces and playing on a number of its tracks. When Gordon asked him in early 2000 to help out with the tapes from the Tiers sessions, O'Rourke readily accepted the challenge.

Hearing the rough tracks, O'Rourke was intrigued. "It was what I would have wanted to hear when I heard *Kill Yr Idols* for the first time," he says. "When this one got aggressive, it was closer to what I thought they sounded like." The actual work of completing the album was easier agreed upon than done. O'Rourke had found himself in many challenging situations before—"I was, 'Here's the guy who can deal with *ridiculous* situations!'"—but what confronted him defied expectations. To O'Rourke, Echo Canyon itself was "a goddamn nightmare." He hated the vintage recording console, which, to him, sounded "like crap"; the console would work one day and not the next, with no clear rationale. On some tracks, it was impossible to tell if there were any drums on the new recordings.

To make sense of the record, O'Rourke moved into the studio for two months, spending his days cleaning up the tracks and his nights sleeping on the couch. Since Gordon was still playing guitar the majority of the time, O'Rourke thought bass lines would enhance some of the tracks, so he overdubbed his own playing onto "Free City Rhymes" and "Small Flowers Crack Concrete." Later, Moore told him that when he heard the beefed-up "Free City Rhymes," everything clicked for him. "At that point," O'Rourke says, "I realized I really *did* understand what they were trying to do." The lack of proper miking of the drums also meant Shelley and O'Rourke had to entirely rerecord some of Shelley's parts, never an easy task in the best of circumstances; in particular, they replaced the original rhythm track on "Nevermind (What Was it Anyway)" with new percussion. "It was really invigorating to have Jim," says Shelley. "He had this manic, workaholic style, and he brought all this enthusiasm with him."

O'Rourke would ultimately receive a coproduction credit with the band, but, he says, "It was a difficult record to mix. It was kind of a salvage thing." The patchwork quality of the album was also felt by art director Frank Olinsky, who was given a seemingly random collection of New York–related images—a few of Ranaldo's city photos, a painting by Gordon, and a screen grab of Patti Smith from Dan Graham's *Rock My Religion*, among others—and told to make a cohesive CD booklet out of it. To Olinsky, it all felt a little disconnected.

The album itself, released by Geffen on May 16, 2000, felt equally disjointed and abstract. Even given a discography that could be challenging at best, *NYC Ghosts & Flowers* was one of their most difficult works. Much more so than on *A Thousand Leaves*, the band attempted to break out of its own formulae. Without many of their custom-tuned guitars, they coaxed new sounds out of their revamped lineup of instruments; the guitars flickered and floated during tracks like "Free City Rhymes." Moore in particular seemed to toy with his customary ways of singing and writing. His vocal during the first half of "Renegade Princess" reeked of glam-rock insouciance; the second half built to a driving incantation reminiscent of Patti Smith. Like other songs on the record featuring his voice, it rarely kicked into the sort of riffy, thrusting rhythms he'd long favored.

But "Renegade Princess" was representative of an album that was often painfully self-conscious in the way it attempted, with varying degrees of success, to mess with the Sonic Youth sound. Some tracks worked overtime to be unfathomable. During the eerily spectral "Side2Side," Gordon's voice, and the abstract poem she read, ping-ponged from speaker to speaker. The improvised "Lightnin'" featured each member of the band grabbing an unusual (for them) instrument: Gordon on trumpet, Moore on a bicycle horn, all of them making a humming, rattling whoosh of clatter for nearly four minutes. Overall, the album marginally recalled the way in which U2, another band that formed during the same period, was also attempting to reinvent itself on albums like *Pop* and *Zooropa*.

At times, the experimentation worked, making for an almost trance-inducing hypnoticism. Gordon rarely sounded as subdued as she did on "Nevermind (What Was It Anyway)," and her voice and the song's tick-tocking riff and beat were subtly seductive. The title track, half recited and half sung by Ranaldo, was the album's penulti-mate centerpiece, one of the band's most evocative fusions of music and poetry. The track slowly surged until, halfway through its seven-minute length, the guitars and drums locked into a repetitive drone-strum that made the influence of Glenn Branca even more apparent.

Poking out from it, Ranaldo's voice—"Will we meet? To run again? New York City ghosts and flowers"—felt like someone giving a eulogy at a wake for a city that had lost its mystery and allure, not to mention cultural history. The song was also inspired by the death of Ranaldo's father, Nicholas, halfway through the sessions.

Yet the album also felt diffuse and, for all its notable restraint, surprisingly low on energy. Sometimes the arrangements were too skeletal, the guitars malnourished, as if the instruments weren't actually playing through plugged-in amplifiers. Moore's "StreamXSonik Subway" touched upon any number of urban images, like missing a subway stop and getting "rousted by a low-beam cop," but at just over two minutes in length, it never ignited. Sonic Youth albums had always had a degree of obscurantism, musically or lyrically, but *NYC Ghosts & Flowers* had more than its share of both; for the first time, the band sounded pretentious.

To friends, the album had a certain logic. "You work hard for a long time, you make a lot of money—relative to the rest of your life, anyway—and you buy yourself a nice house," says Julie Cafritz. "And that becomes your focus. And those records [*A Thousand Leaves* and *NYC Ghosts & Flowers*] were less oriented toward a tight band and more internalized." But not surprisingly, the record was greeted with the most mixed response any Sonic Youth album had received since their first few releases. "There were a few people in the press who said, 'They really crawled up their own ass,'" recalls Perry Serpa, their publicist at the time. "There was a feeling that some people in the press had been okay with them making *A Thousand Leaves* but were now fed up with them." (Even Ranaldo, who supports three quarters of the album, admits, "We were serious about what we were doing, but maybe we didn't work as long or as hard on that record as we could have.")

Perhaps no better example of the album's problematic reception surfaced in the band's performance at the "All Tomorrow's Parties" festival in Essex, England, in April 2000, a month before the album's release. Their set began with a nearly half-hour-long drone improv, called "J'accuse Ted Hughes," and then went on to include many of the songs from the yet unheard *NYC Ghosts & Flowers*. "Play something we know!" someone from the crowd screamed out. When the band finally did, it was during the encore, when they played "Sunday." By then, the audience had thinned considerably.

OVER DINNER at the Lafayette Street apartment one night, Gordon and Moore began kidding O'Rourke. *Who'll play bass on the* NYC *Ghosts & Flowers tour? Guess you'll have to go on tour with us then.* O'Rourke, who'd never been on anything close to a big rock road trip, laughed it off, but he also sensed his new friends weren't completely joking. Besides, O'Rourke was intrigued: He'd been cooped up in recording studios for so long that he hadn't had much of a chance to perform live. Before long, Sonic Youth had lured O'Rourke into its touring lineup.

As someone accustomed to recording for small labels with limited funds, much less touring budgets, O'Rourke was taken aback by the world he entered in the summer of 2000. He felt uncomfortable with techs handing him guitars during concerts. Management asked what he wanted on his backstage rider; baffled, he only requested cigarettes. When hotels were being booked, O'Rourke initially demurred, telling the band's tour manager he'd be happy to sleep on the tour bus. During the early shows on the tour, O'Rourke forgot to tune his guitar in typical Sonic Youth ways, resulting in him playing songs like "Teen Age Riot" in standard tuning. Luckily, Moore and Ranaldo were playing so loud, they didn't initially notice.

The NYC *Ghosts & Flowers* tour would mark the beginning of a schedule the band would stick to for years to come: An album released just before summer, followed by touring that would wrap up by fall in order for their various children to start school in September. In this case, the U.S. tour was fairly short, mostly the month of June, followed by a few weeks in Europe and then the West Coast before winding down in late July. (By then, they'd resumed working with Dutch booking agent Carlos van Hijfte, letting bygones be proverbial bygones.) Initially, everyone thought O'Rourke would be, in Moore's words, "our Eno," someone who would mostly play synthesizer or a laptop computer on stage, contributing bleeps and squiggles to their sound. But O'Rourke ended up adding much more. Alternating between guitar and bass, which allowed Gordon to switch back and forth between instruments as well, O'Rourke quickly added a new (and sophisticated) musical element to the live shows. His bass playing, for one, was far more melodic and smoother than Gordon's. "They wanted me to play things accurately," he says, which would allow Ranaldo and Moore to go off on any number of noise or feedback tangents. "At the same time, I didn't want to play *too* solid, because then it wouldn't match. Some people criticized how I played with them early on, like we were playing too well. But they *wanted* me to play well. It was tough for a while to find a balance."

As expected, the band played a number of songs from the new album; the title track was a regular dramatic (and theatrical) highpoint, and "Nevermind (What Was It Anyway)" and "Small Flowers Crack Concrete" crackled far more than in the studio. Yet as if subconsciously trying to connect those songs to their first, indie era, the band also worked in the likes of "Death Valley '69," "The Burning Spear," and "White Kross." Although "Kool Thing" and "Mote" popped up in the sets, the older, pre-*Daydream Nation* material far outnumbered songs from the early Geffen days.

Whatever the reason—O'Rourke's presence, the change in set lists, or a combination of both—any sluggishness that lingered from the previous tour quickly burned off. Although he was as low-key a presence onstage as at Echo Canyon, mostly standing stolidly behind Gordon, O'Rourke injected vitality into the performances. "The *Thousand Leaves* shows were great, but subdued," says guitar tech Eric Baecht. "But with Jim, they were all excited about playing again. Every show on the *Ghosts & Flowers* tour was ten times more exciting."

"Jim brought in a real change that was really nice," Moore says. "He added a real exciting kind of presence for us. He changed the dynamic quite a bit, in a real positive way." Like a good fledgling rock star, O'Rourke also grew his normally short hair fairly long.

For the last month of the tour, up through Labor Day, they agreed to take an opening-act slot, this one for Pearl Jam. The audiences were more responsive than those of R.E.M. five years earlier, but once more, the band felt a distance from the alt-rock crowds. "I noticed Pearl Jam's audience were, like, a lot of dudes," Moore says. "'*Ed-die!*' Some of them liked us. But they were into basic deliverance, in a way. I didn't see us ever really selling to all those guys." (Coco, however, developed a crush on Vedder that would last until he shaved his head and adapted a less flattering Mohawk, at which point her infatuation abruptly ended.) During the tour, Silva and booking agent Bob Lawton kept asking the band to play a few older songs rather than focus on the taxing *NYC Ghosts & Flowers* material, so Pearl Jam fans might have something to hook into. However, the two men rarely got their wish.

Early the following year, Moore began thinking about making a second album of his own songs; his older brother Gene had shown him a new type of tuning, and Moore had knocked out a batch of material. With O'Rourke helping out, he recorded unplugged versions of a few of the songs at J. Mascis' home studio in Amherst. But when the late spring arrived and another Sonic Youth album needed to get underway, Moore offered up some of the finished and half-finished tunes. With Moore and Gordon spending so much time in Northampton, the days when the band could knock around material for months were drawing to an end. So, in August 2001, they commenced work on their first album with O'Rourke juggling jobs as coproducer, main recording engineer, and band member. For the first time in years, everything in the studio seemed to be in order; perhaps the new, post-gear-theft era wouldn't be such a difficult one after all.

THE FIRST PLANE hurtling into the first tower woke him up. At shortly before 9 A.M. on September 11, O'Rourke was asleep on the couch in Echo Canyon's front room; since he had no permanent city address, he was still using the studio as his home. Even though he was more than familiar with the clattering sounds of New York, he'd never heard a boom like the one that shattered his sleep. Glancing out the window, he saw people streaming out of the building across the way, construction workers at a nearby site staring up at the sky.

O'Rourke took the elevator down to the lobby and saw people on the corner, but the rushes of words out of their mouths didn't make any sense. Still unsure what was happening, he went back upstairs and called Gordon, who was in the Lafayette Street apartment; they were both scheduled to fly to Paris for an experimental-music show. She told him to turn on the TV; a plane had hit the World Trade Center. O'Rourke was still processing the information when the local news-caster started screaming, "Oh, no! Oh, no!" A different plane had slammed into the second tower.

Just then, it felt as if a bomb hit the building. The lights in the studio flickered, and everything started shaking. It was as if he were in the middle of an earthquake. O'Rourke closed the windows to the stu-dio and, thinking he was about to die, grabbed the two small stuffed animals he always carried with him. A fire escape and stairs were situ-ated in the back of the studio, but unaware of them, O'Rourke jumped back into the elevator and returned to the lobby. He headed for the front door of the building, and just as he reached for the han-dle, everything outside turned black. The huge cloud of dust, dirt, and debris was moving right down Murray Street.

Soon enough, the black cloud dissipated, and O'Rourke pushed open the metal door and stepped outside. Everything was covered in what looked like dirty snow. Police shouted for him to get in the sub-way right up the street. He did, but after fifteen minutes, he returned to the street level and began running up Church Street, heading up-town. On the way, he passed people with video cameras and shouted, "Run, you idiots!" ("Even at that moment in time," he says, "my usual hatred for humanity was in full force.") By the time he'd reached Lafayette Street, the sun had come out, yet its presence was only re-motely reassuring.

In his loft around the corner from Echo Canyon, Ranaldo was about to step into the shower and then take his two-year-old son Sage to pre-school when Singer shouted out that a plane had smashed into one of the towers. "Another crazy day in New York," Ranaldo thought to him-self. But when Singer screamed out that a second airplane had hit, they, like most everyone else at that moment, knew something wasn't right.

Sealing the large windows in their second-floor living room, the family—their second child, a boy named Frey, was only two months old—watched as everything outside went black and huge clouds of smoke rushed by. When all four finally emerged from the loft in midafternoon, wearing makeshift masks, the streets were disconcertingly quiet. They too made their way to Moore and Gordon's apartment (Moore himself was in Northampton that week). Ever the Bob Dylan fan, Ranaldo ventured out at one point to the nearby Tower Records to pick up a copy of *Love & Theft*, released that day. ("As absurd as it sounds, I felt I had to go out and buy it," he admits.) Shelley was still in Hoboken; he and alt-chanteuse Christina Rosenvinge, who was making a record for his Smells Like label, were supposed to record at Echo Canyon that day but stayed in New Jersey once they heard the news. While he was speaking with his parents in Michigan, Shelley looked out his window, with its Manhattan view, and saw the towers crumble.

Gordon, her friend Daisy von Furth, and von Furth's husband left for Northampton the next day, but since there wasn't enough room in their car, O'Rourke stayed at the Lafayette apartment by himself for two days. Since he wasn't in possession of any paperwork proving he lived there, he was afraid to leave and not be allowed back into the building by police, who were asking everyone for verification of their residence. Eventually, Don Fleming drove O'Rourke up to Northampton, by which time Tom Verlaine and his significant other had also arrived. The house had become an unofficial refuge for displaced New Yorkers, none more so than O'Rourke. Still traumatized, he settled into a bedroom on the third floor, where he stayed for several months. He would wake up, pour himself coffee, and retreat to the basement, where he would smoke cigarettes all day. He learned that the chunks of metal he had to step over as he left Echo Canyon that morning were parts of one of the planes' engines, which had landed on the building's roof. Keeping to himself in the house, he figured Coco thought of him as her parents' weird friend. Ironically, O'Rourke had just begun feeling better about the studio, thanks to upgrades to the recording console.

Late on the evening of September 11, Ranaldo, Singer, and their children drove out of the city, across empty bridges, and took refuge at his mother's house on Long Island, and then even farther out, on the far eastern tip in Greenport. Alone, Ranaldo returned to the city a few days later to inspect their loft and retrieve a few valuables left behind. The power was off, which was unnerving enough. Using a flashlight, he made his way down darkened hallways and into the apartment.

It was hard to say if anyone remained in the building, and even harder to determine who *was* there. Although the neighborhood was cordoned off, he heard noises outside, people running up and down the hallways. Who were they? Where they *supposed* to be there? He didn't know. He continued packing; he had to escape as soon as possible. He hadn't been so freaked out by the city since that abortive move to his first apartment in the East Village in 1979.

Chapter 13

THE FIRST TO VENTURE back inside the building were Shelley and Aaron Mullan, a young, poker-faced technician who'd taken a job as Echo Canyon's engineer and assistant the year before. From news reports, everyone knew 47 Murray was still standing, but the status of the rooms and equipment remained in doubt. When they reached Chambers and West Broadway, Shelley and Mullen could see a smoldering mountain of rubble in the distance. On the south side of Murray Street, a line of National Guard troops kept outsiders at bay; luckily, the studio lay on the north side of the street, which was patrolled only by city cops.

As FBI agents scoured the roof for pieces of the fallen engine, Shelley and Mullan were told they had five minutes to check on their workplace. With the elevator now out of order, they ran up the four flights of stairs and gingerly stepped inside. A layer of dust coated everything, but, to their relief, nothing had been destroyed, and the large windows weren't shattered. Eventually, they learned one of the generators that powered the console had been fried, but little else had been severely damaged; the tapes for the in-the-works album were intact as well. Even if the tapes had been wrecked, they also knew they had been inordinately fortunate, given the devastation that now surrounded them.

In the months that followed, the city had no choice but to muster some of its old energy and carry on. The same went for the band that had emerged from it twenty years before. Ranaldo and his family returned to their building a month after September 11, the power now restored. Following his extended recuperation time in Northampton, O'Rourke found his way back to the city, eventually relocating to an apartment in Brooklyn. A large cleaning crew scoured Echo Canyon, removing most of the dust and dirt. (For years afterward, though, Mullan would periodically tug on a rarely opened cabinet drawer and find a disquieting layer of white grime.) With its barricades, National Guard troops, and identification checkpoints, the area felt like a war zone. But by November, the band was able to resume work on their next album, even as the stench from the rubble that was once the World Trade Center wafted into the studio.

Ironically, the sessions that had begun the month before September 11 had promised to be the band's most relaxed and technically glitch-free since the *Washing Machine* era six years earlier. The record's basic skeleton had been erected before the attacks, when the solo tapes Moore had worked on quickly evolved into fleshed-out Sonic Youth numbers. "For a while, it was, 'Oh, these are Thurston's acoustic demos he's putting on his album,'" Shelley recalls. "But Thurston starts playing something, he's almost catatonic, just playing it over and over, and then you just play along. It's hard to tell how preformed it is with him. Is it the first time he's playing it or has he played it a hundred times? But it doesn't really matter because everything still went through the Sonic blender." Two songs, "Plastic Sun" and "Sympathy for the Strawberry," evolved differently, out of spontaneous studio jams.

Whether the song was firmed up or not, Mullan, working on his first full Sonic Youth album, was given fairly simple, if vexing, instructions that typified the band's approach to record making. "We didn't always know when we were doing basic tracks," he recalls. "It was kind of unclear. The approach was, 'If it sounds interesting, press 'record.'" For his part, O'Rourke experienced firsthand how songs began with "whatever stuff Thurston brings in," he says, before becoming band collaborations, and how Moore favored first takes while others preferred more completely worked-up later versions. Meticulous when it came to studio setups, O'Rourke noticed the band would sometimes begin playing before everything, including microphones, was in place.

Just as much as he'd helped reboot their live shows, O'Rourke helped liven up Echo Canyon: "I wanted to make up for *NYC Ghosts & Flowers*, so I was very particular about how it was being recorded." His own love of arena rock worked its way into the new music. Reflecting his and Moore's joint interest in what O'Rourke terms "grand, dramatic rock, like Mott the Hoople and Sparks," Led Zeppelin and Doors riffs snuck in and out; O'Rourke referred to one of his contributions as his "Paul McCartney bass part." For "Disconnection Notice," O'Rourke, as coproducer, aimed for a feel reminiscent of David Crosby's "Laughing" from his 1971 stoner-bliss solo album *If I Could Only Remember My Name*. ("That's the shit," O'Rourke says. "I know it's blasphemy. But I like it better than any Neil Young records.")

"We were so used to just kind of playing and not communicating that much," says Gordon. "But Jim was good at saying, 'I don't know what's going on here. What are *you* playing?' He was good at focusing things, and things got very well arranged."

From *Washing Machine* through *NYC Ghosts & Flowers*, the band wasn't so much writing songs as "individual lines that were running along each other," O'Rourke assesses. "Very few of the songs on those albums were ones Thurston could sit down and play on acoustic guitar. It wasn't about that; it was about interlocking parts that added up to the song. You listen to those records [*A Thousand Leaves* and *NYC Ghosts & Flowers*], the songs are constructed like parallel lines running along each other." That scenario wouldn't repeat itself on the new album. To help tighten up the music, O'Rourke played bass on all but two of the songs; Gordon returned to her former instrument on "Rain on Tin" and "Radical Adults Lick Godhead Style."

Moore and O'Rourke had wanted to call the album *Street Sauce*. But as O'Rourke saw, Sonic Youth truly was a democratic state; after a four-to-one band vote, the idea was shot down. (Shelley, the lone objector, felt the title was too insensitive given that the blocks around the studio were still being swept of World Trade Center debris.) They settled on *Murray Street*, which served two purposes. In tandem with Moore's back-cover photo of street signs covered in World Trade Center dust, the title was an obvious allusion to events of the previous year. And in keeping with the subtle nods to music they loved but hadn't always touched upon in their own work, *Murray Street* also intentionally evoked classic-rock album titles like *Abbey Road* and Eric Clapton's *461 Ocean Boulevard*. When album designer Frank Olinsky remarked to Moore that one of the tracks reminded him of Fleetwood Mac, Moore laughed—"almost like, 'you *caught* that!'" Olinsky recalls. Even the photo Olinsky was given for the cover—a shot of Coco Gordon Moore and Carlos van Hijfte's daughter, Stella, taken in a strawberry patch in the Netherlands—reminded Olinsky of the mystical-children cover of Led Zeppelin's *Houses of the Holy*, although no one in the band made the connection explicit.

On one hand the comparisons were silly; nothing Sonic Youth would ever do would be as accessible as a Beatles or Led Zeppelin record. But at least for its first two tracks, *Murray Street* presented a gentler, more melodically inclined band. "The Empty Page" (whose Moore-sung lyric, with lines like "sing out when there's no other way," seemed to hint at post-9/11 uncertainty) had an eloquent, meditative quality and a more traditional rock hook, even when the guitars let it rip midway through. The mood extended to "Disconnection Notice," its lyric inspired by troubles Moore and Gordon's daughter was having in school during that period. "It's about the whole theme of not being 'with the program,'" Moore says, "the idea of a standardized school system geared to children who don't have a standardized existence, and how it doesn't really benefit children much beyond discipline. Just the opposite—it's about uniformity." In its oblique way, the song was, he says, "a response to children being judged by standard testing scores," but it was also about the link he saw between his daughter and his younger self, his own sense of detachment from those around him: "They seem to think I'm disconnected/Don't think I know what to read or write or say," he sang. The melody itself was one of their most languid and elegant, with a sinuous Ranaldo lead guitar slicing through it like a butter knife.

O'Rourke's presence did lend the music what Shelley calls "a new energy. Not that I think *Ghosts & Flowers* or *A Thousand Leaves* were so bad, but *Murray Street* was a big improvement." The vigor was felt in the gritty groove of "Radical Adults Lick Godhead Style," another of Moore's Beat-inspired lyrical riffs, this time on elder rock statesmen like Lou Reed and (in code) Yoko Ono. Reflecting the emergence of free jazz in the band's and especially Moore's universe, Jim Sauter and Don Dietrich of the New York ensemble Borbetomagus (who'd appeared at the Noise Festival with Sonic Youth over twenty years before) contributed elephants-giving-birth saxophones to the song.

One of the band's long-held traditions involved naming early versions of tracks after the band that influenced it; by then, their tape vaults were littered with demos called "Yardbirds," "Voidoids," and "Jim Carroll." One of the new songs was initially dubbed "Celtic Frost" after the Swiss underground dark-metal band. After September 11, it was renamed "Rain on Tin," and Moore's concise lyric—"Gather round/Gather friends/Never fear/Never again"—in part made indirect reference to the Manhattanites who flocked to his Northampton home in the days and weeks after the attacks. (Another was Daisy von Furth, who, with her husband, left the city with Gordon and never returned; they too moved to the Northampton area.) The song opened with crashing, theatrical chords, followed by Moore's brief, almost haiku-style verse. Then the song gave way to an extended instrumental, yet one unlike those in the past: Here, Moore, Ranaldo, and O'Rourke's guitars gradually climbed atop each other, creating a trancelike, dream-weaver quality. In one regard, the instrumental section was a nod to the similarly lattice-work guitars of Television, but in another regard, it conjured the morning of September 11: When a dramatic Shelley drumroll crescendo came crashing in, it was as if they were replicating the sound of a lovely, sunny Manhattan morning suddenly ripped apart by destruction.

Perhaps reflecting the harrowing and confusing time during which it was completed, *Murray Street* felt relatively unguarded yet also pot-holed. "Karen Revisited" was a sequel of sorts to *A Thousand Leaves'* "Karen Koltrane," again about the same college-era Ranaldo friend and her life changes. Phantasmagoric guitars enveloped Ranaldo's voice and melody, but its last nine (of twelve) minutes were devoted to an overlong feedback crunch, part of it recorded at a post-attack benefit concert at the Bowery Ballroom, a downtown club. (The applause at the end of the track gave it away.) In what amounted to unusually lopsided sequencing, the album, which began with three straight Moore-sung numbers, ended with back-to-back Gordon-led tracks. Yet both "Plastic Sun" (its bitchy lyrics, courtesy of Moore, commenting on the way punk had been co-opted by fashion magazines) and "Sympathy for the Strawberry" were lumpy, not entirely well-formed songs. With its sumptuous double-tracking, Gordon's vocal on the latter was one of her most luxurious. But the song also felt shapeless and indeterminate: an unsettled finale to an album that, in its unintended way, also summed up a moment when the world had changed overnight and the future felt less than reassuring.

"WHAT IS THIS THING called the Internet? This 'information super-highway'?" Although Moore was being typically droll and deadpan, there was work to be done on the afternoon of June 9, 2002. In his standard uniform—jeans, sneakers, and long-sleeve buttoned-down shirt over a T-shirt—he was standing at one end of Echo Canyon's rehearsal room. Several guitars, a music stand, and a swarm of snaking wires surrounded him. Facing him in a bumpy semicircle were Ranaldo, Shelley, and O'Rourke, all in casual attire (O'Rourke's striped pants came complete with a large tear in the knee). As usual, Gordon, in blue skirt and blouse and high heels, was the most stylish in the room. Around them were nearly three dozen guitars and a range of effects pedals that looked like boxes strewn around the floor of a shoe store.

With *Murray Street* set for release in the States in a little over two weeks (and earlier in Japan and Europe), the band was driving onto that superhighway with its first-ever Web cast, live from the studio. Nearly six years into their stay there, the once-bare space had become a shrine to their heroes, infatuations, and own history. A Joni Mitchell photo and Captain Beefheart LP cover were tacked onto one wall. In the back hallway, near the shelves packed with boxes of recording tape from old rehearsals and recording sessions, were posters for '80s concerts by Lydia Lunch and LL Cool J—reminders of the city when it was dangerous, unknowable, and almost romantic. One back room was devoted almost entirely to drum cases, another to a table that resembled a handyman's work bench, littered with wires and fuses. Taped mischievously above a toilet in the bathroom was a photo of David Geffen. "Please: Play at a reasonable volume," read a sign (purloined from an old rehearsal space) posted on the studio's front door. (It didn't work: "It's kind of loud up there," groused a tenant walking into the building, as the opening chords of "Candle" floated down four flights of stairs to the lobby.) "Please do not play Sympathy for the Devil," the sign also read.

In the practice room where they stood, kitsch, another part of their heritage, dominated. A Donny and Marie Osmond quilt was draped over a piano; garish posters of Debbie Harry and Stevie Wonder stared down from the walls. A proudly tacky string of chili-pepper lights hung over Shelley's drums. The windowless room had the feel of the basement hideaway of wry, pop-culture-obsessed teenagers.

After "Candle," they casually worked their way through all of *Murray Street*. Between songs, Moore, Ranaldo, and O'Rourke tossed off puns and sarcastic rock-concert banter. "We're gonna play 'em *all* tonight," Ranaldo cracked—a genuine in-joke that referenced the time a teenaged Moore attended a J. Geils Band concert and lead singer Peter Wolf made the same remark to the audience. The band, however, didn't live up to Wolf's vow, leaving the stage after forty-five minutes. (The show, Moore recalls, "was *so* ineffectual.") Gordon mostly kept an alert eye on the proceedings, smiling occasionally in Moore's direction.

They called the Web cast "Rehearsin' for Ya," a name the performances often lived up to. "It's a little bit out of tune, but that's okay," said Moore, who sang from lyric sheets on the stand in front of him. When one song came to a tight close, he said, "That's one. We need at least two songs that stop on a dime." In place of the live drone at the end of "Karen Revisited" (which Ranaldo had also begun calling "Karenology"), Moore grabbed a large metal file and dragged it across the strings for a blaring *grrrrrrrrrg*. As the performance wound down, O'Rourke turned his guitar to face a speaker, creating a torrent of oscillating feedback that enveloped the studio. Ranaldo and Moore joined in, everyone eventually leaving the room until only Moore remained. As he walked out, Shelley patted Moore's guitar as if it were a pet.

In the recording room, everyone began checking postings from fans: "Clap clap stomp stomp," "do 'Free Bird' as an encore," and, in reference to Moore's on-air remark, "a lot of the songs stopped on a dime."

"Well, they didn't stay in *tune*," Shelley cracked, "but they *did* stop."

The session over, the band unwound; Gordon and Ranaldo each put in calls to check on their children. Standing nearby was Cody Ranaldo, then nearing his seventeenth birthday; his oversized T-shirt and baggy shorts were the uniform of the white hip-hop generation, but his short hair and glasses added a bookish touch.

Sitting on the couch, O'Rourke began flipping through the concert listings in the *Village Voice*. "Hey, is it true Rush is playing around?" he said, his voice carrying not a hint of ironic affectation.

Moore chuckled, and Ranaldo, sitting across the room, retorted, with exaggerated but pointed seriousness, *"No one in this room knows."*

"It would be *fun*," O'Rourke said, sounding a little bruised.

A smile that expressed "can you *believe* this guy?" flickered across Moore's face before he added, "I don't think it would be useful."

By the day of the Web cast, O'Rourke's position in the band was more defined than ever. His fill-in role on the *NYC Ghosts & Flowers* album and tour had given way to a full-time membership, the first time the band had added a new member since Shelley's entrance in 1985. No formal announcement was ever made, and O'Rourke himself didn't receive what he calls his "oh, this in-the-band thing is happening" feeling until he saw his photo in the *Murray Street* artwork. "That was probably the first point where I had to face it," he says. "Up to then, I thought, 'This is what I'm doing, and I like doing music and we're doing it together.' I never thought of officially becoming. I

never thought of *not* officially becoming. It just morphed into that."
As part of the arrangement, O'Rourke would share in the songwriting
credits and royalties, receiving one fifth of the band's paycheck, yet he
wouldn't be legally bound in any way: Averse to formal contracts, he
declined to sign any paperwork with the band, their management, or
Geffen Records.

Although the decision to add O'Rourke "ruffled a few feathers" in
the band, according to one friend, it was hard to imagine anyone better suited to joining Sonic Youth. By then, he offered a little something for everyone. His fascination with recording techniques led to a
natural bond with Ranaldo; during the making of *Murray Street*, the
two would often be the last ones in the studio, working until the sun
appeared. Given O'Rourke's supple, more traditional approach to bass
playing, Shelley was able to lock in with him in a way he'd never
quite been able to with Gordon, whose style and sound (an urban,
subterranean rumble) were far different. (Shelley was also relieved he
was no longer called "the new guy" in the band.) Now dealing with a
case of tendonitis in her right arm, Gordon was more than amenable
to having another instrumentalist on stage, allowing her to dance during certain numbers and put less strain on her arm. Having O'Rourke
stand between her and Ranaldo onstage had the additional advantage
of blocking Ranaldo's generally loud amplifier; O'Rourke, not Gordon, would now bear the brunt of the amp's sonic punch.

"I always thought it was about Thurston wanting to have someone to go record shopping with," says Tom Surgal. But like others,
Surgal also sensed O'Rourke's role was more profound: "With Jim, a
lot of it was interpersonal. They needed another person as a buffer.
There are definitely different camps in the band. But it's a statement
of their tenacity and their will that they're there to make music and
not to be best friends." O'Rourke himself realized his additional role
fairly early. "Especially in the beginning, I was a lobbyist," he says.
"It was, 'Tell Lee to turn it down.' They no longer had to say it directly. They could funnel it through me. Something they couldn't
say out loud before, they could now say to me. I was the quirk offi-
cer." ("I don't think people were ever using him as a messenger to

communicate with each other," counters Ranaldo, "but there were occasions when he may have been privy to someone's unhappiness about something.")

As the band relaxed after the Web cast, Shelley—always trying to manage a situation that was perpetually out of his or anyone's control—pulled out a yellow legal pad and pen. With a European tour set to start in less than a week, the set list had to be worked out so that techs Eric Baecht and Nic Close could pack up the appropriate instruments. Shelley knew he had to act quickly; Moore was already stuffing a guitar into a case for a free-jazz improv set in Brooklyn that evening.

But wait—the gear, the *tour*. Shelley pressed again, and Moore, focusing in on the issue for a moment, told him he knew which instruments he'd need. "Don't worry," he said. "I won't fuck up."

"I'm not *convinced*," Ranaldo said offhandedly, with a been-there, *we'll-see* smile.

Moore said nothing in return. He grabbed his guitar and made his way to the elevator. "It's just a bunch of the guys and a lot of noise," he told Gordon. "It's cool if you want to go home." She opted for their apartment; he gave her a quick kiss and was out the door.

ALONG WITH O'ROURKE'S assimilation into the band, many in the Sonic Youth organization sensed another change as the promotion and touring for *Murray Street* were being mapped out. Although they'd rarely spurned the media, giving interviews over the years to everything from *Rolling Stone* and the *New York Times* to *Sassy* and any number of fanzines, Sonic Youth suddenly seemed open to anything. They volunteered for an intense regimen of interviews and photo sessions as well as the kinds of events, like record-store appearances, they'd outgrown years before. "Having seen the industry change at that point, we all started to feel like we needed to do what we could to keep our presence out there, if we were going to survive," says Ranaldo. "We had to think up alternative ways to keep ourselves visible. We had to do what we could to make our presence felt."

Part of the reason was their natural inclination to do the opposite of what came before; the hooks that found their way into *Murray Street* stood in marked contrast to *NYC Ghosts & Flowers'* knottier melodies. But an equally urgent reason was indeed their survival. *NYC Ghosts & Flowers* had sold only forty thousand units, making it the lowest-selling album of their Geffen tenure. The rap-metal vogue that had made them seem anachronistic a few years earlier was on the wane, and a new style of indie or underground guitar band—the White Stripes, the Strokes, the Yeah Yeah Yeahs, and their ilk—were slowly elbowing their way onto the landscape. But the garage-rock aesthetic that most of those bands espoused (and, in the Stripes' case, fascination with blues and country) had little to do with Sonic Youth. Even with rock guitar more viable than it had been in years, they still sounded offbeat and awfully weird.

So they did what they had to—even, in Moore's case, calling Geffen president Jordan Schur to schmooze and communicate the band's excitement with *Murray Street*. Schur was pleasantly surprised; he still knew the band would be a hard sell to the masses. During the tour, which ran through the summer of 2002 and resumed with Japanese dates early in 2003, the band made promotional appearances in record stores (like Waterloo in Austin, Texas) and, after an especially rousing daylight show in New York's Central Park, settled in behind a table and signed autographs. O'Rourke would often accompany Moore to interviews to keep his friend from "getting bored out of his head," O'Rourke recalls. "We have a lot of the same sense of humor. The dynamic was Thurston with his little brother." During the Los Angeles stop of the tour, the two were dispatched to KXLU, the radio station on the campus of Loyola Marymount University. "Hi, I'm Jim O'Rourke, the new guy, and I'm going to take over the band," Moore said at the start.

"And I'm Thurston, the old guy," O'Rourke retorted. (When it was over, after they had answered the usual string of questions about the band's origins and their connection to punk, O'Rourke turned to Moore, and, sounding almost repentant, said, "Sorry I talked so much.

And sorry about that 'old' thing." Moore seemed unperturbed by the crack: "No, that's okay. I liked that.")

Their emphasis on professionalism also emerged during the *Murray Street* concerts. With a nightly repertoire that touched upon nearly every phase of their career—except for the *Thousand Leaves* and *NYC Ghosts & Flowers* material, conspicuous in their absence—the concerts amounted to mini-histories of the band. Two shows at the El Ray Theater in Los Angeles on August 25 and 26 (with, as usual, Keanu Reeves in the crowd) were fairly representative. Newcomers, including the increasingly peach-faced fans starting to appear, heard plenty of songs from their latest record. The entwined-guitars portion of "Rain on Tin" was particularly hypnotic; Sonic Youth actually came across as something approaching a jam band. But the crowd also experienced trips back in time to the pre-Geffen years ("Tom Violence," "Shadow of a Doubt," "Making the Nature Scene"), a tease of *Daydream Nation* ("Kissability"), and, in wire-bristle versions of "Kool Thing" and "Drunken Butterfly," a reminder of their early Geffen semi-pop period. With O'Rourke still handling a number of the bass parts, as well as guitar and effects pedals, Gordon was able to dance onstage during the songs she sang, doing what Chloë Sevigny admiringly referred to as her "jump-rope" move. "People are cringing, probably," Gordon said at the time. More likely they were transfixed: Freed from having to play an instrument, Gordon became a much more sexually provocative presence onstage, adding something truly new, a visual upgrade, to the stage show.

"We're the Rolling Stones or Grateful Dead of our generation, or something," Ranaldo had said a few months before the Los Angeles show. In terms of longevity, he was right; by then, Sonic Youth was celebrating the twentieth anniversary of the release of their initial EP. Each show featured a noise freak-out, usually during "Karen Revisited," and the moment would invariably arrive when Moore would grab a drumstick and scrape it up and down the guitar fretboard. These moves were now as much trademarks as Mick Jagger's onstage finger-pointing jabs or the dual drum solos that had always been part of a Dead set. Yet Sonic Youth's shows, even during the *Murray Street* period, were never completely pat; the tension between who they were (onstage anarchists) and who they had to be at times (a tight, well-oiled rock band) was always in the air.

And even in such settings, they couldn't help but tweak their corporate overseers. In record stores, they'd noticed *Murray Street* was often sold at close to full list price. At several stops on the tour, including both nights at the El Rey, Gordon told the audience, "Don't forget—don't pay more than $13.99 for a CD." Schur, who wasn't in the audience that night, didn't hear about her comment for several months.

"THE ONLY WAY we're going to sell records is if we break up," Moore said one night in the kitchen of the Northampton house as Gordon prepared a lasagna dinner. "Or," he added, "if one of us dies." The summer was over, the majority of the *Murray Street* performances had wound down, and life outside Sonic Youth was again stepping to the fore. As usual, Moore punctuated the remark with a chuckle, a way to deflate the seriousness of what he'd just said. Yet it was clear that their lack of substantial financial reward after two decades in the business stuck in his craw. "I challenge any label out there to sell Sonic Youth records," he said. "I challenge any label out there to get us a gold record. So far it can't be done. Even though they think it might be easy."

Despite the inordinate amount of heavy lifting that had gone into its promotion, *Murray Street* hadn't been the late-period breakthrough the label (and perhaps the band) had hoped. The album had received some of the most welcoming reviews they'd garnered—many of which, to the band's irritation, dwelled on how tuneful and song-oriented the album was compared to its two predecessors. The perception was simplistic: Hooks, albeit of a far subtler type, had crept out of "Hits of Sunshine (for Allen Ginsberg)," "Hoarfrost," and "Nevermind (What Was It Anyway)" on the preceding albums. But the way in which the band talked about the album in relation to old-school rock, down to its title, also fostered the impression that Sonic Youth were now a more accessible band. The album's final sales tally was the ultimate barometer: Reaching approximately sixty-five thousand units by the fall of 2002, the album sold only marginally more than *NYC Ghosts & Flowers*. MTV was rarely playing music videos by then, and even if it had been, the low-budget clips produced for "The Empty Page" and "Disconnection Notice" (directed by friends Chris Habib and Tom Surgal, respectively) wouldn't have stood much chance anyway.

Increasingly, family played a larger role in Sonic Youth life, never more so than in the house in Northampton. The Volvo mini-wagon in the back driveway and the propane grill on the back porch implied suburban normalcy. But the balance between work and family always poked out. In the kitchen, a cookbook called *Too Busy to Cook?* leaned next to a counter full of CDs that ranged from a John Coltrane box and a Paul McCartney and Wings bootleg to albums by Carole King, Lucinda Williams, Pentangle, the Monkees, Neil Diamond, the Saints, and the James Gang. The office's daunting shelves of Beat-era pamphlets now shared space with an eight-year-old's toy Slinky. One of Coco's paintings ("I'm walking to my swimming lessons. I'm feeling good. I chose the colors because they make me happy") was framed in the center hallway. In the kitchen, a calendar featuring the mug of Iggy Pop shared bulletin-board space with their daughter's school schedule. Time was taking its toll on their families as well: A few years after C. Wayne Gordon had passed away, his wife Althea died. Their son Keller resided in a healthcare facility outside Los Angeles.

Coincidentally or not, a music scene had risen up during the same time they had moved to the area. At one of several local clubs, they would see Le Tigre, Fugazi, or Cat Power or do one of their own shows; Moore began working out rough sketches of future Sonic Youth songs at solo performances at spaces like the Flywheel, an intimate club in nearby Easthampton. Moore and Byron Coley opened a combined book and record store that focused on independent records, and Ecstatic Peace!, Moore's long-standing indie label, was relocated to Massachusetts as well. "We felt we could stretch in so many different directions at that point," says Ranaldo; one of them, a natural, was soundtrack music. As a band, they'd first ventured into movie scores in the '80s when, in Los Angeles, they recorded an instrumental score for *Made in USA*, Ken Friedman's ill-fated 1987 teen road movie. Around the time of the *Murray Street* sessions, they'd also written instrumental music for French director Olivier Assayas' *Demonlover* and Allison Anders' *Things Behind the Sun*.

The projects allowed them to stretch out and also gave each a breather from the others; as friends observed, the outside-group projects helped keep the group together. Ranaldo's interest in film and improvisational music led him to merge the two with Text of Light, a loose-knit aggregation usually centered around him, guitarist Alan Licht and saxophonist Ulrich Krieger (Christian Marclay and percussionist William Hooker also joined in from time to time). Starting with its first show, at Tonic in New York in May 2001, Text of Light would emit all-instrumental walls of noise while films (including those of Leah Singer and cult, abstract filmmaker Stan Brakhage) played behind them. Shelley continued to release records on his Smells Like label from the likes of singer-songwriter Chris Lee, his friend Tim Foljahn's Two Dollar Guitar, and Blonde Redhead.

The lasagna eaten, Moore retreated to his study for work and another in an endless series of interviews for one media outlet or another. Eventually, Coco poked her small, blond head in, asking if he could read her a book before bedtime.

"No, I can't," he said. "Mommy's reading to you tonight."

"Boo hoo *hoo*," she shot back with knowing preteen sarcasm.

"Sorry, can't do it," he said.

"Do your interview quickly," she said.

"Okay, I'll do it real quickly. I was born in 1958. The end."

"Well, will it take a long time? Will it?" she demanded.

"It takes how long it takes," he told her, not too forcefully. "If you're still up when I'm done, I'll come up."

"You *have* to."

"Good night," he said.

"And by the way, if you don't have to, you shouldn't do it."

"Wow," he chuckled as she went upstairs. "A future agent."

At the time, their daughter was attending what Gordon referred to with a chuckle as a local "hippie school." Ironically, she did not, at the time, like "loud music," as her mother put it. Other than "The Empty Page" and "Kool Thing," Coco found the music of Sonic Youth too noisy. She was mostly listening to the likes of '90s pop star Vanessa Carlton, which made her parents cringe, but at least someone like Carlton sang and played her own songs. Coco's brief interest in Britney Spears was dampened when her mother told her Spears couldn't actually sing and that older men wrote her songs. ("That was a real turnoff for her," Gordon said.)

Sometimes, Coco would return from school and ask her parents why they weren't working in a store or teaching. They just seemed so *different* from other mothers and fathers. The families of her classmates, as well as neighbors, didn't always know what to make of the new people in town either. Whenever Moore and Gordon were invited to other parents' homes, Moore would naturally gravitate toward their record collections, where he would mostly see CDs by the likes of Macy Gray. Music released on small, independent labels was nowhere to be found, and most of the mothers and fathers had never heard of Sonic Youth. Moore and Gordon would tell them they were "rock musicians" and be greeted with blank stares.

Only when the band played a show in the local park, and a photo made the front page of the local newspaper, did they elicit some reaction. "They were like, 'Oh, my God, what *is* this?'" Moore says. Ironically, it was not unlike the reactions they'd received two decades earlier, during the earliest Sonic Youth performances.

THE FIRST SIGN that things were not fine with O'Rourke came during the mixing sessions for their next album. The writing and recording of the record, which commenced in the summer of 2003 and extended into the early months of the following year, was largely stress-free and enjoyable. Unlike *Murray Street*, many of the songs emerged not from Moore's side projects but from band jamming, much like the old days.

(A few, like "Peace Attack" and "New Hampshire," did start as Moore solo demos, though.) During a rare group outing—off the road, they tended not to socialize with each other—the entire band attended a blues concert at Radio City Music Hall in honor of Martin Scorsese's documentary on the music. At one point, during a jabbing one-note solo by Buddy Guy, Moore looked over and saw Aerosmith's Steven Tyler and Joe Perry mesmerized. Out of the experience came the lyrics to "New Hampshire," the state where Aerosmith first came together.

Much like she'd once been intrigued by Karen Carpenter's quest for bodily perfection, Gordon was now fascinated with another image-driven pop diva, Mariah Carey (and what Gordon refers to as Carey's "overwhelming, psychotic desire to please"); the results were "Mariah Carey and the Arthur Doyle Hand Cream." The incongruous second half of the title was a nod to the revered free-jazz saxophonist, who once sent Moore lotion as a gift. As with "Tunic (Song for Karen)," the song, a musical caboose-on-the-loose ride of a track, was both sympathetic toward, and critical of, its subject. Mildly understanding lines ("Like Miss Monroe your head don't know exactly what your body's doing") were offset with scolding ones ("On Larry King you said you were tired/Time to put to bed the competitive edge").

In the studio, Mullan watched as the band passed around a sheet of paper, each adding a line to a new lyric. "The process was really fun," says Ranaldo of the album sessions. "We were all in a good mood. The heaviness of 9/11 was lifted a little." During the mixing phase, the band shifted work to another studio, Magic Shop, the same place they'd created *Dirty* over a decade earlier. Almost immediately, O'Rourke developed a case of meningitis, his right ear filling up with fluid. Although in deep pain and unable to hear out of one ear, O'Rourke kept working. (Terrified of the results given the circumstances, he didn't listen to the album for at least the first two years after its release.) Perhaps due to his illness, the band noticed that O'Rourke didn't seem to be in as good a mood as he'd been in the past; he was begrudging about making the last-minute aural tweaks they asked of him.

Yet more than just an ear ailment was on O'Rourke's mind. Although he remained close to the band, especially Moore and Gordon, he began realizing that what he calls their long-standing "work habits" weren't about to change. As someone accustomed to working on his own or having final say as a producer, O'Rourke saw the limits of his contributions. "You can't really put one hundred percent into something that's collaborative," he says. "You have to respect other people's input and accept some things you're not into because that's how it goes. I hadn't worked that way in a while." During the sessions, he handed over the engineering reins to Mullan and mostly contented himself with playing bass and guitar.

Despite its problematic wrap-up, *Sonic Nurse* was ultimately an even stronger work than *Murray Street*. The title came from a series of collage-art works by Richard Prince, who himself dated back to the New York scene of the late '70s; Gordon had met him while working at a gallery. Based on covers of old pulp-fiction books, the pieces, collectively dubbed "Nurse Paintings," featured a series of nurses, their mouths covered with surgical masks. The effect was both comforting and, in the way the women seemed muzzled and mysterious, disquieting. (The Center for Nursing Advocacy approved, saying that "despite its irony and gore, the exhibit was a powerful representation of the state nursing is in today. Nurses are gagged and silent, whether through oppression by their employers, physicians, society, or self-silencing.")

The paintings, which graced the front and back covers as well as the inside booklet, lent a unified feel to the packaging, and the music too was cohesive from start to finish. Trickling guitar chords, infuriated noise, and redolent melody had long been components of Sonic Youth songs. But the *Sonic Nurse* material seamlessly integrated all three into nearly every song. The sequencing was more balanced than on *Murray Street* as well: Tracks sung by Moore, Gordon, and Ranaldo were interwoven, rather than bunched together. The result was not merely a more organic and fluid recording, but a late-period high point.

Starting with "Pattern Recognition," featuring a stabbing lead line from Ranaldo and an aggressive O'Rourke bass part, both the songs and the performances were firm and confident. The album was filled with bristling, electrical-socket moments: the moment the three guitars circled around and ensnared each other in "Unmade Bed," the battle between rumblefish six-string guitar and screech in "Stones," Ranaldo's ghostly organ rising up in the choruses of "I Love You Golden Blue," Shelley's range of accents in "Pattern Recognition." The buttery guitars and drum pitter-patter of "Unmade Bed" showed how they'd learned to massage melodies as much as attack them. The drowsily hypnotic, Gordon-sung "Dude Ranch Nurse" (title courtesy a '50s teen novel, the lyric an enigmatic fantasy about George W. Bush as cowboy) demonstrated how they'd learned the art of having a melody lithely, seductively, insinuate itself into one's brain.

The inevitable literary reference arrived in Gordon's lyric to "Pattern Recognition." The song had begun with one of Moore's riffs and vocals: "Instant mayhem!" he sang in the original chorus. But when Gordon took it over, she gave it the title of William Gibson's novel from the year before, which involved a character who'd been missing since the collapse of the World Trade Center. (The "cool hunter" referred to twice in the lyric was taken from the book as well.) "Pattern Recognition" wasn't the only song that conjured September 11. If anything, *Sonic Nurse* was more of a post-attack album than *Murray Street*. Written during an airplane flight as he was reading newspaper accounts of the onset of the Iraq War, Ranaldo's lyric for "Paper Cup Exit" touched on what he calls the country's "collective amnesia" as another Bush took the country to yet another conflict in the region. Moore's "Peace Attack" was a gentle, almost resigned protest song.

When Geffen didn't budget money for any videos, David Markey took it upon himself to make one for "I Love You Golden Blue," a hushed, gorgeous melody with a wistful, whispery Gordon vocal. Markey's video mixed footage of the band performing the song in Los Angeles with home-movie footage of a young boy given to Markey by a friend. Although Gordon never told Markey what the song was about—it could easily be interpreted as a veiled song to her brother Keller, especially in lines like "I can't read your mind . . . I don't have the will"—the video (with its newspaper headlines and gravestone imagery) conveyed an explicit antiwar message.

"Kim never explained the lyric to me," says Markey, "but Thurston's reaction was, 'This is completely evocative of the song.'"

O'Rourke himself was pleased with the end result: "That album had more totally kick-ass songs for me," he says. "I liked it better than *Murray Street*." But by the time the group began its road work to support *Sonic Nurse*, in the now-standard, kids-out-of-school month of June, it was increasingly apparent that O'Rourke wasn't as engaged as he'd been. Once a pleasant break from endless hours in dimly lit recording studios (he calls the *NYC Ghosts & Flowers* tour "a big vacation, like having your butt kissed for nine months"), the road and everything it entailed had become increasingly less attractive. O'Rourke had never been enamored of music-industry schmoozing or after-show parties. The occasional radio-station concert or private party the group would play struck him as "super bogus. I know it's part of that world, but it's not something I ever wanted to be involved with." As much as he liked the members of Pearl Jam—on September 11, Eddie Vedder made a frantic series of phone calls trying to track O'Rourke down—O'Rourke found the concept of being an opening act, for Pearl Jam or anyone else, hard to tolerate. "I never liked it," he says. "*Super*-constraining. When you're a band like them [Sonic Youth] and you're opening for someone, to me, you're telling the audience, 'This is how good we are. We're only good enough to be an opening band.' They disagree with me on that, but that's the way I see it. It's better to do *your* thing—maybe for less money, maybe in smaller places."

Onstage, little seemed amiss. The *Sonic Nurse* tour had to be reorganized at the last minute when a new, revived Lollapalooza, of which Sonic Youth would have been part, was cancelled in light of abysmal ticket sales. (Organizers realized too late that aging fans of PJ Harvey, Morrissey, and other veterans no longer had any interest in standing around in the heat for an entire day.) Once their own tour was underway, though, the shows continued the high of the *Murray Street* gigs, bolstered by the robust songs they were promoting. Some shows were downright manic, Moore climbing onto venue balconies and dangling his guitar over the audience. (The move resulted in more than one dropped guitar and broken neck, which tech Eric Baecht had to repair backstage with Elmer's wood glue and a vise.)

An unexpected peak came in October 2004, when the band made its second appearance at Neil Young's annual benefit for the Bridge School, a facility for children with disabilities cofounded by his wife Pegi. Sonic Youth's first appearance, in November 1991, was a notorious debacle. Since the shows were always unplugged affairs, the band was required to use acoustic guitars. The afternoon rehearsal had gone well, but by the time they took the stage, something had happened to the monitoring system; they couldn't hear themselves play. Completely flummoxed and frustrated by the situation, Gordon yelled "Fuck!," smashed her guitar, and stalked offstage, followed by the others; the audience reacted with boos and catcalls. (Did someone in Young's camp deliberately mispatch cables to exact revenge on the band after they'd complained to Young earlier in the year? Some suspected but never were able to verify.)

The 2004 show went over far better, and, to O'Rourke's delight, the band spent quality backstage time with another of the evening's performers, Paul McCartney. To McCartney's surprise, the band was well aware of his fondness for '60s British avant-garde music and his brother Mike McGear's obscure albums. McCartney seemed relieved to be talking about something other than the Beatles, and he hung out in the Sonic Youth dressing room more than anyone expected. ("I think he was hiding from that wife of his," says O'Rourke.) As if fulfilling a longtime dream, O'Rourke joined in on the "Hey Jude" sing-along.

Overall, though, O'Rourke was growing less enthused about the touring life. Even when the band pulled into exotic European cities, he begged off local expeditions, opting to stay in his room and watch art films, one of his obsessions. A vegetarian with food allergies, O'Rourke also found it hard to find suitable meals on the road, and a problematic personal relationship at home was also wearing on him.

Beyond the wear and tear of a numbing string of hotels and airplane flights, the cumulative effect of five years with a major-label band was taking a toll on O'Rourke. Performing abbreviated opening-act sets was one thing. Having song titles and album art tampered with was another. Although "Mariah Carey and the Arthur Doyle Hand Cream" had been recorded prior to the *Nurse* sessions and released on a split-single seven-inch with Erase Errata in 2003 (complete with an illustration of Carey in the artwork), band lawyer Richard Grabel flagged the title when the time came to include it on *Sonic Nurse*. He couldn't be sure Carey would sue; chances were she wouldn't. But, Grabel told them, a case could be made that they were indulging in unauthorized exploitation of her name for profit. With the vague possibility of a lawsuit in the air—and the thought of having to spend a sizable amount of money to defend themselves—the band begrudgingly agreed to change the title to "Kim Gordon and the Arthur Doyle Hand Cream," although the Mariah-specific lyrics remained intact.

Of them all, O'Rourke was among the most put off by the alteration, which he calls "stupid." Then, when the album art was being assembled, Frank Olinsky was informed by the band's management that he'd have to strip a large "FBI Anti-Piracy Warning" sticker across the bottom of the back cover, on order from Universal Music. He—and others in the band—were startled and displeased. But no one was more offended than O'Rourke, who'd never had to deal with anything comparable during his dealings with independent labels. "I was mortified about that," he says. "What a bunch of bullshit. It sounds crazy, but that might have been a real tipping point for me. I was like, 'Why fucking make records anymore?' You're not even allowed to design your own damn cover. You might as well just make the back an *ad* then. Just sell it as goddamn ad space." The band and Olinsky did compensate by making the back cover reversible for anyone who didn't want to glare at the anti-piracy banner, but to O'Rourke, the damage had been done.

At times, the band didn't know what to make of O'Rourke, either. They never failed to be engaged by his sense of humor and passion for a wide range of music. But they felt he always seemed to be complaining about some technical matter or another, and his casual approach to compensation—he still had uncashed royalty checks taped to his kitchen door in the days before he moved to Japan in the late spring of

2006—was puzzling. As O'Rourke admits, he never billed management for his services and would have to be repeatedly reminded to send invoices; once, he even begged off taking his share of tour merchandise, feeling it wasn't his place to benefit from the band's history.

O'Rourke had fallen in love with Japan and its culture when he'd visited the country a decade earlier, only returning to the States after he'd run out of money. He'd always fantasized about moving there—and, in so doing, devoting himself to his own experimental records and film scoring. In Japan, he wouldn't have to deal with the American music business, the demands of road schedules or people like Jordan Schur, who offended his sensibility as much as any other member of Sonic Youth. He wouldn't have to make appearances on television shows, as the band had done during the *Sonic Nurse* tour, when they played "Unmade Bed" on both *The Tonight Show* and *Late Night with Conan O'Brien*. (During the latter appearance, O'Rourke felt the disapproving stare of house-band leader Max Weinberg on him throughout the performance.) O'Rourke was also making a bigger name for himself as a producer, mixer, and album salvager. Hired to mix Wilco's *Yankee Hotel Foxtrot* in 2001—he and leader and fellow Chicagoan Jeff Tweedy had become friends and occasional collaborators—O'Rourke pulled an overly fragmented album into a coherent whole. In the fall of 2003, O'Rourke produced the band's follow-up, *A Ghost Is Born*, walking away with a Grammy when the band won "Best Alternative Music Album" in 2005.

As gradually as he'd come into Sonic Youth, O'Rourke slowly, inexorably, began to pull out. He put off trips to Northampton for band rehearsals and agonized over his decision. He dreaded telling the band, since he still considered them pals. "It was difficult," he says. "They were exceedingly kind to me. I felt I was insulting them by doing it." But, he says, Japan "was something in my life before I even knew them, and I'd been holding off on it for ten or fifteen years and didn't want to do that anymore. It wasn't so much a decision to leave. It was a decision to change my life." During a series of European shows in 2005, he finally broke the news to the band; as the ones closest with O'Rourke,

Moore and Gordon were the most affected. He helped them fulfill a few more contractual concert obligations—including a show at a festival in Rio de Janeiro in November—and then he was gone.

Given the myriad projects that always seemed to be tugging at O'Rourke, some were surprised he'd lasted in Sonic Youth as long as he had. Within the band, though, some weren't shocked. "Maybe he got as deep into the world of Sonic Youth as he wanted to," Ranaldo says. "It opened his eyes to some things—and to some things he wouldn't be able to change." Even two decades later, Sonic Youth would be Sonic Youth; the odds of anyone altering them or telling them what to do, even a sympathetic colleague like O'Rourke, were slim. On the eve of the twenty-fifth anniversary of the first show ever billed as Sonic Youth, they'd come close to full circle: four people with four different personalities and viewpoints, out of sync with the record industry but back to relying on each other for a way through it all.

Chapter 14

JIM O'ROURKE HAD BEEN OUT OF THE BAND only a few months when the time came to restart the Sonic Youth apparatus. They hadn't been a four-piece since the early stages of *NYC Ghosts & Flowers*, and no one was quite sure how the band would sound without O'Rourke serving in his dual role as aural collaborator and group shock absorber. But their work ethic, not to mention their Geffen contract, beckoned; almost two years had passed since *Sonic Nurse*, and another album, their sixteenth of new songs, needed to fall into place.

To their surprise, the album took shape at a remarkably fast clip. By the early months of 2006, everyone was spread across three different states, so with Moore and Gordon commuting into Manhattan, the material needed to be recorded quickly, on weekends. To make the most of their compressed time, Moore came in with a group of fairly complete songs. They went back to Sear Sound and quickly cut basic tracks, Gordon and Shelley figuring out bass and drum parts for each. Ranaldo played along, then took the raw tapes back to Echo Canyon to painstakingly record his parts, fills, and solos separately from the band. It wasn't his or Shelley's preferred method of making a group album, but they had no other choice. Between family obligations and side projects, too much was taking place outside Sonic Youth to drag out the record-making process any further.

With the exception of Gordon, remarkably fit and lean, the muscle definition in her arms apparent from years of holding a bulky bass

onstage, the band was stockier than in their youth, and age was making itself known in Ranaldo's gray-streaked mop and the glasses
Moore regularly wore offstage. But lounging about the lobby of Sear
Sound in the early months of the year, pecking at laptops or watching
TV as they awaited the completion of a song mix, they also looked
more or less the same. Work shirts, jeans, and sneakers still dominated their wardrobes.

The night's main pop culture event was the Super Bowl, and the half-
time entertainment at Super Bowl XL was none other than the Rolling
Stones. The performance was being sponsored by one of the major telephone companies, and the Stones had agreed to a five-second tape delay
in case any of their songs contained offensive lyrics. By then, it was impossible to imagine anything remotely X-rated about "Start Me Up"
and "(I Can't Get No) Satisfaction," but such were the compromises
that superstar bands, even the Stones, had to make.

With time to kill—and being, as always, captivated by rock history
and their own conflicted thoughts toward celebrity—the four of them
gathered around the TV in the studio's lobby. As the Stones appeared
on the gargantuan stage of the Detroit stadium, Sonic Youth sat and
watched. Their facial expressions ranged from bemusement (at the
spectacle of it all and how ragged the Stones sounded) to awe (at Mick
Jagger's physique and stamina).

The Stones' performance ended just as Sonic Youth needed to resume work. Hoisting themselves up from couches, they filed into the
control room and surrounded John Agnello, the gray-bearded engineer assisting them on the record. Agnello cued up a track, a beatific
and abnormally restrained number called "Do You Believe in Rapture?" The song's steady, metronomic pulse recalled, of all things,
U2's "With or Without You." One by one, everyone chimed in. Shelley thought the cymbal splashes needed a little more definition;
Ranaldo felt his guitar arpeggios could be brightened. Gordon
thought Moore's vocal on the second verse wasn't at the same volume
as his singing in the first verse. Moore, who still had the least amount
of patience for such things, mostly concurred, wandering around the
room as if he couldn't wait to leave it. He was already itching to head

downtown to catch a show by Little Howlin' Wolf, a manic Chicago busker (no relation to the blues icon) known for making a racket all his own.

When they were finished giving their input, Agnello worked his way through each part of the song, twiddling knobs and levers until each tweak was made. After an hour, a track that had already been worked on for many hours seemed complete, although each member would take home a copy to listen once again. Taking another break, Gordon returned to a smaller room to continue fine-tuning her vocals; the others hit their laptops, checking e-mail and watching a bit of YouTube (Crosby, Stills, Nash & Young jamming on "Down by the River" on a vintage TV show).

By that time, their own chances of attaining a Stones-like level of success were slim, and they knew it and accepted it. "I don't know if the band has a desire to sort of really crack anything more, in a way," Moore had said earlier. "Realistically, it can't really happen right now anyway, the way the industry is set up. Unless it's sort of flukish. Anybody will take a fluke any old day to sell a few million records. But it happens extremely rarely, like getting hit by lightning."

But they were still together, an accomplishment in and of itself. To anyone who'd seen them during their earliest days, the idea that a band built on such untidy music would still exist over two decades later was nearly unimaginable. Even stranger was the notion that a band that had sought to dissemble and rebuild rock & roll was now a new generation's classic rock, alongside peers like the Pixies, R.E.M., Dinosaur Jr., the Cure, Hüsker Dü, the Replacements, and many others. And of them all, Sonic Youth, the least accessible of the bunch, were one of the few left standing.

But such was the duality of Sonic Youth. Despite their musical volatility, their lives and careers embodied stability. They retained the same lawyer for twenty years, the same manager for almost as many. (As with any business, they left behind a few burned bridges, a handful of former associates with whom they were no longer close, but there were surprisingly few of them.) In what felt like an unspoken agreement, at least to one of their crew, Ranaldo would sing one song per record and two onstage; Ranaldo himself seemed to accept his role in the band. They remained at once a unified front and a collection of divergent, conflicting personalities. Moore was still the motivator, multitasker, and driving force—part rock-professor academic, part overgrown teenager. Gordon, the group's most complex and often most inscrutable member, remained its vigilant guardian of their aesthetic. She shared the latter duty with Shelley, who was still the most diligent and detailed-oriented when it came to the day-to-day duties. Still the technician at the heart of the group, Ranaldo remained self-confident and alpha but also took on the role of the band's internal negotiator.

They'd grown accustomed to each other's idiosyncrasies and personalities; old grudges and personality clashes had largely subsided. They expressed their exasperation with each other by way of vague wisecracks to outsiders, but for the most part, they'd come to accept each other's contributions and imperfections. After all the years, they knew the four together made a sound they couldn't achieve with any other combination. "People complain," Gordon said, "but they never leave."

As MORE THAN A FEW in their camp observed, the in-progress album was being done in a way that would have made a recording-technique fussbudget like O'Rourke proud. Instead of working at Echo Canyon, which was still reeling from the aftershocks of September 11, the band opted for a more professional studio (and one O'Rourke himself long favored). Every day, assistant Aaron Mullan tuned each of the guitars; longtime associate Don Fleming returned in his recurring role as vocal coach. With engineer and coproducer John Agnello and engineer T. J. Doherty, a particular effort was made to ensure that the singing was in tune. It may have been coincidence, but the meticulous—for them—process was a sign they'd learned a few things from O'Rourke, just as he'd gleaned something about the ins and outs of band consensus and collaboration.

When workdays like those were done, Shelley and Ranaldo often talked about what people would make of the album: It seemed so rudimentary and basic, almost like a standard rock record. When it was released in June of that year, *Rather Ripped*—which had the working title of *Do You Believe in Rapture?*—was indeed the last thing anyone would have expected from them. With its largely concise songs that settled into comfortable verse-chorus structures, it was the album Geffen must have hoped they would've made fifteen years earlier. Addressing sexual attraction, lust, and failed friendships, Gordon's and Moore's lyrics were among their most user-friendly (even when Moore's typically ventured into quasi-Beat turf). In "Reena," "Jams Run Free," and "Turquoise Boy," Gordon sounded as close as she'd ever had to a breathlessly enraptured adolescent; seething sexual lust propelled "What a Waste." Each of the songs Gordon sang had warm, breezy chords and a welcoming ambience. The crunchy swagger and female-predator lyric of the Moore-sung "Sleepin Around" was as close as Sonic Youth had ever come to sounding like, well, the Stones. (The fact that Moore used the same guitar for almost every song also added to the album's cohesiveness.) "Rats," sung by Ranaldo, started as one of his compositions, but Moore's bumpy-road bass line took it into less folk-rock territory.

The Sonic Youth stamp was still heard throughout: in the five instrumental minutes that began the rock-god churn of "Pink Steam" or the way "Incinerate," built on fairly standard love-as-fire metaphors, worked itself into a fret-scorched lather halfway through. "Or" ended the record in the least flamboyant way possible: with Moore running through a list of standard band questions ("How long's the tour? . . . What comes first, the music or the words?") to a softly padding cadence and plucks of Ranaldo's acoustic guitar. But even there, the groove stayed in the pocket. By Sonic Youth standards, the album was almost lightweight. But if they could no longer completely surprise—the shock of noise, volume, and squalor was long gone—they could still startle in other ways: with beauty, melody, and a burnished maturity. They could, simply, play songs.

For the first time in years, the drumbeat began: Sonic Youth maybe, possibly, had a hit album on their hands. From *Rolling Stone* to *Pitchfork*, the reviews of *Rather Ripped* were largely glowing. But once more, the praise didn't translate to the masses. Just as the album reached record stores, two key Sonic Youth–connected executives at Geffen, in A&R and marketing, were laid off. Although Jordan Schur was no longer president of the label, the job had been taken over by a longtime A&R man whose extensive résumé listed distinctly non–Sonic Youth types like Pat Benatar, Huey Lewis, and Christina Aguilera.

The news of the firings arrived on the same day the band was doing a rare gig at their old haunt CBGB, the first show of the American *Rather Ripped* tour. Although disheartened, they had no choice but to play on; road work remained their leading source of income, the way they were able to maintain their lifestyles and partake in side projects. For the tour, they'd recruited former Pavement and Free Kitten bass player Mark Ibold to augment them onstage. Like O'Rourke, Ibold, a rugged forty-four-year-old, was a sensible and natural choice. He'd known the band for years and fit in so naturally that at his first rehearsal, no one told him what parts to play; whatever it was he'd done seemed fine by everyone. Although the shows focused on the new songs, the band would often end the sets with "Or"—the most downbeat possible conclusion for a show—and encore with "Shaking Hell" and sometimes "The World Looks Red," songs so old that most of the crowd had no idea what they were. Although "Kool Thing" had made a comeback on recent tours, it was again relegated to the closet.

Connecting with non-devotees was still thorny; opening for Pearl Jam once again during that tour, they encountered at least one crowd, in San Diego, that reminded them of the Neil Young audiences of sixteen years prior. And in the end, *Rather Ripped* sold about as many copies as each of the two albums that preceded it. Even an appearance by Gordon, Moore, and their daughter on the season finale of the TV series *The Gilmore Girls* (another indication of the way they were still able to pointedly tap into youth culture) didn't make an appreciable difference. The night the show was broadcast, Moore could be found at the Stone, a storefront Lower East Side performance space, where he and O'Rourke played an hour of freeform music. Lurching over his guitar and pulling squealing notes from it as O'Rourke played abstract piano chords, Moore seemed in no hurry to catch his network-series debut. The gig was also an indication that O'Rourke's split from the band was amicable; he also joined them onstage during a Japanese stop on the *Rather Ripped* tour.

Beyond its openness, *Rather Ripped* was a milestone in another regard: It was the last record under their existing, renegotiated contract with Geffen. For the first time since 1989, they were free agents, with no set plan or agenda and conflicting ideas as to where to go next. At such a crossroads, something odd happened; in fact, it happened shortly before the start of the sessions for *Rather Ripped*.

In 2000, Public Law 106-474, R 4846 was passed, creating the National Recording Registry at the Library of Congress; the Registry's goal was to "maintain and preserve sound recordings and collections" of historical import. The first list of inductees, unveiled in 2002, included works by Bob Dylan, Aretha Franklin, and Elvis Presley, as well as "Stars and Stripes Forever." But the 2005 inclusions were particularly head-turning: Alongside songs by Jerry Lee Lewis, Martha and the Vandellas, Nat King Cole, and country legend Roy Acuff, as well as Stevie Wonder's *Songs in the Key of Life* album, was, of all unexpected things, *Daydream Nation*. In effect, the U.S. Government was saying the album fit in with "sound recordings that are culturally, historically, or aesthetically significant." The Registry exalted *Daydream Nation* for its "glorious form of noise-based chaos" and declared that "the group's forays into outright noise always return to melodic songs that employ hypnotic arpeggios, driving punk rock rhythmic figures and furious gales of guitar-based noise." For a moment, it seemed as if rock critics had taken over a branch of the federal government.

The news, along with an invitation for the band to perform the album in its entirety in London, led to a *Daydream Nation* nostalgia wave, culminating in an expanded repackaging of the original record as well as a summer 2007 tour in which the band played the record in its entirety. When the idea was first broached, Moore and Gordon were the most reluctant to sign on. For Moore, the original album

387

remained "thin sounding," in his words, and the idea of turning back the clock, rather than writing new songs or spending time eliciting new sounds from his instrument, was unappealing. But the money was tempting, especially with three young children in the group and college tuitions on the horizon. (No wonder that when HSBC bank recruited Moore to record instrumental tracks for commercials—one of which somewhat recycled the "Kool Thing" riff—he accepted.) The fact that they'd reached a somewhat uncertain moment in their career—did they have a record contract or not?—surely played into the appeal of the shows as well. For a band both confident in its standing yet suddenly on shaky ground, a reminder of its stature couldn't have arrived at a better time.

As all four quickly discovered, relearning *Daydream Nation* was hard work, manual labor; a few of the songs, like "Rain King," had rarely if ever been performed the first time around. Their concentration was evident onstage; during the tour's stop in Brooklyn, New York, they bore down on each song as if in a stage production (which, in a way, the show was). They dutifully worked their way through the album, toying with it at times—"Total Trash" was slowed down, and newly extended instrumental stretches broke out here and there—and after each performance, they seemed relieved it was over. For the encore, they played a mini-set of *Rather Ripped* material, which often elicited as enthusiastic a response as the *Daydream Nation* songs, and sometimes more. As much of a chore as the shows were, they also ideally bookended each other: the older tunes a reminder of what they'd accomplished during their first decade, the newer material an indication of future avenues to explore.

"EVEN IF BANDS REALIZE IT or not, Sonic Youth helped create the environment we live in now," says Gerard Cosloy, the former Homestead Records employee who went on to cofound Matador Records. "If people say they've been influenced by Sonic Youth, that's nice, but if Sonic Youth influenced them to do anything, it's to—and I know this sounds corny—be themselves. And to *not* be like Sonic Youth. I'm not sure they so much 'advanced rock' or advanced free music in any given way, shape, or form. But they've created an environment where people who make music that is even crazier than theirs, and occasionally better than theirs, have a chance to play in front of more than ten people. That's a great thing. If there's nothing else to be proud of, they can be proud of that."

Cosloy was right, of course. Their sound was a blessing but also its own kind of curse. Since so few bands who followed in Sonic Youth's wake sounded like them, putting a finger on their influence wasn't as simple as with Chuck Berry, the Beatles, or the Ramones. Yet when it came to the culture at large, their impact was easier to determine. People they'd championed from the start—or had hired or worked with—seemed to be everywhere, shaping and in some cases transforming pop culture. Upstarts who'd opened for them (Nirvana), followed them to DGC (not just Nirvana but Hole and Beck) or had recorded for Smells Like (Cat Power) were now standard-bearers in their respective ways. When Madonna performed at Live Earth in 2007, she was joined onstage by gypsy world-music rockers Gogol Bordello. The band was led by Eugene Hütz, the young Russian kid who'd seen Sonic Youth in Kiev in 1989 and, so inspired, moved to New York a decade later to pursue his own musical dreams.

Yet in a strange way, their impact was most evident beyond music. Karen Carpenter was no longer mocked but a beloved (if semi-kitschy) icon, appreciated for her dark, sad voice and tragic persona. The newfound (and sometimes aggravating) appreciation of all things tacky had some of its roots in the way Sonic Youth had long championed trash TV and movies or particularly cheesy Top 40 oldies—the way they, like Quentin Tarantino, made junk seem respectable. The ironic wearing of T-shirts with cheesy logos preceded them, but Moore's seemingly endless supply helped legitimize the trend.

Thanks to Sonic Youth album covers, people who'd never been to art galleries or underground comic stores had their first glimpses of the work of Mike Kelley and Raymond Pettibon. Pettibon's work eventually graced the walls of the Museum of Modern Art as he became, in the words of the *New York Times*, "a high-tone collector's darling." Pettibon and Kelley were only two of the alternative artists the band dragged along on its journey from the fringes to the mainstream. During the early '90s, Sofia Coppola seemed directionless; by mid-decade, she'd begun hosting *Hi-Octane*, a short-lived Comedy Central series. One day, she took Moore, a frequent guest, to interview Anna Wintour in the *Vogue* offices. A somewhat puzzled and distant Wintour listened as Moore explained that to help make their hair stand up onstage, rock stars would sometimes use mayonnaise from dressing room buffets. (Wintour was, Coppola says, "slightly horrified.")

But for Coppola, other interactions with Moore were even more fruitful. Once, he handed her a copy of a book with a blond girl's hair on the cover, suggesting she read it. Coppola had never heard of the work, but she wasn't surprised that Moore had: "Thurston has some understanding of teenage girl culture," she says. The book was *The Virgin Suicides*, Jeffrey Eugenides' novel about suburban girls in the '70s (a time period that alone must have spoken to Moore). Coppola not only read and loved the novel, it became the impetus for her eventual career. She'd already directed a short film, *Lick the Star*, for which Gordon had provided soundtrack music. But reading *The Virgin Suicides* was, she says, "a turning point. I didn't think about making a feature film until I read that book. I wanted to make a movie from it, and it was the book that triggered me to make movies." With that film, and its follow-ups *Lost in Translation* and *Marie Antoinette*, Coppola became not just a prestige director but one with a particular skill at delving into the heads of young women.

Coppola's relationship with—and eventual marriage to—Spike Jonze, initiated on the set of the "100%" video, ultimately ran aground. (For a possible metaphor for the breakup, see her *Lost in Translation*.) But as did his ex-wife, Jonze went on to his own illustrious career as a filmmaker (as well as video director and occasional actor). Whether it was meta-movies like *Being John Malkovich* and *Adaptation* or quirkfest videos like the one he directed for Fatboy Slim's "Praise You," Jonze's work, like that of Sonic Youth's, challenged conventional notions of what should or shouldn't happen in art: the thin line between absurdity and seriousness. "They're very inspiring in terms of just doing things their own way," Jonze says of his early days with the band. "It's good to have teachers who are encouraging others that there's not a set way to do something."

Phil Morrison, who'd directed the "Titanium Exposé" clip (as well as a Godard-inspired promotional film for X Girl, starring Chloë Sevigny), went on to direct both the acclaimed Southern-gothic-slice-of-life indie *Junebug* and an iconic series of dork-vs-slacker Apple commercials. In the years after directing the first cut of the "Disappearer" video, Todd Haynes produced a string of arresting films: *Safe*, *Far From Heaven*, and the mesmerizingly weird Bob Dylan biopic *I'm Not There*. (For the latter, Haynes repaid the band for its initial support: The group recorded a version of the title song, Ranaldo organized and produced a handful of Dylan remakes for the soundtrack, and Gordon had a small acting role.) Their circle also included Vincent Gallo—the director, musician, actor, writer, and all-around arts bad boy—and Sevigny, whose on-screen debut in "Sugar Kane" led to a steady stream of roles in films and TV and, with *Boys Don't Cry*, an Oscar nomination for Best Supporting Actress. Tangentially, the list of Sonic Youth college graduates also included Jason Lee, costar of the Jonze-directed portions of "100%," who would graduate from skateboard whiz to, of all things, TV sitcom star.

As the years went on, it became clear that Sonic Youth would never be as commercially successful as some of their protégés. In interviews, Moore's recurring references to how little "coin" the band had made revealed a degree of irritation beneath his laissez-faire attitude. But as they'd learned, integrity (and a lack of compromise) carried a particularly high price. Instead, they had to settle for their influence. If Moore hadn't met Gordon that night at Plugg, it's easy to imagine a world in which Nirvana stayed on an indie label, never making the impact it did; Jonze would still be directing skateboard videos; Coppola would have been best known for *The Godfather: Part III* rather than her own films; and Beck would've remained an oddball playing novelty folk songs in L.A. The odds of each of them succeeding without Sonic Youth were strong—each was driven in his or her way—yet the connecting thread was clear.

THE MORNING'S EDITION of the *New York Times* sat on the dining room table in the Northampton house, and the photo on the front page was hard to miss: Patti Smith standing outside CBGB, a phalanx of photographers around her. Moore picked it up and looked at it, studied it. Part of him wished he'd been there for the last night of the club he'd first ventured into three decades before; after a protracted battle with its landlord, CBGB was finally packing up and leaving town. But he'd heard reports about what a mob scene it was. Being crammed into a stuffy, packed club wasn't as appealing as it had once been, and besides, family obligations were beckoning.

The death of CBGB was not the only sign that the city Moore and Gordon once lived in, which had birthed their sound and sensibility, wasn't the place it once was. So many of the old landmarks in their career were gone. Almost every recording studio where Sonic Youth had put its music on tape had shut down, victim of both the city's real-estate boom and the ongoing collapse of the old-guard music business. Radio City Music Hall Studio, where they made their first album, was now office cubicles. Greene Street, birthplace of *Daydream Nation*, had been turned into retail space once its landlord realized he could charge $12,000 rent every month. Wharton Tiers was forced to relocate his Gramercy Park–area basement studio—where *Confusion Is Sex* and *The Whitey Album* had been created—all the way to Brooklyn when his landlord decided to turn the building into condos. Plugg was still standing but sat empty and forlorn amidst hulking buildings; occasionally, it would host a show or special event, but it was mostly deserted, its phone never picked up. Richard Kern still lived near the East Village apartment where the video of "Death Valley '69" had been filmed, but the block was almost unrecognizable; as with most of the neighborhood, bodegas shared space with upscale restaurants and coffee bars.

Even Echo Canyon—or SYR, or any of the other names they'd given to their own studio—was a part of their past. The building had been sold, the plans for condo or co-op conversion were in the works, and in the spring of 2006, they had no choice but to vacate. After one last session, for Shelley's Smells Like label, they packed up the massive accumulation of guitars, gear, recording equipment, memorabilia, and boxes upon boxes of vintage tapes. Priced out of the city, they hauled all of their belongings out to a building in Hoboken. They called their parcel Echo Canyon West, but the name was, in a way, optimistic; the days when they would congregate for hours on end, filling reels of tape with instrumental jams, were likely as over as CBGB.

With or without a gathering place of their own in Manhattan, the work continued. One night, Moore could be found playing a free-jazz show in the Red Hook warehouse section of Brooklyn with his off-shoot band the Dream Aktion Unit; another night, another month, Gordon was presenting *Perfect Partner*, a live stage collaboration with Morrison and Tony Oursler that combined video and music. (In the way it played off car ads, it was another example of Gordon's ongoing interest in appropriation and collage art.) Ranaldo continued performing at clubs, spaces, and museums with Text of Light, but found the most ideal setting for his guitar rattles and hums in *Drift*, his collaboration with Singer. The couple's most ambitious audio-visual project, it had begun in 1991 as a multimedia visual endeavor merging film and music. After September 11, though, it took on a larger context: Singer's split-screen 16 mm footage of life before and after September 11—a benign downtown ticker-tape parade giving way to images of papers descending from the towers—was merged with Ranaldo's spoken-word narrative of sights and sounds of the neighborhood after the attacks. As the hour-long piece progressed, complete with increasingly despairing imagery, Ranaldo's instrumental score grew increasingly discordant and unsettling.

Just as the Geffen deal was winding down, Ecstatic Peace!—Moore's long-running indie, home to a plethora of freak-rock bands and subterranean skronkers who made Sonic Youth sound like a teen pop band—landed its biggest distribution deal, with, ironically, Universal, Geffen's corporate parent. By way of the new arrangement, the imprint began releasing a varied series of albums: the dark-cloud Americana of Wooden Wand's *James and the Quiet*, the retro psychedelic-rock of Awesome Color's eponymous disc, the freak-commune warbles of MV & EE with the Bummer Road's *Green Blues*. Most surprising of all was the crisp, autumnal acoustic rock of Moore's own *Trees Outside the Academy*, which, in establishing Moore's outside–Sonic Youth voice, was far more successful (and approachable) than his earlier *Psychic Hearts*.

Shelley continued to release records on Smells Like and was the engine behind reissues of the band's back catalogue; it was Shelley who would send preliminary tapes to the others and then wait, patiently, for them to get back to him by deadline. (Sometimes they did, sometimes they didn't.) Somewhere or another in the world, each month seemed to bring another gallery exhibit, experimental noise gig, independently released improv album, poetry reading, museum performance, or published journal. Anyone dropping by Moore's "Street Mouth" exhibit saw collages culled from the rock magazines he'd read as a Connecticut teenager, back when CBGB and other long boarded-up spots like Max's Kansas City and the Mudd Club offered a thrill a night.

With that steady stream of projects, they finally transformed into what they'd aimed to become during *NYC Ghosts & Flowers*: elder counterculture statesmen. They were now keepers of the music-art-literature flame even as, in the culture at large, that flame seemed to grow dimmer with each passing year.

NO ONE, LEAST OF ALL THEM, denied the absurdity of their group name, especially as they each neared or passed their fiftieth birthdays. But they also knew they were stuck with it. "There are two different thoughts about it," Moore said in his home. "Some people say it's ridiculous—'you should change your name.' I think it's a good thing as far as a state of grace, state of mind. It's actually more fun playing the older we get. To be called Sonic *Youth*?" He chuckled. "I'm really looking forward to when we do get really geriatric and exist as Sonic Youth. It'll be *great*."

His daughter's soccer game was about to begin, so he put aside his latest project—organizing, with Byron Coley, a coffee-table book devoted to a history of no wave—and drove her to the nearby field. It was an invigorating late afternoon in the fall, the leaves just turning and a suggestion of dusk in the air. As Coco ran out onto the field and took her position, Moore saw a friend, an actual soccer mom, and went over to chat. They talked about their daughters and the competition ahead.

Then he returned to the bleachers to watch the game. Much like his father, he'd never been interested in sports, but that had changed, too. On the field, his daughter, now twelve, looked like a combination of her parents. She had her mother's youthful athleticism and scrutinizing eyes, and her father's long limbs and emerging height.

After the game, once they'd piled back into the car and Moore dropped one of her teammates off at her parents' house, the car wound its way through the streets of Northampton. On the way home, the topic of dinner arose. Coco wanted Mexican food. Moore told her no. He said her mother was cooking at home.

"Why?" Coco said, as if not understanding the concept.

"Because that's what moms *do*, Coco," Moore replied, a hint of exasperation in his voice. "That's what *dads* do. They cook dinner." In the back seat, Coco frowned and stared out the window.

In his peacoat and glasses, Moore looked like a rumpled, tousled college professor. The look made sense: Even if he and Gordon had rebelled against their academic parents in one way or another, they were still the children of academics.

Soon, talk turned to Coco's band. Despite her age, she'd already begun singing and playing guitar and, with two friends, had formed a power trio, Lightbulb. She even had a stage name, Coko Mo. A few days from now, the girls were going to record a few of their songs in the Moore-Gordon basement.

As far as which songs they'd be putting on tape, Coco said she didn't yet know.

"You should do some of your older songs, your 'hits,'" her father said, in a tone between fatherly pride and bemusement. "Like the one about the fax machine."

Coco gave the disapproving frown of a girl approaching her teenage years. In her mind, she'd already moved on.

"No," she said, "I think we're going to play new songs instead."

ACKNOWLEDGMENTS

(AKA MAKING THE THANK-YOU SCENE)

Most books aren't written overnight, and this one doesn't even come close. I conducted my first interview with Sonic Youth in 1988, then spoke with the band, or individual members, for articles in 1991 and 1992, followed by extensive research and reporting for a feature in *Entertainment Weekly* in 2002.

Three years later, I found myself brainstorming ideas for a new book, although "brainstorming" is probably too high-toned a way to put it: I was walking home from work and pondering my next project when the thought occurred to me that Sonic Youth would be an especially rich topic for a manuscript. A few books on them had been published by then, but the previous one was a decade old, and it felt time to take a fresh look at their music, career, and cultural impact as well as investigate the various musical and career twists from the last decade.

When I first approached them with this idea, both the band and its management company, SAM, were instantly supportive. So it shouldn't come as a surprise that my first note of thanks goes to Kim Gordon, Thurston Moore, Lee Ranaldo, and Steve Shelley. Despite being inordinately industrious people who make even the busiest human feel like a slacker, they carved out time for fresh interviews with me in their homes, recording studios, even cars. God knows why they wanted to subject themselves to even more questioning and interrogation, even on the occasional difficult topic; as their phonebook-thick press kits show, they've done more than their share of interviews over the decades. Yet they began making themselves available almost immediately, with no strings attached and no demands for manuscript approval, and they never flinched when I brought up a name from the past that made them groan. This book couldn't have existed without their generosity and encouragement, and I'm endlessly appreciative of them for all of it.

SAM's John Silva, Michele Fleischli, Michael Meisel, and Jennifer Carrizo were more than obliging when it came to getting this project off the ground. Christine Wolff at Universal generously delved into her files and helped with old articles and video reels.

Although I dipped into my own old transcripts for quotes here and there, the majority of the interviews for this book were conducted between the fall of 2005 and the fall of 2007. My journey into the far-reaching Sonic Youth universe led to my meeting a huge crew of fascinating, helpful, and receptive interview subjects. Former members David Keay, Richard Edson, Bob Bert, Tom Recchion, Jim Sclavunos, and Jim O'Rourke graciously sat down with me (or let me hound them over the phone) in order to probe their contributions to, and interactions with, the band. Bob Bert, a true gentleman and indie rock scholar, was bighearted with his time, archives, memorabilia, and vintage photographs. My thanks also to Leah Singer and family members Eleanor Moore, Susan Erdman, Gene Moore, Josephine Ranaldo, Julia and Ivan Shelley, and Marian Arrington for allowing an outsider, and a journalist at that, to pick their collective brains.

Julie Cafritz, John Erskine, Mark Kates, David Markey, Ray Farrell, Bob Lawton, Nicholas Sansano, Paul Smith, and Carlos van Hijfte gave me hours of their valuable time without hesitation. In alphabetical order, I also offer my gratitude to Vito Acconci, Mark Arm, Eric Baecht, Josh Baer, Peter Baron, David Berman, Janet Billig, Martin Bisi, Glenn Branca, Jeff Cantor, Joe Carducci, Nic Close, Sofia Coppola, Gerard Cosloy, Doc Dart, Tamra Davis, Truus de Groot, Thom DeJesu, Dennis Dennehy, Chuck Dukowski, Danny Elfman, Don Fleming, Tim Foljahn, Marc Geiger, Stefano Giovannini, Michael Gira, Danny Goldberg, Richard Grabel, Dan Graham, Jim Grant, Christine Hahn, Don Hunerberg, Eugene Hütz, Lyle Hysen, Mark Ibold, Spike Jonze, Jonathan Kane, Christina Kelly, Richard Kern, JD King, John Knight, Peter Koepke, Daniel Lanois, Michael Lavine, Alan Licht, David Linton, Steve Loeb, Brian Long, Lydia Lunch, Maurice Menares, Jim Merlis, Bill Mooney, Phil Morrison, Aaron Mullan, David Murphy, Pat Naylor, Frank Olinsky, Tony Oursler, Harold Paris, Terry Pearson, Bonnie Pietila, Steve Ralbovsky, Mark Romanek, John Rosenfelder, David Sanborn, Arleen Schloss, Jordan Schur, Walter Sear, Robin Sloane Seibert, Perry Serpa, Chloë Sevigny, Michael Shamberg, Ned Sublette, Tom Surgal, Wharton Tiers, Butch Vig, Daisy von Furth, Mike Watt, Marnie Weber, Jim Welling, Hal Willner, William Winant, and Ross Zapin. Nicolas and Catherine Ceresole shared both memories and their archive of astounding vintage photos.

For allowing me to rummage through their brains on any number of Sonic Youth–related topics over the years, I tip my hat to Michael Azerrad, Jim Barber, Stephanie Chernikowski, Byron Coley, James Patrick Herman, James Hunter, Glenn Kenny, Michele Romero, Mary Kaye Schilling, Andy Schwartz, Anya Strzemien, and Linda Wolfe. Mark Coleman also provided illuminating perspective on New York in the early '80s; even though I was there too, I only wish my memories were as strong and vivid as Mark's.

For aiding in my quest to track down any number of sources and information, thank you, Holly Anderson, Bill Bentley, Godfrey Cheshire, George Chen at Alternative Tentacles, Mikyl Cordova and Karen Affinito at Radio City Music Hall, Zach Cowie, Allison Elbl and Alexis Henry of ID Public Relations, Dana Erickson, David French and Kevin Mackall at MTV, Rick Fuller, the late Robert Garlock, Andy Greene, Marie-Claude Grenier, Sherri Hill at Western Connecticut State University, Amanda Horton, Regina Joskow, Alice Kim at the Marian Goodman Gallery, Maria Kleinman, Randy Ludacer, Carolyn Lynch, Steve Manning at Sub Pop, Holly Millea, Bill Siegmund at the Audio Engineering Society, Ken Weinstein, and

Howard Wuelfing. Rebecca Coleman and Josh Kline allowed me access to the archives of the Electronic Arts Intermix, a treasure trove of Sonic Youth–connected video footage.

Speaking of archives, Moshe Levy—devoted fan, keeper of the MP3s, and groundskeeper of the excellent Sonic Youth fan site saucer like.com—kindly passed along more vintage concert recordings and studio outtakes than I could have possibly imagined. Moshe's support for my project was as invaluable as the stack of DVRs he sent over from Israel. (And thank you, Yafit Levy, for being such an understanding intercontinental courier.) Chris Lawrence's detailed Sonic Youth discography and concert data base—http://sonicyouth.com/mustang/lp/index.html and http://sonicyouth.com/history/con-set.html—is more than a Sonic Youth biographer could ever ask.

My friend David Hajdu recommended Anna Brenner as a first-rate researcher, and I'm indebted to them both. Anna spent more time than any human should trolling the Web and digging through old microfilm for statistical information and back issues of the *Village Voice*, and I'm grateful to her for her hard work and organizational skills. Sean O'Heir also came to various research rescues, always with the unflappable, easygoing professionalism he brings to any endeavor. Jim Seymore, Rick Tetzeli, and Jay Woodruff either commissioned or edited the *Entertainment Weekly* story that partly inspired this book, and I thank them for supporting the idea and fine-tuning the end result.

Anyone toiling on a book about Sonic Youth has to acknowledge the works that paved the way: Ignacio Juliá and Jaime Gonzalo's *I Dreamed of Noise*, Guido Chiesa's *Sonic Life*, and Alec Foege's *Confusion Is Next: The Sonic Youth Story*. As important documents and historical guides, each laid the groundwork for all the books to follow, including mine, and I bow before them. Thanks to Alec for his support. Richard Nash didn't waver when I asked for permission to quote a few excerpts from *On-Line Diaries: The Lollapalooza '95 Tour Journals* and Lee Ranaldo's *Jrnls80s*, both published by his company, Soft Skull.

Thanks to the magazine, newspaper, and Web editors who kindly kept me employed during the process of researching and writing this book: Doug Brod, Michael Endelman, Kathy Heintzelman, Dave

Itzkoff, Ann Kolson, Tom Kuntz, Nancy Miller, Rebecca Myers, Todd Pruzan, Steve Reddicliffe, Fletcher Roberts, Stephen Thompson, Josh Tyrangiel, Ben Wasserstein, and Emily White. Also, I literally couldn't have finished without the back-repair skills of Wayne Winnick, Leon Aibinder, and Dierdre Browne (no relation), who ensured I could sit upright at my desk and complete this book.

When I first approached my literary agent, Erin Hosier, with this idea, I wasn't sure what her response would be: Was a book on Sonic Youth too cult for anyone to be interested? To my relief and eternal gratitude, Erin was instantly supportive; unbeknownst to me at the time, she was also a fan. As soon as she shared her memory of the first time she heard *Bad Moon Rising*, I knew she was the perfect partner for this project. (Female agent now on duty, indeed.) Thanks also to David Gernert for giving us the initial go-ahead and Henry Dunow, Jennifer Carlson, and Betsy Lerner for picking up the baton. Ben Schafer at Da Capo was immediately up for the challenge and proved to be a kindhearted, attentive editor, colleague, and human being. Thanks also to Kate Burke, Lindsey Lochner, Sean Maher, and Collin Tracy at Da Capo; Albert DePetrillo and Denise Dwyer at Piatkus; and Birgit Schmitz. Martha P. Trachtenberg worked her usual copy-editing magic, exhibiting a knowledge of grammar *and* music notation that mightily improved the manuscript.

My wife Maggie has been a source of encouragement, support, and inspiration for over twenty years, never more so than during this project. Given that her own iPod choices tend toward the pop, it meant even more to me that she would wholeheartedly subject herself to several years of Sonic Youth music around our home (and on her iPod when mine broke and I had to borrow hers—it's all coming off now, Mags!). Maggie also knew what it would take for me to do this book—and how it would impact her—and never flinched. As always, our daughter Maeve had the last word: "Too noisy!" she said more than once, until the afternoon she heard "Incinerate" in the car and realized it was pretty easy to sing along with a one-word chorus. Even if she never learns to love more than that song, Maeve will always be our own incredibly special sonic youth.

INDEX

"Girls Are Short" (Coachmen), 27
Glass, Philip, 23–24, 51, 175
Glenn, Jeffrey, 63, 64
Global Network Booking, 147, 159, 160
Go Girl Crazy (Dictators), 24
Goats Head Soup (Rolling Stones), 115
Godard, Jean-Luc, 206
Godfather: Part III, The, 220, 255
Gold Mountain Management, 214, 218, 246–247, 261, 288
Goldberg, Danny, 214
Gomelsky, Giorgio, 12
Goo, 202–217, 219, 219–223, 259, 268
"Good and the Bad, The," 75, 78, 108, 282
Goodbye 20th Century, 337–340
Gordon, Althea, 29–32
Gordon, Calvin Wayne, 29–32, 325
Gordon, Keller, 29, 31, 32, 113, 116, 167, 295, 375
Gordon, Kim Althea, 6, 60, 62
appearance of, 11, 68, 381–382
background of, 29–38
Bad Moon Rising and, 120, 121–122, 129
Branca, Glenn tour (1983) and, 103–104
Confusion Is Sex and, 97, 98
Daydream Nation and, 178–179, 191
"Death Valley '69" video and, 139, 140
Dirty and, 240, 244, 245–246
EVOL tour and, 160, 161
Experimental Jet Set, Trash and No Star and, 267, 269
family life of, 274–276, 281, 309–312, 335
fashion and, 273, 319
Goo and, 203, 216, 216–217
label problems and, 188, 193
Lollapalooza (1995) and, 287
Lunch, Lydia and,, 92

Moore, Thurston relationship with, 13–14, 38–40, 41–45, 115–117
Murray Street and, 359
NYC Ghosts & Flowers and, 349
personality of, 5, 166–167, 174
Savage Blunder tour and, 89
The Simpsons and, 304
Sister and, 3, 166, 166–167
Smell the Horse tour (1991) and, 225, 228
songwriting and, 113
Sonic Youth and, 77, 86
Sonic Youth, beginning of and, 43–50, 51, 53, 66–68
Washing Machine and, 282–283, 297, 301
The Whitey Album and, 186
See also Sonic Youth
Grabel, Richard, 163, 188, 190, 191, 194, 196, 197, 198, 202, 278, 279, 314
Graham, Dan, 33, 34, 36, 38, 42, 43, 50, 51, 77, 97, 101, 109, 118, 348
Grant, Jim, 201, 202, 208, 212–213, 217
Grateful Dead, 56, 57, 81, 196, 313, 368
Great Gildersleeves, 50, 67
Green, Al, 133, 284
Green Eyes (Shepard), 165
"Green Light," 141, 155, 157
Greene Street, 173–175, 178, 190, 206, 393
Grey, Rudolph, 52, 313
Groening, Matt, 303
Grohl, Dave, 234, 302, 336
Groovy Hate Fuck (Pussy Galore), 158
Gross, Michael, 60, 63
Guided by Voices, 332
Guitar Player, 259
Gumball, 256